Master Clinicians on Treating the Regressed Patient

Master Clinicians on Treating the Regressed Patient

Edited by

L. Bryce Boyer, M.D.

AND

Peter L. Giovacchini, M.D.

JASON ARONSON INC.

Northvale, New Jersey
London

Copyright © 1990 by Jason Aronson Inc.

10 9 8 7 6 5 4 3 2 1

Library of Congress Cataloging-in-Publication Data

Master clinicians on treating the regressed patient.

  Proceedings of the Conference on the Treatment of
the Regressed Patient, held in San Francisco in
March 1987 as a function of the Boyer House Foundation.
  Includes bibliographies and index.
  1. Schizophrenia—Treatment—Congresses.
2. Regression (Psychology)—Congresses. 3. Psycho-
analysis—Congresses. I. Boyer, L. Bryce.
II. Giovacchini, Peter L. III. Conference on the
Treatment of the Regressed Patient (1987 : San
Francisco, Calif.) IV. Boyer House Foundation.
[DNLM: 1. Mental Disorders—therapy—congresses.
2. Psychoanalytic Therapy—congresses. 3. Regression
(Psychology)—congresses. WM 193.5.R2 M423 1987]
RC514.M359 1989   616.89′17   89-6975
ISBN 0-87668-834-2

Manufactured in the United States of America. Jason Aronson Inc. offers books and cassettes. For information and catalog write to Jason Aronson Inc., 230 Livingston Street, Northvale, New Jersey 07647.

CONTENTS

PART II
MASTER CLINICIANS ON THE
THERAPIST-PATIENT INTERACTION

PART III
MASTER CLINICIANS ON THE THERAPIST

CONTRIBUTORS

Christopher Bollas, Ph.D.
Austen Riggs Center, Stockbridge, Massachusetts; Visiting Professor of Psychoanalysis, Instituto di Neuropsichiatria Infantile, University of Rome; Visiting Professor of English, University of Massachusetts at Amherst; member, editorial boards of *The Yearbook for Psychoanalytic Psychotherapy* and *The British Journal of Psychotherapy*.

L. Bryce Boyer, M.D.
Codirector, Center for the Advanced Study of the Psychoses, San Francisco; Director, Boyer Research Institute, Berkeley; Coeditor, *The Psychoanalytic Study of Society*; Honorary Member, Mexican Psychoanalytic Association; Honor Medalist, Argentine Psychoanalytic Association; Recipient, George Devereux Award for psychoanalytic anthropological writings; Elliott J. Royer Award for outstanding contributions to psychiatry. Private practice, psychoanalysis.

Heitor F. B. De Paola, M.D.
Training and Supervising Analyst and faculty, Brazilian Psychoanalytic Society of Rio de Janeiro. Private practice, psychoanalysis.

Renata Gaddini, M.D.
Professor of Psychopathology, University of Padua; Associate Professor, Psychopathology, University of Rome. Private practice, psychoanalysis.

Peter L. Giovacchini, M.D.
Clinical Professor of Psychiatry, University of Illinois College of Medicine, Chicago. Private practice, psychoanalysis.

Peter Goldberg, Ph.D.
Teaching faculty, The Wright Institute Clinic, Berkeley; Supervisory Staff, Children's Hospital of San Francisco and The Wright Institute Clinic. Private practice of psychotherapy.

James S. Grotstein, M.D.
Clinical Professor of Psychiatry, University of California at Los Angeles School of Medicine; Training and Supervising Analyst, Los Angeles Psychoanalytic Institute, California Graduate Institute, and Los Angeles Psychoanalytic Center; Instructor, Southern California Psychoanalytic Institute. Private practice, psychoanalysis.

Joyce McDougall, D.Ed.
Supervising and Training Analyst, Paris Society and Institute of Psychoanalysis; Honorary Member, Association for Psychoanalytic Medicine, New York. Private practice, psychoanalysis.

Thomas H. Ogden, M.D.
Codirector, Center for the Advanced Study of the Psychoses, San Francisco; faculty, San Francisco Psychoanalytic Institute; Assistant Clinical Professor, Psychiatry, University of California School of Medicine, San Francisco; faculty, The Wright Institute, Berkeley. Private practice, psychoanalysis.

David Rosenfeld, M.D.
Training and Supervising Analyst and Faculty, Buenos Aires Psychoanalytic Association; Docent, Psychology, University of Buenos Aires; Docent, Psychosis, Perversions, National Hospital José T. Borda, Buenos Aires. Private practice, psychoanalysis.

Harold F. Searles, M.D.

Training and Supervising Analyst, Washington Psychoanalytic Institute; Lecturer Emeritus, Psychiatry, The National Naval Medical Center, Bethesda, Maryland and The New York State Psychiatric Institute, Columbia University; Clinical Professor, Staff Member Emeritus, Chestnut Lodge Sanitarium (now Hospital), Rockville, Maryland; Clinical Professor Emeritus, Psychiatry, Georgetown University School of Medicine. Private practice, psychoanalysis.

John Steiner, Ph.D.

Psychiatry, Royal College of Psychiatrists; Training Analyst, British Psycho-Analytical Society; Consultant Psychotherapist, Tavistock Clinic; Gaskell Medal; Bronze Medal, R.M.P.A.

Frances Tustin, M.R.C.P.

Honorary Affiliate, British Psycho-Analytical Society; Honorary Member, Association of Child Psychotherapists.

Vamık D. Volkan, M.D.

Training and Supervising Analyst, Washington Psychoanalytic Institute; Professor of Psychiatry and Director of the Division of Psychoanalytic Studies, University of Virginia Medical School; Medical Director, Blue Ridge Hospital, University of Virginia Medical School, Charlottesville. Private practice, psychoanalysis.

PREFACE

The treatment of regressed patients by relatively unmodified psychoanalysis was viewed generally with severe disapproval in the 1950s and early 1960s, especially in the United States. At the same time, the work of those few psychoanalysts who were conducting such therapy experimentally stimulated sufficient curiosity that in 1964, the Program Committee for the Biennial Meeting of the West Coast Psychoanalytic Societies, the chairman of which was Sydney L. Pomer of the Southern California Psychoanalytic Society, arranged for a panel discussion entitled "Psychoanalytic Therapy for Schizophrenic Patients" and invited one member from each of the participating societies to take part, with L. Bryce Boyer of the San Francisco Psychoanalytic Society to serve as chairman.

Boyer, who had long admired the work of Peter L. Giovacchini and had both met and corresponded with him to discuss theoretical and technical issues, persuaded him to co-chair the panel.

Dr. Bernard Brandschaft presented a review of Fairbairnian ideas and Dr. Alfredo Namnum's participation was ultraconservative, reflecting principally the prevalent views of Robert P. Knight. Edward D. Hoedemaker,

Giovacchini, and Boyer presented clinical data and were optimistic. The interest generated resulted in recording the proceedings. *The Psychoanalytic Treatment of Schizophrenic and Characterologic Disorders*, including a chapter by Hoedemaker, thus appeared (Boyer and Giovacchini 1967). A second edition was published in 1980. The present volume is also the product of a conference pertaining to similar treatment of regressed patients and reflects the immense change in the attitude of many psychoanalysts in North America toward the treatment of these patients.

Giovacchini subsequently had become a much sought-after teacher, in Chicago, of the theory and technique pertaining to the therapy of regressed patients. He is a prolific contributor to the literature and has been honored internationally.

Boyer influenced heavily the psychiatric residency training program of Herrick Hospital in Berkeley from its inception in the late 1940s and essentially directed the program during the 1970s until it was discontinued in 1983. Ogden and Boyer then established the Center for the Advanced Study of the Psychoses in San Francisco. The psychoanalytic orientation of the teaching program as it pertained to the treatment of regressed patients was almost unique in northern California and greatly appreciated by the trainees; residencies were sought eagerly.

Because no hospital existed in northern California that facilitated the psychoanalytic psychotherapy of inpatients, after the Herrick program was terminated, a group of ex-residents, initially Helen Ankenbrant, Sara Hartley, Barry Herman, and T. Robert Jones, set up a nonprofit foundation devoted to the building and administration of a suitable facility. Eventually with the help of Thomas Ogden, Drs. Herman and Jones succeeded in establishing such a foundation and honored the senior editor of this book by naming it the Boyer House Foundation.

One of the first public functions of the Foundation was its Conference on the Treatment of the Regressed Patient, held in San Francisco in March of 1987, its participants being, in addition to the editors, Rudolf Ekstein, James T. Grotstein, Harold F. Searles, and Vamık D. Volkan.

The editors agreed to compile the proceedings of the conference and decided to incorporate papers that were written by Europeans already renowned for their work with regressed patients (Christopher Bollas, Renata Gaddini, Joyce McDougall, John Steiner, and Frances Tustin) and to include, as well, contributors from Latin America: David Rosenfeld of Buenos Aires, who has published rarely in English, and Heitor De Paola of Rio de Janeiro, who heretofore has published solely in Portuguese. Finally, we decided to include a contribution by Peter Goldberg, a psychologist whose article was stimulated by the conference.

The chapters in this book illustrate current ideas about the development of internalized object relations, contribute to our knowledge of how those ideas help us understand primitive transference–countertransference relations, and provide information that enables us to improve our therapeutic skills in treating patients who suffer from disorders involving severe states of regression or undergo regression to primitive states during the course of their analyses.

REFERENCES

Boyer, L. B., and Giovacchini, P. L. (1967). *Psychoanalytic Treatment of Schizophrenic and Characterological Disorders*. New York: Jason Aronson.
—— (1980). *Psychoanalytic Treatment of Schizophrenic, Borderline and Characterological Disorders* 2nd ed., revised. New York: Jason Aronson.

L. Bryce Boyer, m.d.

Introduction: Psychoanalytic Intervention in Treating the Regressed Patient

CHANGING ATTITUDES TOWARD TREATMENT

The professional lives of the editors have been devoted largely to the psychoanalytic investigation through treatment in the consultation room of patients who suffered from serious characterological disorders, borderline conditions of all degrees of primitivity, and occasionally individuals who were frankly psychotic, as well as "neurotic" patients who underwent regression to primitive states during the course of their analyses.[1] We have had the opportunity to observe a vast change in the attitude of many psychoanalysts in North America to such use of psychoanalytic therapy of those conditions. As examples, in the middle 1960s, Giovacchini presented a paper illustrating his work at a meeting of the American Psychoanalytic Association and was excoriated as heretical by his discussant.[2] Boyer was openly doubted when on invitation he reported favorable results before a psychoanalytic society and was told that any respectable psychoanalyst

---

[1]Wallerstein (1989) has discussed the thorny question of what constitutes psychoanalysis and psychotherapy. We have sought to use psychoanalysis with the introduction of very few parameters (Eissler 1953).

[2]Various psychoanalytic institutes were invited in the early 1970s to participate in a study of psychoanalytic psychotherapy of schizophrenia, a project of the NIMH. Of those invited, only the San Francisco Psychoanalytic Institute, whence came Giovacchini's discussant, refused to participate, deeming the psychoanalysis of schizophrenia to be "unethical" (Gunderson and Mosher 1975).

would be affronted to be cited by him as a reference. Ten years later no one stirred at a national meeting when an eminent participant, reversing his earlier stand, said psychoanalysis was the treatment of choice for many borderline and psychotic patients and that contemporary psychoanalysis has clearly moved its research interests toward the study of regression.[3] The same position shift is common in print, reflecting, as was noted by E. Gaddini (1982), our having learned from our clinical work that feelings and thinking are based on sense data.

HISTORY

This shift in orientation toward the psychoanalytic treatment of regressed patients has coincided with a gradually heightened understanding of human behavior through the study of early object relationships as a result of child analysis, direct mother–child observations, increasing interest in object relations theory, a more serious consideration of the roles and influences of countertransference, and a gradual inclusion in the thinking of North American analysts of certain conceptualizations of the British Object Relations theorists.[4] I have postulated elsewhere that Kernberg (1972, 1984) played a most important role in making those concepts palatable (Boyer 1987).[5] As early as 1905, Freud set down his criteria for amenability to psychoanalysis, indicating that it should be limited to treatment of patients who suffered from the transference neuroses, have "a reasonable degree of education" (p. 263), are well motivated, "driven to seek treatment by their own suffering" (p. 263), are beyond adolescence but still in the prime of adulthood, are not in a situation of emergency, who possess "a normal mental condition" (p. 264) (Eissler's [1953] "normal ego"), and who are, in Freud's language, not suffering from psychosis, confusional states, or deeply rooted depression.

---

[3]Space does not permit repetition of an earlier discussion of the monumental and instructive efforts made during the first half of this century by various North American psychoanalysts to include psychoanalytic principles in the treatment of severely regressed patients, generally hospitalized (Boyer and Giovacchini 1980).

[4]The editors take an intermediate position regarding object relations, stemming especially from such theoreticians as Jacobson, Erikson, and Mahler within the ego psychological approach, and from the works of Bowlby, Klein, and Winnicott within the so-called British schools of psychoanalysis.

[5]See Greenberg and Mitchell (1983), Grotstein (1981), Ogden (1982, 1986), Winnicott (1958, 1965).

The narcissistic neuroses, if they were treatable at all by psychoanalytic means, required gross modifications from the so-called classical technique. These criteria gradually became dogma, especially in the psychoanalytic training institutions in North America.

At the same time, it is by now well known that Freud's technical procedures scarcely matched the "classical technique" in which the analyst was to behave essentially as a mirror and to deal exclusively with interpretations of transference and resistance (Mahoney 1986). In another place (Boyer and Giovacchini 1980), I have traced the development of Freud's thinking about the psychoanalytic psychotherapy of the narcissistic neuroses and demonstrated that it changed periodically.[6] Suffice it here to note that Freud used unmodified psychoanalysis in the treatment apparently in the early 1930s of a man of whom he wrote to Binswanger (1956). In Freud's words,[7] "The way he treated symbols in his mind, confused identifications, falsified memories and kept to his delusional superstitions made him always psychotic. . . ." Binswanger stated that the patient later had an acute "schizophrenic-manic outburst" and subsequently died of "catatonic fever." Freud abruptly terminated the psychoanalysis, apparently for countertransferential reasons alone, because the patient confessed that he had read notes on Freud's desk when he had stepped out of the room. As is well known, the Wolf Man suffered at times from psychosis, and following Freud's failure, which I have considered to have been due to an unresolved countertransference problem, was analyzed successfully by Ruth Mack Brunswick (1928).[8] Various authors have reexamined Freud's analytic cases and concluded that today they would be diagnosed frequently as borderline or psychotic, as, for example, Reichard (1956). It is of special interest that Tausk (1919) rediagnosed the "hysterical" patient Miss Emma A. as a case of "paranoia somatica" in Freud's presence at a meeting of the Vienna Psycho-Analytical Society, and Freud did not demur. In another place, I have cited dozens of authors, predominantly European, who used psychoanalysis for the treatment of psychoses both before and subsequent to the introduction of the structural theory, some of whom reported successful results (although most

---

[6]Rickman (1926, 1927) listed some 500 references in his discussion of the changes in psychoanalytic thinking about the narcissistic neuroses and their treatment prior to 1927.

[7]Translation through the courtesy of Dr. Dieter Eicke.

[8]While Brunswick (1928) implied that Freud's countertransference enactment created problems with the Wolf Man's analysis, recently Gottlieb (1989) has examined openly Freud's countertransferentially determined behavior with the Rat Man and sought to tie it to details in Freud's early life.

of the authors wrote but a single article) (Boyer and Giovacchini 1980). Of particular importance are detailed case presentations by Laforgue (1926, 1935) concerning his treatment of Odile and her sister. Among other analysts who continued to recommend "classical psychoanalysis" for the treatment of the schizophrenias was Garma (1931, 1978). The vast and often contra-analytic modifications of technique that were advocated by Nunberg (1948) and Federn (1933) are well known.

Robert F. Knight (1953) is credited generally with having popularized the term *borderline states*, although others previously had used similar terms (Hughes 1884 [*borderland patients*]; Rosse 1890 [*borderland insanity*]; A. Stern 1938 [*borderline group*]; Eisenstein 1951 [*borderline states*]; Wolberg 1952 [*borderline patient*]). His stand that psychoanalysis proper was contraindicated for the therapy of "borderline cases" may have been the most influential doctrine pertaining to their treatment by North Americans (Wallerstein 1989).[9] For Knight and the vast majority of North American psychoanalysts, "autistic regression" was to be avoided if at all possible and was not deemed in itself to be a suitable subject of study, even if that regression was limited to the consultation room.[10]

At the same time, although their writings do not state explicitly that they treated patients suffering from the narcissistic neuroses during the 1930s and later psychoanalytically with little manipulation, "support," or suggestion, case fragments presented by many North American analysts, including Deutsch (1933, 1937), Jacobson (1943, 1971), and Lewin (1932, 1937, 1950), leave little doubt that their treatment of regressed patients approached the definitions of psychoanalysis, in contrast to those of psychotherapy, as agreed on by Gill (1954, 1979), Gitelson (1956), Rangell (1954, 1981), and Stone (1954, 1982).

In 1961, Boyer reported on the use of psychoanalysis with few parameters in the office treatment of severely regressed patients, emphasizing the

---

[9]Knight found the patient's associations combined with the analyst's formulations and interpretations frequently to "serve only the purpose of stimulating further autistic elaborations. Psychoanalysis is, thus, contraindicated for the great majority of borderline cases, at least until after some months of successful analytic psychotherapy" (pp. 10–11). Thus his apparently adamant position was softened.

[10]Knight's stand materially influenced the research design for the Menninger Foundation's psychotherapy research project (Kernberg et al. 1972, Wallerstein 1986), obviating the systematic study of regression in treatment.

It is noteworthy that even at Menninger's, where Knight had so very much influence, psychoanalytic treatment and study of adolescent and childhood schizophrenic and borderline patients proceeded apace and dealt with regression and primitive internalized object relations (Ekstein 1955, 1966).

deleterious effects of unresolved countertransference problems, and by 1967, the editors of the current volume published their first book espousing that treatment.[11] In that year, Kernberg (1967) had begun to recommend modified psychoanalysis for the treatment of some borderline patients. It is to be remembered that Kernberg's experience with borderlines was then limited in great part to patients who were being treated at the Menninger Foundation. In 1967 the American Psychoanalytic Association held a panel discussion on severe regressive states during psychoanalysis; the participants agreed generally that regression in treatment was to be avoided (Frosch 1967).

REGRESSION AND INTERPRETATION

One of the major elements that led to Freud's recommendation that psychoanalysis be limited to the treatment of the so-called transference neuroses was that he and many others found the nature of the displacements to the analyst of internalized object relationships from individuals who had been significant to patients during their early pregenital years to be unstable and not amenable to interpretations (A. Freud 1969), a view refuted by Searles (1965, 1979, 1986) and many others.[12] Indeed, the nature of the transference provides data that can be used reliably in establishing a diagnosis (Grotstein et al. 1987, Little 1966, Modell 1963).

As Lewin (1950, pp. 9–19) indicated so cogently, the forms of defense (and resistance) are myriad. Neurotic or psychotic symptoms, organic symptoms or disease processes, character traits, careers, customary or renewed actions, old gratifications, regression itself, and even affects can be used in the service of defense. Citing as his model the first six chapters of Freud's (1900) *Interpretation of Dreams*, Lewin noted that a special principle in the psychoanalytic method is the effort to analyze manifest forms and formal elements in a mental picture into antecedent contents. The conception of the elementary or primary resembles that of the embryologist or geologist. The guiding philosophy of this type of analysis is known as the *genetic principle*. "It does not seek current primordial molecular entities, but may

---

[11]That volume has been succeeded by others dealing with the same subject, published singly or jointly: Boyer (1967, 1983), Boyer and Giovacchini (1980), Giovacchini (1972, 1975a,b, 1979, 1986, 1989), Giovacchini and Boyer (1982).

[12]Elsewhere I have given an example of the beneficial effects of rectifying interpretations so that they dealt properly with dyadic rather than triadic transference relationships after faulty interpretations had led to a static impasse (Boyer 1982).

rest when it establishes a set of early simpler states that are *anlagen* or matrices of later, more developed ones" (p. 13).[13]

In treatment, Lewin (1958) maintained that content and specific transference analysis remained of great importance, in contrast to the philosophy espoused by the Sullivanians including Fromm-Reichmann (1950) and Will (1961) and their students. Other therapists have advocated direct or indirect gratification as essential elements of treatment (Azima and Wittkower 1956, Schwing 1940, Sechehaye 1947). Those who espouse the treatment of regressed states through psychoanalytic means hold in general that the degree of regression to which the patient may be permitted to experience while in the consultation room in the service of understanding those *anlagen* depends, to a great degree, on the tolerance of the analyst himself, whether that tolerance be based on his intellectually derived therapeutic philosophy or upon the nature of his emotional responses to the patient's verbal and nonverbal productions, the degree to which they reawaken within him unconscious conflicts of his own, and his capacity to deal with them in manners that do not create serious countertransferential impediments to the therapeutic process.

Many therapists who treat regressed patients using psychoanalytic principles hold that the interpretation of all regressive phenomena, including psychotic symptoms, at least in part, as defensive and in the service of resistance is a highly important aspect of therapy (Arieti 1959, 1961). Bion (1977), with his concept of not fostering memory, sought to start from the origins in each session. Origins for him, as for others who have studied defensive fantasies as mental processes (E. Gaddini 1982), meant early sense data as relived in the analytic situation, a position consistent with Freud's (1923, footnote added 1927) idea that the ego is ultimately derived from bodily sensations, chiefly those arising from the surface of the body.

INTERNALIZED OBJECT RELATIONS

In Europe, particularly in England, and Latin America, the psychoanalytic treatment of the narcissistic neuroses met generally with less official resistance than in the United States. Interpretation and the growing study of the

---

[13]Willick (1983), writing of the concept of primitive defenses, reminds us that "all kinds of defensive operation may be used by all kinds of individuals. The idea that there are specific primitive defense mechanisms does not seem to be in accord with clinical phenomena" (p. 198).

transference–countertransference relationship were essential elements of therapy of such conditions by some important followers of Anna Freud's school.[14] The followers of the British School of Object Relations assumed that very early internalized object relationships existed in all people and, by and large, included primitive patients, whether hospitalized or otherwise, in their psychoanalytic practice. They assumed that interpretation of phenomena stemming from such relationships was the principal basis of treatment.[15]

In essence, this book depicts the application primarily of psychoanalytic object relations theory to the treatment of severely regressed patients, including those who were diagnosed as psychotic or belonging to the spectrum of borderline disorders (Meissner 1984; see also Abend, Porter, and Willick 1983) and those undergoing serious regressions during analysis for conditions that were considered to be neurotic, Bychowski's (1953) latent psychotics. Clearly, an object relations approach to psychic development permits an easy interplay between psychoanalytic theory and practice, since the principal element of psychoanalytic treatment is a particular object relationship, that between the patient and the analyst, the transference–countertransference relationship (Giovacchini 1979, 1989). In the past, it was said frequently that the task of therapy with the regressed patient was to replace bad internal objects with good ones (Wexler 1951). Today we would speak instead of the need to alter primitive internalized object relationships (Volkan 1976). There is a vast but inconclusive literature dealing with the relative importance of developing actual object relationships with the therapist combined with the development of the transference–countertransference relationship and of the role of interpretation (see Loewald 1960, 1979, 1986).

It is hoped that the essays in this volume will help to clarify to some degree the optimal roles of regression and interpretation in the treatment situation.

Let us begin with a brief review of some current thoughts about the process of internalization of object relationships. These notions are the product of studies that have added to and refined the ideas of structuralization that were developed by Freud (1900), who conceptualized the ego to develop from the id and later wrote, "The ego (the 'I') is first and foremost a

---

[14]See Boyer and Giovacchini 1980, pp. 104–109.

[15]A greatly foreshortened sample of relevant publications follows: Bion (1967), Fairbairn (1941), Guntrip (1968), García Vega (1956), Gioia and Liberman (1953), Grinberg (1967), Khan (1960), Klein (1930, 1948), Meltzer (1967), Nöllman (1953), Rolla (1957), H. A. Rosenfeld (1965), Segal (1950).

bodily ego . . . i.e., the ego (the 'I') is ultimately derived from bodily sensations, chiefly from those springing from the surface of the body" (1923, p. 26, footnote added in 1927).

The thoughts stem primarily from inferences drawn from ongoing caretaker–infant and –child observations, the psychoanalyses of children, and the psychoanalytic therapy of regressed adults. Such studies stress ultimately the building up of dyadic intrapsychic representations, self and object images that reflect the original infant–mother relationship, and their subsequent development into triadic and multiple internal and external interpersonal relationships in general. In this introduction, our discussion will be limited to the effects of very early caretaker–infant relations, preceding the development of the transitional object and phenomena (Winnicott 1953) and potential space (Ogden 1986, pp. 203–232).

The studies of the development of internalized object relations continue to attempt to account for the influences of constitution and heredity as well the effects of caretaker–child interactions.[16] Bowlby (1988) and Emde (1988a, b) have reviewed comprehensively the research knowledge about innate and motivational factors from infancy, gained in disciplines other than psychoanalysis as well as our own discipline in order to advance our own theory. Emde has focused on studies of innate and motivational factors from infancy. He wrote, "Research points to the centrality of the infant–caregiver experience and of emotional availability for establishing both continuity and the potential for later adaptive change. Basic infant motivations are proposed that consist of activity, self-regulation, social fittedness and affective monitoring. These influences are strongly biologically prepared, are necessary for development and persist throughout life" (Emde 1988a, p. 38). He found the psychoanalytic relationship, to the extent that it recapitulates positive aspects of the normative processes involved in the infant–caregiver relationship, to offer a special opportunity for developmental thrust, to offer a "new beginning" (Balint 1948, Loewald 1960, Fraiberg 1980), depending on the emotional sensitivity of the analyst, his or her responsiveness to a range of emotions, and the development and analysis of the transference–countertransference relations.[17]

---

[16]Clinical data too extensive to warrant citation have illustrated that not all primitive patients are amenable to psychological or, for that matter, any known means of treatment. Most observers assume organic causes for such refractoriness to therapy; no doubt inherited modes of organizing experience are relevant (Lorenz 1937; Ogden 1986, pp. 13–15; Tinbergen 1957).

[17]Both Bowlby and Emde provide comprehensive bibliographies.

PRECURSORS OF INTERNALIZED OBJECT RELATIONSHIPS

Observations and postulations pertaining to the beginnings of internalized object relations have found their precursors in body sensations and the sense of being. As Freud (1914) and Spitz (1965) note, the beginning of human life is probably characterized by a purely physiological existence, and sensory impressions have as yet no psychological meaning. Meaningful sensations, depending on the accumulation and reduction of tension, constitute the first primitive engrams. "The first mnemic registrations take place in an entirely undifferentiated sphere and it is usually not until the second half of the first year when there will be evidence of the infant's mental representations having become grouped into the first crude images of self and an object" (Tähkä 1988, p. 231). Jacobson (1974) suggests that psychic life originates in physiological processes that are independent of external sensory impressions but "From birth on, however, the discharge processes expand with the opening up of biologically predetermined and preferred pathways for discharge in response to external stimulation" (p. 11).

Of importance in clarifying this area are the clinical and observational work of Meltzer (Meltzer 1975, Meltzer et al. 1975) and Tustin (1972, 1981, 1986), developed in the context of their work with autistic children, and the clinical work of Bick (1968, 1986) and D. Rosenfeld (Rosenfeld 1982, 1984, Rosenfeld and Pistol 1986). Ogden (1986, 1988), too, writes of the precursors of mother–infant interactions. He considers the development of British object relations theory over the past twenty years to contain the beginnings of an exploration of a realm of experience that precedes the states addressed by Klein, Winnicott, Fairbairn, and Bion. Ogden (1989) has coined the term *autistic-contiguous position* as a way of conceptualizing a psychological organization more primitive than either the paranoid–schizoid or the depressive position, a mode of organizing experience that stands in a dialectical relationship to the paranoid-schizoid and depressive modes, holding that each creates, preserves, and negates the others. The autistic-contiguous mode is highly germane to an exposition of the development of internalized object relations. It is a sensory dominated, presymbolic mode of generating experience that provides a good measure of the boundedness of human experience and the beginnings of a sense of the place where one's experience occurs. It is beyond the purview of this chapter to discuss further the autistic-contiguous position beyond noting some of its properties. "Anxiety in this mode consists of an unspeakable terror of the dissolution of boundedness resulting in feelings of leaking, falling, or dissolving into endless, shapeless space," as has been described by Anzieu (1970), Bick (1968,

1986), Boyer (1988), and D. Rosenfeld (1984).[18] It will be seen below that Ogden's views are consonant with the presumed presymbolic mentation ascribed by the Gaddinis (R. Gaddini 1970, 1978, 1985) to infants before they have reached the transitional phase, a position with which Giovacchini (1980) agrees.

At this point a view of caretaker–infant relationships and internalization will be offered.[19] First explored is the area where body ends and mind begins. Let us start with fantasy, remembering that thought begins with fantasy. Freud (1923, p. 21) told us that what becomes conscious is the concrete subject matter of the thought, and that thinking in pictures is but a very incomplete form of becoming conscious; that it stands nearer to unconscious processes than does thinking in words. The concept of fantasy, when it begins and its vicissitudes, remains unsettled. McDougall (1989, introduction, p. 9) writes: "Since babies cannot yet use words with which to think, they respond to pain only psychosomatically." E. Gaddini (1982) postulated that before fantasy can become visual, there is an experience of it *in* the body. It might be more accurate to designate such experiences as protothoughts.[20, 21] On this basis, a physical function can be altered according to

---

[18]In Chapter 3 of this book, Steiner posits the existence of a borderline position to lie between the paranoid-schizoid positions.

[19]Thanks are gladly given to Dr. Renata Gaddini for her assistance in the preparation of this portion of the Introduction.

[20]Wilson and Mintz (1989) hold that deep defensive regression renders a renewed merger of psyche and soma in which whatever capacity to symbolize remains is expressed predominantly through somatic avenues.

[21]Such "fantasies in the body" had been inferred previously by Isakower (1938, 1954), Lewin (1946, 1950, 1953), and Spitz (1955). Here I cite Wangh's (Boyer 1956, pp. 19–20) paraphrasing of Spitz.

"Lewin deduces logically that if a regression occurs from the visual imagery level at which the dream functions, then there should be memory traces older than these pictures. Thus, as I do, he sees these memory traces 'more like pure emotion,' made up of deeper tactile, thermal and dimly protopathic qualities which are in their way 'memory traces' of early dim consciousness of the breast or of the half-sleep state. And, if I read him correctly, he believes it to be at this level of integration that the subject regresses in the so-called blank dream. It follows that the level of regression involved in the Isakower phenomenon harks back to an earlier period, that which precedes the reliable laying down of visual mnemic traces or at least to a period at which a significant number of visual mnemic traces has not yet been accumulated. I would be inclined to say that while the regression of the dream screen goes to the level of the mnemic traces laid down somewhere between the ages toward the end of the first half year and reaching to the end of the first year, in the Isakower phenomenon the regression reaches to the traces of experiences preceding this period. Obviously, these ages represent extremely wide approximations."

its mental significance, and meaning can be given to its somatic expression. Such "fantasies in the body" are not available to elaboration as are visual fantasies and account for early somatic pathology and psychophysical syndromes that begin in infancy and continue into adulthood as well as cases of alexithymia (Demers–Desrosiers 1982, Marty et al. 1963, Taylor 1984).[22, 23] Such crude, unvisualized fantasies in the body occur during the period of "personalization," one of Winnicott's (1971) terms for "infant being at one with mother," a time for which he used also the term *subjective-object* (Winnicott 1969). They are followed by fantasies *on* the body that represent the first mental image of the separate self. The earlier fantasies are linked to an elementary image of the body, "roundish-shaped," resulting from a linear continuity of the peripheral sensations deriving from maternal care (E. Gaddini 1986, Greenacre 1958). The roundish image represents the relations between the various elements of Freud's "concrete subject matter," child care and the sensations associated with it. The intrabody or intraoral precursor of object that may focus on the mouth is the concrete matter that can develop in the images of visual thought. The earlier work of Abraham (1924), Isakower (1938), and Lewin (1950) can be interpreted to support this idea.

Mahler's (Mahler 1968, Mahler et al. 1975) studies have established, as have so many others, that continuity of consistent care that is sensitive to the needs of the infant makes it possible for him or her to move away from earlier essential concern with needs and sensations toward a capacity of desiring where the time factor is involved, toward individuation. The work

---

[22]Lipowski (1988) reminds us that Stekel (1911) introduced the term *somatization* to refer to a hypothetical process whereby a "deep-seated" neurosis could cause a bodily disorder and Menninger (1947) defined "somatization reactions" as the "visceral expression of the anxiety which is thereby prevented from being conscious."None of the recent contributors to *Psychosomatic Symptoms* (1989), edited by Wilson and Mintz, agrees with Nemiah and his collaborators (Nemiah et al. 1976), nor does McDougall (1989), that a hereditary constitutional defect in psychosomatic patients results in a failure of the ego's capacity to fantasize and dream. Wilson (Wilson and Mintz, p. 133) holds that such failure to report constitutes an analyzable resistance, and McDougall adds that some patients can develop the capacity to verbalize fantasies theretofore unexpressed in words during the analysis of regressed states. The data of the current contribution seem to affirm that position.

[23]The relevant work of Viktor von Weizsäcker (1946, 1954, 1956) is rarely mentioned in the literature written in English, but has stimulated a school of psychoanalysts in Argentina (Centro de Consulta Médica Weizsäcker) whose work is devoted primarily to studying the psychosomatic border and its affects in early object relations development and the treatment of patients with psychosomatic disorders (Chiozza 1976, Chiozza et al. 1979).

of Mahler and the many other observational students such as Roiphe and
Galenson (1981) of caretaker–child interactions concern themselves primarily with later periods of development than those being considered here.
R. Gaddini (1987) stresses "the basic value that internalization of precursor
physical sensations connected with early care have for the infant in his first
months. Whatever is concretely done to care for a needy baby and to console
him for his lost union with his mother has to be included among these basic
sensations connected with care aspects" (p. 322).

Sucking and skin contact are for the neonate and the young infant the
main consolers, the main physical precursors. The nipple or its substitute
and the mouth together reestablish continuity and cohesion. R. Gaddini
(1987) thinks of the existence of the intraoral precursors (nipple and substitutes) as a step toward relating to the transitional object and reestablishing
continuity. While orality has always been thought of in terms of eroticism
and sexuality, sucking, even on a nonnutritive object, more importantly
reestablishes ideas of continuity with the mother, not only in infants but,
regressively, in adults as well (Gaddini and Gaddini 1959). The mouth's
original function is sensory and only later (when separation has begun)
does it become a potentially incorporating organ. It is then that instinctual orality can be mentioned (E. Gaddini 1981). Of greatest importance:
The mouth is essentially the place where physical and mental models
convene.

To repeat, these precursors (of transitional objects) are based on tactile
sensations of continuity, be they intraoral or clearly based on epidermic
sensations, such as mother's nipple or its substitute, whether nutritive or
otherwise, mother's hair or other parts of her body, "or also the infant's
body which is the same at this early stage of development" (R. Gaddini
1987, p. 324). The precursor's model is the "illusion" of the baby that it *is*
the mother and mother *is* baby (Winnicott 1953b). Here we deal with
fantasies *in* the body, those imageless fantasies that are closer to bodily
sensations and functioning than to thinking.

In our investigation of earliest development, the value of precursors is
paramount because, being so primary, their study allows us to understand
significant vicissitudes of the initial sense of being. Because of the equation
early = severe in psychopathology, we find that the pathology that is
based on the failure of their development or on their premature loss is
particularly severe: perversions (especially fetishism), fixed ideas, compulsions, adulthood conviction of the reality of the imaginary companion, and
so on. In these cases the precursor has not led to the bridge between me and
not-me, the transitional object. When the precursor is prematurely lost, the

early self is lost, and the accompanying sensation is presumed to belong to the "primary agonies" or "catastrophe" which is at most organized in the mind in a very elementary way. The sense of loss experienced by the child who has been deprived of his or her transitional object is closer to mourning.

A mother's pathological symbiotic ties to her infant may interfere with symbolization of reunion with her after loss. Children do not create a transitional object if the mother remains available physically, as sometimes occurs if the mother's symbiosis with her baby is excessive. The protracted use of precursors, substitutes for the breast and tactile contact, interferes with the development of symbolization. Psychosomatic patients rarely create a transitional object, because of their impaired capacity for symbolization. "Psychosomatic symptoms appear when the child's use of the object has been adversely affected, and in later development, language and symbolization prove to be impaired by this early interference with prestages of object relationship, mind–body differentiation and interaction, symbolization and communication with the object" (R. Gaddini 1987, pp. 324–325). Precursors, thus, can be viewed also as defenses against differentiation, against the development of the transitional phase and phenomena and an early sense of self. Such objects and phenomena during the subphase of differentiation, when mind and mental operations are on their way, are described by Mahler, Pine, and Bergman (1975) as typical of "hatching."

Pathology based on the the deficiency or loss of these precursors, not-yet symbols (see also Segal [1957]), consistent with the equation early = severe, includes, as mentioned formerly, some cases of psychosomatic syndromes that persist from infancy into adulthood: at least some cases of autism, perversions (especially fetishism), compulsions, persistence into adulthood of a belief in the imaginary companion, and fixed thinking.

At the same time, reseachers have found little predictability in behavior from infancy to later ages and Emde (1988a) wrote of a "central developmental paradox." Pointing to the degree of flexibility and plasticity that has been found in infants, he stressed the influence of the environment, the "matching" of the growing infant and its caretaker. "The developmental orientation, in fact, indicates a particular view about adaptation and pathology. What is not adaptive is a lack or variability in an individual who is faced with environmental demands necessitating alternative choices and strategies for change" (Emde 1988a, p. 24). Freud (1937) felt that one of the reasons for poor results of psychoanalysis was the rigidity of some analytic practitioners and poor matching between patient and therapist.

IMPLICATIONS FOR TREATMENT
OF REGRESSED PATIENTS

The psychoanalytic relationship, occurring later in life, to the extent that it recapitulates or offers positive aspects of normative processes involved in the infant–caretaker relationship, offers a special opportunity for a "new beginning," a developmental thrust. A "corrective emotional experience" takes place, one that is based on the emotional availability of the analyst and the constancy of the therapeutic environment, rather than the therapist's manipulation. To a degree that has been underrecognized in our literature, the optimal availability of analysts is based on their emotional sensitivity and their security and responsiveness to a wide range of emotions. Stated otherwise, the analyst must be able to tolerate emotionally the patient's need to regress to very primitive psychological, even psychosomatic states, including in some cases those in which the fantasies are *in* the soma. It is in this type of atmosphere that a therapeutic alliance can develop within which appropriate interpretations will be effective. In Emde's (1988b, p. 291) words, "If the process goes well, the analytic relationship becomes fortified by a new executive sense of 'we' and an analytic 'we-ego.'"

Freud's (1910) "countertransference" came to be considered as the repetition of the analyst's irrational, unconscious, previously acquired attitudes, now directed toward the patient. Today, most analysts would consider this view to be Racker's (1953) countertransference neurosis. The literature on countertransference is vast and burgeoning; the most comprehensive review in English is that of Langs (1976). Hann–Kende (1933) may have been the first to have suggested that the countertransference could be turned to purposes beneficial to therapy. Today, countertransference is viewed generally as the analyst's total emotional response to his patient's needs (Little 1957).

COMPLEMENTARY REGRESSION
OF PATIENT AND THERAPIST

Analysts have long sought to understand what constitutes Reik's (1948) "listening with the third ear," or Isakower's "analyzing instrument." Spiegel (1975) noted that both analyst and analysand operate in similar states of mind (free-floating attention and free association, respectively) and noted that this results in a type of conversation that is unique to psychoanalysis. Balter, Lothane, and Spencer (1980) speak of the analyzing instrument as operating within a subsystem of the ego of the analyst who "is more likely to perceive connections between words, ideas and images which are products of the patient's primary process, because his subsystem is itself in part freed from the constraints of secondary process thinking, reality testing, and so on" (pp. 490–491).

Boyer (1986) notes that analysts' awareness of the fantasies, emotional states, and physical sensations that occur during their free-floating attention (and, at times, their subsequent dreams) enables them to be more in tune with their patients' communications, and that such awareness is especially useful in working with regressed patients. Their tolerance of patients' primitive regressions, those that might lead to or involve the fantasies *in* the body as well as transitional relatedness and subsequent developmental phases as they are relived in the analytic situation, entails their capacity to regress concomitantly with their patients, while simultaneously retaining the observing function of their ego (Searles 1979).

I conclude the introduction with a clinical fragment.

A 54-year-old immigrant Levantine, still physically beautiful, had been periodically hospitalized as "schizophrenic" in her native country from the ages of 16 to 20, under the care of a renowned psychoanalyst. She had perceived herself as having no will of her own, but rather as her mother's "organic extension" and "barbie-doll puppet." During one interview, she said, consecutively, "Until I was 4, I was an autonomous body protecting itself against becoming a dead puppet"; "At 13 I turned into nonanimate matter, dead bits of a popped balloon, that is, broken bits of body boundaries swaying helplessly in the waves of an ocean, my mother, without autonomous movement"; "At 33 I turned into a rotting piece of flesh, organic matter, devoured by maggots, fragments of my mother"; and, "A few years later I was a dead puppet whose mother was pulling the strings which made it look alive, but there were some signs of hidden life at the core, a secret woven with guilt."

At 21 she decided to live with a rich and influential foreigner old enough to be her father, as *his* puppet. She called him "daddy" and he called her "baby." He made no demands on her beyond the satisfaction of his lust and that she dress magnificently and behave appropriately at embassy functions, while serving as his highly efficient secretary.

For her, as had been true for her mother, others' external reality was but a dream, and her reality consisted of an inner dream life that continued during the day. While she had intense orgasms and her physical activities were graceful and appropriate, her conscious mental life was unassociated with such outer events. Her privately experienced alienation from the world and others' experience was recognized but vaguely by them. During this period of her life, she lived in the same country as did her extended family and visited them frequently. No one appears to have recognized her as odd.

When the consul returned to his homeland, she inexplicably became terrified that she would be mysteriously annihilated. At the same time, she was terrified that if her family were to learn of her fear, her mother would "seduce" her to return home where she believed she would become a zombie, living her mother's life as a fantasied "martyr world-saver." Thus, she lived alone, supporting herself as a secretary. She secretly sought orthodox psychoanalysis from her former therapist but was seen instead vis-à-vis once weekly, receiving advice and support that accompanied interpretations that seemed to her "to belong to the private mythology" of her therapist, as they presumed that the patient's view of reality coincided with the therapist's, and that when the patient talked about lust and sexual activities, "she [the therapist] thought I was confusing the man with my father while I was trying to fuse with my mother again, after I had become afraid our protective membrane had ruptured."

In desperation, she left treatment and soon found and immediately married another man old enough to be her father, a renowned scientific investigator whose expectations of her were similar to those of the consul, and who took her abroad as his assistant.

It was a very strange marriage, again involving the names "daddy" and "baby." She served brilliantly as his "puppet," as she had done previously for her other male protector and, while overtly psychotic, her mother. She discovered important data that furthered her husband's career, but she claimed no credit for them because she believed they belonged to an irrelevant reality. So far as she was concerned, she was content in her life of puppetry while her inner mental reality consisted of being the world's heroine savior, an idolized martyr or, literally, a sun or other planet. Periodically, she was quite aware that the "world" symbolized her mother, but that knowledge was of no use to her. At the same time, her husband spent months on end with his "mummy" in another country, apparently living some sort of symbiotic or psychologically fused relationship with her.

Following "my psychotic break" when she was 12 or 13, she was convinced that she was literally a physical and mental extension of her mother, whose existence depended on the patient's thoughts and actions, as, reciprocally, hers did on her mother's. She was consciously aware of believing that she and her mother inhabited the same skin and, during brief periods when she simultaneously transiently perceived them to be separate, that any injury, physical or psychical, to either of them would result in bleeding out their bodily contents and ceasing to exist. This emphasis on the skin and its implications of continuity with the mother is reminiscent of the Gaddinis' position that the intrapsychic preservation of such continuity is a precursor that precedes and defends against the development of the transitional object, and of Rosenfeld's psychotic body image (see Chapter 6). This patient never had a transitional object.

At 35 she had the first of two daughters, born three years apart, both of whom she perceived to be literal extensions of herself. She believed their every anxiety to be the product of uncontrollable and insatiable physical needs. Like her, they were capable solely of "animal and not human communication" and were continuous with her as she was with her mother, inside a membrane that changed character from time to time but clearly symbolized fragile skin. "Animal communication," as I learned after many months, meant unwitting, reflex response to internal physical needs, particularly alimentary and tactile needs. Now she was terrified that her daughters would eat her up from inside, and she became aware that she had feared earlier that her mother and she would empty each other by devouring from the inside.

She interpreted her husband's fear of impregnating her to mean that he was terrified that orgasm would destroy him by literally turning him into an animal whose flinty eyes were those of a prehistoric reptile, as she saw her mother's eyes at times, and that were he to become sexually excited he would become unable to revert to human rather than animal communication; her sympathetic response would result in their fusion into a fragile membrane, the contents of which would consist of unbridled instinctual urges, largely cannibalistic. Thus, she refused sexual relations following the birth of their second daughter, apparently to her husband's relief, and had no further intercourse, although she masturbated frequently, with sadomasochistic fantasies in which she was raped serially and endlessly while tied to a post, as an unpaid victim, a white slave.

Her husband's work took them to various European countries in which she received transient reduction of anxiety from psychotherapists so long as she could hope that they would communicate with her on a "human" rather than an "animal" level, where the "intelligence of the organism" prevailed. Then her husband left her for two years for reasons apparently pertaining solely to his work. She returned to her parents' home and seemingly became fused anew with her mother, as now she was incapable of any activities beyond looking after the welfare of her daughters. Otherwise, she vegetated in a darkened room where her mental life consisted of fantasies she believed she was sharing with her mother.

When her husband rejoined her, they and their daughters moved to the United States where she was hospitalized and medicated as psychotic, with no apparent amelioration. During this period, her parents died and she responded to their deaths by using the negation defense. After a year, her husband's work took them to California where she continued to live in isolation, bestirring herself solely to cook for and otherwise look after her husband's and daughters' physical needs, or to attend and hostess social functions necessary to her husband's work. At such times she functioned in totally appropriate ways, secretly smiling to herself because everyone about her, it seemed to her, lived in an unreal reality. At the same time, she considered her activities automatic or "robotic." She was quite consciously aware of both realities, and at times was mildly curious about her need to keep them separate. Her family seemingly were unaware that she was seriously disturbed. When alone, she spent much time writing stream of consciousness ideation in a secret code, a shorthand of an actual language unknown to her husband and children. Once her ideas were recorded, their content was repressed, but she saved the many written volumes in hopes that at some future time she would be able to face her fantasies and memories if she could comprehend the reality of others around her. Her family believed she was writing a novel for publication and respected her privacy.

Although she hid her fears of reciprocal cannibalism from her family, and her husband did not perceive her anxiety, he "babied" her "whim" to seek treatment once again. She was seen by a psychoanalyst vis-à-vis, one to three times weekly, for some seven years. Treatment consisted of bringing her secret writings to her analyst's office and trying to learn the meanings of what she discovered she had written. Apparently, her therapist became discouraged and eventually sought to deal with her by arguing about what constituted reality. After the fourth year, she interpreted his behavior to mean he was anxious and wanted to stop his care, but by then she believed that they had fused and that were she to leave him, their enclosing membrane would rupture and their beings would leak out. Nevertheless, after seven years, she had come to the conclusion that taking care of her family had more priority than taking care of her psychoanalyst and asked to be transferred to my care, having heard I treated patients everyone else had given up on, and was "tough."

The highly abbreviated material that follows deals with data pertaining to her psychological precursors.

I offered to see her in orthodox psychoanalysis on an experimental basis. She agreed, although she was terrified that the deprivation of eye contact would make all human communication impossible and that "the intelligence of the organism" would prevail. Her insatiable animal needs would make her burrow into my body like a baby rodent and my eyes would become her mother's eyes, those of a prehistoric cold-blooded reptilian, totally impersonal and inhuman, watching for any evidence of her stirring, which would give me–mother an opportunity to devour her. She likewise feared that if she were not to be allowed to translate her writings to me she would have nothing to say, as without them to come between us and protect us, the "bridging function of words" would lead to our fusion. Our words carried different realities and their fusion would cause our physical fusion.

Although much of what she said made very little sense to me, at no time did I feel uncomfortable with her and my principal initial activity consisted of asking her to restate in different words what she meant for me to understand; I frequently iterated to her what I believed I had understood she sought to communicate and asked for further clarification.

Despite her terror, she was intrigued that I encouraged rather than impeded her efforts to verbalize aloud her contorted thinking and images, "the remaining cerebration that has persisted inside me since my mental breakdown when I was 13. I've kept it secret from everyone but my psychoanalysts and they've all discouraged me from trying to tell them about it and to learn about myself from it." She sensed that for the first time she had met someone who was not afraid that her "looniness" was contagious, and therefore she did not believe she would harm him with her experiences, thoughts, dreams, or hallucinations. She said, "No one has ever encouraged me to look further inside of me. I've never known before that I could say aloud things I've thought and not have the verbalizing make our reality change, that is, turn you or me literally into what I had only become aware I thought after hearing my words." She said that she had always known that her only hope for salvation was to learn to understand her unconscious motivations and conflicts, and consequently each of her previous seventeen therapists had been a certified psychoanalyst. None, however, was willing to give her the experience of seeking a psychoanalytic experience. She had believed that she had to take care of them as well as herself.

After some weeks, she revealed a secret that she had previously imparted to no one, namely that she lived in constant pain "due to the stirring of animal life" in her lower brain and spinal cord, sometimes extending to her "tail." Her higher, "human" brain was nonfunctional. Her nervous system was the repository of her previous mental life, which had become fused with it "as it was in the beginning before I learned human rather than animal communication."

She quite literally believed that she was motivated solely by neurophysiological manifestations of primitive animal urges, primarily insatiable hunger, which could be gratified solely through physical fusion and devouring a mother–surrogate from the inside.

Soon after she reported the pain in her "lower brain and spinal cord," it became apparent to me that anxiety resultant from any conflict whatsoever was quickly dissipated and replaced by physical symptoms. Thus, my interpretive efforts were directed toward helping her understand this somatization as a defense. As an example, I would recall for her that she had been speaking of uneasiness, fear, or anxiety and then the emotional discomfort had disappeared and been replaced by the pain in her lower brain and spinal cord. I said that her body was colluding with her mind in seeking to protect her from feeling discomfort and in learning what internal conflicts had caused the emotional discomfort. Intrigued, she was nevertheless frightened and incredulous, but gradually she came to understand the defensive maneuver.

Sometimes, screaming and writhing, she described endless permutations of pain radiation, and whenever I sought to trace her systems of logic and to learn against what such regressive episodes during her interviews served to defend her, she used material taken from her extensive reading of neurophysiological literature to support her position. As to be expected, the majority of her reported pain radiations followed hysterical paths, and her associations to the pains and the syndromes they reportedly caused revealed fused orality and genitality (Marmor 1953). But at that time she was impervious to useful knowledge of symbolism.

Later, of course, we would learn that her "tail" gained symbolic meanings having to do with sexual and perineal activities and desires. Sometimes such knowledge would emerge when she hallucinated my taking an actual active role in the consultation room in her relivings of her sadomasochistic fantasies or dreams of being serially raped. At the same time as she screamed with pain as I raped her vaginally and anally, she retained a grasp on reality and laughed aloud as she told me she had to regress to relive her childhood properly this time and I should know that to gratify her sexually at this period of her development would be indulging in "child molestation."

Her life outside the consultation room held no interest for her during her interviews and I had but the vaguest idea what she did. From time to time she briefly commented that her husband and daughters had said that she was more energetic and communicative than previously.

It was over a year after she entered treatment with me before she remembered that her pains had begun when she moved with her husband and children to the United States, a move she feared would rupture the membrane surrounding her mother and her, and result in their bleeding into nothingness. She reasoned that so long as she spent much of her time isolated and in a dream state, she was effectively dead, and being "asleep–dead" would prevent her mother's death in fact.[24]

She had interpreted her previous analyst's willingness to let her use her writings as a protective screen between them to mean that he feared that spontaneous recital of her thoughts would damage him. She took my position that she was to speak rather than read as evidence that she did not have to take care of both of us and that she had a better chance to regain the capacity for "human communication" in her work with me.

A change in her symptomatology that occurred six months into her treatment frightened and encouraged her: She began to have "spasms" and "contractions" in her lower brain and spinal cord and interpreted them to mean that humanity was stirring concurrently with her animality, "the intelligence of the organism." She reported a dream: "A baby's hand came out through my navel inside the membrane skin from the womb. I was awed and amazed. I showed it to my husband, my beginning emergence as a human." She then talked of mother animals' kicking hungry babies away and became afraid. My interpretation that she had become fearful that her growing human wishes pertaining to me as a representative of her mother would lead to my rejection of her alleviated her anxiety.

During the next few months, continuing spasms frightened and encouraged her; at the same time, her periods of self-isolation became briefer and she undertook many activities, now being able to experience consistently both realities concurrently. She was greatly encouraged. Subsequently, intermittent periods occurred when there were no pains

---

[24]See Lewin (1950, chap. 4).

ascribed to her lower brain and spine, and when the symptoms recurred, interpretations that they served defensive purposes were effective. Then came some sessions in which her dreams and fantasies involved her as an infant or a small child who had a security blanket; she said, "It's hard to believe that my reliving of my past even includes being happy the same way my daughters were." Subsequently, she bought and privately treasured a teddy bear.

About a year into her analysis, following a period of several weeks during which she had experienced no pains or spasms from her lower brain or spine, she delightedly told me one day that she had reacted to an insensitive act of her husband's by experiencing spasms and finally knew that what she had called the intelligence of the organism had a psychological meaning and served psychological purposes, that it was not solely a reflex, organic symptom related only to "neurophysiological metabolism." At the following session she presented data that support Gaddini's notion of fantasies in the soma: She said, "I woke up with 'sick' pain in my shoulders, arms, neck, and tail. It has a life of its own. It's coming out. It used to be stronger than I was. Then I saw a latent, blurred image which meant I was closer to being able to talk about it." Suddenly, she cried, as the blurred image became a clear picture that she later identified as an actual memory of herself sewing and unable to remember what she was doing because she was fearful of her mother's vitriolic ridicule. After talking of having read that men are sexually excited by cripples and thus Chinese men bind women's feet so that they'll be crippled and helpless, she sobbed loudly, saying, "She *smelt* cripples, and her power gave her immense sexual excitement. I can see her. She made everyone and everything dependent on her and then got so excited when she tortured the helpless ones. She had cats and kept them caged and wouldn't let anyone else feed them. Then she'd take them food and just before they'd get to the food, she'd kick them with her sharp, highheeled shoes that look like those deformed Chinese women's feet, and she'd flush and quiver with what must have been an orgasm." Startled, she became aware that her physical pains had left. She said, "They became a blurred image, then a clear image, and finally words."

Another time, after she told me with delight and awe that she could now risk loving and trusting me as someone separate from her and not use me solely as a "container for the parts of me that are my mother and torture me," and repeating that she knew for her to get over her "looniness" she had to relive her past "from its beginning" in her experiences with me, she described in another way how she perceived her sensations becoming words that made human communication possible. "I wake up (from dreams that are only feelings) thinking in images. This morning I saw myself sitting beside a pile of my inner content, content made up only of sensations and emotions; it is quite a big pile. I am taking small pinches of stuff from the pile and hammering it into small containers, rather than bringing it here and believing it is inside you; the containers look like dental crowns. They are strung to each other to form a visible pattern but there are no actual teeth any more. I know what I am doing, I am putting my inner content into containers of words. I am separating and diffusing the content of the heap. . . . I wonder why I have to hammer the stuff so forcefully into inflexible containers, why it takes so much effort to force my inner content into ready-made shapes. My inner content becomes visible when it is put into the small, hard containers that are how I see words. Nothing in this world can be visible and used for human communication unless it is put into matter and thus given the form of words. As long as energy is loaded with emotions and the meaning that is my inner content is not related to matter, it remains invisible, that is, unconscious, to me, refuse in a pile, unusable and shapeless. Nothing can be distinguished and identified. As long as patterns of emotions and thoughts are fused together into small knots in a pile made of sensations, nothing can become visible; human communication through words does not really exist."

REFERENCES

Abend, S., Porter, M., and Willick, M. S. (1983). *Borderline Patients: Psychoanalytic Perspectives.* New York: International Universities Press.

Abraham, K. (1924). The influence of oral eroticism on character formation. *Selected Papers on Psycho-Analysis.* London: Hogarth, 1942.

Ainsworth, M. D. (1985). Patterns of infant–mother attachments: antecedents and effects of development. *Bulletin of the New York Academy of Medicine* 61:771–791.

Anthony, E. J. (1958). An experimental approach to the psychopathology of childhood: autism. *British Journal of Medical Psychology* 31:211–225.

Anzieu, D. (1970). Skin ego. *Psychoanalysis in France,* ed. S. Lebovici, and D. Widlöcher, pp. 17–32. New York: International Universities Press, 1980.

Arieti, S. (1959). Schizophrenic thought. *American Journal of Psychotherapy* 13:537–552.

—— (1961). Introductory notes on the psychoanalytic therapy of schizophrenics. In *Psychotherapy of the Psychoses*, ed. A. Burton, pp. 69–89. New York: Basic Books.

Azima, H., and Wittkower, E. D. (1956). Gratifications of basic needs in schizophrenia. *Psychiatry* 19:119–120.

Balint, M. (1948). Individual differences of behavior in early infancy and an objective way of recording them. *Journal of Genetic Psychology* 73:57–117.

Balter, L., Lothane, Z., and Soencer, J. R., Jr. (1980). On the analyzing instrument. *Psychoanalytic Quarterly* 49:474–504.

Bick, E. (1968). The experience of the skin in early object relations. *International Journal of Psycho-Analysis* 49:484–486.

—— (1986). Further considerations on the function of the skin in early object relations. *British Journal of Psychotherapy* 2:292–299.

Binswanger, L. H. (1956). Freud's psychosentherapie. *Psyche* 10:357–366.

Bion, W. R. (1962). *Learning from Experience*. New York: Basic Books.

—— (1967). *Second Thoughts. Selected Papers on Psychoanalysis*. New York: Jason Aronson.

—— (1977). Attention and interpretation. In *Seven Servants. Four Works by Wilfred R. Bion*. New York: Jason Aronson.

Bower, T. G. R. (1977). The object in the world of the infant. *Scientific American* 225:30–48.

Bowlby, J. (1988). Developmental psychiatry comes of age. *American Journal of Psychiatry* 145:1–10.

Boyer, L. B. (1956). Maternal overstimulation and ego defects. In *The Regressed Patient*, pp. 3–22. New York: Jason Aronson, 1983.

—— (1961). Provisional evaluation of psychoanalysis with few parameters in the treatment of schizophrenia. In *The Regressed Patient*, pp. 63–89. New York: Jason Aronson, 1983.

—— (1967). *Die Psychoanalytischer Behandlung Schizophrener*. Munich: Kindler Verlag.

—— (1982). Analytic experiences in work with regressed patients. In *The Regressed Patient*, pp. 187–216. New York: Jason Aronson, 1983.

—— (1983). *The Regressed Patient*. New York: Jason Aronson.

—— (1986). Technical aspects of treating the regressed patient. *Contemporary Psychoanalysis* 22:25–44.

—— (1987). Psychoanalytic treatment of the borderline disorders today: a brief review. *Contemporary Psychoanalysis* 23:314–328.

Boyer L. B., and Giovacchini, P. L. (1967). *Psychoanalytic Treatment of Schizophrenic and Characterological Disorders*. New York: Science House.

—— (1980). *Psychoanalytic Treatment of Schizophrenic, Borderline, and Characterological Disorders*, 2nd ed., revised and enlarged. New York: Jason Aronson.

Brazelton, T. B. (1981). *On Becoming a Family: The Growth of Attachment.* New York: Delta/Seymour Lawrence.

Brunswick, R. M. (1928). A supplement to Freud's *A History of an Infantile Neurosis. International Journal of Psycho-Analysis* 9:439-476.

Bychowski, G. (1953). The problem of latent psychosis. *Journal of the American Psychoanalytic Association* 1:484-503.

Chiozza, L. A. (1976). *Cuerpo, Afecto y Lenguaje. Psicoanálisis y Enfermedad Somática.* Buenos Aires: Editorial Paidós.

Chiozza, L. A., Aizenberg, S., Bahamonde, C., et al. (1979). *La Interpretación Psicoanalítica de la Enfermedad Somática en la Teoría y en la Práctica Clínica.* Buenos Aires: Ediciones Universidad del Salvador.

Demers-Desrosiers, L. (1981). Influence of alexithymia on symbolic formation. *Psychotherapy and Psychosomatics* 38:103-120.

Deutsch, H. (1933). Zur psychologie der manisch-depressiven Zustände, insbesondere der chronischen Hypomanie. *Internationale Zeitschrift Für Psychoanalyse* 19:358-371.

—— (1937). Absence of grief. *Psychoanalytic Quarterly* 6:12-22.

Eisenstein, V. M. (1951). Differential psychotherapy of borderline states. *Psychiatric Quarterly* 25:379-401.

Eissler, K. R. (1953). The effect of the structure of the ego on psychoanalytic technique. *Journal of the American Psychoanalytic Association* 1:104-143.

Ekstein, R. (1955). Vicissitudes of the "internal image" in the recovery of a borderline schizophrenic adolescent. *Bulletin of the Menninger Clinic* 19:86-92.

—— (1966). *Children of Time and Space, of Action and Impulse. Clinical Studies of the Psychoanalytic Treatment of Severely Disturbed Children.* New York: Appleton-Century-Crofts.

Fairbairn, W. R. D. (1941). A revised psychopathology of the psychoses and psychoneuroses. *International Journal of Psycho-Analysis* 22:250-279.

Federn, P. (1933). The analysis of psychotics. *International Journal of Psycho-Analysis* 15:209-215.

Fordham, M. (1977). *Autism and the Self.* London: Heinemann.

Fraiberg, S. (1980). *Clinical Studies in Infant Mental Health: The First Year of Life.* New York: Basic Books.

Freud, A. (1969). *Difficulties in the Path of Psychoanalysis.* New York: International Universities Press.

Freud, S. (1905). On psychotherapy. *Standard Edition* 7:255-268.

—— (1914). On narcissism: an introduction. *Standard Edition* 14:67-102.

—— (1910). The future prospects for psycho-analytic therapy. *Standard Edition* 11:141-151.

—— (1923). The ego and the id. *Standard Edition* 19:12-18.

Frosch, J. (1967). Severe regressive states during analysis. *Journal of the American Psychoanalytic Association* 15:491-625.

—— (1983). *The Psychotic Process.* New York: International Universities Press.

—— (1988). *Psychodynamic Psychiatry.* 2 vols. New York: International Universities Press.

Gaddini, E. (1969). On imitation. *International Journal of Psycho-Analysis* 50:475–484.

—— (1981). Il problema mente-corpo en psicoanalisis. *Rivista di Psicoanalisi* 27:3–29.

—— (1982). Early defensive fantasies and the psychoanalytic process. *International Journal of Psycho-Analysis* 63:369–388.

—— (1986). La maschera e il cerchio. *Rivista di Psicoanalisi* 32:175–186.

Gaddini, R. (1970). Transitional objects and the process of individuation. *Journal of the American Academy of Child Psychiatry* 9:347–365.

—— (1974). Early psychosomatic symptoms and the tendency toward integration. *Psychotherapy and Psychosomatics* 23:26–34.

—— (1976). Formazione del sé e prima realità interna. *Rivista di Psicoanalisi* 2:206–225.

—— (1985). The precursors of transitional objects and phenomena. *Journal of the Squiggle Foundation* 1:49–56.

—— (1987). Early care and the roots of internalization. *International Review of Psycho-Analysis* 14:321–333.

Gaddini, R., and Gaddini, E. (1959). Rumination in infancy. In *Dynamic Psychopathology in Childhood,* ed. E. and L. Pavenstedt and L. Jessner, pp. 166–185. New York: Grune & Stratton.

García Vega, H. (1956). Algunos aspectos del análisis de una psicosis paranóide. *Revista de Psicoanálisis* 11:77–92.

Garma, Á. (1931). La realidad exterior y los instinctos en la esquizofrenia. *Revista de Psicoanálisis* 2:56–82.

—— (1962). La esquizofrenia. In *El Psicoanálisis. Teória, Clínica y Práctica.* Buenos Aires: Editorial Paidós.

Gill, M. H. (1954). Psychoanalysis and exploratory psychotherapy. *Journal of the American Psychoanalytic Association* 2:771–797.

—— (1979). The analysis of the transference. *Journal of the American Psychoanalytic Association* 27 (Suppl.):263–273.

Gioia, G., and Liberman, D. (1953). Una sesión psicoanalítica de un paciente esquizofrénica. *Revista de Psicoanálisis* 10:372–378

Giovacchini, P. L., ed. (1972). *Tactics and Techniques in Psychoanalytic Therapy.* New York: Science House.

—— (1979). *Treatment of Primitive Mental States.* New York: Jason Aronson.

—— (1980). Primitive agitation and primal confusion. In *Psychoanalytic Treatment of Schizophrenic, Borderline and Characterological Disorders,* 2nd ed., revised and expanded, ed. L. B. Boyer and P. L. Giovacchini, pp. 299–340. New York: Jason Aronson.

—— (1986). *Developmental Disorders. The Transitional Space in Mental Breakdown and Creative Integration.* Northvale, NJ: Jason Aronson.

—— ed. (1975a). *Psychoanalysis of Character Disorders.* New York: Jason Aronson.

—— (1989). *Countertransference: Triumphs and Catastrophies.* Northvale, NJ: Jason Aronson.

—— (ed., with the collaboration of A. Flarsheim and L. B. Boyer. [1975b]). *Tactics and Techniques in Psychoanalytic Therapy. Vol. II: Countertransference.* New York: Jason Aronson.

—— (1979). *Treatment of Primitive Mental States.* New York: Jason Aronson.

Giovacchini, P. L., and Boyer, L. B. eds. (1982). *Technical Factors in the Treatment of the Severely Disturbed Patient.* Northvale, NJ: Jason Aronson.

Gitelson, M. (1956). Psychoanalyst, USA. *American Journal of Psychiatry* 112:700–705.

Gottlieb, R. M. (1989). Technique and countertransference in Freud's analysis of the Rat Man. *Psychoanalytic Quarterly* 58:29–62.

Greenberg, J. R., and Mitchell, S. A. (1983). *Object Relations in Psychoanalytic Theory.* Cambridge, MA: Harvard University Press.

Grinberg, L., ed. (1977). *Prácticas Psicoanalíticas en las psicosis.* Buenos Aires: Editorial Paidós.

Grotstein, J. S. (1981). *Splitting and Projective Identification.* New York: Jason Aronson.

Grotstein, J. S., Solomon, M. F., and Lang, J. A. (1987). *The Borderline Patient.* 2 vols. Hillsdale, NJ: Analytic Press.

Gunderson, J. G., and Mosher, L. R. (1975). *Psychotherapy of Schizophrenia,* p. xxvii. New York: Jason Aronson.

Guntrip, H. (1968). *Schizoid Phenomena, Object Relations and the Self.* New York: International Universities Press.

Hann-Kende, F. (1933). On the role of transference and countertransference in psychoanalysis. In *Psychoanalysis and the Occult,* ed. G. Devereux, pp. 158–167. New York: International Universities Press.

Hughes, C. H. (1884). Borderland psychiatric records—prodromal symptoms of psychical impairment. *Alienist and Neurologist* 10:276–288.

Isakower, O. (1938). A contribution to the pathopsychology of phenomena associated with falling asleep. *International Journal of Psycho-Analysis* 19:331–345.

—— (1954). Spoken words in dreams. *Psychoanalytic Quarterly* 23:1–6.

Jacobson, E. (1943). Depression. The Oedipus conflict in the development of depressive mechanisms. *Psychoanalytic Quarterly* 12:541–560.

—— (1971). *Depression. Comparative Studies of Normal, Neurotic and Psychotic Conditions.* New York: International Universities Press.

—— (1974). *The Self and the Object World.* New York: International Universities Press.

Kernberg, O. F. (1967). Borderline personality organization. *Journal of the American Psychoanalytic Association* 15:641–685.

—— (1972). Critique of the Kleinian School. In *Tactics and Techniques in Psychoanalytic Therapy,* ed. P. L. Giovacchini, pp. 62–96. New York: Science House.

———— (1986). *Severe Personality Disorders. Psychotherapeutic Strategies.* New Haven: Yale University Press.

Kernberg, O. F., Burstein, E. D., Coyne, L., et al. (1972). Psychotherapy and psychoanalysis. Final report of the Menninger Foundation's psychotherapy research project. *Bulletin of the Menninger Clinic,* vol. 35.

Khan, M., and Masud R. (1960). Clinical aspects of the schizoid personality: affects and technique. *International Journal of Psycho-Analysis* 41:430–437.

Klein, M. (1930). The psychotherapy of the psychoses. *British Journal of Medical Psychology* 10:242–244.

———— (1968). *Contributions to Psycho-Analysis, 1921–1945.* London: Hogarth.

Klein, S. (1980). Autistic phenomena in neurotic patients. *International Journal of Psycho-Analysis* 61:395–401.

Knight, R. P. (1953). Borderline states. *Bulletin of the Menninger Clinic* 17:1–12.

Laforgue, R. (1926). Scotomization in schizophrenia. *International Journal of Psycho-Analysis* 8:473–478.

———— (1935). Contribution à l'étude de la schizophrénie. *Évolution Psychiatrique* 3:81–96.

Langs, R. (1976). *The Therapeutic Interaction,* vol. 2. New York: Jason Aronson.

Lewin, B. D. (1932). Analysis and structure of a transient hypomania. *Psychoanalytic Quarterly* 1:43–58.

———— (1937). A type of hypomanic reaction. *Archives of Psychiatry and Neurology* 37:868–873.

———— (1946). Sleep, the mouth and the dream screen. *Psychoanalytic Quarterly* 15:419–434.

———— (1950). *The Psychoanalysis of Elation.* New York: Norton.

———— (1953). The forgetting of dreams. In *Drives, Affects, Behavior,* ed. R. M. Loewenstein, pp. 191–202. New York: International Universities Press.

———— (1958). *Dreams and the Uses of Regression.* New York: International Universities Press.

Lipowski, Z. J. (1988). Somatization: the concept and its clinical application. *American Journal of Psychiatry* 145:1358–1368.

Little, M. (1957). "R"—the analyst's total response to his patient's needs. In *Transference Neurosis and Transference Psychosis,* pp. 51–80. New York: Jason Aronson, 1981.

———— (1966). Transference in borderline states. In *Transference Neurosis and Transference Psychosis,* pp. 135–154. New York: Jason Aronson, 1981.

Loewald, H. (1960). The therapeutic action of psychoanalysis. In *Papers on Psychoanalysis,* pp. 221–256. New Haven: Yale University Press, 1980.

———— (1979). Reflections on the psychoanalytic process and its therapeutic potential. In *Papers on Psychoanalysis,* pp. 372–383. New Haven: 1980.

———— (1986). Transference-countertransference. *Journal of the Psychoanalytic Association* 34:155–167.

Lorenz, K. (1937). *Studies in Animal and Human Behavior.* London: Methuen.

Mahler, M. S. (1968). *On Human Symbiosis and the Vicissitudes of Individuation.* New York: International Universities Press.

Mahler, M. S., Pine, F., and Bergman, A. (1975). *The Psychological Birth of the Human Infant.* New York: Basic Books.

Mahoney, P. (1986). *Freud and the Rat Man.* New Haven: Yale University Press.

Marmor, J. (1953). Orality in the hysterical personality. *Journal of the American Psychoanalytic Association* 1:656–671.

Marty, P., M'Uzan, M., and David, C. (1963). *L'Investigation Psychosomatique. Sept Observations Cliniques.* Paris: Universitaires de France.

McDougall, J. (1978). *Plea for a Measure of Abnormality.* New York: International Universities Press.

—— (1989). *Theaters of the Body: A Psychoanalytic Approach to Psychosomatic Illness.* New York: Norton.

Meissner, W. W. (1984). *The Borderline Spectrum. Differential Diagnosis and Developmental Issues.* New York: Jason Aronson.

Meltzer, D. (1967). *The Psychoanalytical Process.* London: Heinemann.

—— (1975). Adhesive identification. *Contemporary Psychoanalysis* 11:289–310.

Meltzer, D., Bremner, J., Hoxter, S., et al. (1975). *Explorations in Autism.* Perthshire: Clunie.

Menninger, W. C. (1947). Psychosomatic medicine: somatization reactions. *Psychosomatic Medicine* 9:92–97.

Modell, A. H. (1963). Primitive object relationships and the predisposition to schizophrenia. *International Journal of Psycho-Analysis* 44:282–292.

Nemiah, J. C., Freyburger, H., and Sifneos, P. E. (1976). Alexithymia: a view of the psychosomatic process. In *Modern Trends in Psychosomatic Medicine,* vol. 3, ed. O. W. Hill, pp. 403–409. New York: Appleton-Century-Crofts.

Nöllman, J. (1953). Consideraciones psicoanalíticas acerca de un enfermo esquizofrénico con mecanismos hipocondríaco-paranóides. *Revista de Psicoanálisis* 10:37–74.

Nunberg, H. (1948). *Practice and Theory of Psychoanalysis.* New York: Nervous and Mental Disease Publishing Co.

Ogden, T. H. (1982). *Projective Identification and Psychotherapeutic Technique.* New York: Jason Aronson.

—— (1986). *The Matrix of the Mind. Object Relations and the Psychoanalytic Dialogue.* Northvale, NJ: Jason Aronson.

—— (1989). On the concept of an autistic-contiguous position. *The Primitive Edge of Experience.* Northvale, NJ: Jason Aronson.

Racker, H. (1953). The countertransference neurosis. *International Journal of Psycho-Analysis* 34:313–324.

Rangell, H. (1953). Similarities and differences between psychoanalysis and dynamic psychotherapy. *Journal of the American Psychoanalytic Association* 2:734–744.

—— (1981). Psychoanalysis and dynamic psychotherapy: Similarities and differences twenty-five years later. *Psychoanalytic Quarterly* 50:655–693.

Reichard, S. (1956). A re-examination of "Studies in Hysteria." *Psychoanalytic Quarterly* 25:155-177.

Reik, T. (1948). *Listening with the Third Ear. The Inner Experience of a Psychoanalyst.* New York: Farrar, Straus.

Rickman, J. (1926). A survey: the development of the psycho-analytical theory of the psychoses, 1894-1926. *British Journal of Medical Psychology* 6:270-294.

—— (1927). A survey: the development of the psycho-analytical theory of the psychoses, 1894-1926. *British Journal of Medical Psychology* 7:94-124, 321-374.

Roiphe, H., and Galenson, E. (1981). *Infantile Origins of Sexual Identity.* New York: International Universities Press.

Rolla, E. (1957). Análisis de una esquizofrénica. *Revista de Psicoanálisis* 14:72-75.

Rosenfeld, D. (1982). The notion of a psychotic body image in neurotic and psychotic patients. Paper presented before the Norwegian Psychoanalytic Society, Oslo.

—— (1984). Hypochondriasis, somatic delusion and body schema in psychoanalytic practice. *International Journal of Psycho-Analysis* 65:377-388.

Rosenfeld, D., and Pistol, D. (1986). Episodio psicótico y su detección precoz en la transferencia. Paper presented at the XVIth Latinamerican Psychoanalytic Congress, Mexico City, July.

Rosenfeld, H. A. (1965). *Psychotic States: A Psycho-Analytical Approach.* London: Hogarth.

Rosse, I. C. (1890). Clinical evidences of borderland insanity. *Journal of Nervous and Mental Disease* 17:669-683.

Schwing, G. (1940). *A Way to the Soul of the Mentally Ill.* New York: International Universities Press.

Searles, H. F. (1965). *Collected Papers on Schizophrenia and Related Subjects.* New York: International Universities Press.

—— (1979). *Countertransference and Related Subjects. Selected Papers.* New York: International Universities Press.

—— (1986). *My Work with Borderline Patients.* Northvale, NJ: Jason Aronson.

Sechehaye, M. A. (1947). *Symbolic Realization.* New York: International Universities Press, 1951.

Segal, H. (1950). Some aspects of the analysis of a schizophrenic. *International Journal of Psycho-Analysis* 31:268-278.

—— (1957). Notes on symbol formation. In *The Work of Hanna Segal*, pp. 49-68. New York: Jason Aronson.

Spiegel, L. A. (1975). The functions of free association in psychoanalysis: their relation to technique and therapy. *International Review of Psycho-Analysis* 2:379-388.

Spitz, R. A. (1955). The primal cavity: a contribution to the genesis of perception and its role for psychoanalytic theory. *Psychoanalytic Study of the Child* 10:215-240. New York: International Universities Press.

—— (1965). *The First Year of Life.* New York: International Universities Press.

Stekel, W. (1911). Zür Differentialdiagnose organischer und psychogenischer Erkrankungen. *Zentralblatt für Psychoanalyse und Psychotherapie* 1:45–47.

Stern, A. (1938). Psychoanalytic investigation of and therapy in the borderline group of neuroses. *Psychoanalytic Quarterly* 7:467–469.

Stern, D. N. (1985). *The Interpersonal World of the Infant.* New York: Basic Books.

Stone, L. (1954). The widening scope of indications for psychoanalysis. *Journal of the American Psychoanalytic Association* 2:567–594.

—— (1982). The influence of the practice and theory of psychotherapy on education in psychoanalysis. In *Psychotherapy: Impact on Psychoanalytic Training,* ed. E. D. Joseph and R. S. Wallerstein, pp. 75–118. New York: International Universities Press.

Tähkä, V. (1988). On the early formation of the mind. I: differentiation. *International Journal of Psycho-Analysis* 68:229–250.

Tausk, O. (1919). On the origin of the "influencing machine" in schizophrenia. *Psychoanalytic Quarterly,* 1933 2:519–556.

Taylor, G. T. (1984). Alexithymia: concept, measurement, and implications for treatment. *American Journal of Psychiatry* 141:725–732.

Tinbergen, N. (1957). On anti-predator response in certain birds: a reply. *Journal of Physiologic Psychology* 50:412–414.

Tustin, F. (1972). *Autism and Childhood Psychosis.* London: Hogarth.

—— (1981). *Autistic States in Children.* Boston: Routledge and Kegan Paul.

—— (1986). *Autistic Barriers in Neurotic Patients.* New Haven: Yale University Press, 1987.

Volkan, V. D. (1976). *Primitive Internalized Object Relations.* New York: International Universities Press.

Wallerstein, R. S. (1986). *Forty-Two Lives in Treatment: A Study of Psychoanalysis and Psychotherapy.* New York: Guilford Press.

—— (1989). Psychoanalysis and psychotherapy: an historical perspective. *International Journal of Psycho-Analysis,* in press.

Weizsäcker, V. (1946). *Casos y Problemas Clínicas.* Barcelona: Editorial Pubul.

—— (1954). *Natur und Geist.* Göttingen: Vandenhoeck & Ruprecht.

—— (1962). *El Círculo de la forma.* Madrid: Editorial Morate.

Wexler, M. (1951). The structural problem in schizophrenia: therapeutic implications. *International Journal of Psycho-Analysis* 32:157–166.

Will, O. A. (1961). Process, psychotherapy, and schizophrenia. In *Psychotherapy of the Psychoses,* ed. A. Burton, pp. 10–42. New York: Basic Books.

Willick, M. S. (1983). On the concept of primitive defenses. *Journal of the American Psychoanalytic Association* 31:175–200.

Wilson, C. P., and Mintz, I. L. (1989). *Psychosomatic Symptoms: Psychodynamic Treatment of the Underlying Personality Disorder.* Northvale, NJ: Jason Aronson.

Winnicott, D. W. (1953a). Transitional objects and transitional phenomena. In *Collected Papers. Through Paediatrics to Psycho-Analysis,* pp. 229–242. New York: Basic Books, 1958.

—— (1953b). Psychosis and child care. In *Collected Papers. Through Paediatrics to Psycho-Analysis*, pp. 219–228. New York: Basic Books, 1958.

—— (1956). Primary maternal preoccupation. In *Collected Papers. Through Paediatrics to Psycho-Analysis*, pp. 300–305. New York: Basic Books, 1958.

—— (1958). *Collected Papers. Through Paediatrics to Psycho-Analysis*. New York: Basic Books.

—— (1960). The theory of the parent–infant relationship. In *The Maturational Process and the Facilitating Environment*, pp. 37–55. New York: International Universities Press, 1965.

—— (1965). *The Maturational Process and the Facilitating Environment*. New York: International Universities Press.

—— (1969). The use of an object. *International Journal of Psycho-Analysis* 50:711–716.

—— (1971). *Playing and Reality*. New York: Basic Books.

Wolberg, A. R. (1952). The borderline patient. *American Journal of Psychotherapy* 6:694–710.

PART I

MASTER CLINICIANS ON THE REGRESSED PATIENT

PETER L. GIOVACCHINI, M.D.

Interpretation, Fusion, and Psychic Synthesis

Infantile trauma impedes the ordinary course of emotional development; that is, it leads to fixation points to which the patient may regress later in life when facing stresses that are associatively connected to these early disruptive experiences. When one is dealing with patients suffering from primitive mental states, the definitive developmental stages that Freud (1905, 1916) postulated are difficult to observe, and we seldom, if ever, witness a neat regression to an easily discernible fixation point. Rather, ego states are amorphous and chaotic, and they are reflected in the way patients perceive themselves.

Emotional development is viewed as a series of hierarchically ordered sequences. There is a relatively smooth progression from global unstructured psychic states to highly differentiated ego states, a movement from an amorphous to a discrete organization. Freud (1905) outlined a developmental course beginning with autoerotism, to primary and secondary narcissism, and then traversing the various psychosexual stages that deal with part objects to a final whole-object genital phase. The structuralizing process achieves unity, but within higher states of greater organization there is also considerable compartmentalization.

Analysts think in terms of subsystems that have specific functions, but they are integrated with one another and contribute to ego synthesis (Nunberg 1932) and cohesiveness. Mental functioning can be divided into two fundamental activities, perception and action, that occur in an increasingly sophisticated secondary process fashion as the mind matures. The progression from amorphous to differentiated psychic states leads to a more discriminated awareness of external reality and a distinction between the inner and outer world. As subsystems are constructed, the ego learns how to move in that outer world, and how to adapt, cope, and satisfy inner needs. This is an adaptation that occurs within the context of object relations.

Freud (1912, 1913) postulated that the goal of psychoanalytic treatment is resolution of intrapsychic conflicts, particularly those dealing with oedipal issues. Whether he was dealing with oedipally based neuroses is a moot point (Giovacchini 1986, Reichard 1956), but analysts, in their dealing with a group of patients commonly designated as borderline, find that the effects of faulty psychic structure play a significant role in the production of psychopathology and have to be dealt with in the treatment setting. Interpretation within the transference context, considered to be the essence of the psychoanalytic method (Gill 1982), makes the unconscious conscious and subject to control by the ego's synthetic forces. This is known as *working through*, which Freud (1914) discussed primarily in terms of the patient's resistance to allowing this type of synthesis to occur. Patients are generally afraid of giving up their resistance to free association, which is designed to bring unconscious derivatives into consciousness. Brenner (1987), on the other hand, refers to the analysis of all components of psychic conflict, even those that place themselves in direct opposition to the goals of treatment.

Since the modus operandi of the analytic method is interpretation and an exploration of the transference-countertransference axis, clinicians may question how verbal exchange will have an effect on psychic structure, since the patients confronting us seem to have problems because of faulty psychic structure. When one is dealing with patients described as character disorders (Giovacchini 1979, 1986), the aim of treatment is to attain some character change, since it is the structure of the psyche that creates emotional pain, misery, and difficulties in relating to the external world. This goal seems to be markedly different from that of resolving intrapsychic conflict and could easily be thought of as requiring more than interpretation alone.

Thus we are faced with two questions. The first relates to a more precise concept of defective structure, and the second requires us to explore in greater detail just what is meant by interpretation, especially interpretation within a transference context. As clinicians, we are most concerned about the insight-promoting qualities of interpretation and how they lead to beneficial changes in psychic equilibrium. This will require an expansion of our understanding of the psychopathological discontinuities of psychic structure as well as the interpretative interaction.

STRUCTURAL PSYCHOPATHOLOGY
AND THE BORDERLINE STATE

Regardless of the voluminous literature on the borderline patient, we still are bewildered as to what, exactly, we mean by borderline. At a conference in 1975, Masterson, Kernberg, Searles, and I spent an entire day presenting theoretical and technical viewpoints, as well as ample clinical material that we believed would help elucidate the problems we face when diagnosing and treating borderline patients. At the end of the day, we were all convinced that we were speaking about different patient populations, though there were some similarities in our descriptions of the manifestations of psychopathology (see Masterson 1977).

Ordinarily, psychoanalysts are not too concerned about precise diagnostic distinctions. We usually follow Freud (1912), who stated that we should not have any preconceived notions about our patients and should be surprised at every "turn" in the material. Still, he paid some attention to diagnosis when he distinguished between the transference and the narcissistic neuroses (Freud 1914) and made such a distinction the determinant of whether psychoanalytic treatment is possible. Thus, in psychoanalysis, as in other clinical areas, diagnosis has some relevance to treatability.

Patients suffering from structural or characterological psychopathology, more easily referred to as character disorders, do not form a homogeneous group. I propose the term *character disorders* as a general category that can be placed alongside, and at the same level, as the psychoneuroses. These two categories highlight the distinction between structural and instinctual conflict, which can be compared to anatomical and physiological disorders. As is true generally, there are very few "pure" diseases.

Within the category of character disorders, the diagnostician includes borderline states and the psychoses (Giovacchini 1979). The latter frequently have been viewed as examples of structural defects. As Freud's approach to diagnosis was multidimensional, in that he included levels of fixation and regression and specific conflicts and groups of defenses, the differences among various types of character disorders are examined in terms of the quality of object relationships, specific adaptive mechanisms, and the cohesiveness of the self-representation. These refer to, respectively, phenomenology, psychic processes, and structural factors.

In a recent book (Giovacchini 1979), I subdivided character disorders into five clinical entities: (1) schizoid states, (2) borderline states, (3) character neuroses, (4) affective disorders, and (5) psychoses. The first four can be considered to be on a continuum from the most primitive schizoid states that exhibit severe structural problems, primarily a lack of structure, to the affective disorders, which in addition to faulty structure principally involving the superego, can also be understood as the outcome of intrapsychic forces. The psychoses do not belong on this continuum in spite of the structural defects they exhibit. They have to be studied in a different frame of reference (Giovacchini 1986), but this is not the purpose of this chapter.

As is usually true of continuums, the extremities are clear-cut. It is what lies in between that is hard to perceive clearly; in this instance, this includes borderline states and character neuroses. Schizoid states and affective disorders are, for the most part, easy to distinguish.

Briefly, schizoid states refer to patients who lead a dull, drab existence. They relate only minimally to the surrounding world, unable to deal with its complexities. Their chief mode of relating or, better stated, nonrelating, is withdrawal; hence the label *schizoid*. They do not have the complexity of structure required to form an elaborate delusion. They are constricted, infantile, dependent persons who frequently cannot subsist on their own. They may require custodial care.

The borderline states and the character neuroses are difficult to differentiate. I believe that the blurred distinctions between these two groups explains our bewilderment about borderline patients.

The patients I prefer to call borderline make a borderline adjustment to the outside world. Their psychic structure is not sufficiently developed for them to deal with the complexities of daily life. As one patient aptly put it, he had an arithmetic mentality but was living in a world of calculus complexity. Still, unlike the schizoid patient, they relate to their environment, but they try to change it so that it will be in tune with their needs and adpative capacities. There is a lack of synchrony between their psychic organization and what is required to get along in the outside world. As is true of all emotional disorders, it is the degree of asynchrony that determines the type and extent of psychopathology.

Inasmuch as the cohesiveness of the self-representation is determined by how a person functions, these patients, because of their relative lack of adaptive capacities and their inner discontinuities, have an insecure identity sense. The lack of adaptive capacities includes defensive adjustments. I distinguish this group from the character neuroses in that the character neuroses have fairly well-organized defenses that help them maintain self-esteem and cope with the vicissitudes of the outer world.

All patients with character disorders have identity problems and, at times, difficulties in relating to external objects and the surrounding milieu. They can become transiently psychotic, which, from some clinicians' viewpoints, would qualify them for the label borderline. Borderline then would be a phenomenological diagnosis. The patients I have designated as borderline are borderline in two respects; they can become psychotic, and they make a borderline adjustment to the external world. Furthermore, they have a paucity of defenses in comparison to the next group in the diagnostic hierarchy, the character neuroses.

I am emphasizing the borderline qualities of this group of patients in contrast to the character neuroses group, who can have rather complex defenses that enable them to maintain a degree of intrapsychic equilibrium and narcissistic supplies. Borderline patients have some defenses and may be able to use splitting and projective defenses, but they are, to a large measure, unsuccessful. They suffer from a pervasive sense of inadequacy and make only a marginal adjustment.

The character neuroses are able to make some type of adaptation to the external world and to maintain narcissistic supplies. They may make extensive use of projective and splitting mechanisms, their prominent concern often being the maintenance of self-esteem. Frequently, they overcompensate for latent feelings of inadequacy. In some instances, their narcissistic defenses fail, and these patients suffer from low self-esteem and feel insecure in their identity sense.

Patients with character neuroses differ from borderline states, however, in that they do not sense a lack within themselves. They may view themselves as self-defeating or inhibited, but they do not complain that they do not know how to deal with a situation. They may be conflicted as to what to do, but they attribute this to ambivalence, since they know the alternatives.

Their psychopathology chiefly involves the self-representation in a specific fashion. Similar to borderline patients, they have a poorly defined identity sense, but they are more conflicted about themselves rather than bewildered as to who or what they are. Basically, they do not approve of themselves. If their narcissistic defenses work, they aggrandize their status, an overcompensation protecting them against their inner disapproval. Otherwise, they openly reveal and sometimes act out of their fundamental sense of inadequacy.

The self-representation suffers from inner conflict. It is better constructed than that of the borderline patient, but it is not able to tolerate intimacy. They view intimate relationships as they have experienced the mother–child fusion. Their mothers, as a rule, did not abandon them, as has frequently happened with borderline patients. Rather, their mothers used them as narcissistic extensions of themselves, sometimes projecting their self-hatred into the child. There are many variations of the mother–child bond, but patients suffering from character neuroses conceive of the maternal symbiosis (fusion) as destructive.

Borderline patients appear to be psychically disjointed. Various parts of their psyche are not integrated with one another. There is a lack of continuity between inner needs and the ego's executive system's techniques to gratify those needs. In some instances, inner needs are not fully developed so that they can be expressed or felt (Giovacchini 1979, 1986), but, nevertheless, the patient senses a need and is often overwhelmed by the disruptive feeling that something is missing without being able to define that feeling further. This inability to identify feelings only adds to the patient's disruption.

Ordinarily, the child, even during infancy, is prepared to deal with the outer world. The infantile environment is not particularly different from the adult world. Borderline patients, by contrast, have been raised in a world that was radically different from the contemporary milieu. Sometimes, the infantile world strikes us as so alien that the patient seems to have been raised on another planet.

Thus, the inner world of borderline patients, because of their early surroundings, is not congruent with the world they have to live in. They cannot cope with the exigencies all of us have to face routinely. Normally the psyche finds the contemporary world familiar because, to some extent, it has related to various facets of reality since infancy. The infantile environment is *externalized* and becomes blended with the surrounding world. The ego can cope with the environment because it has appropriate adaptive techniques that have been gradually acquired since childhood. By contrast, borderline patients, because of the alien world of their infancy, cannot achieve a smooth adaptive externalization. The inner discontinuity of various layers of the psyche hampers the functioning of the executive system, and this is reflected in the clumsy, disjointed, and unsatisfying fashion the patients relate to the external world and objects.

I have often referred to the hypothetical and legendary master sergeant as an excellent example of externalization (Giovacchini 1972, 1979, 1986, 1987). The sergeant's parents may have been violent, volatile persons who were physically abusive both to themselves and their children. The sergeant was raised in an atmosphere of violence, and his defenses and adaptations were able to deal with dangerous situations. During battle, the sergeant is calm and efficient and knows how to survive in settings the ordinary person would find terrifying. The sergeant has externalized the violent infantile milieu into the world of war. In a world of peace, however, the sergeant may feel himself in a quandary. It is an unfamiliar world in which he feels inept and gauche; it is a world that cannot integrate the infantile ambience.

STRUCTURAL DISCONTINUITY

The character structure of the borderline patient can be conceptualized in terms of a vertical axis. As mentioned, I am referring to a lack of hierarchically ordered, smoothly blended layers of psychic structure. Freud (1915) stressed that in the course of emotional development, earlier levels do not disappear; they continue to exist alongside later, better-developed stages, as he described when he compared the maturation of the psyche to various layers of lava moving down the volcano, the forward layers gradually incorporating those behind them. Some borderline patients demonstrate structural discontinuity. There is little connection between early and later developmental stages; there are relatively few or no connecting bridges. The effects of such a defect can be striking.

> For example, a young adult male seemed to adapt well to the psychoanalytic ambience. He was comfortable on the couch and did not seem to have any particular difficulties in free associating. Having become accustomed to a relatively quiet treatment environment, I was surprised when this suddenly changed.
>
> After three months of treatment, after speaking calmly and quietly for ten minutes, he spasmodically twisted his body and neck and screamed. The scream would start as a soft sob or moan and then gradually increase in intensity, a slow crescendo culminating in a vocal explosion. At the same time, his body would convulse and twist, and he would grimace as if he were feeling severe pain. On occasion he might twist his arms around his face or head as if he were warding off a blow. At the beginning, these episodes occurred two or three times per session, but as time went on they increased in frequency to every two or three minutes. His sessions became a series of such explosions.
>
> I asked him whether he were afraid I might attack him, since he seemed to be both protecting himself and acting as if he had been struck. He replied that he was not afraid of me and did not see me as wanting to hit him. Rather, he was dismayed at what he considered to be his inability to communicate and make contact with me.
>
> He described an intense but inchoate feeling being generated deeply inside himself. He felt it first as an indescribable sensation building up somewhere in his abdominal area. He experienced it as a relentless, disruptive force that he was struggling to restrain and confine. His twisting and grimacing were the manifestations of this struggle. He believed he could tame this turmoil if he could only put it in words, but it was experienced as a quantum jump, incapable of being

tamed and suddenly exploding in his mind when it reached its greatest intensity. He would then scream.

We compared this sequence with the operations of a Van der Graef generator, which consists of two metal poles that act as stands for two spheres that are several inches apart. Electricity is pumped into one pole until it reaches a certain intensity of potential energy. After peaking, the electrical buildup creates a spark that jumps the gap between the spheres. Potential energy is converted into kinetic energy and is manifested by a spark. Because there is no connecting bridge between the two spheres, there is no smooth dynamic flow of electric current. Energy is transported in quantum jumps.

The patient, in a similar fashion, lacked connecting bridges between upper and lower levels of the psyche. Primary process forces did not undergo secondary process revision by transforming feelings into words, thoughts, and concepts. They burst through in their raw and unbridled form into consciousness. The patient had a relative lack of intermediary zones that tame or, as Hartmann (1955) would state, neutralize elemental forces. This young man was usually capable of processing feelings and had connecting bridges between reality-attuned and primary process-oriented personality levels. In the regression stimulated by the treatment process, however, his defective psychic continuity became manifest.

The patient who has nothing to say or who vigorously seems to avoid becoming involved with instinctual derivatives is often another example of specific structural defects involving a lack of continuity and characteristic of the borderline state.

A single man in his early 30s described his mother as an astute, intuitive woman. She had recognized that he had some bizarre ideas, believed that he was schizophrenic, and insisted that he get into treatment. Since she was his only source of income, he felt forced to see me. Their relationship had been more like two "pals" throughout his life rather than that of mother and child. He described her as hating children or childish activities; on the other hand, she could be charming and perceptive at the adult level. However, he could not trust her. If he allowed himself to feel helpless and vulnerable, she would turn away from him and even stop giving him money. The patient believed she would control the treatment because she was paying for it and I would find her more interesting than he was.

Session after session he would lie on my couch and lament the fact that he was there. He would usually start by stating that he had nothing to say. Since his mother had picked me as his therapist, I was not the right person for him. He had had the same experience with every therapist he had seen, regardless of who chose them. He saw no value whatsoever in what we were trying to do, and he disavowed that there was anything of significance in his unconscious; in fact, he denied he had an unconscious. The few times he spoke he went into concrete details about mundane everyday events. He spoke with such a detachment that it caused me to feel that I was not there.

I learned that he had to denigrate what he found to be valuable. This became apparent in his dreams and with an acute psychotic breakdown that required hospitalization after I left on a two-week trip. He could not allow himself closeness, that is, infantile dependence, because he felt he would be "dropped." I learned subsequently that his mother actually had dropped him and was very awkward and clumsy holding him when he was an infant.

In a sense, he had succeeded in decathecting the primitive parts of the psyche. When he said he had nothing to say, he really had nothing to say. He was not repressing unconscious derivatives or withholding or resisting free associating. I accepted his pronouncement at face value. Since he was not able to bring to life his infantile yearnings and conflicts, he felt lifeless. His attitude toward life was mechanistic and concrete and nonpsychologically oriented.

He did not cathect me either, and that is why I felt obliterated. In a sense, he was correct. Since he could not use me as a target for projection except to view me as he did his mother, I was a person who could relate only to higher ego levels. Therefore, I was useless. I had a picture of his unconscious as being a dark room. If he lit a lamp, I would come into existence as I became visible, but if he kept the room dark, then my presence would no longer be perceived. My existence depended on his energizing early psychic states. To cathect me, he had to cathect his unconscious first.

It may seem redundant to speak of a cathexis of the unconscious, since the unconscious has been viewed as an energic source, a seething cauldron (Freud 1916–1917, 1923). In this instance, I am giving the ego a central position in that if it does not exactly serve three masters, it at least relates to them: the external world, the superego, and the id (Freud 1923). In other words, the ego is connected to all psychic systems.

My patient's lack of such connections is part of a structural defect and differs from repression. Psychoneurotic patients who count on repression as a dominant defense reveal in dreams and associations unconscious derivatives that are frequently expressed in primary process terms. The patients I am describing often present themselves as concretely oriented, rigid persons who, if they report dreams, usually dream of segments of reality. Their dreams are also concretely structured, to the degree that the analyst finds it difficult to discover id derivatives. As these patients are extensively studied, this inability to get in touch with various parts of the self turns out to be the outcome of an inner fragmentation, a structural discontinuity, rather than an adaptive defense such as repression.

STRUCTURE-PROMOTING INTERPRETATIONS AND FUSION

Clinicians have devoted considerable attention to the curative factors in psychoanalysis. Often, the therapist postulates that an effective interaction with the patient has to go "beyond interpretation." Alexander and French (1946) wrote about the "corrective emotional experience," an adoption of a role that is contrary to the patient's self-defeating and painful expectations. The classic example of a corrective emotional experience is that of the priest who has been robbed of his silverware by the escaped convict Jean Valjean in Victor Hugo's novel *Les Miserables*. The police apprehend the thief with the stolen goods and bring him to the priest's house. Apparently Jean had been given dinner by the kindly priest and repaid him by stealing his silver. The priest, on seeing Jean with the gendarmes, surprises him and his guards when he says, "But Jean, you have forgotten the candlesticks," indicating that what Jean had taken was a gift. This event changed the course of Jean's life, and he became a prosperous and respected citizen.

In Chicago, there was considerable enthusiasm about what was considered to be a new technique that eventually led to insight, but was distinct and different from interpretation. The enthusiasm was short-lived; it was difficult to create "Jean Valjean" situations in treatment, and the analyst's interventions were often awkward because of his discomfort with the deliberate assumption of a role. Today, there is little reference to the corrective emotional experience. It has acquired a negative connotation, and within the analytic context is is considered to be a manipulation that hampers the therapeutic relationship.

Kohut (1971) and his followers believe that they have discovered a new therapeutic approach that does not exactly eschew interpretation, but it does not emphasize it either. The key word is *empathy*, which, like the corrective emotional experience, provides patients with something they have never had in their traumatic infantile backgrounds. A proper amount of empathy and mirroring (furnishing the patient with narcissistic supplies) supposedly sets the fixated developmental process in motion once again. I need not point out the obvious fallacies to this approach, since I have already critically discussed them (Giovacchini 1977, 1979). Interpretation is not a prominent aspect of Kohut's technique, that is, interpretation in the traditional sense.

Dealing with patients suffering from structural defects causes many clinicians to feel inadequate if they rely only on the insight-producing effects of interpretation. There is more to the treatment of such patients than simply making the unconscious conscious. In fact, some borderline patients seem to be completely immersed in their unconscious, not having a repressive barrier of any consequence. Often, the analyst quickly senses that the patient already knows a good deal about his inner world and that this knowledge has not, in any way, helped. The therapist may feel that he does not have or know the proper treatment techniques that will enable him to deal with a perplexing clinical situation; he feels as if he were a *borderline analyst*, a feeling that, if sufficiently intensified, may cause him to abandon the analytic method and to seek substitutes for interpretation.

It has been especially recommended for the treatment of patients suffering from character disorders that the analyst concentrate on interpreting the transference. The patient may be well acquainted with primitive forces within the self and the manifestations of faulty psychic structure, but he may not know how his psychic state and past infantile traumatic experiences are reflected in his attitudes toward and relationship with the analyst. Gill (1982) believes that the only therapeutically effective interpretation in any analysis is interpretation of the transference.

Discussing different types of interpretations highlights that there are various levels of meanings to such interactions. An interpretation is more than just a disembodied stream of words. More than intellectual content is communicated. The interpretation of the transference implies that, along with content, there are also powerful feelings that are being transmitted, which at times cannot be put into words. These feelings, however, could be instrumental in the creation of inner structural changes that can lead to the acquisition of psychic structure, which enables the patient to relate better to the outer world, an adaptive improvement that, in turn, achieves further integration, a positive feedback sequence. Such interactions are subtle and cannot be understood only in terms of the total content of the interpretation.

INTERPRETATION AND DEFINITION
OF THE ANALYTIC SETTING

Some exchanges between the patient and therapist do not appear to have any resemblance to interpretation. For example, Winnicott (1972) in his paper "Fragment of an Analysis" describes his reaction to the patient's material, which, I believe, had considerable interpretative significance, although on the surface what Winnicott said did not seem to be at all related to what the patient was feeling or doing (Giovacchini 1972). Rather, it seemed to be a description of what Winnicott was experiencing. The patient, a youthful professional man who generally felt inadequate, reported to Winnicott a rare instance of feeling good about himself. Apparently, he had achieved something in his daily life of which he was proud, and with enthusiasm, reported his triumph to Winnicott. The patient was disappointed with Winnicott's response because he felt that his therapist was not sufficiently sharing and reflecting back his good feeling. Winnicott's reply was interesting as he stated, "I made an interpretation," and then he went on to explain that he did not, at the moment, feel as enthusiastic as the patient, but then, at other times, he did not feel as despondent or as depressed about the patient's material. This reply does not sound like an interpretation, since Winnicott seemed to be talking only about his feelings and responses rather than the patient's. At most, it could be considered to be a remark about countertransference and not a transference interpretation.

Nevertheless, Winnicott believed that his response was an interpretation as indicated by his words, "I made an interpretation." I believe he was correct and that, in an indirect fashion, he had made a transference interpretation. In my mind, Winnicott was emphasizing that he had a spectrum of reactions to the patient's material. He did not get as elated or as depressed as the patient. Winnicott's spectrum was narrower than the patient's, but Winnicott represented the analytic setting. Anything the patient felt that went beyond the boundaries of the setting, either in the upward extremes as elation or the downward side of the spectrum as depression, belongs exclusively to the patient. Whatever expectations he may have of his analyst that go beyond the boundaries of Winnicott's reactions can be considered to be transference expectations or simply transference. I believe Winnicott understood this intuitively.

I have called this type of interpretation a *definition of the analytic setting* (Giovacchini 1972), which, I believe, can be useful to patients suffering from faulty psychic structure and who have poorly constructed ego boundaries. Borderline patients, especially, find it difficult to relate to new settings because, as with everything else, they find them incomprehensible.

Part of their dilemma is based on a relative lack of discrimination between the inner world of the psyche and reality. Defining the boundaries of the analytic setting can be reassuring.

INTERPRETATION AND THE REPETITION COMPULSION

To discuss further the content of interpretations, the classical approach concentrated on id impulses or the defenses against such impulses. Defenses were often entwined in the patient's resistance. Freud did not make precise distinctions between resistances and defenses, and because of the lack of such a differentiation, aspects of his therapeutic approach can be difficult to understand. He advocated the analysis of defenses, but, in actuality, he forbade resistance. When he (Freud 1912–1914) insisted that analysis be conducted in a state of abstinence, he was trying to hinder the expression of resistance, which often took the form of acting out (Freud 1914). He also recognized the importance of the repetition compulsion as it dominated the transference and determined the patient's feelings and reactions toward the analyst (Freud 1920).

The recognition of the repetition compulsion as a salient feature of the patient's psychopathological behavior and feelings and its role in constructing the transference expands our concept of the psychoanalytic treatment process. It also extends our concept of interpretation beyond interpreting hidden instinctual impulses, defenses, and resistances. Although the "compulsion to repeat" (Freud 1920) is an intrinsic quality of an instinctual impulse, the repetition compulsion is a much broader process that describes an infantile frame of reference. The patient has developed certain defenses and adaptive techniques to deal with the traumatic infantile environment. In life he recreates the trauma so that he can master it. If his total environment resembles the early dangerous and threatening relationships (usually assaultive or abandoning), then the patient has managed to externalize a milieu. The repetition compulsion is the motivating force behind externalization and includes many other elements in addition to instinctual impulses.

The purpose of the repetition compulsion, although it often seems to be a repetition of a self-defeating sequence, is to master trauma and to convert a state of passive vulnerability to active mastery. It represents an attempt at self-regulation and the establishment of psychic equilibrium. When the infantile trauma has become part of the transference, in that the analyst has been assigned the threatening role, the patient can shift his attitude, now manifested as negative transference, as he recognizes the extent of his projections. He can also use the therapist as an ally to help him actively master the dangerous infantile past that is being reenacted in the present.

Interpretation in this context deals with this reenactment. The therapist reveals to the patient how the analyst is viewed as a person of the traumatic past, a role that has been projected into him. There are many variations as to how patients use the therapist. Roles may be reversed, so they may treat their analyst as they, themselves, were traumatized by their caretakers. Still, however, the patient externalizes the infantile environment. He is trying to achieve some resolution of a painful early orientation.

Without the help of treatment, the patient would keep repeating the traumatic past in the same self-defeating fashion. He may be able to make a minimal adaptation but at the cost of achieving higher satisfying, autonomous levels of psychic integration. During treatment the analyst interprets the total scenario the patient has created, not all at once, of course, but the eventual therapeutic purpose is to understand how the patient perceives the world in terms of early traumatic constellations and is using infantile adaptations and outmoded defenses that are inappropriate and self-destructive in the current setting. The insights acquired pertain to how the patient is maladaptively relating to the external world rather than to forbidden instinctual wishes and intrapsychic conflicts.

The patient is then free to acquire more efficient, effective reality-attuned adaptations. Patients develop a capacity to make use of helpful sectors of their external world that were previously unavailable to them when they were operating under the pressure of the repetition compulsion. They learn new techniques that are now capable of being incorporated into the ego's executive system. This often occurs through identification, sometimes an incorporation of the analyst's values.

The distinction between interpretations dealing with psychodynamic vectors and the scenario of the repetition compulsion is not as clear as I have implied. Within the context of the repetition compulsion, we often encounter conflicting destructive feelings and considerable ambivalence. Superego restrictions may also play a prominent role, as well as forbidden incestuous impulses. Still, with many patients, the analyst has to demonstrate how all these elements are involved in their general misery and alienation from the external world. Simply identifying conflicting feelings is not enough.

Interpretation for patients suffering from character disorders cannot be separated from countertransference attitudes. Countertransference may interfere with the interpretative process because neither the patient nor the analyst is aware that they are participants in the repetition compulsion scenario. The analyst is not aware of being a participant precisely because he is a participant and, therefore, is unable to help the patient understand what is happening. I do not wish to discuss countertransference extensively, since my focus is on interpretation, but inasmuch as it is part of the interpretative process, its presence and effects have to be acknowledged. I am confining my description of countertransference to the situation in which the analyst absorbs the patient's projections in that he assumes the role assigned to him and then acts it out in the context of the repetition compulsion. He becomes either the persecutor (the parental imago) or the victim (the patient). I will briefly present a patient who illustrated how the repetition compulsion was involved in the treatment interaction.

A 20-year-old college student was repeating a pattern to fail both in his daily life and in treatment. He sought therapy because nothing in life had ever turned out well for him. Though of superior intelligence, he did poorly in school, and now at the university he was getting very poor grades or failing his courses. He also was rejected by the fraternity he wanted and was constantly turned down when he tried to date or asked a girl for a dance. He stated that his whole life had been one constant failure but now he was aware of how much pain and misery he felt because he could not get along in the world he lived in. As a child, his failures did not bother him as much.

The patient had learned how to live in an environment punctuated by his failures. His parents were intellectuals, and they held high aspirations for their children. His father began pushing him to learn when he was two years old and by the age of four, he could read and write and had mastered addition, subtraction, and some multiplication.

In spite of his achievements, the family gave him very little attention. Instead, they were devoted to his four-years-older brother, upon whom they lavished all their admiration and concern. The brother was also considered to be very bright and the mother, especially, enjoyed basking in his limelight. The brother also had a delicate constitution and was frequently sick; he had most of the contagious diseases of childhood and had been diagnosed as having a rare congenital muscular disease. The patient felt he had been rejected and abandoned, and he saw no point in being successful.

His negative attitude about success was discovered during his therapy, where he repeated with me the reactions he had toward his parents. Somehow, he managed to make me feel concerned about his academic progress. In part, this was related to the preservation of the treatment, because if he failed all his courses, he would not be allowed to return to school, and he would have to leave the city and return home. I became aware of such concerns later in treatment. He would start a course with considerable promise and report to me his successes. He might even get an A on a midterm examination. Then his work would precipitously deteriorate and he would either fail or nearly fail the course. I felt extremely frustrated, and my feelings vacillated between wanting to urge him to try harder or to reprimand him for what, at times, I believed were attempts to sabotage his academic career and future ambitions. He was planning on applying to law school, and he needed a superior academic record to gain admission. His father, a lawyer, was very anxious that he be accepted to a prestigious law school.

I finally realized that my reactions were similar to his father's. I would start out with hope and perhaps even move on to complacency, since it seemed that his superior intelligence would gain him success; then I reacted with shock at his first failure, followed by concern, frustration, and finally indignation. This progression was repeated several times, and though I should have been familiar with this sequence, I nevertheless continued reacting.

While writing a summary of this patient for a seminar in which the participants discussed what they considered to be their difficult patients, I was impressed by the persistence of my reactions after so many identical episodes. I was also struck by how, for a while, I regularly felt complacent and recalled that the patient bitterly complained about it. He remonstrated that he was needy and I was not responding to his needs. His complaints seemed to usher in his series of failures.

Although I did not understand as fully as I would have liked the significance and manipulative aspects of the patient's destructive and self-destructive behavior, I recognized that somehow I was allowing myself to be pulled into his infantile frame of reference. I had lost analytic objectivity and had moved away from the observational position as I reacted to the content of his material. I became aware of my misdirected involvement after I wrote the summary of the clinical material for the seminar.

During the next session, the patient began the litany of his failures. He had reached the stage in which his previous successes had suddenly crashed as he sought the road to failure. Since I had reached some conclusions, tentative as they were, as to what was happening, I felt considerably more detached than I had been in the past. The patient sensed that something was different, and he asked me about my reactions to his current failure. Spontaneously, I replied that I found it interesting that he had to build up hope and expectations and then suddenly dash them. I added that this was a hostile pattern that had to be understood and, as far as I was personally concerned, it no longer mattered whether he failed or succeeded. I was simply interested in how his mind worked and what he was trying to accomplish by his behavior. I also acknowledged that in the past I had been concerned to the extent that I had lost my analytic focus, but now my viewpoint about what he was doing had changed. The patient was bemused and replied: "Man, you're playing it cool," and I felt considerably relieved. The patient's demeanor also lost some of its edginess, and he gradually developed an interest in learning more about his motivations and manipulations.

As with Winnicott, my reply does not seem to be an interpretation. It refers to my feelings and reactions, a countertransference admission, rather than leading to insights about the patient's self-defeating behavior. Reflecting further on this interaction, I concluded that it was an example of a definition of the analytic setting. I was covertly pointing out that he had been trying to make me part of his infantile environment, and, indeed had succeeded. Later I related his behavior to the repetition compulsion. Our relationship had submerged our purpose of analytic inquiry and, in a sense, obliterated the therapeutic setting. I was trying to reestablish it, and by acknowledging my countertransference participation, I was also emphasizing his transference projections. This must have been done in a noncritical fashion as evidenced by his response, "Man, you're playing it cool."

The course of analysis took on a different focus after this exchange. The crucial factor involved my feeling of complacency after the patient had demonstrated his intellectual capabilities. It was then that his family took him for granted and, from the patient's viewpoint, abandoned him as they turned their attention toward the needy and sickly older brother. In treatment, I had been content to rest on his laurels as I felt complacent about his achievements, taking them for granted as his family had done. He, in turn, had to recapture the parents' and now my interest and concern. He also wanted revenge so, if he could not be loved for achieving, he would make an impact by failing, and shattering our complacency. He was competing with his brother, but not on the basis of winning. To lose was his aim because, in a paradoxical fashion, it meant victory. It was a Pyrrhic victory, however, that made life difficult and unrewarding.

We were eventually able to understand his "compulsion to repeat" or, better stated, his "compulsion to fail," as a reaction to the terrifying fear of abandonment. Furthermore, his rage became overwhelming as he faced the oxymoron that "to be strong is to be weak" which, when carried to its extreme, became "to be alive is to be dead." His brother, in fact, died when the patient was sixteen, and he believed his parents regretted that he had not died instead of his brother. He was furious at them but, at the same time, he felt intense guilt about being the survivor. This combination forced him to choose a self-defeating life pattern that incorporated both his need for revenge and his guilt.

Over the next several years, the analysis dealt with various facets of the patient's infantile orientation and how, through the repetition compulsion, he had recreated it, that is, externalized it, in both the academic and treatment setting. As he began seeing me more in the role of observer rather than participant, succeeding and failing meant less to him, as it did to me. He gave up his ambition to enter law school and settled for a liberal arts degree. He then found a position in an advertising agency, a setting in which his creative talents have flourished.

As is true of any analysis, there were many facets to the transference that involved id impulses and projections of inner feelings. Still, these particular interpretations had to be fitted into the broader framework of the infantile setting that was characterized by idiosyncratic attitudes regarding success and failure, strength and weakness, and life and death. I believe Freud (1937) was referring to a similar situation when he discussed the wider gestalt of constructions in analysis as various interpretations are integrated with each other. Freud was interested in reconstructing the past and lifting infantile amnesia. Constructions in analysis are not always the outcome of lifting infantile amnesia. They can be formulated by putting together bits and pieces of insight derived from transference–countertransference interactions. I believe the recognition of the reenactment of the infantile environment in the transference is for patients suffering from character disorders equivalent to the lifting of infantile amnesia, which Freud felt was the goal of treatment for patients suffering from psychoneuroses.

The patient I have just discussed had a fairly intact ego, although he lacked a stable and cohesive self-representation. His confusion about life and death and success and failure hampered the development of a consistent ego-ideal that would have given him a sanguine outlook and goals that he would find worthwhile and gratifying. To be fixated on the concern about being abandoned and surviving narrowed his focus and interfered with the development of satisfying adaptive techniques. Still, his self-representation and his ego's integrative capacities were sufficiently structured so he could retain a coherent representation of the infantile environment and be able to externalize it in the analytic setting. Interpreting the scenario of the repetition compulsion as it was reenacted in the analysis freed him from the constricting adaptations and defenses against the trauma of rejection and abandonment and later crushing guilt feelings.

The patient's acquired freedom is related to inner structural changes. He always had the capacity to be a successful student, but he had not carried his abilities to relationships with the outer world. His executive techniques were hindered and underdeveloped because whenever he achieved a modicum of academic success, he would have to inhibit any further progression. Thus, he restricted himself to the academic area and did not develop any interpersonal skills. Analysis permitted him to pursue an autonomous scholastic program, autonomous in that he had no particular compulsion to excel, to gain admiration, or to fear being rejected. He took pride in his work, but he felt he was doing it for himself. The self-confidence he gained helped develop effective methods of relating to his male friends and girls. He has reached a higher level of integration of the ego's executive system and perceives the external world on its own terms rather than those of infancy and childhood.

Putting the gestalt of the repetition compulsion in an interpretative interaction can lead to the lifting of infantile constrictions that interfere with or distort the developmental process. Thus, such interactions are particularly apt for patients suffering from structural problems. The college student I have described can be considered an example of a character neurosis with some structural deficiencies. I believe similar situations in treatment can also be useful for patients who have very few structural problems, whose psychopathology is primarily the outcome of intrapsychic conflict. More severely disturbed patients, such as borderline disorders whose characterological problems include structural discontinuity, can also benefit from such interpretations aimed at understanding the extent of the patient's externalization of the infantile environment and the definition of the analytic setting. The more disturbed patient, however, emphasizes other features of the treatment process that involve specific forms of patient–analyst interactions, such as fusion.

BACKGROUND AND FOREGROUND ELEMENTS OF INTERPRETATION

Insofar as interpretation leads to the acquisition of further psychic structure, it has some similarities to the mother–infant nurturing relationship. Infants grow both physically and emotionally because they have been properly nurtured. An effective interpretation has been compared to a good feed, indicating that it is directed to gratifying basic needs.

Both the nurturing relationship and interpretation can be divided into two components: a foreground of nurturing and a background of soothing. The nurturing element refers to the satisfaction of the need, such as food, shelter, the removal of irritants, and other caretaking activities. The mother also soothes her child by holding him with warmth and tenderness. She constructs a calm, pleasant atmosphere in which optimal nurturing can occur. The analytic process through interpretation provides nurture in the context of a background, soothing, holding environment. As discussed, I believe the construction of the holding environment is also part of the interpretative process, particularly with interpretations that are directed toward the definition of the analytic setting.

The college student patient illustrates how the repetition compulsion was an impediment to the development of psychic structure and executive ego functions that would have permitted him to deal effectively with the external world. Other patients remain fixated at primitive developmental stages because they have not received adequate soothing. The creation of a holding environment in the analytic setting can be a structure-promoting experience. In these instances, improvement is not the outcome of a specific intervention; rather, the therapist's interest and exploratory nonjudgmental approach creates a calm, objective environment that helps soothe the patient's inner disruption. I recall a middle-aged woman who no longer needed to drink vodka to calm what had been almost constant agitation. Her analytic sessions achieved the same effect, so she no longer needed to drink.

A supervisee reported how his patient, a young, agitated 24-year-old woman, reported that the water in her aquarium became murky. She bought a new filter and the water once again became clear. The therapist saw himself as the filter that had the potential of clearing up the murkiness within the patient. The patient was a very disturbed young lady who had a marked tendency to act out. She had, however, calmed down considerably, and her life became better organized after she bought the new filter for the aquarium. The therapist had discussed how he saw himself functioning in a fashion similar to the filter, and the patient agreed that she felt that the treatment had an organizing and cleansing effect. The patient had succeeded in attributing to the therapist the capacity to stabilize her. Previously, she was not able to achieve inner regulation, that is, to clear up psychic murkiness.

How did this soothing relationship develop? In the past, the patient had not been able to find a person who could help her regulate her inner turmoil, and she had seen several other therapists. This therapist is obviously different from those she had seen in the past, but it is difficult to understand precisely what he did to be able to exert such a beneficial influence on her. This patient had the capacity to create chaos and provoke anxiety in persons who were involved with her. She could be intrusive to a degree that disrupted treatment. This occurred when she refused to leave at the end of the session. Her current therapist is an exceptionally stable person who is not easily provoked or frightened. Regardless of the turmoil she tried to create, he could maintain a therapeutic focus and deal, for the most part, with her behavior in a calm, nonjudgmental analytic fashion. He would not, however, allow her to be destructive or physically abusive, and he would have picked her up, literally, and thrown her out of his office if she tried to carry out her threat not to leave at the end of the session. I believe that his nonanxious, matter-of-fact approach must have been reassuring and calming.

Taming disruption, that is, the background soothing element of the therapeutic interaction, creates a situation in which the patient can strive for higher levels of psychic integration. The supervisee did not absorb his patient's disruption.

INTROJECTION OF EGO DEFECTS AND THE TREATMENT PROCESS

In some instances, the therapist introjects the patient's ego defect. The absorption of the patient's projections is a well-known phenomenon in treatment, but usually clinicians think in terms of projections of impulses or parts of the self such as the superego. The introjection of an ego defect is a different phenomenon from what occurs in the usual introjective-projective interaction. Nevertheless, in the treatment of some patients who have serious structural problems, it can become the basis for a helpful therapeutic relationship that involves both the foreground and background elements of the interpretative interaction.

The patients I am referring to do not exactly project. They have not achieved sufficient psychic structure to be able to do so. Still, the analyst is able to make certain structural configurations of the patient his own and then rearrange them in a more integrated fashion; this will help the patient. On the surface this process sounds similar to projective identification. It is different, however, in that the patient does not project and the final interaction is the outcome of fusion rather than the more complex process of identification.

For example, at the beginning of treatment, a patient in her late thirties gave me a wooden statuette to care for. It was about eighteen inches tall, with a rectangular head and face with no definite features. The body was thin, the thinnest spot at the waist. The hips flared out and were the widest portion. There was a primitive quality to this statuette, but it had some artistic merit and resembled a Giacometti sculpture. I have discussed this patient several times in various contexts (Giovacchini 1979, 1986); here I wish to emphasize a specific ego defect that I, after a fashion, absorbed. The patient set it up by giving me the statuette.

The statuette represented the way she viewed herself. It was her self-representation—primitive, amorphous, without arms to embrace. She was jagged with hard angles. At first, I thought she gave it to me because she wanted me to understand her. This was true, but she also wanted me to have it so I could keep her in my mind, so I would not forget or lose her. Whatever reluctance I may have had in accepting her offer of the statuette must have quickly vanished, because I was certain there would be no treatment if I refused.

The patient began treatment by asking me when I would be going away for a vacation or a speaking engagement. Though I would not be leaving for several months, she insisted on knowing every detail of the trip and indicated how painful it was going to be for her. She constantly attacked me for my intention to desert her.

She revealed that she had only a minimal capacity to retain and hold a mental representation. Out of sight literally meant out of mind. She had not achieved the capacity for evocative memory as described by Fraiberg (1969). She could not maintain a mental representation unless it was either in her visual field or she could form an image of that person in a particular place. If she knew that he or she was not there, she could not conjure such an image. I had to be in my consultation room twenty-four hours a day, seven days a week, sitting in a chair with the statuette in an alcove next to me. She became very upset when my activities upset that image.

Throughout the course of treatment, she would periodically get angry at me, usually when she felt I was threatening to wander beyond her psychic range. Usually in a rage state she would grab the statuette and break it. It was easy to break because the waist was very thin, and it always snapped in two at the umbilicus. I felt anxious and upset at such moments, but my tension would quickly subside after I glued it back together. The patient would have these outbursts at the end of the session.

After eight years of treatment and not having threatened the integrity of the statuette for several years, she once again became angry. I do not recall the reason, but it was not the same anger she had previously felt. Nevertheless, she started reaching for the statuette, but, to my surprise, I had no feelings about what she was doing. She noticed my lack of reaction immediately and suddenly put her arm down. Startled, she asked me how I felt, and without deliberation I said, "It's O.K.; I don't need her anymore." She nodded, took the statuette but did not break it, and I have not seen it since.

The patient, over the course of eight years, had developed the capacity to hold a mental representation without external reinforcement. She no longer questioned me about my trips, and sometimes even felt enthusiasm if she thought I was attending a worthwhile and exciting conference. She had read some of my writings and had attended several clinical seminars. At that time, she was seriously thinking of becoming a psychotherapist.

Apparently, within the context of the treatment, I was also unable to hold a mental representation of the patient without external reinforcement, in this case the statuette. I was uneasy and upset every time she broke it and would regain my composure only after I mended it. At the beginning of treatment, the patient assumed I would have the same difficulty she had when she entrusted the statuette to my care.

I do not actually have any problems with evocative memory, but in terms of our relationship I adopted an orientation toward her that reflected her ego defect. This was evidenced by my concern for the statuette as well as by my having forgotten on one occasion to tell the patient I would be out of town. I forgot to cancel her appointment. In fact, I did not remember her at all when I left. Partly, this was my revenge for the anticipated attack about my leaving, but I believe that, for the moment, I had also lost her mental representation.

Though it is difficult to be certain, I doubt that the patient's projections played much of a role in my reactions. Unlike the college student, she lacked the psychic structure and organization to sustain even such a primitive mechanism as projection. Again, this is a question of degree because, to some extent, she used many defensive adaptations, but compared to persons with better-structured personalities, she made only minimal use of projective defenses. When she gave me the statuette, she simply assumed that everyone was like herself and not able to form and hold a mental representation. She could not appreciate the fact that there were minds different from her own that could relate to her at higher levels of psychic organization.

Nevertheless, even if the patient were unable to project effectively, I still managed to "absorb" her ego defect during certain periods of our relationship. Though she had not projected, I was able to introject certain aspects of her lack of psychic structure. The mechanism I used, introjection, was at a higher level of ego integration than the modalities she used to maintain emotional balance. Still, recreating a similar psychic state within myself enabled me to be in resonance with many of her feelings. I understood and at times could feel the anguish she experienced in many situations that would otherwise have seemed trivial. I could also finally appreciate her need to have me constantly present, although I could, at the same time, obliterate her from my mind.

She gradually developed the security that I would not abandon her, and if I went on a trip, she could rely on me to return. Previously, she found my returning as painful as my leaving since, as she had lost my mental representation with my departure, she found it painful to re-structure it because there was very little residual of a memory trace on which to rebuild an image of me. After seven years of treatment she became somewhat casual about my trips and no longer required a detailed itinerary of my whereabouts. This occurred so gradually that neither one of us was aware of any particular improvement. The inci-dent of my lack of concern about the fate of the statuette turned out to be an important and revealing interaction. Without direct verbaliza-tion, we both realized that she had developed the capacity for evocative memory. I regained mine in my orientation toward her treatment, and she had somehow fused with me as she developed a similar capacity for the retention of mental representations. What began as a difference in levels of relating, my introjecting while she was not capable of project-ing, had now reached an equilibrium in which we were participating with somewhat similar functional modes.

The resonance of our ego states seemed to be an essential feature of the therapeutic process that led to the acquisition of psychic structure. This was not an active interpretative interaction, but it became a type of bonding that stabilized our relationship and that gradually evolved in a soothing holding environment. The patient had many moments of regression and affective volatility but, in spite of her disruption, she was attached to the treatment. I made many interpretations about how she related to people and how her inability to hold mental representations created panic and forced her to be demanding of her friends and me. We were able to relate her current feelings to their genetic antecedents, but I believe that the soothing bond we had established created sufficient structure so that she could now fuse with me, that is, fuse with the more integrated aspects of my psyche.

This patient presented many paradoxical features that were the manifestations of psychic discontinuity. I have emphasized the primitive aspects of her personality, because that was how she generally presented herself. I also knew, however, that on occasion she could function in a highly competent manner. She had a remarkable memory for music, being able to recognize various compositions, the orchestra, and often the soloists. She could also be very adept socially, bringing people together, introducing them, and facilely remembering names. The patient lamented that this part of her personality was seldom available to her. She could behave as an adult, but she did not believe this was her true self.

Like some other patients I have discussed, she did not view herself as having connecting bridges between the primitive and advanced levels of the psyche. Unlike many psychoneurotic patients, she had no problem in getting in touch with the primitive self; she had difficulties in remaining in contact with higher levels. Apparently I juxtaposed myself with her unstructured orientation and, as she fused with me, helped her develop connecting bridges to establish better reality-adapted ego orientations. I had incorporated, to some extent, her lack of structure, but I was able simultaneously to function at higher levels of analytic functioning and integration. Her spectrum of psychic functioning expanded because of her fusion with me, and gradually she incorporated, that is, she superimposed higher areas of psychic structure and connecting bridges to remain in touch with her capacity to function effectively. Eventually we discussed these processes, which enabled her to register the interaction indelibly in her mind. Our interaction then had become clearly interpretative as it led to lasting effective insight.

FUSION, PROJECTION, AND EXTERNALITY

In the treatment of patients with structural defects, fusion with the healthier aspects of the analyst's personality leads to structure-promoting identifications. This leads to changes in psychic structure that are similar to the effects produced by mutative interpretations (Strachey 1934).

Borderline states and other patients who have characterological problems often have difficulties fusing with potentially helpful external objects. They are not open to and cannot avail themselves of beneficial experiences in the outside world. They have similar problems in the treatment setting in that they cannot internalize various aspects of the analytic process that would be helpful in achieving ego integration and resolution of intrapsychic conflicts. The inability to fuse and fear of fusion are equivalent to resistance, which usually refers to a resistance to some aspect of the therapeutic procedure or specifically to a meaningful interpretation.

Freud (Breuer and Freud 1895) viewed resistance as an impediment to treatment that had to be overcome as quickly as possible. Patients suffering from character disorders cannot consciously suppress or control their impulse to fend off the analyst's interpretations or not to follow the prescribed procedure, because such an impulse is deeply rooted in their psychopathology. Freud (1923) wrote about such situations when he described the negative therapeutic reactions, recognizing that some patients could not let the analyst succeed because it made them feel beholden and vulnerable, and threatened their integrity. Borderline patients, for example, may need to fuse with the therapist to acquire psychic structure, but the process of fusion is perceived as destructive.

As discussed, the borderline patient's self-representation is not cohesive; it is poorly structured (relatively amorphous) and tenuously held together. It is difficult for these patients to integrate new experiences within their psyches because they do not have sufficient structure to form an introject of that experience or to fuse with an external object without disrupting the minimal cohesiveness of the self-representation. Inasmuch as interpretation occurs within the context of the patient's fusing with the analyst, these patients present special technical problems because they have intense fears of annihilation if they do not maintain a vigilant degree of separateness. They cannot relax their precariously formed ego boundaries. To internalize or to be incorporated into another psyche provokes an existential catastrophe. Thus, the therapeutic process is in opposition to the maintenance of psychic equilibrium. Some clinicians have judged that these patients are not suitable for analysis because they cannot survive the regression that is characteristic of the therapeutic process.

We encounter similar problems even with patients with higher degrees of psychic structure, the character neuroses. As discussed, they also have problems with their self-representations, but these are usually the outcome of structural conflicts. The self-representation may feel vulnerable, for example, in forming intimate relationships. Because of an early destructive fusion with their mothers, these patients, as adolescents and adults, are afraid to form close ties although they feel alienated and lonely without them. They are afraid of being exploited, manipulated, or even mutilated. These fears are the manifestations of conflicts that stem from higher psychic levels than those experiencing existential crises and the terror of annihilation. In treatment, they also resist fusion and other aspects of the analytic interaction because they are perceived as relinquishing control.

Patients who fear relinquishing control and view fusion as destructive often demonstrate a discontinuity of psychic structure and hierarchies, as previously discussed. Their characterological configurations lead them to view the world in a concrete fashion and to be isolated from the primitive parts of their personality. They may relate to the world on the basis of a false self-compliance (Winnicott 1960).

To continue with Winnicott's viewpoint, the true self, if it exists to any significant degree, is not connected to the false self. There is little continuity between higher and lower psychic levels. In other words, there is a lack of connection between the functioning adaptive aspects of the psyche and the inner world of affects. The patient relates almost exclusively to the external world.

These patients are not psychologically minded; they often have no concept of psychic determinism. They seek the sources of their behavior, feelings, and adaptations in the external world. Consequently, they do not take responsibility for what happens to them. They are not aware, indeed they vehemently deny, that they have any control over their destinies. Inasmuch as they are constantly involved with the surrounding world and blame it for all their mishaps, they seem to be constantly projecting. This is not, however, projection in the ordinary sense; and, to repeat what I have said earlier, patients with such primitive orientations have not yet achieved the capacity to project.

To project means that there is some distinction between the inner world of the psyche and external reality. it also means that the patient is able to place some aspects of the inner world (psychic structure, feelings, id impulses) into the outer world. The patients I am describing have no access, relatively speaking, to the inner world, and, therefore, cannot project it.

Still, many of these patients demonstrate all the features of paranoid characters. They are querulous, suspicious, and often immersed in a litany of complaints, constantly blaming others for their endless misfortunes. Rather than projecting in the classical sense, these patients are demonstrating the consequences of an ego defect, psychic discontinuity, that renders them incapable of getting in touch with the deeper recesses of the psyche. Consequently, all understanding and explanation, all etiological sources are confined to only one frame of reference, the superficial context of visible phenomena. They have little or no concept of psychic reality.

Understandably, this would make psychoanalysis difficult if not impossible. Inasmuch as interpretation is directed toward understanding psychic reality, such interpretations would be meaningless to these patients. Yet in some instances therapists can work with them, even though from what I have described the situation seems impossible—and it often is.

Clinicians are familiar with the rigidity of the paranoid, and the patients I am describing may appear to be extremely rigid. It is a rigidity, however, that is founded on a lack of options and an inability to make connections. They can connect only external events and conscious reactions, and this frequently appears to be paranoid. It is, nevertheless, the only way they can relate and maintain psychic synthesis.

It is an extremely precarious synthesis, at best. Because the larger portion of their psyches operates on the basis of a false self, they do not feel themselves as whole persons; in extreme instances they do not have any assurance that they exist. Sometimes we are aware of the poignant nature of their adaptations, adaptations based on self-effacement and constrictions.

Some novelists intuitively appreciate the dilemma of surviving with such constrictions. I turn to an unlikely source of data, a mystery novel written with unprecedented sensitivity. The main character is a writer who pretends to be a certain detective so that he can continue his mission of following a person who is wandering the streets of New York in an apparently senseless fashion, picking up all sorts of meaningless items and junk, such as stones, pieces of dirt, twigs, bottle caps, even dried dog excrement, and collecting them in a carpetbag. It is interesting that the writer in the novel has to assume the identity of another person so that he can effectively function. The author of the novel writes:

> By flooding himself with externals, by drowning himself out of himself, he had managed to exert some small degree of control over his fits of despair. Wandering, therefore, was a kind of mindlessness. . . . he was obliged now to concentrate on what he was doing, even if it was next to nothing. Time and again his thoughts would begin to drift, and soon thereafter his steps would follow suit. This meant that he was constantly in danger of quickening his pace and crashing into [the person he was following]. . . . to guard against this mishap he devised several methods of deceleration. The first was to tell himself that he was no longer Daniel Quinn. He was Paul Auster now, and with each step he took he tried to fit more comfortably into the strictures of that transformation. Auster was no more than a name to him, a *husk without content*. To be Auster meant being a man with no interior, a man with no thoughts. And if there were no thoughts available to him, if his own inner life had been made inaccessible, then there was no place for him to retreat to. As Auster, he could not summon up any memories of fears, any dreams of joys, for all these things as they pertained to Auster, were

a blank to him. *He consequently had to remain solely on his own surface, looking outward for sustenance.* [Auster 1985, pp. 98–99; emphasis mine]

This quote stresses the adaptive nature of this type of externality and the lack of inner connections. The outcome of this adaptation is not always a paranoid outlook. Some patients find this "husk without content," the state of a "mindless zombie," as a patient described himself, intolerably painful, a misery that causes them to seek therapy and makes treatment possible in spite of the inaccessibility to the inner life.

Again, we can ask how a transference can be established if the primitive parts of the patient cannot be projected. It does occur, however, but it is based on fusion rather than projection. Ordinarily, we view the mechanisms of projection and fusion as being interrelated as Klein (1946), Ogden (1982), Grotstein (1981), and others have written in their descriptions of projective identification. But this does not mean that fusion cannot occur with only a minimal amount, if any, of projection. Fusion need not involve all levels of two personalities merging with each other. The patient can feel that only the surface layers of his character are incorporated by his therapist and, in turn, internalize, in a limited fashion, the superficial elements of the analyst's psychic structure. As discussed in the previous section, the patient could not project, whereas I could introject her ego defect of being unable to maintain mental representations. Eventually, however, the patient could merge with the healthier surface elements of my personality. Projective identification includes deeper as well as superficial elements of the psyche. Inasmuch as the patient has to remain solely on his *own surface, looking outward for sustenance* means that there is a potential for fusion, at least of surface levels of the psyche, which can then lead to structuring a transference. In turn, the construction of transference helps establish a connection with the inner world, and this makes interpretative discourse possible.

The concrete personality has achieved a certain amount of psychic stability. Other persons are, to some extent, aware of the lack of connections with the inner world and lament their false self status (see Boyer 1983). They revile themselves for "lacking character" as they constantly mold themselves to the contours of the surrounding reality, in itself a fusion. They are disturbed by their lack of identity, their as-if qualities (Deutsch 1942).

The former therapist of a patient currently in treatment with another analyst compared his patient to the main character in a Chekhov short story, "The Darling." The story contained a remarkable description of the as-if character. The patient agreed that, at that time, she did not have a distinct personality; she stated that she had no mind of her own and that she had an intense need to please her first therapist. She also indicated that she had fused with him. There was also considerable evidence that the therapist had fused with his patient. Gradually, the patient began to feel she was developing feelings of her own. The general impression was that within the context of fusion, the patient had begun to consolidate an identity of her own; that is, there was an emerging inner core. However, for extraneous reasons, the treatment relationship had to terminate, and some years later she sought further therapy.

She emphasized in her second treatment relationship that she had fused with her former therapist. This was particularly evident in her dreams, but it was a fusion based on deadness. Her therapist, a depressed character, lamented that psychoanalysis was dead and that the only way to preserve it was to stuff himself and the patient and put themselves on perpetual display in a museum. This prospect was agreeable to both patient and therapist. Now she reevaluated her former treatment and began viewing it on the basis of its destructive potential.

She reached the startling conclusion that what she had viewed as an emerging sense of self based on newly felt feelings was an illusion. She now knew that she was not experiencing her own feelings; rather, her reactions were the feelings her therapist put into her. She had believed that she was both "The Darling" as well as having become a distinct person later. Her having achieved autonomy was her therapist's belief, however, which became hers when they fused with each other. Nevertheless, she did not experience much vitality or autonomy. She felt tied to him, enveloped by a pervasive feeling of deadness.

One of the most impressive moments in her former treatment was the analysis of a dream. Briefly, the dream involved frogs, which, to her therapist, indicated that childish patterns were surfacing and released so that they could be integrated by the ego, thereby achieving higher levels of psychic organization. She told her second therapist that she, as a young child, was impressed by her mother's bathrobe, one covered with pictures of tiny frogs. In her associations she felt she would be smothered by this bathrobe, and her dream was, in fact, a nightmare. Apparently her therapist was unaware of the patient's fear of being devoured by the frogs of her internal world, but she outwardly accepted his attributing a sense of identity to the logo of the frog. True, she had made some connections with the inner world that were lacking when she felt like an "as-if" character, but, in spite of some accessibility to deeper levels of the personality, she was still reacting, at least toward her therapist, in an "as-if" fashion. She was adapting herself to his viewpoint and from a surface level was fusing with his feelings of deadness.

With her present analyst, she was able to understand the subtle facets of her previous therapeutic relationship. She also fused with him, but it was based on a sense of aliveness rather than deadness. I have discussed fusion in the context of deadness and aliveness elsewhere (see Giovacchini 1986). Here, I simply wish to stress that her understanding about what had happened occurred when she was merging with her second therapist. She was involved in his sense of aliveness and though this appeared to be a superficial interaction, the patient sometimes complaining and blaming herself that her material dealt only with surface phenomena, she nevertheless was able to formulate various elements of her character in depth.

When the treatment of patients suffering from character disorders is discussed, processes such as projection and fusion must be understood as thoroughly as possible. What part and what level of psychic structure is being projected or merged with must be identified, and the therapist's contributions must be evaluated. Sometimes what appears to be an interpretation is a disruptive countertransference reaction (Boschan 1987).

To summarize briefly, the investigative atmosphere of the analytic setting can be supportive and reassuring for both types of patients—borderline states and character neuroses. Patients learn that being helped does not mean that they are vulnerable and will be exploited. Like the patient who cannot hold or integrate mental representations, these patients gradually acquire the capacity to incorporate the integrative aspects of the analytic interactions. The soothing background holding qualities, which include the analyst's observational stance of the therapeutic relationship, allow patients to develop the security that eventually permits them to fuse with their therapists. The communicative, that is, insight-promoting, qualities of interpretation are absorbed by patients with structural defects as they fuse with their analysts. To incorporate the analysts' insights is an achievement and represents a structural accretion. The patient has developed security about his capacity to incorporate helpful experiences and still exist, or he has, to a large measure, overcome his fear of intimacy and losing control. Thus, the act of being able to let the analyst relate on an interpretative basis helps overcome basic conflictful attitudes that are the outcomes of a poorly structured and conflicted self-representation. The act of interpreting is itself a structure-promoting experience.

CONCLUSION

The majority of patients who seek treatment suffer from psychopathology based on structural defects rather than intrapsychic conflict due to clashes between the ego and the id. These patients have been classified as borderline states, emphasizing that they are hovering on the edge of psychosis.

This chapter stresses that patients suffering from character disorders have to be studied more precisely in terms of specific ego defects, an approach that goes beyond phenomenology.

I described a type of structural defect that is characterized by a discontinuity between the primitive and higher integrated levels of the personality. These patients lack connecting bridges between various parts of the self, and this creates specific symptoms and behavior as well as particular technical problems during treatment.

To understand such patients in the treatment context, the concept of the interpretative interaction must be expanded. I discussed various types of interpretation that involve countertransference elements and changes within the therapist. As these patients acquire the capacity to fuse with the analyst's therapeutic and interpretative activity, they achieve integrity of the self-representation, which is a structure-promoting experience.

REFERENCES

Alexander, F., and French, T. (1946). *Psychoanalytic Therapy*. New York: Ronald.

Auster, P. (1985). *City of Glass: New York Trilogy*—1. Los Angeles: Sun and Moon Press.

Boschan, P. (1987). Dependence and narcissistic resistances in the psychoanalytic process. *International Journal of Psycho-Analysis* 68:109-119.

Boyer, L. B. (1983). *The Regressed Patient*. New York: Jason Aronson.

Brenner, C. (1987). Working through: 1914-1984. *Psychoanalytic Quarterly* 56:88-109.

Breuer, J., and Freud, S. (1895). Studies on hysteria. *Standard Edition* 2:1-252.

Deutsch, H. (1942). Some forms of emotional disturbances and their relationship to schizophrenia. *Psychoanalytic Quarterly* 11:301-321.

Fraiberg, S. (1969). Libidinal object constancy and mental representation. *The Psychoanalytic Study of the Child* 24:48-70. New York: International Universities Press.

Freud, S. (1905). Three essays on the theory of sexuality. *Standard Edition* 7:122-243.

—— (1912). Recommendations to physicians practicing psychoanalysis. *Standard Edition* 12:109-121.

—— (1912–1914). Papers on technique. *Standard Edition* 12:85–175.

—— (1913). On beginning the treatment. *Standard Edition* 12:121–145.

—— (1914). Remembering, repeating and working through. *Standard Edition* 12:145–157.

—— (1915). Instincts and their vicissitudes. *Standard Edition* 14:103–140.

—— (1916). Introductory lectures on psycho-analysis. *Standard Edition* 15–16:13–481.

—— (1923). The ego and the id. *Standard Edition* 19:1–60.

—— (1937). Constructions in analysis. *Standard Edition* 23:257–269.

Gill, M. (1982). *Analysis of Transference: Theory and Technique I*. New York: International Universities Press.

Giovacchini, P. (1972). *Tactics and Techniques in Psychoanalytic Therapy I*. New York: Jason Aronson.

—— (1977). A critique of Kohut's theory of narcissism. *Adolescent Psychiatry* 5:213–235.

—— (1979). *Treatment of Primitive Mental States*. New York: Jason Aronson.

—— (1986). *Developmental Disorders: The Transitional Space in Mental Breakdown and Creative Integration*. New York: Jason Aronson.

Grotstein, J. (1981). *Splitting and Projective Identification*. New York: Jason Aronson.

Hartmann, H. (1955). Notes on the theory of sublimation. *Psychoanalytic Study of the Child* 10:9–29. New York: International Universities Press.

Klein, M. (1946). Notes on some schizoid mechanisms. *International Journal of Psycho-Analysis* 27:99–110.

Kohut, H. (1971). *The Analysis of the Self*. New York: International Universities Press.

Masterson, J. (1977). *Treatment of the Borderline Adult: A Developmental Approach*. New York: Brunner/Mazel.

Nunberg, H. (1932). *Principles of Psychoanalysis: Their Application and the Neuroses*. New York: International Universities Press.

Ogden, T. (1982). *Projective Identification and Psychotherapeutic Technique*. New York: Jason Aronson.

Reichard, S. (1956). A re-examination of "Studies in Hysteria." *Psychoanalytic Quarterly* 25:155–177.

Strachey, J. (1934). The nature of the therapeutic action of psychoanalysis. *International Journal of Psycho-Analysis* 15:127–160.

Winnicott, D. W. (1960). Ego distortion in terms of true and false self. In *The Maturational Process and the Facilitating Environment*, pp. 29–37. London: Hogarth, 1958.

—— (1972). Fragments of an analysis. In *Tactics and Techniques in Psychoanalytic Therapy 1*, ed. P. L. Giovacchini, pp. 455–693. New York: Jason Aronson.

.2

Thomas H. Ogden, M.D.

On the Structure of Experience

> The other one, the one called Borges, is the one things happen to.
> . . . I know of Borges from the mail. . . . It would be an exaggera-
> tion to say that ours is a hostile relationship; I live it, let myself go
> on living, so that Borges may contrive his literature, and this
> literature justifies me. [J. L. Borges, "Borges and I"]

Borges's prose poem, "Borges and I" (1960), delicately teases apart what
ordinarily comprises the illusion of unity of experience. In an infinitely
more clumsy way I would like to propose a psychoanalytic framework with
which to think about the components of the dialectical process generating
human experience. I will explore the idea that human experience is constituted by the dialectical interplay of three different modes of generating
experience: the depressive mode, the paranoid-schizoid mode, and the autistic-contiguous mode. The concept of the first two of these modes was
introduced by Melanie Klein,[1] while the third represents my own synthesis,
clarification, and extension of ideas introduced primarily by Frances Tustin,
Esther Bick, and Donald Meltzer. Each of these modes of generating experience is characterized by its own form of symbolization, mode of defense,
quality of object relatedness, and degree of subjectivity. The three modes
stand in a dialectical relationship to one another, each creating, preserving,

---

[1]Although I am not a Kleinian, I have found many of Klein's ideas, when
viewed independently of her developmental timetable, her concept of the death
instinct, and her theory of technique, to be pivotal to the development of psychoanalytic thought. Two of her most important contributions to psychoanalysis are the
concepts of the paranoid-schizoid and depressive positions. Neither concept has been
integrated into the main body of the American psychoanalytic dialogue.

and negating the others. The idea of a single mode functioning without relation to the other two is as meaningless as the concept of the conscious mind in isolation from the concept of the unconscious mind; each is an empty set filled by the other pole or poles of the dialectic.

I will describe each of the three modes of generating experience with particular reference to the analytic experience. What I hope will become apparent is that every psychological event is overdetermined, not only in terms of layers of unconscious content, but also in terms of modes of experience generating the psychological matrix within which mental content exists. Psychological change ("structural change") will be discussed in terms of shifts in the nature of the dialectical interplay of modes of generating experience.

Paradoxically, the elements of the synchronicity of experience will, for the sake of clarity, be presented sequentially in this chapter. Like a novice juggler who requires the patience of his audience while he gets his first baton into solitary flight, I ask for the reader's indulgence while I launch the initial sections of this chapter. In the end, the reader must become the juggler, holding in generative tension the multiplicity of modes constituting human experience.

EXPERIENCE IN A DEPRESSIVE MODE

The concept of the depressive position was introduced by Melanie Klein (1935, 1958) to refer to the most mature form of psychological organization. Although this organization continues to develop throughout life, Klein believed that it has its origins in the second quarter of the first year of life.[2] Bion (1962) modified this concept to emphasize not its place in a developmental sequence, but its place in a dynamic relationship with the paranoid-schizoid position. In this chapter, I will focus on the depressive mode not as a structure or a developmental phase, but as a process through which perception is attributed meaning in a particular way. This is what I have in mind by a mode of generating experience. The qualities of experience in each mode are interdependent, each providing the context for the other.

In the depressive position, the mode of symbolization, termed *symbol formation proper* (Segal 1957), is one in which the symbol represents the

---

[2]As will be seen, the debate over Klein's developmental timetable loses much of its significance when her "positions" are viewed not as developmental phases, but as synchronic dimensions of experience.

symbolized and is experienced as different from it. Symbolic meaning is generated by a subject mediating between the symbol and that which it represents. It could be said that it is in the space between the symbol and the symbolized that an interpreting subject comes into being. It could also be said with equal validity that it is the development of the capacity for subjectivity, the experience of "I-ness," however subtle and unobtrusive, that makes it possible for the individual to mediate between symbol and symbolized. Both are true. Each constitutes the conditions necessary for the other; neither "leads to" or "causes" the other in a linear, sequential sense.

The achievement of symbol formation proper allows one to experience oneself as a person thinking one's thoughts and feeling one's feelings. In this way, thoughts and feelings are experienced to a large degree as personal creations that can be understood (interpreted). Thus, for better or for worse, one develops a feeling of responsibility for one's psychological actions (thoughts, feelings, and behavior).

As one becomes capable of experiencing oneself as a subject, one at the same time (via projection and identification) becomes capable of experiencing one's "objects" as also being subjects. That is, other people are viewed as being alive and capable of thinking and feeling in the same way that one experiences oneself as having one's own thoughts and feelings. This is the world of whole object relations in which one exists as more or less the same person over time in relation to other people, who also continue to be the same people despite powerful affective shifts and mixtures of affect. New experience is added to old, but new experience does not undo or negate the past. The continuity of experience of self and other through loving and hating feeling states is the context for the development of the capacity for ambivalence.

Historicity is created in the depressive mode as the individual relinquishes his reliance on omnipotent defenses. When, in a paranoid-schizoid mode, one feels disappointed or angry at an object, the object is no longer experienced as the same object that it had been, but as a new object. This experience of the discontinuity of self and object over time precludes the creation of historicity. Instead, there is a continual, defensive recasting of the past. In a depressive mode, one is rooted in a history that one creates through interpreting one's past. Although one's interpretations of the past are evolving (and therefore history is continually evolving and changing), the past is understood to be immutable. This knowledge brings with it the sadness that one's past will never be all that one had wished. For example, one's early relationships with one's parents will never be all that one has hoped. At the same time, this rootedness in time also brings a depth and stability to one's experience of self. One's relation to the history that one has created interpretively is an important dimension of subjectivity without which one's experience of "I-ness" feels arbitrary, erratic, and unreal.

In a psychological state in which other people are experienced as subjects and not simply as objects, it is possible to care about them as opposed to simply valuing them as one would value a prized object or even essential objects like food or air. Objects can be damaged or used up; only subjects can be hurt. Therefore, it is only in the context of the experience of subjective others that the experience of guilt becomes a potential human experience. Guilt has no meaning in the absence of the capacity for concern for other people as subjects. Guilt is a specific sort of pain that one bears *over time* in response to real or imagined harm that one has done to someone about whom one cares. One can attempt to make reparation for that about which one feels guilty, but this does not undo what one has done. All the individual can do is to attempt to make up for what he has done in his subsequent relations with others and with himself. Empathy becomes possible in this mode of experience, since others are experienced as subjects whose feelings can be understood to be like one's own.

Once the other is experienced as a subject as well as an object, one has acknowledged the life of the other outside the area of one's omnipotence. In a world of subjects whom one ambivalently loves and cannot fully control, a distinctively new form of anxiety (not possible in the more primitive modes of experience) is generated: the anxiety that one's anger has driven away or harmed the person one loves. Sadness, the experience of missing someone, loneliness, and the capacity for mourning become dimensions of human experience as a consequence of the interplay of the qualities of experience in the depressive mode described above. As will be discussed, in a paranoid-schizoid mode, magical restoration of the lost object short-circuits these experiences. There is no need for, or any possibility of, missing or mourning a lost object when absence can be undone through omnipotent thinking and denial.

The nature of the transference in a depressive mode has its own distinct qualities. In a paranoid-schizoid mode transference is based upon the wish and the belief that one has emotionally recreated an earlier object relationship in the present relationship; in a depressive mode, transference represents an unconscious attempt to recapture something of one's experience with an earlier object in the present relationship. This latter form of transference is rooted in the context of the sadness of the knowledge that the relationship with the original object is a part of the past that one will never have again. At the same time, the past is never lost completely in a depressive mode, in that one can repeat something of the experience with the original object in a relationship with the new object (Ogden 1986). This, for example, under normal circumstances, makes the waning of the Oedipus complex possible. The little girl, for example, experiences sadness in the eventual acceptance of the fact that she will not be able to have the unconsciously wished-for romantic and sexual relationship with her father. The pain of this renunciation is bearable in part because the experience with the father is kept alive in relationships with new objects transferentially and will form an important core of her mature, adult love relationships (cf. Loewald 1979, Ogden 1987).

The depressive mode of generating experience that has been schematically described constitutes a dialectical pole that exists only in relation to the paranoid-schizoid and autistic-contiguous poles. In the never-attained ideal of the depressive mode, analytic discourse occurs between interpreting subjects, each attempting to use words to mediate between himself and his experience of the other.

This discourse between subjects is frequently blocked by unconscious thoughts and feelings that the subject finds too frightening or unacceptable to put into words. I am thinking here not only about frightening and unacceptable sexual and aggressive wishes, but also about other sorts of fears, such as the unconscious anxiety that aspects of oneself are so private and so central to an endangered sense of being alive that the act of communication will endanger the integrity of the self. Still another form of anxiety that disrupts the intersubjective discourse is the fear that one's life-sustaining ties to one's internal objects may be jeopardized through any sort of discourse in which one relinquishes control over one's internal object world by sharing knowledge of it with another (Ogden 1983).

The analyst and analysand attempt to understand the "leading edge of anxiety" that constitutes the principal source of the disruption of the intersubjective discourse at a given moment. In a depressive mode, that anxiety is always object-related in that the unconscious reasons for feeling fearful, guilty, ashamed, and the like have to do with overdetermined unconscious fantasies involving internal and external objects. The derivatives of these unconscious object-related fantasies constitute the content of the analytic transference–countertransference experience.

The analyst has no means of understanding the patient except through his own emotionally colored perceptions of and responses to the patient. Of these perceptions and responses, only a small proportion are conscious, and it is therefore imperative that the analyst learn to detect, read, and make use of his own shifting unconscious state as it unfolds in the analytic discourse. For example, a patient, Mr. M., early in analysis was talking with apparently great intensity of feeling about his affection for and loyalty to his wife and the fulfillment he found in their sexual relationship. I had no conscious reason for doubting his sincerity. However, I noted a passing thought of my own that was as ephemeral as a dream as it recedes on waking. I made a conscious attempt to struggle against the weight of repression in an effort to recapture it. The thought that I was repressing was infused with a somewhat smug pleasure in the self-protective privacy inherent in the role of analyst vis-à-vis the analysand. I was feeling safe in this peculiar relationship wherein only the "dirty laundry" of the patient is aired. My thoughts then went to the question of what dirty laundry I thought I was pretending to be free of at that moment.

These questions helped alert me to the possibility that the patient was at the time disavowing anxiety in relation to the ideas he was discussing. As Mr. M.'s associations continued, his fears concerning his wife's genitals were very subtly hinted at as he discussed their sexual intercourse the previous night. He said that he very much enjoyed their lovemaking in "complete darkness" and mentioned in passing that he had washed his penis after intercourse.

This use of the intersubjective resonance of unconscious processes of individuals experiencing one another as subjects is paradigmatic of the unconscious-preconscious level of empathy in a depressive mode. This process can be thought of as involving the analyst's unconscious projection of himself into the patient's unconscious experience of himself and his internal objects, an unconscious identification with the patient's unconscious experience of himself and his internal objects, and the creation of an unconscious intersubjective third ["the Other" (Lacan 1953)] between the patient and analyst. However it is described, it is a process in which analysts make available to patients their own unconscious chain of symbolic meanings through which they attempt to experience something similar to the unconscious experience of patients, but in a less intense way and in a less conflicted and less powerfully repressed or split-off way.

Having described a conception of the depressive mode of experience, I must reiterate that no such entity exists; every facet of human experience is the outcome of a dialectic constituted by the interplay of depressive, paranoid-schizoid, and autistic-contiguous modes. As will be discussed later, even symptomatology generated in response to a conflict of subjective desire (for example, conflicted oedipal desires, fears, and loyalties) is only partially constructed in a depressive mode. At this point, I will delineate features of each of the other two poles of the dialectic of experience. Again, for purposes of clarity, this will be done as if each mode could be isolated from the other and viewed in pure form.

EXPERIENCE IN A PARANOID-SCHIZOID MODE

The paranoid-schizoid position is Melanie Klein's (1946, 1952, 1957, 1958) conception of a psychological organization more primitive than the depressive position, which she conceived of as having its origins in the first quarter of the first year of life. Again, the emphasis in this chapter will be shifted from Klein's diachronic conception of a sequence of structures or developmental phases to a consideration of the dialectical interplay of synchronic modes.

The paranoid-schizoid mode of generating experience is based heavily upon splitting as a defense and as a way of organizing experience. Whereas the depressive mode operates predominantly in the service of containment of experience, including psychological pain, the paranoid-schizoid mode is more evenly divided between efforts at managing psychic pain and efforts at the evacuation of pain through the defensive use of omnipotent thinking, denial, and the creation of discontinuities of experience.

In a paranoid-schizoid mode, the experience of loving and hating the same object generates intolerable anxiety that constitutes the principal psychological dilemma to be managed. This problem is handled in large part by separating loving and hating facets of oneself from loving and hating facets of the object. Only in this way can the individual safely love the object in a state of uncontaminated security and safely hate without the fear of damaging the loved object.

Splitting defensively renders object-related experience of a given emotional valence (e.g., the relationship of a loving self to a loving object) discontinuous from object-related experience of other valences (e.g., the relationship of a hating self to a hating object). Each time a good object is disappointing, it is no longer experienced as a disappointing good object, but as the discovery of the bad object in what had been masquerading as a good object. Instead of the experience of ambivalence, there is the experience of unmasking the truth. This results in continual rewriting of history so that the present experience of the object is projected backward and forward in time, creating an eternal present that has only a superficial resemblance to time as experienced in a depressive mode.

The defensive use of a discontinuity of experience (splitting) is commonly encountered in work with patients suffering from borderline and schizophrenic disorders. When the patient is disappointed, hurt, angry, jealous, and the like, he feels that he sees with powerful clarity that he has been duped by the analyst and that he is finally perceiving the reality of the situation as it is and as it always has been: "The fact of the matter is that I've deluded myself about you for a long time. It is obvious to me now that you have absolutely no regard for me; otherwise you wouldn't forget fundamental things about me like my girlfriend's name that I've mentioned a thousand times."

Rewriting history leads to a brittleness and instability of object relations that are in continual states of reversal. There is no stable, shared experience of the history of the relationship between patient and analyst that can form a framework and container for present experience. In this mode of experience there is an almost continuous background of anxiety deriving from the fact that the individual unconsciously feels as if he or she is perpetually in uncharted territory in the presence of unpredictable strangers. Analytic theory need not appeal to the concept of the death instinct to account for anxiety experienced in such a brittle container for psychological experience.

In a paranoid-schizoid mode, there is virtually no space between symbol and symbolized; the two are emotionally equivalent. This mode of symbolization, termed *symbolic equation* (Segal 1957), generates a two-dimensional form of experience in which everything is what it is. There is almost no interpreting subject mediating between the percept (whether external or internal) and one's thoughts and feelings about that which one is perceiving. The patient operating in a predominantly paranoid-schizoid mode may say, "You can't tell me I don't see what I see." In this mode, thoughts and feelings are not experienced as personal creations but as facts, things-in-themselves, that simply exist. Perception and interpretation are experienced as one and the same. The patient is trapped in the manifest, since surface and depth are indistinguishable. That which would be viewed as interpretation from the perspective of the depressive mode would be experienced in a paranoid-schizoid mode as an attempt to "twist the facts," to distract, deceive, and confuse through the "use of psychological bullshit."

Transference in a paranoid-schizoid mode has been termed *delusional* (Little 1958) or *psychotic* (Searles 1963) transference. The analyst is not experienced as *like* the original childhood object; he *is* the original object. For example, a therapist made some inquiries during a therapy hour about the details of a physical complaint his patient, A., was discussing. The patient experienced this as an anxious, intrusive overreaction on the part of the therapist that led her to experience him as having become her mother (not simply similar to her mother). The following day the patient consulted her internist, who later in bewilderment called the therapist and said that A. had introduced herself by saying, "I'm A.'s mother. I'm very worried about

A.'s illness and would like to ask you some questions about it." In this way, the patient became her therapist-mother and enacted the overanxiousness and intrusiveness of the therapist-mother.

In the absence of the capacity to mediate between oneself and one's experience, a very limited form of subjectivity is generated. Predominantly, the self is a self as object, a self that is buffeted by thoughts, feelings, and perceptions as if they were external forces or physical objects occupying or bombarding oneself. An adolescent schizophrenic patient would violently turn his head in order to "shake" (get rid of) a thought that was tormenting him. Another schizophrenic patient requested an X ray in order to be able to see what it was inside of him that was driving him crazy. Still another patient "took a big shit" in the therapist's waiting-room toilet before each session in order not to harm the therapist with his toxic inner contents during the session.

When working with patients generating experience in a predominantly paranoid-schizoid mode, one must couch one's interventions in language that reflects the concreteness of the patient's experience; otherwise patient and analyst have the experience of talking in a way that, in the words of one such patient, "completely misses one another." One does not talk about the patient's feeling that he is like a robot; one talks with the patient about what it feels like to be a robot. One does not talk with the patient about the patient's feeling that he is infatuated with a woman; one talks with him about what the patient feels when he believes he is possessed or haunted by a woman. One does not talk about the patient's wish to be understood by the therapist; one talks about the patient's conviction that the therapist must think the patient's thoughts and feel the patient's feelings if he is to be of any value at all to the patient.

Psychological defense in a paranoid-schizoid mode is based in large part on the principle that one secures safety by separating the endangered from the endangering. (This is the psychological meaning of splitting.) All defenses in a paranoid-schizoid mode are derived from this principle; for example, projection is an effort to place an endangering (or endangered) aspect of self or object outside of the self while retaining the endangered (or endangering) aspect of self or object within. The other defenses in this mode of generating experience—introjection, projective identification, denial, and idealization—can be seen as variations on this theme.

The paranoid-schizoid mode is characterized by omnipotent thinking through which the emotional complexities of loving and hating are magically "resolved," more accurately, precluded from psychic reality. In this mode, guilt (as it exists in a depressive mode) simply does not arise; it has no place in the emotional vocabulary of the more primitive mode. Since one's objects, like oneself, are objects as opposed to subjects, one cannot care about them or have concern for them.[3] There is little to empathize with, since one's objects are not experienced as people with thoughts and feelings so much as they are felt to be loved, hated, or feared forces or things that impinge on oneself. Other people can be valued for what they can do for one, but one does not have concern for even the most important of one's possessions. As described earlier, an object can be damaged or used up, but only a subject can be hurt or injured.

In a paranoid-schizoid mode, what might become a feeling of guilt is dissipated, for example, through the use of omnipotent reparative fantasies. The injury to the object is denied through the use of a magical remedy that is intended to expunge from history the harm that one has done. History is rewritten, and the need for guilt is obviated. For instance, a patient operating heavily in a paranoid-schizoid mode often would laugh and say that he was only kidding after having said something extremely cruel to his wife. Having said, "You know I was only kidding," he felt that he had undone the damage by magically changing the assault into something humorous (by renaming it). When his wife refused to participate in this magical rewriting of history, the patient would escalate his efforts at joviality and begin to treat her with contempt, accusing her of being a baby for not being able to "take it."

This attempt to make use of paranoid-schizoid defenses (magical reparation, denial, and rewriting of history) for the purpose of warding off depressive anxiety (guilt and the fear of the loss of the object due to one's destructiveness) constitutes a manic defense. Loewald (1979) has described the way in which self-punishment similarly can be used to dissipate feelings that threaten to become an experience of guilt. In self-punishment, one uses an omnipotent fantasy that the punishment eradicates the present and past existence of the crime, and there is therefore no reason to feel guilty.

Similarly, in a paranoid-schizoid mode one does not miss a lost or absent object; one denies the loss, short-circuits the feeling of sadness, and replaces the object (person) with another person or with oneself. Since the new person or aspect of self is emotionally equivalent to the lost object,

---

[3]Since the paranoid-schizoid mode never exists in isolation from the depressive mode (and the autistic-contiguous mode), the concept of the self-as-object (completely dissociated from the experience of self as subject) is meaningless phenomenologically. Due to the dialectical structure of experience, self-experience is never completely devoid of a sense of "I-ness," and one's objects are never simply objects altogether devoid of subjectivity.

nothing has changed; there is no need to mourn what is still present. For example, a patient explained that my vacation turned out to be a "blessing in disguise," since he had learned that he was not nearly so dependent on me as I had led him to believe. In this case, an aspect of self was used to magically replace the absent object. In work with this patient, my absences were regularly followed by an enactment of manic defenses in the form of a threatened disruption of treatment (which he "no longer needed") or a grudging agreement to continue analysis "if that's what you think is best" or "for the sake of the completeness of the analysis," which he was convinced was in its termination phase.

Object relatedness in a paranoid-schizoid mode is predominantly in the form of projective identification (Grotstein 1981, Klein 1946, Ogden 1979, 1982). This psychological-interpersonal process reflects many of the other facets of the paranoid-schizoid mode discussed so far. It is based on the omnipotent fantasy that an aspect of self (which is either endangered or endangering) can be placed in another person in such a way that "the recipient" is controlled from within (Klein 1955). In this way, one safeguards an endangered aspect of self and at the same time attempts to omnipotently control an object relationship by treating the object as an incompletely separate container for aspects of oneself. This facet of the process of projective identification involves an evacuative method of managing psychological strain.

In projective identification, the projector by means of actual interpersonal interactions with the "recipient" unconsciously induces feeling states in the recipient that are congruent with the "ejected" feelings. In addition to serving defensive purposes, this constitutes a fundamental form of communication and object relatedness. The recipient of the projective identification can sometimes retrospectively become aware that he is "playing a part . . . in somebody else's fantasy" (Bion 1959, p. 149). Projective identification is a "direct communication" (Winnicott 1971, p. 54) in that it is unmediated by interpreting subjects; instead, it is predominantly a communication between the unconscious of one person and that of another. For this reason, it is often experienced by the recipient as coercive. There is no choice; one not only finds oneself playing a role in someone else's internal drama, one feels unable to stop doing so. The recipient feels controlled from within. If he is able to contain the induced feelings without simply dumping them back into the projector, a shift in the relationship between the projector and the recipient can occur that leads to psychological growth. The "processing" of a projective identification by the recipient is not simply a matter of returning modified psychological contents to the projector. Rather, it is a matter of altering the intersubjective mode of containment generated by the interacting pair, thus generating a new way of experiencing the old psychological contents. It is not so much that psychological contents are modified; it is the intersubjective context that is modified.

This conception of psychological change is not limited to the understanding of projective identification. Rather, what we have arrived at in the course of this discussion is a basic principle of all psychological growth, including that which occurs in the analytic process. Psychological growth occurs not simply as a result of modification of unconscious psychological contents; in addition, what changes is the experiential context (the nature of the containment of the psychological contents). Unconscious fantasy is timeless and is never destroyed (Freud 1911). It is therefore misleading to talk about the eradication of an unconscious fantasy, since that implies that the old fantasy is destroyed or replaced by a new one. It is not the unconscious fantasy that is destroyed or replaced; rather, the fantasy is experienced differently due to a shift in the psychological matrix within which it exists.

The idea that it is not only content but context that shifts in psychological growth was elegantly articulated by a schizophrenic patient when asked if he still had his hallucinatory voices. He replied, "Oh yes, they're still there; they just don't talk anymore." Similarly, in the course of analysis, one does not destroy the thoughts and feelings constituting the Oedipus complex (Loewald 1979); instead, one experiences the component object-related feelings differently. A patient, Mr. K., said in small bits over the course of his fourth year of analysis, "I am still aware that when I am with women teachers I could become extremely anxious if I were to allow myself to experience them (as I used to) as mothers whom I am afraid of having sexual feelings and fantasies about. But I do have some choice in the matter now, and I realize that there was some pleasure and excitement in imagining that I could be sufficiently special (more special than my father and brothers) to get my mother to stop being a mother and start being a wife to me." What had been achieved by this patient was not simply a change in the content of his unconscious fantasy. The Oedipus complex had not been "destroyed" or "overcome." Rather, the psychological context for the experiencing of oedipal wishes and fears had undergone change. Previously, the set of unconscious oedipal desires and prohibitions had been characterized by powerful concreteness and immediacy. Mr. K. initially said he had no idea why he had anxiety "attacks" when talking with women teachers. "It is something that just happens to me and there is no reason for it. I know there is no real danger. The anxiety just goes through me like electricity." The patient had developed compulsive study habits in an effort to become a perfect student and became terribly anxious before exams even though he had prepared in a way that he recognized to be "overkill."

Oedipal feelings and fantasies are always generated in part in a depressive mode. There would be no power or poignancy to the oedipal dilemma if it were not the problem of a subject (for example, the boy) who hates, and wishes to be forever rid of, the same father he loves. In other words, it is a dilemma rooted in subjectivity, whole object relations, ambivalence, and historicity. However, important facets of the unconscious conflict and resultant symptomatology (e.g., anxiety attacks) are experienced largely in a paranoid-schizoid mode. For example, Mr. K. initially experienced his anxiety attacks not as a form of, or reaction to, his feelings and fearful thoughts, but as a force sweeping over him that frightened him. The patient's female teachers were unconsciously experienced as not simply like his mother, but the same as his mother; otherwise the full power of the incestuous danger would not have presented itself in such a concrete way. (Dream material in this phase of analysis included the frightening shifting back and forth of the identity of older women figures, resulting in a feeling on the part of Mr. K. that he "didn't know who was who.") The patient was clearly not psychotic, but the transference to his female teachers was simultaneously experienced in both paranoid-schizoid and depressive modes with a tendency for the dialectical interplay between the two to "collapse" in the direction of the paranoid-schizoid mode during anxiety attacks (Ogden 1985). In the "attacks" of anxiety, there was very little of a subject mediating between the patient and the terrifying thing happening to him.

From this point of view, psychoanalysis is a method of treatment designed not only to help the patient modify unconscious fantasy content, but also a process aimed at helping the patient to experience unconscious content differently. That is, it is a process directed at helping the patient shift the balance of the dialectical interplay between modes of generating experience in relation to specific unconscious contents. What must happen in analysis is not a simple translation of psychological contents from one mode to another. The therapeutic process as I understand it involves the establishment, reestablishment, or expansion of a dialectical relationship between different modes of experience.

There is a tendency among analytic thinkers, including Klein herself, to valorize the depressive mode and villainize the paranoid-schizoid mode. As Eigen (1985) has pointed out, the depressive mode is too often viewed as the full realization of the human potential. In the depressive mode, it is held that man develops the capacity for abstract symbolization, subjectivity and self-reflection, concern for others, guilt, and reparative wishes that lead to cultural productions. On the other hand, the paranoid-schizoid mode is understood as generating a psychological state in which the individual relies on splitting and projective identification for the purpose of evacuating feelings and denying reality. Such a depiction of these modes is based on a diachronic conception of the relationship between the two and fails to appreciate the fundamental dialectical nature of their relationship. The paranoid-schizoid and depressive modes serve as essential negating and preserving contexts for one another. The depressive mode is a mode of integration, resolution, and containment, and if unopposed, leads to certainty, stagnation, closure, arrogance, and deadness (Bion 1962, 1963, Eigen 1985). The paranoid-schizoid mode provides the necessary splitting of linkages and opening up of the closures of the depressive position, thus reestablishing the possibility of fresh linkages and fresh thoughts. The integrative thrust of the depressive mode in turn provides the necessary antithesis for the paranoid-schizoid mode in limiting the chaos generated by the fragmentation of thought, the discontinuity of experience, and the splitting of self and object.

THE AUTISTIC-CONTIGUOUS MODE
OF GENERATING EXPERIENCE

The conceptions of the paranoid-schizoid and depressive modes discussed so far represent ideas derived predominantly from the work of Klein and Bion. The conception of a dialectic of experience constituted exclusively by these two modes is incomplete insofar as it fails to recognize an even more primitive, presymbolic, sensory-dominated mode that I will refer to as the *autistic-contiguous mode*. The conception of an autistic-contiguous pole of the dialectic of experience represents an integration, interpretation, and extension of aspects of the work of Bick (1968, 1986), Tustin (1972, 1980, 1981, 1984, 1986), and Meltzer (Meltzer 1975, 1986, Meltzer et al., 1975). Each of these authors was strongly influenced by Bion's (1962, 1963) conception of the container and the contained as well as his theory of thinking. (A very incomplete list of other important contributors to this line of analytic thought includes J. Anthony [1958], Anzieu [1970], Brazelton [1981], Eimas [1975], Fordham [1977], E. Gaddini [1969], R. Gaddini [1978], S. Klein [1980], Mahler [1952], Milner [1969], D. Rosenfeld [1984], Sander [1964], Spitz [1965], Stern [1977, 1985], Trevarthan [1979], and Winnicott [1960].) In this chapter, space allows for only a brief introduction to a discussion of this mode of experience.

The autistic-contiguous position is a primitive psychological organization operative from the beginning that generates the most elemental form of human experience.[4] It is a sensory-dominated mode in which the most inchoate sense of self is built upon the rhythm of sensation (Tustin 1984), particularly the sensations at the skin surface (Bick 1968). The autistic-contiguous mode[5] of experiencing is a presymbolic, sensory mode and is therefore extremely difficult to capture in words. Rhythmicity and experiences of sensory contiguity contribute to the earliest psychological organization in this mode. Both rhythmicity and experiences of surface contiguity are fundamental to the earliest relations with objects: the nursing experience and the experience of being held, rocked, spoken to, and sung to in the arms of the mother. These experiences are "object-related" in a very specific and very limited sense of the word. The relationship to the object in this mode is certainly not a relationship between subjects as in a depressive mode, nor is it a relationship between objects as in a paranoid-schizoid mode; rather, it is a relationship of shape to the feeling of enclosure, of beat to the feeling of rhythm, of hardness to the feeling of edgedness. Sequences, symmetries, periodicity, skin-to-skin "molding" are all examples of contiguities that are the ingredients out of which the beginnings of rudimentary self-experience arise. The experience of "self" at this point is simply that of a nonreflective state of sensory "going on being" (Winnicott 1956, p. 303)

---

[4]The autistic-contiguous position is conceptualized in this paper not as a prepsychological (biological) phase of development in which the infant lives in a world cut off from dynamic relations with external objects; rather, it is conceived of as a psychological organization in which sensory modes of generating experience are organized into defensive processes in the face of perceived danger. Under circumstances of extreme, protracted anxiety, these defenses become hypertrophied and rigidified and come to constitute a pathologically autistic psychological structure. The development of a normal autistic-contiguous psychological organization can occur only within the unfolding relationship with the mother as environment and the mother as object (cf. Winnicott 1963).

[5]I have termed the most primitive of the modes of experience the *autistic-contiguous mode* in order to parallel roughly the method of naming the paranoid-schizoid mode, which takes its name from the form of psychological organization and defense associated with it. In the autistic-contiguous mode, psychic organization is derived in large part from sensory contiguity; that is, connections are established through the experience of sensory surfaces "touching" one another. Breakdown of this organization leads to the implementation of autistic defenses that will be described.

It must be borne in mind that throughout this chapter the term *autistic* is being used to refer to specific features of a universal, sensory-dominated mode of experience and not to a form of severe childhood psychopathology. It would be as absurd to view infants or adults as suffering from pathological autism while relying heavily on an autistic-contiguous mode of generating experience as it would be to think of infants or adults as paranoid-schizophrenics while organizing experience in a paranoid-schizoid mode, and depressed when operating in a predominantly depressive mode.

derived from "body needs" which only "gradually become ego needs as a psychology gradually emerges out of the [mother–infant's] imaginative elaboration of physical experience" (p. 304).[6]

Early experiences of sensory contiguity define a surface (the beginnings of what will become a sense of place) on which experience is created and organized. These sensory experiences with "objects" (which only an outside observer would be aware of as objects) are the media through which the earliest forms of organized and organizing experience are created.

Contiguity of surfaces (e.g., "molded" skin surfaces, harmonic sounds, rhythmic rocking or sucking, symmetrical shapes) generate the experience of a sensory surface rather than the feeling of two surfaces coming together either in mutually differentiating opposition or in merger. There is practically no sense of inside and outside or self and other; rather, what is important is the pattern, boundedness, shape, rhythm, texture, hardness, softness, warmth, coldness, and the like.

A 29-year-old patient, Mrs. L., came to an analytic hour just after having spent time with her mother and felt, for reasons that she "could not put her finger on," as if she were in a state of such severe anxiety and diffuse tension that the only way to end the state of tension would be to cut herself with a razor all over her body. It had taken great effort on her part to come to the session instead of cutting herself as she had done in the past. The patient cried uncontrollably in the hour. I interpreted as much of the situation as I thought I understood on the basis of what I knew about the patient's relationship to her mother and the connection between these feelings and the transference–counter-transference anxieties of the previous few sessions. Mrs. L. said that she felt as if she were "coming apart at the seams." I said that I thought that she was feeling as if she were coming apart in the most literal way and that she felt as if her skin were already lacerated in the way she had imagined lacerating herself.

It was late in the afternoon and getting cold in the office. I said, "It's cold in here," and got up to turn on the heater. She said, "It is,"

---

[6]Stern (1985), from a psychoanalytic developmental-observational vantage point, states, "Infants [from birth] . . . take sensations, perceptions, actions, cognitions, internal states of motivation and states of [nonself-reflective] consciousness and experience them directly in terms of intensities, shapes, temporal patterns, vitality affects, categorical affects, and hedonic tones" (p. 67). This earliest mode of experience operates throughout life "out of awareness as the experiential matrix" (p. 67) for all succeeding subjective states.

and seemed to calm down soon after that. She said that for reasons that she did not understand she had been extremely touched by my saying that it was cold and by turning the heater on. "It was such an ordinary thing to say and do." I believe that my putting the heater on acknowledged a shared experience of the growing coldness in the air and contributed to the creation of a sensory surface between us. I was using my own feelings and sensations in a largely unconscious "ordinary way" (perhaps like "an ordinary devoted mother" [Winnicott 1949]), which felt to the patient as if I had physically touched her and held her together. The sensory surface mutually created in that way was the opposite of the experience of "coming apart at the seams"; it facilitated a mending of her psychological-sensory surface, which felt as if it had been shredded in the course of the patient's interaction with her mother.

This sensory "holding" (Winnicott 1960) dimension of the analytic relationship and setting operated in conjunction with the binding power of symbolic interpretation (formulated on the basis of the intersubjectivity of the transference–countertransference).

Clearly, the experience just presented was not an example of "pure and undiluted" experience in an autistic-contiguous mode. As is always the case, the autistic-contiguous mode "borrows from" (interpenetrates with) the paranoid-schizoid mode in the creation of fantasy representations for sensory-dominated experience as well as borrowing upon features of a depressive mode, including elements of subjectivity, historicity, and symbolization proper.

There is a crucial distinction between a purely physiological reflex arc and experience in an autistic-contiguous mode despite the fact that both can be described in nonsymbolic, bodily terms. Although the reflex has a locus (from an outside observer's point of view), a locus is different from the beginnings of a sense of a place in which experience is occurring; the reflex may to an observer have periodicity, but periodicity is different from the feeling of rhythm; the reflex may have a temporal and spatial beginning and end, but that is not the same as a feeling of boundedness. The rudiments of sensory experience of self in an autistic-contiguous mode have nothing to do with the representation of one's affective states either idiographically or fully symbolically. The sensory experience *is* the infant in this mode, and the abrupt disruption of shape, symmetry, rhythm, skin moldedness, and so forth is the end of the infant.

Tustin (1980) attempted to communicate the nature of experience at the infant's skin surface by asking us to try to experience the chair we are sitting on not as an object, but simply as a sensory impression on our skin: "Forget your chair. Instead, feel your seat pressing against the seat of the chair. It will make a 'shape.' If you wriggle, the shape will change. Those 'shapes' will be entirely personal to you" (pp. 281–282). In the autistic-contiguous mode, there is neither a chair nor one's buttocks, simply a sensory "impression" in the most literal sense of the word. Tustin describes two sorts of sensory impressions constituting normal early experience: soft impressions, which she terms *autistic shapes* (1984), and hard angular impressions, which she terms *autistic objects* (1980). The difference between these experiences of sensory surface constitutes forms of definition of experiential content within this mode. Experience of an autistic shape is the feeling of softness that much later we associate with ideas like security, safety, relaxation, warmth, and affection. The words that seem to me to be closest to the sensory level of the experience are the words *soothing* and *comforting*. It is not a matter of mother comforting me—it is simply a soothing sensory experience.

A relationship to an autistic shape is different from a relationship to a transitional object (Winnicott 1951) in that the "otherness" of the autistic shape is of almost no significance. In transitional phenomena, the experience centers on the paradox that the object is at the same time created and discovered by the subject and therefore always has one foot in the world outside the individual's omnipotence. This is clearly not the case in relationships to autistic shapes and objects.

> Mr. R. began analysis and found to his great distress that he literally could not think of anything to say. He felt utterly blank and empty. He had looked forward to the beginning of analysis but found the analytic experience terrifying. He had expected to be able to talk without difficulty. Mr. R. unconsciously managed to create a sensory base for himself by filling what he later called the "holes" in himself (his inability to think or talk) and in the analytic relationship (which he experienced as nonexistent) by focusing intently on a rectangular shape that he discerned in the pattern of lines and textures on the ceiling above the couch. These "holes" were subsequently understood in part as derivatives of the patient's early experience of the "holes" in the early mother-infant relationship associated with his mother's profound postpartum depression, for which she was briefly hospitalized. She told him during the course of the analysis that she had held him as a baby only when "absolutely necessary." He had been allowed to cry in his crib for hours on end while his mother hid in her room.

In contrast, the experience of an autistic object is the feeling of a hard, angular impression upon the skin that is experienced as if it were a hard shell-like quality of the skin. It is associated with the most diffuse sense of danger and with what may be represented in a paranoid-schizoid mode by fantasies of a hard shell formed by the skin surface to be used as a protective armor.

Mrs. M., a 35-year-old attorney, during an acute regressive phase of treatment, developed extreme muscular rigidity that led to cramping of her muscles, particularly in her neck. She would frequently massage her cramped muscles in the sessions. These symptoms clearly had features resembling a catatonic state wherein defense against unconscious anger is usually central. However, the current transference–countertransference experience in this case did not center around the patient's fears of her destructiveness in relation to herself or to me. Rather, the material just prior to the acute regression had been organized around feelings of utter vulnerability represented in dreams by images of being a pincushion. This was understood as a derivative of Mrs. M.'s (previously discussed) feeling of being powerless to resist being taken over by her mother's (and my) projections of ourselves into her. As a result, over time I interpreted the acute regression in Mrs. M.'s analysis as an effort by her to create hardness in her body that would serve as a way of resisting my attempts to get inside of her in order to control her and turn her into what I needed her to be for me. Mrs. M.'s massaging of her muscles was viewed as a way of both creating a sensory surface on which to locate herself and a way of reassuring herself that the surface was a hard protective one. (During the regressed phase of analysis under discussion, the patient presented no fantasies or dreams of being invaded or having a shell; experience was predominantly in a sensory mode.) The tension diminished as the sensory experience was reconnected with words by means of verbal interpretation.

I conduct all phases of analysis and psychoanalytic therapy (despite major shifts in the dialectical balance of the three modes of experience) on the basis of the principle that there is always a facet of the personality, no matter how hidden or disguised, operating in a depressive mode and therefore capable of utilizing verbally symbolized interpretations (Bion 1957, Boyer 1967). Often the succession of the patient's associations in conjunction with affective shifts in a given meeting or series of meetings serves as evidence that the patient has heard and made use of the analyst's interpretation. Sometimes one must wait for years before the patient gives direct evidence (e.g., by reminding the analyst of an interpretation made at a time when the patient seemed incapable of operating in a depressive mode) that he or she has utilized the interpretation.[7]

The breakdown of the continuity of sensory-dominated experience being described results in the anxiety that Bick (1968) and Meltzer (Meltzer et al. 1975), on the basis of their work with pathologically autistic children as well as with healthier children and adults, describe as the experience of one's skin becoming a sieve through which one's insides leak out and fall into endless, shapeless space devoid of surface or definition of any sort (see also Rosenfeld 1984). Bion (1959) refers to experience stripped of containment and meaning as "nameless dread." (Perhaps the term *formless dread* might better reflect the nature of anxiety in the autistic-contiguous mode, since the experience of shapes, rhythms, and patterns are the only "names" that exist in this mode.)

> Mrs. N., a 52-year-old woman with an extremely unstable sense of continuity of being, spent long periods of time in every therapy hour silently attempting to picture phone numbers, birth dates, street numbers, and the like of all of the people that she had known since childhood. In the middle of one of these extended ruminative silences, the phone in my office rang and was promptly answered by my answering machine. Mrs. N. was clearly shaken by this and left the office for the first time in the treatment. She returned in about five minutes. Much later in the therapy, Mrs. N. told me, with a mixture of shame and relief, that she had left the room to go to the bathroom because she had had the feeling that she had soiled herself with feces or urine. This experience was not represented at the time in the form of thoughts and was primarily a physical sensation. Only in retrospect could the patient describe it as a feeling of having been "cut into" by the unexpected disruption of her ruminative thoughts. Mrs. N. had a long history, beginning in early childhood, of violent disruptions of self-experience. For example, the patient reported that when she was 6 years old her mother would tie her arms and legs to the bedposts in order to prevent her from masturbating at night.

---

[7]I believe that while there is always an aspect of the patient functioning in a depressive mode (a "nonpsychotic part of the personality" [Bion 1957]), there are always at the same time other aspects of experience that are defensively foreclosed from the realm of the psychological, for example, by means of the creation of psychosomatic illness (McDougall 1974), alexithymia (Nemiah 1977), and forms of "nonexperience" (Ogden 1980).

The terror ensuing from disruption of continuity of sensory experience calls into play forms of defense specific to this mode of experience. Bick (1968, 1986) describes a type of defense that she refers to as "second skin formation." This is a self-protective effort at resurrecting a feeling of the continuity and integrity of one's surface.[8] An example of pathological second skin formation is the development of infantile eczema that Spitz (1964) understood as a psychosomatic disorder resulting from insufficiency or inadequacy of holding in the first weeks and months of life. The continual scratching (often leading to the necessity of wrapping the infant's hands in gauze to prevent severe skin damage and infection) is understood from this perspective as the infant's desperate attempt to restore (through heightened skin sensation) a surface by means of which the terror of leakage and falling into shapeless space is allayed.

Wrapping a hospitalized patient snugly in sheets (while he is continually accompanied and related to by an empathic staff member) is an effective and humane way of treating a patient experiencing the terror of impending annihilation in the form of the dispersal of the self into unbounded space. This form of intervention represents an attempt to supply the patient almost literally with a second skin by means of the provision of a firm, palpable, containing sensory and interpersonal surface.

Common forms of second skin formation encountered clinically with adult patients in psychotherapy and analysis include unremitting eye contact that begins in the waiting room and is only painfully disrupted at the closing of the consulting room door at the end of the hour; constant chatter on the part of the patient filling every moment of the session, leaving hardly a moment of silence; continual holding of one object or another that is

---

[8]Meltzer (Meltzer et al. 1975), building upon the work of Bick (1968), introduced the term *adhesive identification* to describe a form of identification more primitive than either introjective or projective identification. In an autistic-contiguous mode (which Meltzer refers to as the "world of two-dimensionality" [p. 225]), one utilizes adhesive identification in an attempt to create or defensively reconstitute a rudimentary sense of cohesiveness of one's surface. The surface of the other is utilized as a substitute for an incompletely developed or deteriorating sense of one's own surface. Examples of the means by which the surface of the object is defensively "adhered to" in adhesive identification include imitation, mimicry, and clinging forms of sensory connectedness to an object that "can hold [one's] attention and thereby be experienced, momentarily at least, as holding the parts of the [sensory dominated] personality together" (Bick 1968, p. 49).

Tustin (1986) prefers the term *adhesive equation* to *adhesive identification*, since the individual's body is equated with the object in the most concrete, sensory way in this defensive process.

either brought to the session or picked up from the analyst's office (e.g., a tissue); perpetual humming or repeating of sentences or phrases, particularly when a silence might otherwise ensue.

Tustin (1980, 1981, 1984, 1986) has explored the defensive use of autistic objects and shapes in the face of threatened disruption of sensory continuity of self. Autistic shapes and objects offer a form of self-soothing that is "perfect" in a way that no human being can possibly be. The self-soothing activity, whether it be hair twirling, stroking the lobe of the ear, thumb sucking, sucking on the inner surface of the cheek, rocking, tapping one's foot, humming, imagining symmetrical geometric designs or series of numbers, is absolutely reliably present. These activities always have precisely the same sensory qualities and rhythms, never evidencing shifts in mood, never once being a fraction of a second late when they are needed, and so on. No human being can provide such machinelike reliability. The individual has absolute control over the autistic activity; at the same time the autistic activity can tyrannize the individual (Tustin 1984). The tyrannical power of the activity derives from the fact that an individual relying on an autistic mode of defense is absolutely dependent on the protection of the perfect recreation of the sensory[9] experience to protect him against unbearable terror ("formless dread"). I have been impressed by the way in which both aspects of this tyranny play important roles even in the psychoanalysis of adult patients who have achieved the capacity for stably generating experience in a predominantly depressive mode.

A 42-year-old patient, Dr. E., a psychotherapist, became enraged if I were a minute late in beginning his analytic hour. (He wore a digital watch.) Dr. E. said that he knew that I knew the importance of "the frame" and if I violated it in this egregious way, I must not care about him or the analysis in the least. The "frame" was not just an idea for this patient, but a palpable feeling as tangible, hard, and enclosing as the metal frame around a picture. This man had indeed become addicted to the analytic frame as an autistic object. Dr. E. made it clear that he needed not simply reliability in our "relationship," but absolute certainty. As a result, he attempted to control everything, including

---

[9]Boyer's (1986) version of the "fundamental rule" incorporates a full appreciation of the sensory dimension of the analytic experience. He at times directly and at times indirectly (e.g., through the questions he poses) asks his patients to attempt to notice and put into words the thoughts, feelings, and *physical sensations* that they experience in the sessions. He also asks the same of himself in his efforts to utilize his countertransference experience (Boyer 1983, 1987).

my thoughts and feelings. He would continually tell me what I was thinking and feeling and in that way could attempt never to be surprised or disappointed by me. Interpretations that incorporated an idea or perspective that Dr. E. had not yet thought of were extremely distressing to him, because they reflected the fact that I had thoughts that he had not created and therefore did not control in an absolute way. This set of feelings and form of relatedness are usually understood in terms of anal-erotic obsessionality, omnipotence, and projective identification. These are no doubt accurate descriptions of the symptomatology and form of relatedness, but need to be supplemented by an understanding of the way in which the experience also involves tyrannizing relatedness to an autistic object.

The topic of countertransference responses to analytic experience in an autistic-contiguous mode can be touched upon only briefly here. The analyst's feelings often include feelings of being tyrannized by an automaton (as in the case of Dr. E.), feelings of inadequacy for having no compassion with the patient or for being unable to make any connection whatever with the patient, and intense feelings of protectiveness of the patient. This relatively familiar range of feelings is not unlike the group of responses one has to patients operating in predominantly paranoid-schizoid and depressive modes. More specific to the autistic-contiguous mode of experience is countertransference experience in which bodily sensation dominates. Somatic experiences like twitching of one's hand and arm, stomach pain, feelings of bloatedness, and the like are not uncommon. Very frequently the countertransference experience is associated with skin sensations such as feelings of warmth and cold (see discussion of Mrs. L.) as well as tingling, numbness, and an exaggerated sensitivity to skin impressions like the tightness of one's tie or one's shoes. At times, the space between the patient and myself has felt as if it were filled with a warm, soothing substance. Frequently, this is associated with a drowsy countertransference state that has nothing to do with boredom. It is a rather pleasant feeling of being suspended between sleep and wakefulness. (Perhaps this is the sensory dimension of Bion's [1962] idea of "reverie," a concept referring to the analyst's state of receptivity to the patient's unconscious experience and the mother's receptivity to her infant's symbolic and asymbolic [or presymbolic] experience.)

From the perspective developed in this chapter, the autistic-contiguous mode, under normal circumstances, can be seen to provide the bounded-sensory "floor" (Grotstein 1987) of experience. It offers sensory enclosure that exists in dialectical tension with the fragmenting potential of the paranoid-schizoid mode. The danger of psychosis posed by the fragmenting and evacuative processes of the paranoid-schizoid mode is contained in two ways: (1) "from above" by the binding capacity of symbolic linkages, historicity, and subjectivity of the depressive mode, and (2) "from below" by the sensory continuity, rhythmicity, and boundedness of the autistic-contiguous mode.

CONCLUSION

In this chapter, human experience is conceived of as the outcome of a dialectical relationship among three modes of experience. The autistic-contiguous mode provides a good measure of the sensory continuity and integrity of experience (the sensory "floor"); the paranoid-schizoid mode is a principal source of the immediacy of concretely symbolized experience; the depressive mode is a principal medium through which historical subjectivity and the richness of symbolically mediated human experience are generated. Experience is always generated between the poles represented by the ideal of the pure form of each of these modes.

These modes of generating experience are analogous to empty sets, each filled in their relationship with the others. Psychopathology can be thought of as forms of collapse of the richness of experience generated between these poles. Collapse may be in the direction of the autistic-contiguous pole, the paranoid-schizoid pole, or the depressive pole. Collapse toward the autistic-contiguous pole generates imprisonment in the machinelike tyranny of attempted sensory-based escape from the terror of formless dread by means of reliance on rigid autistic defenses. Collapse into the paranoid-schizoid pole is characterized by imprisonment in a nonsubjective world of thoughts and feelings experienced in terms of frightening and protective things that simply happen and cannot be thought about or interpreted. Collapse in the direction of the depressive pole involves a form of isolation of oneself from one's bodily sensations and from the immediacy of one's lived experience, leaving one devoid of spontaneity and aliveness.

REFERENCES

Anthony, J. (1958). An experimental approach to the psychopathology of childhood: autism. *British Journal of Medical Psychology* 31:211-225.

Anzieu, D. (1970). Skin ego. In *Psychoanalysis in France*, ed. S. Lebovici and D. Widlöcher, pp. 17-32. New York: International Universities Press, 1980.

Bick, E. (1968). The experience of the skin in early object relations. *International Journal of Psycho-Analysis* 49:484–486.

—— (1986). Further considerations on the function of the skin in early object relations. *British Journal of Psychotherapy* 2:292–299.

Bion, W. R. (1957). Differentiation of the psychotic from the nonpsychotic personalities. In *Second Thoughts*, pp. 43–64. New York: Jason Aronson, 1967.

—— (1959). Attacks on linking. *International Journal of Psycho-Analysis* 40:308–315.

—— (1962). *Learning from Experience*. New York: Basic Books, 1964.

—— (1963). *Elements of Psycho-Analysis*. London: Heinemann.

Borges, J. L. (1960). Borges and I. In *Labyrinths*, pp. 246–247. New York: New Directions, 1964.

Boyer, L. B. (1967). Office treatment of schizophrenic patients: the use of psychoanalytic therapy with few parameters. In *Psychoanalytic Treatment of Schizophrenic and Characterological Disorders*, ed. L. B. Boyer and P. L. Giovacchini, pp. 143–188. New York: Science House.

—— (1983). *The Regressed Patient*. New York: Jason Aronson.

—— (1986). Technical aspects of treating the regressed patient. *Contemporary Psychoanalysis* 22:25–44.

—— (1987). Countertransference and technique in working with the regressed patient: further remarks. Presented at the Boyer House Foundation Conference, The Regressed Patient, San Francisco, March 21, 1987.

Brazelton, T. B. (1981). *On Becoming a Family: The Growth of Attachment*. New York: Delta/Seymour Lawrence.

Eigen, M. (1985). Toward Bion's starting point: between catastrophe and faith. *International Journal of Psycho-Analysis* 66:321–330.

Eimas, P. (1975). Speech perception in early infancy. In *Infant Perception: From Sensation to Cognition*, vol. 2, ed. L. B. Cohen and P. Salapatek, pp. 193–228. New York: Academic Press.

Fordham, M. (1977). *Autism and the Self*. London: Heinemann.

Freud, S. (1911). Formulations on the two principles of mental functioning. *Standard Edition* 12:213–226.

Gaddini, E. (1969). On imitation. *International Journal of Psycho-Analysis* 50:475–484.

Gaddini, R. (1978). Transitional object origins and the psychosomatic symptom. In *Between Reality and Fantasy*, ed. S. E. Grolnick, L. Barkin, and W. Muensterberger, pp. 109–131. New York: Jason Aronson.

Grotstein, J. (1981). *Splitting and Projective Identification*. New York: Jason Aronson.

—— (1987). Schizophrenia as a disorder of self-regulation and interactional regulation. Presented at the Boyer House Foundation Conference, The Regressed Patient, San Francisco, March 21, 1987.

Klein, M. (1935). A contribution to the psychogenesis of manic-depressive states. In *Contributions to Psycho-Analysis, 1921–1945*, pp. 282–311. London: Hogarth, 1968.

—— (1946). Notes on some schizoid mechanisms. In *Envy and Gratitude and Other Works, 1946–1963*, pp. 1–24. New York: Delacorte, 1975.

—— (1952). Mutual influences in the development of ego and id. In *Envy and Gratitude and Other Works, 1946–1963*, pp. 57–60. New York: Delacorte, 1975.

—— (1955). On identification. In *Envy and Gratitude and Other Works, 1946–1963*, pp. 141–175. New York: Delacorte, 1975.

—— (1957). Envy and gratitude. In *Envy and Gratitude and Other Works, 1946–1963*, pp. 176–235. New York: Delacorte, 1975.

—— (1958). On the development of mental functioning. In *Envy and Gratitude and Other Works, 1946–1963*, pp. 236–246. New York: Delacorte, 1975.

Klein, S. (1980). Autistic phenomena in neurotic patients. *International Journal of Psycho-Analysis* 61:395–401.

Lacan, J. (1953). The function and field of speech in psychoanalysis. In *Écrits*, trans. A. Sheridan, pp. 30–113. New York: Norton, 1977.

Little, M. (1958). On delusional transference (transference psychosis). *International Journal of Psycho-Analysis* 39:134–138.

Loewald, H. (1979). The waning of the Oedipus complex. In *Papers on Psychoanalysis*, pp. 384–404. New Haven: Yale University Press, 1980.

Mahler, M. (1952). On childhood psychoses and schizophrenia: autistic and symbiotic infantile psychoses. *Psychoanalytic Study of the Child* 7:286–305. New York: International Universities Press.

McDougall, J. (1974). The psychosoma and the psycho-analytic process. *International Review of Psycho-Analysis* 1:437–459.

Meltzer, D. (1975). Adhesive identification. *Contemporary Psychoanalysis* 11:289–310.

—— (1986). Discussion of Esther Bick's paper, "Further considerations on the function of the skin in early object relations." *British Journal of Psychotherapy* 2:300–301.

Meltzer, D., Bremner, J., Hoxter, S., et al. (1975). *Explorations in Autism*. Perthshire: Clunie.

Milner, M. (1969). *The Hands of the Living God*. London: Hogarth.

Nemiah, J. (1977). Alexithymia: theoretical considerations. *Psychotherapy and Psychosomatics* 28:199–206.

Ogden, T. (1979). On projective identification. *International Journal of Psycho-Analysis* 60:357–373.

—— (1980). On the nature of schizophrenic conflict. *International Journal of Psycho-Analysis* 61:513–533.

—— (1982). *Projective Identification and Psychotherapeutic Technique*. New York: Jason Aronson.

—— (1983). The concept of internal object relations. *International Journal of Psycho-Analysis* 64:227–241.

—— (1985). On potential space. *International Journal of Psycho-Analysis* 66:129–141.

—— (1986). *The Matrix of the Mind: Object Relations and the Psychoanalytic Dialogue*. Northvale, NJ: Jason Aronson.

————— (1987). The transitional oedipal relationship in female development. *International Journal of Psycho-Analysis*, 68:485-498.

Rosenfeld, D. (1984). Hypochondria, somatic delusion and body scheme in psycho-analytic practice. *International Journal of Psycho-Analysis* 65:377-388.

Sander, L. (1964). Adaptive relations in early mother–child interactions. *Journal of the American Academy of Child Psychiatry* 3:231-264.

Searles, H. (1963). Transference psychosis in the psychotherapy of chronic schizophrenia. In *Collected Papers on Schizophrenia and Related Subjects*, pp. 654-716. New York: International Universities Press, 1965.

Segal, H. (1957). Notes on symbol formation. *International Journal of Psycho-Analysis* 38:391-397.

3

JOHN STEINER, Ph.D.

The Defensive Function of Pathological Organizations

For some time psychoanalysts have been interested in types of defensive organization that give rise to analyses that become stuck and resistant to change. In these patients, defenses do not operate singly but seem to be organized into a defensive system that is represented internally as an organization of internal objects. While different types of organization have been described (Steiner 1988), they all seem to be based on a narcissistic type of object relationship in which projective identification leads to a lack of distinction between self and object. See, for example, Rivière (1936), Meltzer (1968), Segal (1972), Riesenberg-Malcolm (1981), O'Shaughnessy (1981), Sohn (1985), and Steiner (1985, 1987), but especially Rosenfeld (1964, 1971). Spillius (1983) has reviewed some of these studies and has also edited a reprinting of some of them with a useful commentary (1988).

In a previous paper (1987) I discussed the nature of such pathological organizations of the personality and have emphasized the rigid structure of the organization and the way it leads to the creation of a third position, the *borderline position*, which exists in equilibrium with the two basic positions, viz.

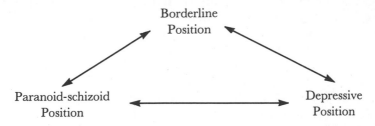

Borderline Position

Paranoid-schizoid Position   Depressive Position

The main application of these ideas is clinical, and I suggested that this kind of equilibrium diagram can help us to orient ourselves more precisely to the patient's material. We can use it to remind ourselves of the need to assess whether the patient is functioning primarily at a paranoid-schizoid level, primarily at a depressive level, or in the borderline position under the sway of a pathological organization. Once we have oriented ourselves in this way, we can also try to follow the shifts between the borderline position produced by the organization and the other two positions.

When we do this it becomes clear that the pathological organization functions as a defense, not only against fragmentation and confusion, but also against the mental pain and anxiety of the depressive position. It acts as an intermediate area between the other two positions, where the patient believes he can retreat if either paranoid or depressive anxieties become unbearable.

In this and other previous work emphasis has been given to description of the organizations, the mechanisms they employ, and the object relations that result. Although it is generally recognized that they are defensive, the purpose to which they are put has not been examined in detail; in this chapter I will look at some of the anxieties against which the organizations operate.

THE DEFENSE AGAINST SEPARATENESS

An important idea in this context was put forward by Rosenfeld (1971), who suggested that narcissistic organizations protect the patient from the experience of separateness. Narcissistic object relations are based on projective identification in which unwanted parts of the self are disowned and projected into objects and, at the same time, desirable parts of the object are taken over, possessed, and controlled. The reality of what belongs to self and what belongs to objects is obscured, and both good and bad aspects of the object may be idealized and identified with so that they are viewed as belonging to the self. This may result in manic states or in the superior withdrawal characteristic of the narcissistic patient. However, a much wider range of patients employs essentially similar organizations of defenses that may emerge as primarily obsessional, or infantile and dependent, or hysterical or even psychotic in their manifestations. The particular type of clinical picture seems to depend on the nature of the defenses and the types of forces that hold the defenses together in an organization. All of them to varying degrees have profound effects on the individual's relationship with reality.

Despite the varied clinical presentation, all of these states depend on projective identification for their structure, and this results in an incomplete experience of separateness between self and object. Sometimes only a part of the self appears to be disowned and attributed to the object, while at other times the whole self seems to be unconsciously experienced as residing within an object. This may lead to claustrophobic anxieties but the alternative, namely emerging into separateness, seems to be equally or more frightening. Rey (1979) has referred to this situation as the *claustro-agoraphobic dilemma.*

Rosenfeld (1971) discusses the question of why separateness should be so terrifying and suggests that the reason has to do with the fact that both good and bad aspects of the object become more clearly visible as the patient begins to emerge from a fusion with the object. This leads to an appreciation of reality, and the retreat to live inside the object is essentially a retreat to an omnipotent world where reality need not be faced.

If we consider the reality of the bad qualities of the object, it is understandable that frustrations arise whenever shortcomings become evident. Sometimes, if the patient is emerging from an idealized state of fusion, the shortcomings have a particularly painful coloring connected with a sense of betrayal. It often seems as if the patient feels that he was promised a perfect object and the reality of disappointment seems unfair and unbearable. This is particularly true of those frustrations that arise in the oedipal configuration, since they emphasize that the patient does not possess and control his objects as he was previously led to believe.

Perhaps even more important, because of the primitive nature of the feelings that are provoked, is the way reality leads to an appreciation of the good qualities in the object that stimulate envy. Here Rosenfeld suggests we find the expression of the death instinct, which may have catastrophic results for the patient's ego and for his object relationships. The pathological organization of defenses by protecting the patient from a recognition of the distinction between self and object can effectively protect the patient from both these consequences of separateness, but at a considerable cost. When envy predominates, the defenses seem to become both a defense against the envy and an expression of it.

PARANOID-SCHIZOID AND DEPRESSIVE ANXIETIES

The type of anxiety experienced depends in part on the nature of the defensive organization, which creates its own problems for the patient, but it also depends on the purpose for which the defenses were mounted. Here again the equilibrium diagram can be useful, because the anxieties that threaten the patient can be broadly grouped into those connected with the paranoid-schizoid position and those connected with the depressive position. The organization can create a borderline area that protects the patient from the anxieties of either of the two basic positions, but at any one time the threat may be predominantly paranoid-schizoid or predominantly depressive. The diagram can be used to remind us that the distinction is important and we can try to judge whether the patient is primarily operating in the area:

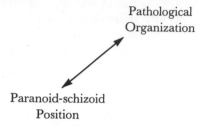

or more centrally in the area:

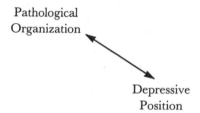

In other words, are his anxieties to do with the fear of fragmentation and disintegration or more in the area of depressive pain, guilt, and loss?

Some of these issues are, of course, relevant in the case of all defenses that serve to lessen anxiety, but I am particularly concerned with those situations where defenses are deployed, not singly in isolation, but as part of a defensive system or organization, because it is these organizations that seem to produce states of mind that tend to become so fixed and rigid.

To look at this question I will briefly outline the sequence of anxieties, defenses, and object relations that have to be gone through in the course of normal development, and emphasize those that seem to be so difficult to endure that they call for the deployment of a pathological organization of defenses.

THE TWO BASIC POSITIONS

Melanie Klein's differentiation of two major groupings of anxieties and defenses, the paranoid-schizoid and depressive, has allowed us to identify different types of anxieties that the developing infant has to face. I will only summarize them briefly here as follows.

In the paranoid-schizoid position anxieties of a primitive nature threaten the immature ego and lead to the mobilization of primitive defenses. Splitting, idealization, and projective identification operate to create rudimentary structures made up of idealized good objects kept far apart from persecuting bad ones. The individual's own impulses are similarly split, and he directs all his love toward the good object and all his hatred against the bad one. As a consequence of the projection, the leading anxiety is paranoid, and the preoccupation is with survival of the self. Thinking is concrete because of the confusion between self and object, which is one of the consequences of projective identification (Segal 1957).

The depressive position represents an important developmental advance in which whole objects begin to be recognized and ambivalent impulses become directed toward the primary object. These changes result from an increased capacity to integrate experiences and lead to a shift in primary concern from the survival of the self to a concern for the object upon which the individual depends. Destructive impulses lead to feelings of loss and guilt, which can be more fully experienced and which consequently enable mourning to take place. The consequences include a development of symbolic function and the emergence of reparative capacities, which become possible when thinking no longer has to remain concrete.

The distinction between the two positions has an impressive clarity but does sometimes make us forget that, within the positions, mental states with very different qualities exist. In the paranoid-schizoid position the type of splitting described above can be considered as normal and distinguished from states of fragmentation that result from disintegrative splitting. Projective identification of a violent kind may then lead to both the object and the projected part of the ego being splintered into minute fragments, creating persecutory states often with depersonalization and extreme anxiety (Rosenfeld 1947, Bion 1957, Segal 1964). Such states may result when hostility predominates and especially if envy stimulates attacks on good objects.

When this happens the normal split between good and bad is likely to break down, leading to a confusional state (Rosenfeld 1950, Klein 1957). It makes some sort of sense after all to have hostile feelings to bad objects, but hostile feelings to good objects lead to the good objects being turned bad, either as a defense or as a consequence of envious attacks, and the whole distinction between good and bad may be difficult to maintain. These states seem to be particularly difficult to bear and may lead to disintegrative splitting. Such states of confusion and fragmentation make the patient particularly vulnerable to the influence of a pathological organization that offers a kind of pseudo-structure to help deal with the confused and chaotic state of mind (Meltzer 1968, Rosenfeld 1971).

THE DEFENSE AGAINST ANXIETIES OF THE PARANOID-SCHIZOID POSITION

I will now try to illustrate some of these themes by presenting clinical material, and I will begin by discussing situations where the borderline position seems to act as a defense against paranoid-schizoid anxieties. In the following section, by contrast, I will try to illustrate how the borderline position can serve as a defense against depressive anxieties.

Patient A

A patient I saw in a consultation interview seemed to be consumed with anger. His wife had had several breakdowns requiring hospital admission, and a social worker had been seeing them as a couple. She had then arranged for his wife to have individual treatment and the patient had been furious and had arranged his own referral to the Tavistock Clinic. He was able to say very little about himself, and when I pointed this out he became indignant, saying that he thought it unreasonable for a patient who had problems in communication to be expected to communicate. After several attempts to get through to him that led nowhere, I asked for a dream. He described one in which he met a friend and was offered a lift home on his motorbike. They drove all over London and ended up at the river, which was nowhere near his home. In the dream he got angry and said it would have been quicker to go home by himself. I interpreted that this was the feeling in the session where I seemed to be taking him all over the place but not where he wanted to go. I suggested that he was fed up and wondered why he had come at all. To this he said, "Very clever."

When I asked for an early memory, he described several vaguely, but when pressed for detail he recalled a time as a small child when someone gave him a glass to drink from. He bit completely through it and ended up with pieces of glass in his mouth. Before that he thought he had been used to flexible plastic cups. I linked this with his rage in the session and his fear that things around him were cracking up. I interpreted that he was afraid I couldn't be flexible like the plastic cup, but might crack up as his wife had done. He was able then to acknowledge his violence and to admit that he hit his wife and also smashed the furniture at home. It remained impossible to work with him, since to be flexible seemed to mean to become completely pliable and allow him to dictate how the session and his treatment should be conducted.

I felt that his arrogant and demanding nature reflected his need to avoid his internal chaos and confusion. He did not know how to cope with his wife's illness, perhaps because it reminded him so vividly of his own. Any relinquishment of his angry omnipotence threatened to expose the chaos and confusion. He seemed to be operating on the left-hand limb of the equilibrium diagram, where anxieties of a paranoid-schizoid kind led to his need to adopt the protection of a pathological organization, which was in fact not adequately dealing with his anxiety so that he felt threatened with a breakdown.

Patient B

Another patient was extremely aloof and complained about the secretaries, who he said had messed up his appointment. He insisted that I worked in an incompetent, unsatisfactory institution, but he exempted me from blame, dissociating me from my "inefficient underlings," and he clearly wanted me to agree with him and apologize for them. He summarized it all by insisting that I lived in a house of straw, which I ought to be able to acknowledge. I found I could not get near him, and after I tried many different approaches I eventually suggested that he was afraid that *he* was the one who lived in a house of straw, which he had to defend vigorously with his haughty coldness.

Not surprisingly this did not help, and when I asked for a dream, he thought it was a stupid request. He did, however, recall that he had had a dream some ten years previously about a horse that won the National, and all he could remember was that it was called Arctic Prince. Although he could not accept my interpretation that this was how he felt, the image seemed to fit so precisely with his cold superiority that I felt it indicated a kind of unconscious insight. He could communicate this insight to me, but was unable to accept it back into himself. If he let me through to him, it seemed that his house of straw would actually be threatened.

Patient C

A 25-year-old artist would become irrationally terrified that his plumbing would leak, that his central heating would break down, that his telephone would be cut off, and so on. He was extremely anxious to start analysis and immediately became very excited, convinced that he was my star patient, and wondered if I was writing a book about him. Very quickly, however, he felt trapped and insisted on keeping a distance by producing breaks in the analysis, which created an atmosphere where I was invited to worry about him and prevent him from leaving. The extent of his claustro-agoraphobic anxieties was illustrated when he went to Italy for a holiday. Because of his country of origin he needed a visa, and although he knew this, he had simply neglected to get one. When the immigration officials in Rome told him that he would have to return to London, he created such a scene, crying and shouting, that they relented and let him in. Once in the country, however, he became frightened that he wouldn't be allowed out because the officials would see that his passport had not been stamped. Therefore, he managed to cajole his friends to take him to the French border, which he crossed in the trunk of their car; then he obtained the necessary visa and reentered in the normal way to continue his holiday.

It is clear that he regularly left me to carry the worry and concern for him, and this became particularly so when he behaved in a similar way as he prepared to take a holiday to the Soviet Union. This time he found that his visa did not correctly match the departure date, so he simply took a pen and altered it. He did return safely and soon after had the following dream. He was in a Moscow hotel with a homosexual friend and wanted to masturbate with him. Two lady guides, however, refused to leave the room and indeed seemed proud of their work and of the hotel, even arranging to serve excellent meals in the room. The patient complained about this because he felt trapped, not even being allowed to go to the restaurant, and even began to suspect that the guides had connections with the KGB.

The panic that constantly afflicted this patient was basically that which resulted when things got out of control, in the form of central heating breaking down or the telephone being cut off, for example. His defensive organization was an attempt to deal with this chaotic anxiety by omnipotent methods in which he would force himself into his objects and then feel claustrophobic and have to escape in great anxiety. His dream of the Soviet Union did seem to contain a representation of a good object in the form of the two lady guides, but his basic reaction to these was persecutory, and he complained that he was imprisoned and not allowed to go to the restaurant. What the guides did was interfere with his homosexual activity by their presence, and I think this is what the analysis was beginning to do. He became afraid that the organization would be weakened by the analysis and had to escape to reassert its potency.

Sometimes the organization that rescues the patient from the chaos and confusion is a psychotic one, which may result in a delusional state. Although paranoid delusions may themselves be frightening, it is often remarkable that a patient in a vague and ill-defined persecutory mood with terrible anxiety and depersonalization may actually become quite calm when his anxieties have been organized into a delusional system. What appeared as a nameless and vague dread becomes converted into a clear-cut delusion of persecution with apparent relief.

These examples have illustrated how chaos, confusion, violence, and panic can become extremely difficult to bear and can consequently become the occasion for the development of a pathological organization. These organizations may then protect the patient from such experiences and may lead to an equilibrium in which the patient can cope albeit at the cost of a considerably restricted life. It is often when such an equilibrium breaks down that the patient seeks treatment, and he may then try to reestablish the equilibrium in his analysis (Rivière 1936, Joseph 1983). It may be the dread of such persecutory states that contributes to the need to maintain the defensive organization.

THE DEFENSE AGAINST ANXIETIES
OF THE DEPRESSIVE POSITION

Another point of maximal anxiety arises in the depressive position, where it is easy to forget that splitting also plays an important role. Klein (1935) emphasizes how splitting is resorted to again when the good object has been internalized as a whole object and ambivalent impulses toward it lead to depressive states in which the object is felt to be damaged, dying, or dead, and "casts its shadow on the ego" (Freud 1917). Attempts to possess and preserve the good object are part of the depressive position and lead to a renewal of splitting, this time to prevent the loss of the good object and to protect it from attacks. The aim in this phase of the depressive position is to deny the reality of the loss of the object by concretely internalizing it, possessing it, and identifying with it. This is the situation of the bereaved person in the early stages of mourning and appears to be a normal stage that needs to be passed through before the subsequent experience of acknowledgment of the loss can take place.

A critical point in the depressive position arises when the task of relinquishing control over the object has to be faced. The earlier trend, which aims at possessing the object and denying reality, has to be reversed if the depressive position is to be worked through, and the object is to be allowed its independence. In unconscious fantasy this means that the individual has to face his inability to protect the object. His psychic reality includes the realization of the internal disaster created by his sadism and the awareness that his love and reparative wishes are insufficient to preserve his object, which must be allowed to die with the consequent desolation, despair, and guilt. These processes involve intense conflict, which we associate with the work of mourning and which seem to result in anxiety and mental pain. This seems to be another critical point for the patient, and if these experiences cannot be faced, a pathological organization may again be called into play to deal with the conflict.

Patient D

A student was referred for psychotherapy by a psychiatrist following an admission to hospital because of depression and suicidal ruminations. He gradually improved and returned to his home, but was undecided if he should continue his studies. He came to the consultation obviously anxious and within a few seconds became extremely angry, perhaps because I had so far remained silent. When I asked him if he wanted to begin, he grimaced and snapped, "No!" At first I thought he looked quite psychotic, since his lips were trembling with rage and he had great difficulty controlling himself. After a few minutes he got up and walked about the room, looking at my books and pictures, and eventually stopped and picked up a picture of two men playing cards and said, "What game do you think these two are playing?" I interpreted that he felt he and I were playing a game and he wanted to know what was going on. He relaxed slightly and sat down again. He then said he felt I was adopting a technique that had been imposed on me by the Tavi-

stock Clinic and that I expected him to go along with it. I interpreted
that he saw me as a kind of robot who mechanically did what I was told,
and he agreed.

When I asked for a dream, he described one he had when he was 15
and which remained extremely vivid. In the dream he was standing in a
city that had been completely destroyed. Around him were rubble and
twisted metal, but there were also small puddles of water and in these a
rainbow was reflected in brilliant colors. I interpreted that he felt a kind
of triumph if he could destroy me and make out of me a robot, which
meant to him that I was simply twisted metal with nothing human
about me. He admitted that the mood in the dream was ecstatic, and I
suggested that the triumph and exaltation were a way of denying the
despair and destruction. He relaxed perceptibly, and with additional
work we could link the catastrophe in the dream to a time at the age of
15 when he returned home to be told that his parents were going to
separate.

In contrast to the earlier examples I think the underlying situation in
this patient was fundamentally a depressive one. His internal world contained damage and destroyed objects, which gave it the desolated appearance of a destroyed city. This filled him with such despair that he could not
face it and was led to deploy manic mechanisms as a defense. If the mania
and omnipotence could be contained, he was able to make contact with his
depression and work with the therapist. The analytic work could schematically be located on the right-hand arm of the equilibrium triangle. As he
found depressive anxieties to be too much to cope with, he turned to an
arrogant manic organization as a means of escaping from them.

Patient E

Another young man also came with manic features as well as elements
of schizoid superiority. He was a 28-year-old youth worker who complained of being unable to find meaning in life, of anxiety attacks, of
self-consciousness, and an inability to experience what was happening
around him. He was a tall, good-looking man, dressed with a hint of
being down and out without actually being so.

The first part of the interview was rather challenging, since he
really interviewed me, asking for my reaction to him and his condition.
Did I realize, for example, that he talked about himself with his tongue
in his cheek? Eventually I asked for a dream, and he described one that
occurred after a recent time in the Lake District, where he stayed high

up in the hills, coming down only occasionally and mostly sleeping rough. In the dream he was climbing up a steep hill, got into the clouds, and then saw a road that branched so that he did not know which direction to take. At this point he got more excited and spoke very quickly, describing all sorts of features like railway stations containing clocks and barometers, and linking these in an elaborate way with events in his childhood. He explained that the crossroad had a symbolic meaning representing his freedom of choice and his doubts about the direction his life should take. Eventually I interpreted that he seemed to be trying to draw me into the clouds with him and inviting me to get very involved in the meaning of the dream symbolically. I suggested that the real communication was that he did feel down and out, sleeping rough, and that he had to get high to get away from some very depressed feelings. This slowed him down temporarily, and he could tell me that he had applied for thirteen jobs without success and that his girlfriend had recently rejected him.

Later he mentioned that he was cut off from his childhood, and this led me to ask what his earliest memory was. He described one in which his brother, who was six years older, was throwing him to a friend. This memory brought tears to his eyes, and he explained that his brother had died some seven years before, apparently in an accident after coming home drunk from a party. The gas outlet in the bathroom was blocked by snow, and he was killed. At the same time he added that his brother was down and out, was taking drugs, and had reached the end of his tether, so that it was clear that the patient felt that it was really a suicide. I was able to interpret his identification with his brother and his fear of showing me how depressed and suicidal he was.

I think it is often possible to make contact with depressive anxieties even in consultation interviews such as these, and in this way to get a glimpse of a state of mind that the patient dreads and that he uses all means at his disposal to avoid. Often the most effective means of defense against these anxieties is again the deployment of a defensive organization.

FURTHER THOUGHTS ON DEPRESSIVE ANXIETIES

Despite the fact that the anxieties of the depressive position were described with detail and vividness by Melanie Klein (1935, 1940), they have not always been given sufficient emphasis, and some authors speak as if the patient's problems are virtually over when he can pass from the terrors of the paranoid-schizoid position to the depressive position. Because of this I will look at the depressive position in greater detail.

Klein (1936) describes how during development the organization of the ego changes from the relative fragmentation typical of the paranoid-schizoid position to a more organized state in which it is able to identify more fully with good objects. "The dread of persecution, which was at first felt on the ego's account, now relates to the good object as well, and from now on preservation of the good object is regarded as synonymous with the survival of the ego" (Klein 1935).

This change is accompanied by a change in object relations, namely from a relationship with part-objects to one that involves whole objects, and it is through this step that the ego arrives at a new position, which forms the foundation of the situation called the "loss of the loved object" (Freud 1917). Not until the object is loved *as a whole* can its loss be felt as a whole.

She goes on to emphasize that this is the situation that is fundamental for the experiences connected with the depressive position—namely, when the ego becomes fully identified with its good internalized objects, and at the same time becomes aware of its own incapacity to protect and preserve them against the internalized persecuting objects and the id. This anxiety is psychologically justified.

Because it does not abandon its earlier defenses, omnipotent attacks continue to be mounted in an attempt to annihilate and expel the object. Splitting is then used to try to preserve the good object by deflecting the attacks away to a bad object. A breakdown of splitting is, however, constantly threatened, for every access of hate or anxiety may temporarily abolish the differentiation and thus result in a "loss of the loved object."

She goes on to say, "It seems to me that only when the ego has introjected the object as a whole, and has established a better relationship to the external world and to real people, is it able fully to realize the disaster created through its sadism and especially through its cannibalism, and to feel distressed about it. . . . It requires a fuller identification with the loved object, and a fuller recognition of its value, for the ego to become aware of the state of disintegration to which it has reduced its loved object." This realization leads to despair.

In this paper Melanie Klein describes some of the states of mind and some of the conditions that the patient who is facing a depression finds in his internal world and the consequent feelings of guilt and despair that accompany them. She recognizes how difficult it is for the patient to face such experiences and describes how defensive processes are mounted to help evade this psychic reality. If we understand this, we are closer to understanding the patient's need to mount such defenses.

MOURNING

We can, however, ask further questions, and we are helped by Klein's discussion of mourning (1940). It is interesting to ask what happens in the course of normal development to allow a patient to pass through an experience such as that of having his object destroyed. If it is true that he is dependent on his object, and if his object is lost, then where can he find the resources to continue to live?

I think this is the central paradox of the depressive position. It does seem that psychic reality demands that the patient must face first that his object is destroyed, and next that he is dependent on the object and has to face his own destruction and demise so that all hope of the survival of his object and thus of himself has to be abandoned. This is the state of affairs at the beginning of mourning and leads to a hopelessness that demands the most powerful defenses. These defenses are designed to deny either the reality of the loss of the object or the reality of the subject's dependence on it.

If, however, psychic reality *is* faced, a new situation arises. First the object is gradually relinquished and the reality of the loss is acknowledged as mourning proceeds; next, if mourning is allowed to continue, the subject begins to recognize that by detaching himself from his object he is able to survive the loss and gradually engage once more in life. The dependence on the object is a psychic reality but not an actual reality. Only if the psychic reality is faced can the actual reality be subsequently experienced.

Freud (1917) has described the process of mourning in beautiful detail and emphasizes that in the work of mourning it is the reality of the loss that has so painfully to be faced. In the process every memory connected with the bereaved is gone over and reality testing is applied to it until gradually the full force of the loss is appreciated. If successful, this process leads to an acknowledgment of the loss and a consequent enrichment of the mourner. I think we are in a position to speculate in more detail about what this involves; it is helpful to consider it in two stages.

First, in the early phases of mourning the patient attempts to deny the loss by trying to possess and preserve the object. One of the ways he does this is by projecting parts of himself into the lost object and identifying with it. This involves a form of projective identification. Every interest is abandoned by the mourner except that connected with the lost person; this total preoccupation is designed to deny the separation and to ensure that the fate of the subject and the object are inextricably linked. If the subject dies, then I die; conversely if I am to survive, then the reality of the loss of the object has to be denied.

This is where the patient has somehow to overcome the paradox I have described, and this process demands a separation of self from object. If this can be achieved, the parts of the self are extracted from the object and returned to the ego. In this way the object is viewed more realistically, no longer distorted by projections of the self, and the ego is enriched by reacquiring the parts of the self that had previously been disowned.

Klein (1940) has described this vividly in the patient she calls Mrs. A., who lost her son and after his death began sorting out her letters, keeping his and throwing others away. Klein suggests that she was unconsciously trying to restore him and keep him safe, throwing out what she considered to be bad objects and bad feelings. At first she did not cry very much, and tears did not bring the relief that they did later on. She felt numbed and closed up. She also stopped dreaming, as if she wanted to deny the reality of her actual loss and was afraid that her dreams would put her in touch with it.

Then she dreamed that she saw a mother and her son. The mother was wearing a black dress, and she knew that her son had died or was going to die. This dream put her in touch with the reality not only of her feelings of loss but of a host of other feelings that the associations to the dream provoked, including those of rivalry with her son, who seemed to stand also for a brother, lost in childhood, and other primitive feelings that had to be worked through. Later she had a second dream in which she was flying with her son when he disappeared. She felt that this meant his death—that he was drowned. She felt as if she too were to be drowned—but then she made an effort and drew away from the danger back to life. The associations showed that she had decided that she would not die with her son, but would survive. Even in the dream she could feel that it was good to be alive and bad to be dead, and this showed that she had accepted her loss. Sorrow and guilt were experienced but with less panic, since she had lost the previous conviction of her own inevitable death. (This description is particularly poignant, because Melanie Klein wrote this paper shortly after she lost her own son in a mountaineering accident, and it seems likely that Mrs. A. is actually herself.)

We can see that the acknowledgment of the reality of the loss and the differentiation of self from object are the critical issues that determine if mourning can proceed to a normal conclusion. This involves the task of relinquishing control over the object and means that the earlier trend, which was aimed at possession of the object and denying reality, has to be reversed. In unconscious fantasy this means that the individual must face his inability to protect the object. His psychic reality includes the realization of the internal disaster created by his sadism and the awareness that his reparative wishes are insufficient to preserve his object, which must be allowed to die with the consequent desolation, despair, and guilt. These processes involve intense conflict, which is part of the work of mourning to resolve.

The act of relinquishment and the recognition of the possibility of survival despite the loss seem to be particularly difficult to face. They lead to the deployment of a pathological organization of defenses and these in turn prevent mourning from proceeding because they deny the very reality that has to be faced.

One reason for this seems to be that when defenses are organized in this systematic way they have a rigidity that prevents the very separation of self from object, which is necessary for mourning to proceed. We might suppose that if projective identification is a simple isolated mechanism, it retains a kind of flexibility so that albeit with pain, the projections can be withdrawn as reality is faced. If, however, the projection is rigidly fixed, the separation of self from object cannot be achieved and the loss of the object cannot be differentiated from loss of the self. This is the situation when narcissistic object relationships such as those described by Rosenfeld (1971) prevail.

Patient F

Another patient had a long and very stuck analysis dominated by the conviction that it was imperative for him to become a doctor. In fact, he was unable to get a place at medical school, and after various attempts to study dentistry had to be content with a post as a hospital administrator, which he hated. Session after session was devoted to the theme of his wasted life and the increasingly remote possibility that studies at night school might lead to a place at a medical school, perhaps if not in this country, then overseas.

I was repeatedly able to link his need to be a doctor with his conviction that he contained a dying object in his inner world that he considered he had to cure and preserve, and that he could not accept his inability to do so. He could not recognize that this task was impossible and quite beyond his power, and he could not get on with his life and let his object die. He had a terrible fear that he would not be able to cope when his parents died and also a great fear of his own aging and death. Somehow he was convinced that if he could be a doctor, it would also mean that he would be immune from illness.

When he was 14, his grandfather developed cancer and over the next two years became progressively more ill and died in a most painful way. My patient could not bear to see him suffer and especially could not bear to watch the loving way his grandmother cared for his grandfather. When the doctor first broke the news to the family, he had run out of the house in a panic. I had heard different references to this tragic experience over the years, and one day I interpreted that his wish to be a doctor was an omnipotent wish to reverse this death and that he believed he could even now keep his grandfather alive and was doing so inside himself through the fantasy that as a doctor he would cure him.

He was able to follow this and seemed touched, but a few minutes later he explained that his wish to be a doctor had occurred not then but years earlier at the age of 5 after he had his tonsils out. He described his panic as the anesthetic mask was applied, and I have no doubt that he was afraid that he was going to die. The wish to be a doctor was therefore connected with the wish to preserve his own life as well as that of his object, and the two were so inextricably linked that he could not consider that he could survive if his object were to die. The task of mourning could not proceed, and the idea of relinquishing the ambition of being a doctor was tantamount to giving up the wish to live.

TECHNICAL CONSIDERATIONS

It is important, and by no means always easy, to identify which group of anxieties the patient is defending against at any particular time, and it is suggested that a recognition of the defensive role of pathological organizations as depicted in the equilibrium triangle is a help in this direction.

It may turn out that future work will reveal that the type of organization deployed against paranoid-schizoid anxieties is significantly different from that used against depressive anxieties, but at present they seem similar. It seems likely that in the course of development a pathological organization was initially deployed against the anxieties of the paranoid-schizoid position and, once established, was later brought into play to defend against depressive anxieties.

In the course of treatment it often turns out that as patients improve, they continue to insist that they need the organization to prevent a catastrophe; although this may have been true once, a closer view may reveal that it is really depressive pain that they are finding difficult to bear. At other times it may be the analyst who gets it wrong and interprets to patients that they are afraid to face depression when the underlying anxiety is actually more in the area of disintegration and survival of the self.

These ideas address the deep roots of the anxiety, and I think they are extremely important to the understanding of pathological organizations. In practice it is often necessary to examine the anxieties, to study how they affect the patient and how they provoked the defensive organizations that now protect the patient. It is often the breakdown of the organization that leads the patient to seek treatment, and he or she may use the analysis to try to reestablish the organization and hence the status quo. At other times it is progress in treatment that leads to a recognition that the organization is not providing the patient the help that was formerly needed and that it is actually a hindrance masquerading as a help. As the patient tries to turn to other sources of strength, intense anxieties are often awakened and it is important for the analyst to try to understand what it is that the organization is defending against.

This approach does, however, have its dangers if it is not seen in the overall task of making ourselves available to patients as a means of understanding their experiences and communications, and it may lead us away from the primary task of attending to those anxieties that are currently active in the session.

Indeed, we have learned to be cautious about the question of why the patient uses a particular set of defenses. At one time this would be the usual way to approach the analysis, and a complete interpretation would describe the defense and then describe the anxiety with which the defense was designed to deal. The analyst would say, "You are doing this because if you did not do it, such and such a situation would arise." More recently we have realized that such double-barreled interpretations can be misleading and can divert the attention of both analyst and patient from an understanding of what is actually happening (Joseph 1983). It is often a great relief to turn to why something is happening and away from what it is that is actually happening. Moreover, it is premature to ask why something has arisen if we do not have a clear idea of what it is we are trying to understand.

Nevertheless, it is possible that we have become too afraid of these issues, and it is interesting to consider and investigate why defenses are mounted. When we have a clearer idea of what is happening in the transference, I believe it helps us and the patient to take the investigation deeper to the antecedent causes. This may mean trying to trace the history of a particular pattern of behavior, investigating its roots in childhood, for example. But a simpler question has to be asked in the first instance, namely, what is the function of a particular mental mechanism? From what

anxiety is it protecting the patient? In this way we are concerned to understand not only the current state of affairs during the operation of a system of
defenses, but also the state of affairs that might exist if those defenses were
not deployed.

CONCLUSION

I have looked at the function of pathological organizations from the point
of view of the anxieties from which they serve to defend the patient. These
can be grouped into anxieties that arise in the paranoid-schizoid position
and those that arise in the depressive position. I have suggested that it is
clinically important to distinguish between these two groups of anxieties
and that pathological organizations protect the patient from both groups by
creating a borderline position that exists in equilibrium with the two basic
positions. The equilibrium diagram I have put forward may help the
analyst make such distinctions and consequently may help him follow the
patient's material more precisely.

REFERENCES

Bion, W. R. (1957). Differentiation of the psychotic from the nonpsychotic personali-
    ties. *International Journal of Psycho-Analysis* 38:266–275. Reprinted in *Second
    Thoughts*, pp. 43–64. New York: Jason Aronson, 1984.
Freud, S. (1917). Mourning and melancholia. *Standard Edition* 14:237–258.
Joseph, B. (1983). On understanding and not understanding: some technical issues.
    International Journal of Psycho-Analysis 64:291–298.
Klein, M. (1935). A contribution to the psychogenesis of manic-depressive states.
    International Journal of Psycho-Analysis 16:145–174. Reprinted in *The Writ-
    ings of Melanie Klein* 1:262–289. London: Hogarth, 1975.
——— (1940). Mourning and its relation to manic-depressive states. *International
    Journal of Psycho-Analysis* 21:125–153. Reprinted in *The Writings of Melanie
    Klein* 1:344–369. London: Hogarth, 1975.
——— (1952). Some theoretical conclusions regarding the emotional life of the
    infant. In *Developments in Psychoanalysis*, ed. J. Rivière pp. 198–236. Re-
    printed in *The Writings of Melanie Klein* 3:61–93. London: Hogarth, 1975.
——— (1957). *Envy and Gratitude.* London: Tavistock. Reprinted in *The Writings
    of Melanie Klein* 3:176–235. London: Hogarth, 1975.
Meltzer, D. (1968). Terror, persecution and dread. *International Journal of Psycho-*

Analysis 49:396–401. Reprinted in *Sexual States of Mind*, pp. 99–106. Perthshire: Clunie, 1973.

O'Shaughnessey, E. (1981). A clinical study of a defensive organization. *International Journal of Psycho-Analysis* 62:359–369.

Rey, J. H. (1979). Schizoid phenomena in the borderline. In *Advances in the Psychotherapy of the Borderline Patient*, ed. J. LeBoit and A. Capponi. New York: Jason Aronson.

Riesenberg-Malcolm, R. (1981). Expiation as a defense. *International Journal of Psychoanalysis and Psychotherapy* 3:549–570.

Rivière, J. (1936). A contribution to the analysis of the negative therapeutic reaction. *International Journal of Psycho-Analysis* 17:304–320.

Rosenfeld, H. A. (1947). Analysis of a schizophrenic state with depersonalization. *International Journal of Psycho-Analysis* 28:130–138.

—— (1950). Notes on the psychopathology of confusional states in chronic schizophrenia. *International Journal of Psycho-Analysis* 31:132–137.

—— (1964). On the psychopathology of narcissism: a clinical approach. *International Journal of Psycho-Analysis* 45:135–140.

—— (1971). A clinical approach to the psychoanalytic theory of the life and death instincts: an investigation into the aggressive aspects of narcissism. *International Journal of Psycho-Analysis* 52:169–178.

Segal, H. (1957). Notes on symbol formation. *International Journal of Psycho-Analysis* 38:391–397. Reprinted in *The Work of Hanna Segal*, pp. 49–65. New York: Jason Aronson, 1981.

—— (1964). *Introduction to the Work of Melanie Klein*. London: Hogarth.

—— (1972). A delusional system as a defense against the reemergence of a catastrophic situation. *International Journal of Psycho-Analysis* 53:393–401.

—— (1983). Some clinical implications of Melanie Klein's work: the emergence from narcissism. *International Journal of Psycho-Analysis* 64:269–276.

Sohn, L. (1972). Narcissistic organization, projective identification and the formation of the identificate. *Bulletin of the British Psychoanalytic Society* 59:33–40.

Spillius, E. B. (1983). Some developments from the work of Melanie Klein. *International Journal of Psycho-Analysis* 64:321–332.

—— (1988). *Melanie Klein Today: Developments in Theory and Practice, Vol. 1: Mainly Theory*. London and New York: Routledge.

Steiner, J. (1979). The border between the paranoid-schizoid and the depressive positions in the borderline patient. *British Journal of Medical Psychology* 52:385–391.

—— (1982). Perverse relationships between parts of the self: a clinical illustration. *International Journal of Psycho-Analysis* 63:241–251.

—— (1987). The interplay between pathological organizations and the paranoid-schizoid and depressive positions. *International Journal of Psycho-Analysis* 68:69–80.

4

FRANCES TUSTIN, M.R.C.P.

Autistic Encapsulation in Neurotic Patients

. . . one might say perhaps that there lives not one single man who after all is not to some extent in despair, in whose inmost parts there does not dwell a disquietude, a perturbation, a discord, an anxious dread of an unknown something, or of something he does not even dare to make acquaintance with, dread of the possibility of life, or dread of himself, so that . . . this man is going about and carrying a sickness of the spirit which only rarely and in glimpses, by and with a dread which to him is inexplicable, gives evidence of its presence within. [Kierkegaard 1849, p. 155][1]

In my book *Autistic Barriers in Neurotic Patients* (Tustin 1986) it was suggested that some neurotic patients, particularly phobic and obsessional patients, had a hidden encapsulated part of the personality that impeded psychoanalytic work with them. There I sought to demonstrate that intensive psychotherapy with psychogenic autistic children had increased our understanding of such worrying, hard-to-reach patients. Since the publication of that book, various people either have written to me or been to see me about such patients. I want to share their reports with you, and also the further thinking they have stimulated.

---

[1]My thanks are due to Alexander Newman for introducing me to this book.

117

OTHER WRITERS' FINDINGS

So far as I know, Sydney Klein is the only psychoanalyst who specifically uses the term *autism* in relation to the sealed-off part of the personality of certain neurotic patients. In his seminal paper, "Autistic Phenomena in Neurotic Patients" (1980), he writes:

> The sooner the analyst realises the existence of this hidden part of the patient, the less the danger of the analysis becoming an endless and meaningless intellectual dialogue and the greater the possibilities of the patient achieving a relatively stable equilibrium. Although the analyst has to live through a great deal of anxiety with the patient, I feel ultimately the results make it worthwhile. [p. 401]

After I had written *Autistic Barriers in Neurotic Patients*, I came across Winnicott's (1974) paper "The Fear of Breakdown," in which, although he did not use the term *autism*, he was obviously referring to the psychic happenings I had been trying to understand.

He wrote as follows: "I can now state my main contention, and it turns out to be very simple. I contend that the clinical fear of breakdown is the fear of a *breakdown that has already been experienced*. It is the fear of the original agony which caused the defence organisation which the patient displays as an illness syndrome" (p. 104). In speaking of a "breakdown that has already been experienced," Winnicott referred to the "breakdown" experienced by an infant who, in an immature state of neuromental development, becomes aware of his bodily separateness from the suckling mother, in a nursing situation that cannot help him to cope with the intense feelings that this arouses.

In an earlier paper Winnicott (1958) had written about this situation, and had said that the infant had not reached the "stage of emotional development which could provide the equipment for dealing with loss." He went on to say, "The same loss of the mother a few months later would be a loss of object without this added element of loss of part of the subject" (p. 222).

My early training did not, unfortunately, include Winnicott's ideas. Thus, after I had written my first paper on autism, which was about John, the autistic child who taught me about the "black hole" of bodily separateness from the mother, it was an eye-opener when colleagues pointed out to me that Winnicott had already written about this situation and had called it "psychotic depression." I realize now that although I don't agree in detail with all that Winnicott has said, my work with autistic children is leading me into areas that were so courageously explored by him. As Juliet Mitchell, in a recent lecture to the Squiggle Foundation, has said, "Winnicott was charting something other than Freud or Klein." However, as we shall see, this chapter touches on much that was adumbrated by Freud (1920) in his most controversial book, *Beyond the Pleasure Principle.*

But to return to Winnicott's (1974) paper, "The Fear of Breakdown," the "breakdown" to which he refers is the one that occurred in infancy, about which he has written so succinctly in his paper, "The Mentally Ill in Your Case Load" (1963). The "defence organisation" is the closing down of awareness, for which I shall use the notion of encapsulation, and the "illness syndrome" is psychogenic autism. This has been precipitated by what Winnicott called "psychotic depression," for which Edward Bibring (1953) used the term "primal depression," a depression in which feelings of helplessness and hopelessness predominate. This was John's "black hole with the nasty prick."

In writing about "the breakdown that had already been experienced," Winnicott tells us that in the analytic situation, an adult neurotic patient "remembers" something that happened "near the beginning of the patient's life." However, in work with autistic children, who are much closer to infancy than adult patients, we get similar elemental recollections of this crucial situation in infancy when they had become prematurely aware of their bodily separateness from the suckling mother. I have come to realize that this poignant experience had been traumatic. Freud (1920) has told us a good deal about buried traumas. This trauma, associated with premature awareness of bodily separateness from the mother, has been lying in suspension as it were, and comes up in treatment in an attempt to assimilate the "undigested" experience (Freud's "repetition compulsion").

The striking thing about these elemental unconceptualized "memories" is their detailed nature and their vividness and clarity. John's dramatic reliving of the "black hole" of bodily separateness from the suckling mother has been quoted many times in my books and papers (Tustin 1966, 1972, 1986). This was a very significant experience for me. It surprised me because it could not be related to the Kleinian formulations in which I had been trained.

I would now like to give you a similarly striking example of a reliving of this crucial situation in infancy. It occurred in the analysis of an autistic child who was being treated by a trainee child psychotherapist whose work I was supervising at the time. This child's material indicates that, as an infant, the nipple of the breast (or teat of the bottle) had been experienced as being continuous with his tongue. When awareness of bodily separateness impinged prematurely, this "teat-tongue" was felt to be broken in two.

Colin was a 5-year-old autistic boy who was being treated by Gideon Harari. Gideon saw Colin four times a week. When the incident to be reported occurred, Colin had been in treatment for two months. After one month, Colin experienced the first break in the continuity of his therapy, due to the Christmas holidays. In the month after Christmas, in the week prior to the session to be reported, Colin had a two-day absence due to a cold.

When Gideon came to his supervision with me, he told me in a concerned way that there was a piece of Colin's material that he felt he had not adequately understood, because Colin had repeated it on each of the four days he had come. This consisted of the child coming into the therapy room and going straight to the water faucet, which he sucked vigorously. Colin, who had been mute when he entered therapy, then turned and faced his therapist, saying, "Loo-oo-ook," as if trying to transmit something very important. He stood looking at his therapist with his tongue lolling loosely out of his mouth, with water dripping from it as if he had lost control of it, and as if he had lost something.

In supervision, I suggested that perhaps Colin was telling Gideon about a time when, as a little baby, he had found that the lovely sucking thing was not part of and controlled by his tongue, to be there whenever he wanted it. This made him feel that an important bit of his tongue had gone. "Oneness" had become "twoness."

When he next came to see me, Gideon reported that, as the result of interpreting along these lines, the puzzling piece of repetitive behavior had stopped. Gideon felt convinced that the interpretation had been very meaningful to Colin. He felt then, and still feels, that this was a critical turning point in Colin's psychotherapy, the outlook for which seems good.

Gideon was well in touch with the atmosphere of the session, for he went on to tell me that after Colin had made the spectacular demonstration with his tongue, which had not been sufficiently understood, he had turned his back on Gideon and had engaged in repetitive controlling activities such as opening and shutting the door and putting the light switch on and off. This had caused Gideon to feel very cut off from Colin. He had felt that there was a barrier between them that prevented them from being in touch with each other. Many mothers of autistic children have told me that they feel that their child is in a shell all the time, and that they are barred from getting in touch with him (or her). I have come to realize that this is the result of such children's attention being concentrated upon controlling activities that distract their attention from situations that distress them.

Let us think about this illusion of a barrier or a shell.

THE BARRIER OR THE SHELL

Such barriers are the result of repetitive auto-generated procedures. In order to be able to talk about and to think about these protective procedures, I have conceptualized them as "autistic objects" and "autistic shapes," or "sensation objects" and "sensation shapes." But for the autistic child, these sensation-dominated, repetitive, and stereotyped procedures are unconceptualized. They are part of their system of concretized delusion and, as such, they are "tactile hallucinations" (Aulangier 1985, Tustin 1980, 1984, 1985). I can only give thumbnail sketches of them here.

As the result of working with autistic children, I first of all became aware of what I have called "autistic objects" or "sensation objects."

AUTISTIC OBJECTS OR SENSATION OBJECTS

After I had written about these "objects," I was relieved to find that Winnicott had written about them also. He referred to them by a paradox, calling them "subjective objects." These objects are experienced as being part of the subject's own body, and, as such, shut out awareness of bodily separateness. They are hard objects that are clutched tightly. They make the child feel hard, impenetrable, in absolute control, and thus safe. (Sadly, these children feel that they are solely responsible for their own safety.)

AUTISTIC SHAPES OR SENSATION SHAPES

Following Winnicott's lead, these could be called "subjective shapes." They are not classified or objectivized shapes associated with specific objects, nor are they experienced in terms of spatial relationships, as are objective

shapes. Experienced solely on body surfaces, they are soothing and tranquil-
izing. They are experienced in a tactile, concretized way.

When children's attention is riveted upon these autogenerated tactile
hallucinations, their attention is distracted away from the outside world to
such an extent that they seem to be "in a shell." This is what I refer to as
autistic encapsulation.

AUTISTIC ENCAPSULATION

As we have seen, the delusion of encapsulation arises from the autogenerated concretized procedures of "autistic objects" and "autistic shapes."
These procedures arise from the human being's inbuilt propensities for
object-seeking and shape-making, which, in autistic children, are used in
such an idiosyncratic way that they amount to an aberration. The resulting
delusion of encapsulation protects the subject from the effects of traumatic
happenings that have been insufferable, but they prevent cognitive and
emotional development.

The insufferable traumatic situation is shut away from the rest of the
personality by these autogenerated procedures. As Klein (1980) has said, it is
"a hidden part of the patient." The traumatic incident lies as it were in
suspension, unassimilated and unchanged. Since it was experienced before
the patient could speak, it seems to be out of the reach of the "talking cure"
of psychoanalysis. However, some patients are driven to try to tell us about
this traumatic breakdown in their infancy. They do it through a kind of
psychodrama in the analytic session, as Colin and John did. Others do it by
what they call "acting out." For instance, a supervisee told me about a
patient who, while she was encountering problems of separation in their
work together, fell and broke her ankle. After this "acting-out" was interpreted, the patient came the next day and reported a dream by which she
"contained" and worked over the experience. In the dream, she was a tiny
vulnerable figure crawling out of the plaster cast that encircled the break in
her ankle. She said that it was as if she were being born. She was now able to
think about the experience instead of experiencing it in an acting-out,
concretized way.

It is certainly the case that, if the break in their continuity of "being"
occasioned by the trauma awareness of bodily separateness is understood
and worked over, the patient experiences a kind of psychic birth. Ongoing
psychological functioning, which had previously been blocked by the auto-
generated encapsulation, is freed. For example, mute or echolalic autistic
children begin to speak meaningfully and even fluently.

A DEFENSE AGAINST TRAUMA

Autistic encapsulation seems to be a defense specifically against trauma. From his supervision of work with Holocaust victims, David Rosenfeld (1985) has written to me from Argentina, saying that the encapsulation of the trauma suffered by these patients seemed to have had the positive effect of preserving it, so that it could be worked over and thought about in the analytic situation. Yolanda Gampel (1983a,b, 1988) has sent me papers from Israel in which she has also found this to be the case. These were traumas that were suffered later in life, but which seemed to have called forth the same elemental defense as those experienced in infancy, perhaps because they have been similarly "unthinkable" and "unspeakable."

Winnicott (1974) writes of the way in which "the original agony" comes into focus in the analytic situation. He says that the neurotic patient "remembers" something that happened near the beginning of the patient's life. He suggests that: ". . . this outcome is equivalent of the lifting of repression which occurs in the analysis of a psycho-neurotic patient (classical Freudian analysis)" (p. 105). Autistic encapsulation seems to be an elemental concretized forerunner of "repression," of "denial," and of "forgetting." I see it as being a protomental protective maneuver rather than a psychological defense mechanism.

The "remembering" of such a patient is the reevocation of the encapsulated traumatic experience by a situation in the outside world to which it has a rough-and-ready correspondence. This need not necessarily be in psychotherapeutic treatment. For example, the woman in the next illustration was not in treatment, but her experiences showed that the same traumatic infantile situation as that which was depicted by Colin was being reenacted.

THE REENACTMENT OF INFANTILE BREAKDOWN

This woman was describing the incident that precipitated her depressive breakdown. She told how she went to pick up a pencil, which *broke in two in her hand.* At this, she said that something snapped inside her head. She described poignantly how she wanted the walls to close around her, both to protect and obliterate her. (Note the concretized nature of her reaction.) She felt completely helpless, out of control, and in despair. She contemplated suicide. Significantly, she said that her mother had died two years before, but she had not been able to mourn her death. She now felt that she was losing her confidence, her faith, and her beliefs. She said that she felt she needed someone alongside her who would enter into her state of mind, insofar as was possible. She needed, she said, for someone to "take her suffering and heal it."

It has been my experience that patients who have felt so bereft must go through primitive processes of "mourning," or "grief," as Margaret Mahler (1961) has called it. They are grieving about the loss of they know not what. They have an agonized sense of loss and brokenness that is unthinkable and inarticulate. In psychotherapy, as the shutters of their autistic encapsulation begin to open, the infantile transference to the therapist enables them to dramatize their traumatic infantile sense of loss, and to talk about it. But they are difficult patients; because they have a powerful effect upon those who treat them, psychotherapists are liable to be drawn into their speechless dramas.

Let me give you an example in the treatment of an adult patient.

BROKENHEARTEDNESS

Recently, a psychiatrist came to see me about a patient, a physics teacher, who gave the appearance of functioning quite well in the outside world, but who told this psychiatrist, "There are three of me, two are all right, but the third one is sealed off and won't let anyone near. This part is leading me to destruction." The very experienced medical director of the clinic in which this psychiatrist worked said to his junior colleague, "You should never have taken on such a patient. These patients break therapists' hearts."

As the result of what I have learned from autistic children, I was able to help this psychiatrist to see that these patients threaten to break therapists' hearts because they themselves are heartbroken. Their heartbreak goes beyond what we usually mean by the term. The feeling of brokenness goes into the very fabric of their being. As we have seen, the "original agony" of the breakdown was when the sensuous experience of the "oneness" of the "teat-tongue" was felt to break into "twoness." Because the sucking rhythm had become associated with the beating of the heart, it was the "teat-tongue-heart" that was felt to be broken. Of course, all this was wordless, and to put it into words seems clumsy and even absurd. But it helps us to understand that for these patients, bodily awareness of their separateness had been experienced as an interruption to the pulsing rhythm of their "going-on-being" (Winnicott, personal communication). Their sense of "being" was felt to be threatened. Annihilation stared them in the face. Some very desperate steps had to be taken to combat it. To combat it and to cover over their brokenness, they have developed the plaster cast of autism. This has impeded the development of the "psychic envelope," as described by Anzieu (1987).

This concretized experience of encapsulation spells death to the psyche. Of their suicidal states, Winnicott (1974) has said to these patients: " . . . they are intent on sending the body to death which had already happened to the psyche. Suicide is no answer, however, it is a despair gesture" (p. 106). This means that they are some of our most worrying patients.

Doctor Grotstein of Los Angeles has generously written to me as follows about one such patient:

> Your concepts have been of enormous importance particularly with a young man I am now analyzing. The breakthrough came about when I realized that he believes himself concretely to have hidden himself in an upstairs closet in his bedroom where he cried his eyes out as a child but was unheard by his parents. I came to realize early on that he was an encapsulated personality—now currently practicing as a gifted architect. Well, we are now getting through the encapsulated hall-closet-self and there is nothing but tears—and hope! Thank you.

Grotstein's account of his patient illustrates that hidden behind the hard callousness of the autistic encapsulation we find tears and heartbreak. We need to prepare ourselves to bear this suffering if these patients' alienation from humankind is to be modified.

However, as well as compassion for the suffering of these patients, we need tough realism about their evasive and domineering techniques. In a hidden part, these patients are in the grip of their reactions to past events. Stemming from this past, they have a submerged sense of grievance about what they feel they ought to have had, and this has become deeply entrenched. At a certain stage in treatment, they talk of "holes," and these are "black holes" because of the tantrum of frustration about what they feel they have lacked. At this stage, such a patient gets very annoyed with the therapist, as he had been very annoyed with his mother when she would not be formed in his terms. They cannot "put up" with people as they are. It is quite difficult for the therapist to "put up" with these patients at this stage. Understanding their underlying sense of agony helps us to do so. But we should not be soft and sentimental with these patients. We point out how they are treating us and explain that this must come from some unhappiness they have experienced that has been stirred by events in the analytic situation. But we can't hurry them to show their underlying sense of breakdown. This will only come when the patient is ready to reexperience it. In the meantime, we need to be compassionate but realistic about what is happening. Sentimentality is death to psychic development.

As well as being unduly aware of other people's shortcomings, such people are unduly aware of their own. They lack a robust self-respect. As therapists we must not be bowled over by such patients' criticism of us, rational though this may be—for these patients needle us in our weak spots (Giovacchini and Boyer 1975)—nor must we be drawn into their abyss of despair. For a long time, this despair is unacknowledged by the patient, but it comes out in the form of "atmospheres" that are very disturbing to the therapist.

PSYCHOTHERAPY WITH ENCAPSULATED PATIENTS

As the result of his work with grossly deprived and neglected children, Winnicott has emphasized the environmental failure in infancy that precipitates such a breakdown. My work with autistic children, who have not experienced such crude and gross environmental failures, has led me to concentrate on the child's reactions that have contributed to the breakdown. In autistic psychopathology, the child's own nature seems to have played a significant part. In order to cope with what they have felt to be their unmet expectations, these hypersensitive children have developed encapsulating and idiosyncratic ways of behaving. These have usurped the functions of the mother. Their sense of grievance about what they feel they have not had, legitimate though this may be, has deprived them of what they could have had, even though their mother was depressed and underconfident. Although these autistic reactions have a preservative and protective function, the idiosyncratic and overdeveloped body-ego practices associated with them are deleterious to ongoing development. This is because they become more important to the child than the mother, the father, and other people.

To have a "self" we need to have awareness of "others." Obliterating awareness of others as separate and needed beings results in the obliteration of the sense of self. Instead, in autistic states a precocious and inflated body ego has developed that shuts out awareness of others. This can take the form of cerebral egghead pretensions, as well as a secret use of "sensation objects" and "sensation shapes" (Tustin 1980, 1985, 1986). This means that in working with these patients, we must not allow ourselvs to be canceled out by their hidden egotistic grandiosity. Behind their passivity, these patients seek to weaken us, to undermine us, and to overpower us. We need to be realistically aware of this to prevent it happening, even though we also have compassion for the origin of this behavior in overwhelming feelings of enraged helplessness and hopelessness in infancy. But we cannot help the patient with these feelings until their hidden autistic encapsulation is realized and modified, and they experience the overpowering neediness that gave rise to it.

Although such patients need to feel that we care deeply whether they live or die, for a dreadful terror of annihilation is part of the syndrome, we must not seem to entangle them with our care and concern. This is because, in some of these patients, autistic reactions have developed in part as a protection against being smothered by what they felt to be an engulfing mother who needed them as a solace for her loneliness. When we first meet them, these neurotic patients may have a superficially good relationship with their mother, but it soon becomes clear that deep down they have a chronic aversion to her that uses her actual defects to seem rational. This turning away from the protection of the mother exposes them to states of frozen panic (Giovacchini 1967). When elemental dangers threaten them, they lack a "background of safety," as both Sandler (1960) and Grotstein (1980) have called the maternal protection of early infancy. A paper by Marc (1987) had made me realize that after birth the rhythm of the beating of the mother's heart is part of the "background of safety," as recent work is showing it to be in the intrauterine situation. In order to feel safe and to feel that they exist, autistic children have resorted to the beating of their own heart, and have become averted from the reassuring, comforting aspects of the mother.

Let me now give you details of a session that illustrates this in a patient for whom success and progress provoked frozen panic. This was the patient called Ariadne, who, toward the end of her analysis, coined the phrase "the "rhythm of safety," which became the title of one of the chapters in *Autistic Barriers in Neurotic Patients* (Tustin 1986). The following session was not included in that book, and came a year before she developed a sense of a "rhythm of safety." Our joint understanding of her hidden autistic encapsulation had paved the way for the development of this more flexible and authentic sense of safety and of self.

ARIADNE

Ariadne was charming and likable. Like all such patients, she was obsessional and phobic. Potentially, she was a joyful and creative person, but much of her joy and creativity was frozen away in an autistic capsule. Indeed, Ariadne, whom I had treated when she was a little girl, came back to me aged 25 because she had had a frightening episode when she became completely frozen like a corpse. She had spent the night in great terror begging her cousin, who nobly stayed with her throughout this terrible ordeal, to take her to a mental hospital because she was sure that she was going mad. This episode followed her personal success in her career as an actress, when she had taken over the role of the leading lady, who suddenly became ill. This situation had triggered the somewhat analogous one of her infancy, when she felt that she had taken over her mother's role. Also, in the present situation, the other members of the cast, who she felt were in rivalry with her, had been experienced as savage predators against whom she had no protection. She feared these predators would bite off parts of her body, particularly the protective and sensation-giving bits. This is a form of "castration anxiety" of a more generalized kind than that which Freud has described.

Ariadne's Early History

When Ariadne was an infant, her mother had been very depressed due to the previous death of a boy child at 2½ years old. In her early infancy, Ariadne and her mother were abnormally close to each other, and the father was shut out, a situation with which he had colluded, since he was very engrossed in his own professional work. In treatment, it became clear that, in the depths, Ariadne felt that she had been able to belittle and undermine her malleable, depressed mother, who desired to be a particularly good mother out of guilt about the death of the boy. As you can imagine, Ariadne's reactions to this situation had many facets, but the one I want to focus on is her feeling that in order to counter her sense of bodily loss, she felt that she had bitten off the mother's special bit that enabled her to function as a mother. She had then ignored her mother's separateness as a person in her own right, and had manipulated her as if she were part of her body-stuff, so that she could show off and attract to herself the attention she felt that she needed in order to bolster up her confidence.

The Session

In the session to be reported, which occurred two years after she had started her second psychotherapy, Ariadne began by telling me that at school she never wrote an essay on her own; her mother had always written it for her. She told me that at her mother's suggestion she had started a debating society at school, and that she had been the chairperson. "I just went along and said what my mother had told me. I didn't really understand it. I wasn't even really interested in it. I just wanted to show off, like snipping off a rose from someone else's garden, without their knowing, to put in my buttonhole to show off with and to draw attention to myself."

Thinking of John's revelations to me about "the red button on the mummy's breast," I said, "Yes, you felt that you bit off the red button, the rose, from the mummy's breast, which enabled her to function as a mother, so that you could draw attention to yourself in order to be reassured that you really existed. You then used her as a thing, as if she were a part of your body and not a person in her own right. You did this because when, as a little baby, you found that your mother's body was separate from yours, you felt helpless and hopeless. You felt that you went 'flop.' Your very existence seemed to be threatened. You felt that you were lost. You tend to do this to me at times of separation. But this way of behaving saps your own initiative and confidence."

She said, "But I remember one occasion at school, which stands out vividly in my mind, when I did something on my own initiative. I wrote a poem—it was about rain or something—and the teacher liked it very much and asked me to read it to the class."

I started to say, "So you can be creative in your own right," but Ariadne interrupted and said, "But after I had read the poem to the class, I was afraid that something terrible was going to happen to me."

I pointed out that a similar thing had happened when she got into a frozen panic after she had successfully taken over the role of the leading lady in the play. It seemed to me that this had triggered the infantile situation when she had felt that she snipped off bits and pieces from her soft, depressed mother in order to make herself feel big and important, because deep down she felt so lacking, little, and helpless. (Autistic children often try to bite off parts of the therapist, or they stick bits of cardboard or paper onto themselves to give themselves an extra bit.) But she was always afraid of being found out. She felt that this belittled, soft mother could easily turn into a hard, retaliatory mother who grabbed back her bits and pieces, that is, "took the shine out" of her creative efforts. I went on to say that she was always afraid that something would happen to her when she asserted herself and did something creative. At times of separation, she felt that her mouth was in deadly rivalry with other mouths for the sensation-giving "tit-bit." When, as an infant, she found that the nipple was not part of her controlling tongue, but was separate from it, in a wordless way she had felt that it had been bitten off by these other mouths. She was always struggling to get the pulsing bit that made her feel alive, special, and in control. At times of separation, psychotherapy became a savagely competitive situation rather than a cooperative one. Her reaction was to try to shut out awareness of others who she felt were intent on having the special sensation-giving bit that seemed to ensure both her safety and her existence.

Ariadne then went on to tell me about an actual present-day happening that had analogies with an unresolved psychic situation. It was a kind of "acting-in." The actual situation became a psychic theater in which she worked over her hidden encapsulated states and realized their dangers. For Ariadne the "world" was often "a stage" on which she acted out the unassimilated elemental dramas of her infancy in an effort to come to terms with them.

In the reported session she said, "I went to have my head done for a play I'm to be in. I have to have a false head because at the end of the play my head explodes." She went on, "First of all, the man who is making this head put latex over my head and shoulders. I had two straws up my nose in order to be able to breathe. I felt all right about this because the latex was elastic. Inside the latex, I listened to my breathing and the beating of my heart, and that was companionable." (Note the comforting nature of the heartbeat, though it was autistic comfort unrelated to others.) She went on, "But when he put the plaster of paris over the latex I felt panicky. That was hard, and I knew I couldn't get out of it unless he cut me out of it. I was absolutely dependent on his doing that. I was helpless if he didn't." I took up how panicked she felt when she realized that she had to be dependent on someone else whom she had to trust, especially when her trust was impaired by living in terms of the delusory extremes of there being a soft, manipulable mother, who could so easily turn into a hard, unyielding mother who would punish her for exploiting and belittling her in such a big-headed way.

She replied by saying that she thought it would be a good murder story. Another woman had the job of making a head for someone and, in doing so, blocked up the straws that gave air to the nose, and then the one whose head was being done "would die from suffocation. She would be smothered." I said that she was afraid that I was this woman. She feared that when I was kind, I was being soft, seductive, and smothering—spreading around her like the latex. She feared that I might suddenly become resentful of what she felt to be her monopolizing and exploiting of me, and turn nasty, hard, and murderous. These misconceptions from her infantile past meant that she feared to use me and to make progress in her analysis. She feared that she had charmed and manipulated me, treating me not as a separate human being, but as plastic material like latex to be manipulated. Then she felt immured by a soft latex mother who seemed part of her body stuff, with whom she could have all her own way, and whom she did not have to share with a father or other children. She was afraid that the improvements she had made as a result of the analysis had come about by her going through me like a knife through butter, or latex, to cut out of me all that she wanted. She then felt that she left me "cut up," in both senses of the term, shrunk and dying. An amusing raconteur, she was warning me not to be seduced by her entrancing talk, not to become too soft and malleable, because then there was the threat that I would become hard and encircle her, as in a plaster cast, and she would be entombed. She would be psychically dead, and all her potentialities for being creative would be lost.

CLINICAL DISCUSSION

In the reported session it seemed to me that Ariadne's experience of the making of the false head evoked infantile bodily-cum-mental states that were hidden away. As she recounted to me her experience of the false head being made, she was enabled to work over these feelings. They were no longer shut away from being recognized. As an infant, in a state in which her existence had seemed to depend upon bodily continuity with her mother, she had experienced traumatic discontinuity. This was the breakdown she had already experienced in which she felt she lost a vital part of her body. She was always straining to get this extra bit so that she could be extraordinary, perfect, and complete. Humpty-Dumpty-like, she had a puffed-up sense of her own importance in order to draw to herself the extra attention she felt she needed.

But it was an insecure sense of importance in which there lurked the threat of breakdown, of the "great fall" from which there was no hope of being "put together again." For her, disillusionment had become unduly associated with despair.

In this session, it became clear that Ariadne felt that by the use of her seductive charm, she magically controlled and manipulated the outside world and the people in it to spread around her in an unduly supportive way, as she felt that she had manipulated the depressed mother of her infancy as if she were soft body stuff like latex, with no identity of her own as a separate person. Thus, the alarming sense of discontinuity when extinction seemed imminent was avoided. Vulnerable "black hole" states were shut away from conscious awareness by the encapsulation. But they were provoked in other people. Her life was mainly a manipulative controlling strategy that stifled her genuine creativity. She froze with terror when it seemed that her protective cerebral pretensions would be exploded, to disclose the naïveté, vulnerability, helplessness, and nothingness within.

The reaction was to hide away from this "black hole" of bodily separateness by feeling covered with the mother's body stuff experienced as if it were her own. Thus, she could rise to the challenges and pressures of the outside world, and could get away from feeling defective, broken, and no good. Other patients, in coming out of the protection of autism, have shown that they felt like "babes in the wood," who needed to cover themselves with leaves, fur, feathers, grass, tufts of carpet, or the chenille of the sofa. . . . These hypervulnerable children feel that their skin is paper-thin or nonexistent. They have a desperate need to protect their "going-on-being."

When Ariadne used her own creative initiative, she was afraid that she had secretly bitten it off or seduced it from an exploited soft mother. In treatment, as she began to feel big, creative, and rich, she felt that I shrank and became smaller and smaller. As a belittled-mother surrogate, I might retaliate and certainly would not protect her. It became clear that she felt she was at the mercy of savage rivals who took on the character of predatory animals limned by our phylogenetic past. She feared that she would be bitten and killed. These delusory terrors were hidden away because they were too dreadful to contemplate. They constituted what she called "the undertow." This had a devastating effect upon her functioning. It froze a normal psychic birth. It kept her in a state of pessimism arising from her unrecognized black despair. Without the uplift of hope, she found it difficult to make decisions. She flinched away from taking even justifiable risks. As she said, "Everything has to be tied up with a bow on top," because at depth, she was in a state of "fear, trembling, and sickness unto death." If we are to help patients with their hidden "heartbreak," we have to "make acquaintance with" this despairing part of ourselves. The plate glass window of our bland complacency has to be shattered. Inflated ideas about ourselves have to be sloughed away.

And now let me present some clinical material that generously was sent to me by Dr. Fail, a psychoanalyst in training in Australia. It illustrates very well the way in which findings from psychotherapy with psychogenic autistic children can stimulate psychological growth in neurotic adult patients.

CLINICAL MATERIAL

Dr. Fail writes as follows:

> For some weeks prior to reading your books, the patient had been discussing themes that had become familiar from her previous years of psychotherapy. In particular was a fear of doing her postgraduate exams. She had failed on a number of occasions a postgraduate qualification for fear of cannibalising my brains and my babies. Passing exams also meant growing up and "parents die when children grow up," and passing exams also meant termination of therapy in her mind. The whole courtyard scene that could be seen from my waiting room excited her. This was very similar to her excitement and rapture she felt on hearing my voice—she wrapped my words (the content seemed irrelevant) around herself. [Compare this with Ariadne's latex, which was manipulated around her.[2]] And she talked about hanging on to me like a barnacle. [Ariadne's latex meant that she felt stuck to me. I call this *imitative fusion*.[2]]

Dr. Fail continues:

> At this stage, I had been reading your two books and began to see the material in a different light and to make some interpretations along the lines of the painfulness of realisations of our separateness and that the barnaclelike adhesions were to obliterate the awareness of the gap between us.
>
> I have made more detailed notes about her responses to this and I thought you'd be particularly interested in these responses.
>
> Initially, she responded by saying that she felt her skin was being peeled away, and if we were separate, then who was I. She feared she would shrivel away and die and I would not be able to survive; she weighed the same as both of us put together and if I were separate I would have to get a body from somewhere else. I said that it seemed I was the nipple in her mouth that belonged to her. She replied that she thought that way because if she didn't, she would feel as if something very significant was missing. She saw me as a thief with a black mask, robbing her of her illusions and her weight, and she was now terrified that any further weight loss would signify a total disappearance. She became detached and despairing, and felt crippled and empty like a scooped-out husk.

---

[2]Author's insertions.

She dreamt of a babaco—exotic-looking cucumber fruit with hard skin, but very disappointing when cut in half, because they were just cucumbers. The babaco seemed to symbolise the loss of exotica, the loss of rapture of the fused state when cut in half. The skin also symbolised the hard skin she had to grow around herself to hold herself together for fear she would disappear into nothingness. She had nightmares of a football stadium full of dead bodies disposed of in the Tibetan way, where the bodies are cut up for the vultures to eat.

She now began to perceive me differently. She stated that previously I was a diffuse presence, the way that people talk about God—God is everywhere; but now that I was in my own skin, and I had a shape of a person, she felt alone and left out in the wilderness like someone who had lost his faith. She used to feel God's arms around her and now there was only a man behind her.

An A. A. Milne rhyme in which a little boy lost his mother kept repeating itself in her head. She would stop the rhyme and add, "I feel I mislaid my mother. I don't like this separation business; it feels like something you're doing to me to get rid of me."

My presence was now felt to be an unwanted intrusion, and my voice irritated her now, compared to the previous feeling of excitement and delight as she wrapped herself around the sounds of my words. Now she felt as if she were on a window ledge, about to fall and shatter into little pieces, and that I was prodding her.

She had never felt sad about the end of the sessions before and for the first time she heard the peals of the nearby school bell, which always rang five minutes before the end of our sessions, and now it sounded like a death knell. She had persistent fantasies of me with a feather boa around my neck. This seemed to represent an attempt to regain the soft and fluffy, dreamy, fused state and the anger when this paradise is lost; the boa turns into a boa constrictor that swallows its prey whole. [Compare this with Ariadne's feeling that the soft manipulable mother could so easily turn into the hard murderous mother.[3]]

She saw herself on an ice floe, a broken piece of glacier, out in the cold. She saw herself as brain damaged, having no mind, or something being missing if we didn't share the same mind.

---

[3]Author's insertion.

She then became preoccupied with Siamese twins who were receiving publicity at that time. The twins were joined at the pelvic region, so they had one body and two brains. It was distressing her that when they were going to be separated, one would lose something, because one was going to be made a female, although genetically he was male, but there was not enough male genitalia for the two. "Even Eve was made from Adam's rib." "If we separate, then I lose." The twins symbolised her fears that there must be a division of property, and that she would be left with something missing. Previously we had perceived this lack, this feeling of inadequacy, the feelings of something missing, as the lack of a penis, but now it could be further seen as a result of an awareness of separateness. At the same time there was this fear that I would be left damaged with this division of property, in particular brain damaged due to her envy of my creativity in our work together. Now that there was an awareness of separateness, agonising feelings of envy predominated the sessions. (I would see this more as "rivalry" than envy. I would see it as being in competition for the vital sensation-giving bit which gives her a sense of "being.")

These excerpts from sessions occurred over a two-and-a-half-month period. The significance of these reactions and this period of her therapy is, I think, best demonstrated by a simple statement she made some subsequent three months to the period described above. She stated, "I come to see you these days, rather than to be here." This meant for her for the first time in her life to actually experience loneliness. This, I think, was a significant development.

CONCLUSION

I have come to think that a sense of bodily separateness is the heartbreak at the center of all human existence, and that some people experience it in a more drastic way than others. How it is dealt with seems to affect the development of the whole personality. Insight into the pathological states associated with agonizing experiences of bodily separateness, such as were described by Kierkegaard at the beginning of this chapter, can seem like a baptism of fire. However, if this fiery baptism is survived, and the autistic scales fall from our eyes, thinking becomes clearer and a sense of individual identity more firmly established. This occurs for both analyst and patient.

REFERENCES

Anzieu, D. (1987). *Les Enveloppes Psychiques.* Paris: Dunod.

Aulangier, P. (1985). "Hallucinatory withdrawal." Is it the same as "autistic withdrawal"? *Lieux de L'enfance,* No. 3. Toulouse (privately published). (*Proceedings of the Congress Approche Psychanalitique de l'Autisme et des Psychoses Infantiles Précoces.* Monaco, 1984.)

Bibring, E. (1953). The mechanism of depression. In *Affective Disorders,* ed. P. Greenacre, pp. 13-48. New York: International Universities Press.

Freud, S. (1920). *Beyond the Pleasure Principle. Standard Edition* 18:7-66.

Gampel, Y. (1983). I was a holocaust child: now I am fifty. In *The Holocaust Survivor and Their Family,* ed. A. Wilson. New York: Praeger Scientific.

―――― (1988a). The psychoanalyst at work. *International Review of Psycho-Analysis,* in press.

―――― (1988b). Facing war, murder, torture and death in childhood. *International Journal of Psychoanalytic Psychotherapy,* in press.

Giovacchini, P. L. (1967). The frozen introject. In *Psychoanalysis of Character Disorders.* New York: Jason Aronson.

Giovacchini, P. L., and Boyer, L. B. (1975). The psychoanalytic impasse. *International Journal of Psychoanalytic Psychotherapy* 4:25-47.

Greenacre, P. (1941). The predisposition to anxiety. Part 1. *The Psychoanalytic Quarterly* 10:66-94.

Grotstein, J. S. (1980). Primitive mental states. *Contemporary Psychoanalysis* 16:479-546.

―――― (1985). Personal communication.

Kierkegaard, S. A. (1849). *Fear, Trembling and the Sickness unto Death,* trans. W. Lowrie. Princeton: Princeton University Press, 1941.

Klein, S. (1980). Autistic phenomena in neurotic patients. *International Journal of Psycho-Analysis* 61:395-401.

Mahler, M. S. (1961). On sadness and grief in infancy and childhood: loss and restoration of the symbiotic love object. *The Psychoanalytic Study of the Child* 16:332-351. New Haven: Yale University Press.

Marc, V. (1987). Jeu, rhythmes et création. *Le Journal des Psychologues* 48:54.

Rosenfeld, D. (1985). Personal communication.

Sandler, J. (1960). The background of safety. *International Journal of Psycho-Analysis* 41:352-356.

Tustin, F. (1966). A significant element in the development of autism. *Journal of Child Psychology and Psychiatry* 7:53-67.

―――― (1972). *Autism and Childhood Psychosis.* London: Hogarth.

―――― (1980). Autistic objects. *International Review of Psycho-Analysis* 7:27-39.

―――― (1981). *Autistic States in Children.* London: Routledge and Kegan Paul.

―――― (1984). Autistic shapes. *International Review of Psycho-Analysis* 11:280-288.

—— (1985). Autistic shapes exemplified in adult psychopathology. *Topique* (May), pp. 9–23.

—— (1986). *Autistic Barriers in Neurotic Patients.* New Haven: Yale University Press.

Winnicott, D. W. (1958). *Collected Papers. Through Paediatrics to Psychoanalysis.* London: Tavistock.

—— (1963). The mentally ill in your caseload. In *The Maturational Processes and the Facilitating Environment*, pp. 217–229. New York: International Universities Press, 1965.

—— (1974). The fear of breakdown. *International Review of Psycho-Analysis* 1:103–107.

5

JAMES S. GROTSTEIN, M.D.

Invariants in Primitive Emotional Disorders

As I began to survey my experiences in treating patients with primitive mental disorders, I felt able to identify a group of elements that seemed to cohere as invariant occurrences, whether these patients were in the psychotic or in the upper or lower level borderline categories. Further, these syndromic elements seemed to be clustered around cataclysmically disorganizing regressive phenomena, which constitute self-regulatory attempts to compensate for these regressions and/or are the symptomatic residues of compensatory failures. I am referring to the transformations that the self undergoes as one experiences absolute *knowable* terror (perception or fantasy) across *nameless dread*, as well as the *terror beyond knowing*, and even *beyond being*.

It is these transformations that underlie the pathognomonic *discontinuity of being* (Winnicott's [1960] "failure to go-on-being"). These patients feel a certainty that the veritable holocaust they experience (frequently as a "domino-wave front") signals to them that their internal fault lines are reactivated, a phenomenon that Balint (1968) has so cogently addressed. In former times this phenomenon was referred to as the "loss of innocence," by which was meant that the victim had been stripped of any vestige of innocence, protection, or any expectation of fairness. He was now helplessly vulnerable to whatever predator chose him as its prey. God was dead! This profound sense of anticipated or actualized helplessness links primitive mental disorders, particularly the borderline personality disorder and patients with psychotic states, with the posttraumatic stress disorders, with which there is commonly a considerable overlapping in origins and in symptomatology.

The mental elements comprising meaninglessness have been termed "beta elements" by Bion (1962) to designate their quality of "nameless dread" (Grotstein 1989c). Grotstein (1989a,b,c) relates this to the phenomenon of randomness or entropy in psychotic, borderline, and other disorders. Stone (1988) studied these elements and relates them to the phenomenon of chaos, and, more specifically, believes that borderlines are characterized by a generalized hyperirritability that can be related to chaos. Langs (1988a) has studied chaos independently as a generalized field theory for psychoanalysis. The term *chaos* seems now to be a misnomer for the phenomenon of what hitherto was a synonym for randomness. Even though the laws of chaos are now being scientifically formulated, the individual experience of chaos is still that of randomness, which corresponds to the experience of the borderline and the psychotic of not being able to determine the meaningfulness of the self and of the self's relationships—and, for that matter, of experiences generally.

It is my penultimate thesis that patients suffering from primitive mental disorders can be universally characterized as being *disregulated* in a variety of self functions. Their attempts to self-regulate from their disasters are ill-fated and result in their belief that they are doomed. The hope*ful*ness of more benign disorders and the hope*less*ness of primitive disorders are reflected in their respective patterns of controlled versus uncontrolled regressions in psychoanalysis and psychotherapy; the former regress with confidence of "being caught." They frequently conjure Paradise. The latter seem only to anticipate their return to Nemesis, because Paradise has either been destroyed (deprivation) or never existed at all (privation).

Some of the leading elements just alluded to are as follows:

(1) Failure to one degree or another in the continuing processes of *bonding* and/or *attachment* (Bowlby 1958, 1969, 1973, 1980) with primary and subsequent objects, experienced especially in terms of failure of attunement, as indicated by deficits in the formation of the *emerging self, a core self, and a subjective self* (Stern 1985). This includes difficulties in bonding and attachment to oneself.[1] The types of bonding and attachment may be secure, insecure, and avoidant, and the latter two ("failed attachments")

---

[1]I employ the term *bonding* as the attitude of the mother (and father, and so on) toward the infant, whereas *attachment* is the attitude of the infant toward mother, a distinction made by Bowlby (1969, 1973, 1980). At the extremes, "invulnerable infants" can attach to mothers who have difficulty in attachment, whereas many mothers can bond to "irritable infants" who have difficulty in attachment.

frequently transform into perverse attachments of psychological bondage ("binds"). The most immediate and absolute experience of a sudden rupture in the attachment-bond is *separation anxiety*. Separation anxiety is mitigated by bonding and attachment, especially when the images, schemata, and memories of the attachment-bonding objects are internalized as functions. I find it useful to think of three internal objects in particular: the background presence of primary identification (Grotstein 1980), the transformational object (Bollas 1987), and the object of destiny (i.e., superego/ego ideal: Grotstein 1983c). The first of these includes Winnicott's (1960) "holding environment," Bion's (1962, 1963) "container-contained," Sandler's (1960) "environment of safety," and Ogden's (1986) "matrix." The second represents the object that transitionally escorts the infant to its future identity, which, in turn, is represented by the third object. These objects together also cover virtually all the beneficent internal object functions conceived of by Klein, Fairbairn, Winnicott, and Kernberg and also include all the self-object functions conceived of by Kohut and his followers.

(2) *Stranger anxiety*, which is discontinuous from separation anxiety but coeval with it, seems to furnish the frightening scenarios that fill the gap of separation. It is my belief that the inherent fear of the stranger is a transformation of our inherent, atavistic fear of being a prey to the immemorial predator (Bowlby, personal communication). The nature of these prey-predator scenarios is phylogenetically honed and first emerges, I believe, as inherent preperceptions as well as preconceptions, which are *released* by experiences of abandonment, neglect, or impingement to produce apocalyptic phantasmagoria (Ostow 1986) and which are relentlessly repeated in separations that these patients experience from their treatment in what has been termed the "gap." Stranger anxiety, which has neurodevelopmental roots (Jones 1988), is probably the format of the persecutory fantasies that Klein (1940) postulates comprise the paranoid-schizoid position. From another point of view, one can see how infants and primitive personalities may unwittingly superimpose prey or predator ("stranger") imagery onto the images of their parents or loved ones, as in a montage, and thereby comingle the strange with the familiar.

(3) The precocious development of a dissociation in the personality of permanent alter egos or second selves, the commonest forms of which are *true* and *false selves* (Winnicott 1952), following which there may develop more labyrinthine internal objects, the latter of which may also be recognized as the *mad omnipotent self* (Rosenfeld 1965, 1987) or the *pathological grandiose self* (Kernberg 1975, Kohut 1971, 1977). This internal object has

many derivatives and may occupy manic, depressed, perverse, psychotic, hyperlibidinal, hyperaggressive-destructive perspectives. Fairbairn (1952) refers to them as *endo-psychic structures*, which are organized amalgams of internalized objects and split-off selves.

These altered attachments, which seek to compensate for or regulate the failed attachment and bonding, become manifested as *pathological identifications*, which ultimately begin to function as independent, autonomous *alter egos*. The pathological identifications may be of the concordant[2] (e.g., identification with the aggressor), complementary (e.g., identification with the role prescribed by the aggressor), and oppositional type (e.g., locked into a counteridentification of combat with the object). These internal objects and their external projections exert enormous authority over the patient, who seems to behave toward them as if in a trance state or locked into an identificatory posture. The nature of the interaction may be sadomasochistic (cruel), slave-master (dependent), or "need-fear" (loving), the last of which describes a rapid oscillation between the claustrophobic anxiety of too much closeness alternating with the extreme anxiety of aloneness.

Furthermore, many of these patients may develop "screen identities" (Greenson 1958), which defensively mask these pathological structures. The nature of the two most important alter egos, the frantically assertive and the withdrawn ones, correspond to Bowlby's (1969, 1973, 1980) protest and withdrawal patterns and may probably be created by the release of inherent potentialities to respond to critical object absence or neglect (Engel and Schmale 1972, Hofer 1973a,b, 1975a,b, 1976, 1980, 1982, 1983, 1984, 1987, Hofer and Shair 1978, 1980, 1982).

These patients suffer from an incomplete development both of a sense of a *special* or *unique self* and a sense of a *normal, ordinary, human, needy self* in dialectical balance with the former. Their normal omnipotent gran-

---

[2] I have borrowed the terms *concordant* and *complementary* from Racker (1968), who ascribes them to the two classes of countertransference. To him, a concordant identification by the analyst represents a direct translocation of the patient's *ego* experience, whereas a complementary identification would represent the translocation into the therapist of an *internal object* within the patient. I employ the concept of *complementary identification* somewhat differently. To me it represents any kind of identity on the part of a second person that behaves in unconscious accord to the wishes, beliefs, or dictates of the first person. It is the essence of *"folie à deux."* Additionally, I add the third term, not employed by Racker, of *oppositional identification*, to designate an identification that takes the form of rebellion or reaction formation but which is still locked into a slavish relationship to the first object.

diosity is ill-fated, denied them, or purloined by a pathological alter ego, while their normal, ordinary, human, needy self has been overtainted by circumstances to render it a source of profound vulnerability and therefore heir to shame, humiliation, and the danger of foreclosure. Thus, they seem to need to manipulate others to perform excessive self-object functions for them so that their needs can be met with little or no extending of themselves beyond the arbitrary picket lines of their sense of encapsulated or entangled safety.

(4) The formation of a *skin boundary frontier representation* represents the infant's confidence in having a skin container that can sustain affect states and hide deficits in a state of volitional privacy from the potentially judgmental stares of others (Bick 1968); in other words, it is a prophylactic to the experience of shame. Conversely, blushing is one of the worst fears of patients with primitive mental disorders. There is also the experience of a sharply demarcated *"me/not me" interface* or of states of extreme *boundarylessness* and *confusion with objects* (defective in the development of the skin boundary frontier representation [Grotstein 1980]). The most important consequence of this is a *low threshold* to the impingement of internal and external stimuli and a *compromise* of the patient's ability to be a *private self*.

In either case, these patients suffer from an inability to undergo *transition* between states and can therefore not tolerate change. Giovacchini (1987a) explicates Winnicott's (1951) concept of transitional objects and phenomena in psychotic and borderline symptomatology. He demonstrates how these patients use their therapists as transitional (nonhuman, servicing) objects and how they seem to be arrested in transitionalness without being able to transcend it.

(5) As an extension of the preceding, these patients seem to have difficulty with *repression*, both *primal* and *secondary*, and consequently are more vulnerable to the irruptions of primitive (maybe even atavistic) imagery, as, for instance, in night terrors. In my experience, many, if not most of them, seem to have been born with an inherent predisposition toward hyperarousal-hyperalertness-hypersensitivity, confirming the work of Bergman and Escalona (1949), who found unusual sensitivities in children who were "at risk" for later psychotic illness. They seem to have no "rheostat" to modulate their reception of internal and external experiences. This is especially true for affects.

Boyer (1956, 1971) also has investigated this area of the relationship between hyperexcitability in the infant and later psychotic illness. He offers

the following formula for the interrelationship between the infant's constitutional givens and the nurturing environment: ". . . stimulus barrier plus
maternal protective barrier plus growing psyche yield normal ego development" (1956, p. 241). Psychotics, borderlines, and psychosomatic patients
seem to be virtually "possessed" by primitive preaffect enactments, that is,
by affects that have not yet been transformed into signal affects (affect
representations). These preaffective "feelings" have not been sufficiently
contained and continue to be disregulating in turn. A particular variety of
patients possessing this hypersensitivity is unusually vulnerable and sensitive to the suffering of others and seems to be predisposed to be altruists and
healers.

(6) There is a frequent history of infant and *child abuse* when one
considers the entire range or spectrum of traumatic impingement sexually or
aggressively by parents or environment, some of the results of which may be
identification with the aggressor, characterological submission to aggressors
to get love, hyperarousal states, and the like. From another perspective,
patients with primitive mental disorders *always* suffer from abuse, whether the
abuser is a real external person or an internal phantom inescapably conjured
because of relatively inadequate attunement in the presence of a low threshold
to experience. As a consequence, we must be all the more vigilant for the
simultaneous presence of the *posttraumatic stress disorder* in our patients.

(7) As a consequence both of hypersensitivity *and* a deficit in their
ability to access a normal mother's "rheostat" function, they experience a
failure in the ability to regulate or modulate and therefore to transform
internal and external events into meaningful experiences (*failure of data
processing* and of *transformation into personal experiences* [Bion 1965]).
This deficit includes: failure of absorption and/or intake of data, failure of
gating, failure of prioritization, and failure of being able to assign meaning
and significance to the data of events to transform them into emotional
experiences.

(8) They seem to demonstrate a *failure to be able to experience gratitude
toward one's objects, therefore obviating their ability to mourn them*, and to
adjust to loss, change, growth, weaning, and so forth. The consequence of
this failure is the handicapping of their capacity for symbolic function, that
is, the capacity to transform affective experiences with objects into *representations* (failure of object permanence and object constancy—and particularly a failure of rapprochement [Bion 1962, 1963, 1965, 1970, Klein 1940,
Mahler 1968, Searles 1987]).

(9) An *alexithymic* disposition to experiences, one where there is either a coarctation of feelings and fantasies or an uncontrolled superabundance of primitive prerepresentational feeling (Krystal 1977, 1982, McDougall 1974, 1980a,b, 1982, Rapaport et al. 1946, Rickles 1981, 1983, 1986, Taylor 1977). Alexithymia conveys not only not knowing the names of feelings, but also a disorganization or nonorganization of the generation of feelings, fantasies, and pleasure. Thus, patients with primitive emotional disorders suffer from *danger* rather than from excesses of *pleasure*. Further, it follows that they suffer from *deficient "alpha function"* (Bion 1962), which can be translated as *deficient primary process* as well as *deficient secondary process* (Grotstein 1977a,b, 1980, 1983a,b, 1986, 1987). Further, the concept of alexithymia implicates the *faulty development of autosensualism* (Tustin 1981a,b, 1986) and, as a consequence, a faulty sensual linking to objects. Thus, these patients suffer from alexithymia, anhedonia, affective disregulation, abnormal autosensualism, abnormal attention and arousal, and pathological formation, processing, transforming, and communicating of associations.

(10) The sense of *shame, humiliation, stigmatization, alienation, and ostracism* corresponds to the sense of fatalism that characterizes the philosophies of these patients. To the extent that primary process mechanisms still function in these patients, the victimizations they experience, whether internal, external, or both, seem to be quickly "rectified" and organized into a fatalistic but strangely "correct" cosmic "pecking order" in which they believe that what happened to them constitutes a group signification of their rank in that group. This signification then seems to be their tattoo or fingerprint of true identity and is difficult to foreswear in treatment despite protests to the contrary.

(11) A state of *trance-like submission* to the arrogated authority of internal objects and other "alter egos" or their projected transformations onto external objects seems to necessitate that these patients behave with command obedience to the capricious whims and dictates of these objects. By invoking the conception of trance, I am hinting at the hitherto infrequently mentioned phenomenon of *consciousness* and its important components, such as *arousal, attention, awareness, background-foreground relationships (figure-ground)*, all of which seem to be impaired in these patients.

(12) Interpenetration to one degree or another by significant neurobiological factors, sometimes primary (hereditary or congenital) or secondary but, in either case, often permanent or quasi-permanent, constitutes a significant subtext of *psychological meaninglessness* to deceive our hermeneu-

tic intention to apply psychological meaning to all experiences. The neuro-biological impairment may be genotypal (hereditary) and may or may not require phenotypal (environmental) releasing to become activated. It is now being learned that a significant percentage of patients with primitive mental disorders may suffer from neuro-perceptual-cognitive disorders, affective disorders, schizotypal disorders, and posttraumatic stress disorders, any or all of which occupy an either primarily or secondarily neuroanatomical, neurophysiological, and neuropsychological substrate. Ultimately, the psy-chopathological contribution of neurobiological factors can be divided into specific and general deficits, the latter of which is most often manifested in terms of a lowered threshold to stimuli.

(13) A sense of having been *imprinted* with and therefore bonded to a nonnurturing and/or impinging family environment *and* to a self that has varyingly molded to its exigencies. This experience can be thought of as a detrimental but obligatory bonding ("binding") to a negative background experience of primary identification. It is particularly with the latter that psychoanalytic treatment has difficulty. The challenge to this entity produces the *negative therapeutic reaction*, which is a result of the fear of change.

(14) *Neophobia*, the fear of change, is a prime characteristic of these patients. They seem to have a belief that they are concretely rooted to infancy (or even are unborn) and cannot change. Any contemplated change threatens to rip them away from their objects and from themselves. They conceive of any and all changes as a fundamental danger to their very existence; that is, "If I change, I am no longer me!" This neophobic anxiety is yet another manifestation of their inability to transitionalize their expe-riences; that is, their underlying inability to employ transitional techniques in order to gradualize or adjust to separation experiences.

(15) The ultimate preoccupation of these patients is with the achieve-ment and/or maintenance of *safety* rather than the pursuit of pleasure, contrary to previous psychoanalytic formulations, and this goal of safety is in line with their constant quest for self-regulation and/or modulation, either for stimulus hunger or for stimulus overload.

(16) In light of the shift of psychoanalytic perspective from the intra*personal to the inter*personal, especially as it has been elaborated in infant development studies (Stern 1985, Trevarthen 1983), we are now con-strained to think in terms of *interactionism* and *intersubjectivity*. Because of this shift, I should like to reinvoke the ancient but long-disused concept of

"folie à deux," both in its positive and in its negative sense, to explain all normal and pathological varieties of intimate bonding and attachment and their distortions and failures as seen in collusive states. For instance, Apprey (1987) has conducted longitudinal outcome studies on infants and mothers from pregnancy through the fourth year postnatally in which he sought (a) to determine the degree of health or pathology in the mother's unconscious fantasies about her child (particularly projective identification) and (b) to determine the outcome of infant–child response to these fantasies. *Folie à deux*, then, would be the result of the infant's readiness to accept and to counteridentify with the mother's projective identifications. It is my belief that this is an important source of benevolent and pathological influence.

(17) The experience by the therapist of critical and critically important projective *counteridentifications* and *countertransferences*, the presence of which highlights the special employment of a primitive, preverbal communication by these patients. It is as if they remained fixated at the threshold of preverbal/verbal language development, the former phase characterized by projective identification (Bion 1962) and the latter by the successful acquisition of symbols (Stern 1985). Projective counteridentification, first described by Grinberg (1962, 1979), emphasizes patients' projections, which are foreign to the analyst, into the analyst's experience. Boyer (1986, 1987) presents case material of borderline patients that beautifully demonstrates this phenomenon. In one example he experienced his right forearm unconsciously pronating as if poising to serve with a tennis racquet, only to find that this corresponded to a crucial buried memory of his patient. Countertransference per se is more common. There is hardly a therapist alive who can remain dispassionate in the face of his patient's "orgies" of self-mutilation and manipulative (and nonmanipulative) suicide attempts. Mention must also be made of the pioneering work in countertransference by Searles (1979, 1986), Giovacchini (1975, 1979), and Boyer (1983).

REGRESSIVE CONSTELLATIONS

The regressive process may be dramatic or silent. In the former case one is reminded of borderline patients, patients with panic disorders and traumatic neuroses, as well as patients who suffer from depressive, manic, and/or schizophrenic psychotic breaks. Others may experience a silent descent, by which I mean that they seem to disappear imperceptibly into a "walking-dead" state in which they have all but forfeited their pride, hope, innocence, and vitality. Some of these patients conform to what Winnicott (1973) referred to as those who fear having an imminent mental breakdown, but who really have already suffered from a silent one and employ the future tense rather than the past tense as a protective denial. Their very employment of this disavowal bears poignant testimony, however, to the depth of their feelings of shame.

I postulate that failure of "good enough attachment and bonding" precludes the emergence of the *background presence of primary identification* (Grotstein 1980), which Winnicott (1960, 1963) terms the *subject* or *environmental mother*, Sandler (1960) terms *the background of safety*, and Ogden (1986) calls the *matrix*. The failure of this background support to emerge precipitates the experience of an infantile catastrophe and is characterized by a foreclosure over all remaining links to the object. It is as if the infant (and his later analogue) would then experience a sense of disorientation and of falling (or being pulled downward) into nothingness, chaos, randomness, or meaninglessness. One of the most immediate consequences of this cataclysmic regression is the bizarre alteration of perceptions. There is no object behind them or underneath them to hold them up or to give them perspective. The very floor of their psychic space disappears, and the vast maw of chaos opens up to pull them in. In perceptual terms, figure and ground become indistinguishably commingled. I consider this experience to constitute the *infantile psychosis*[3] (Grotstein 1980, 1989c).

The first state of arrestment or of restitution of this regressive catastrophe is, due to the sequential release of inherent "programs" of phylogenetically honed adaptive strategies, the development of permanent anxiety-panic or depressive states. This not only is manifested in the overt behavior of these infants, but is also revealed in their developing a proclivity toward pathological autosensuality (autoerotism) in which sense impressions, rather than linking up with objects, *actually become the restituted autosensual object in lieu of the object* (Tustin 1981a,b, 1986). The development of a primary pathological autosensual self results in the experience of dissociation or alienation and the formation of an abnormal alter ego (or second self) which, because of precocious closure, is cut off from the rest of the personality and operates by its own idiosyncratic rules and values. It may relate to but is not necessarily identical to the false self.

Another consequence of this actual or anticipated catastrophe is the formation of a sharp demarcation or absence of demarcation between the self and other ("me/not me" boundary). The foreclosure of the background

---

[3]I consider the *infantile psychosis* to be a meta-psychological concept, not a chronological one. Thus "infantile" is a statement of depth of regression or state of primitiveness, not necessarily of earliness.

presence of primary identification precipitates a state in which the infant must become neophobic. Any change means falling into uncontrollable regression. They therefore seem either to encapsulate themselves or to entangle themselves indiscriminately into the fantasied substance of the object. Encapsulation and entanglement are the forerunners of dissociation and projective identification respectively and seem to characterize alternative organizations to all psychopathology. The phenomenon of transitionalness, especially as associated with transitional objects, transitional phenomena, and transitional space (potential space), is the antithesis to the absoluteness of the sharply demarcated boundary. Transitionalness represents the combined work of the common enterprise of mother and infant to construct a mythic blanket of faith in a mid-area of experience ("potential space," Winnicott 1971) between fact and fiction, between creation and discovery, that allows the infant to feel himself to be upheld during absences until such time as he can develop a "rhythm of safety" (Tustin 1986), one that heralds the internalization, not of the object per se, but of the experience with the object that constitutes a "blessing" from the object in its absence—as opposed to its curse. It may also be true that *memory* itself is, in its origins at least, a prime example of a transitional phenomenon insofar as it constitutes a mental icon, as it were, of the object.

From the perspective of infant observation studies, Stern (1985) offers new conceptualizations that take issue to one extent or another with all previous psychoanalytic reconstructive theories of infant development. At issue from Stern's point of view is not the capacity for the newborn infant to be separate enough to experience trauma. (Stern repudiates primary narcissism, autism, symbiosis, the stimulus barrier, and infantile wish-fulfillment-in-fantasy.) Stern concludes instead that there are *senses of self* that develop in both sequential *and* parallel lines in terms of a *sense of an emergent self*, a *core self*, a *subjective self*, and a *verbal self*, all a function of self and interactional regulation and attunement in an intimate relationship with a bonding caretaker in the following sets: the *domain of emergent relatedness*, the *domain of core relatedness*, the *domain of intersubjective relatedness*, and the *domain of verbal relatedness*. The senses of self that develop along these lines are the *senses of agency, physical cohesion, continuity, affectivity, subjective self–intersubjective self, organization-creating, and transmission of meaning*.

Using Stern's perspective, one can hypothesize that psychosis develops in the incomplete or abnormal outcome of an emergent self in the domain of emergent relatedness. The borderline disorder would be the outcome of the incomplete emergence of a core self in the domain of core relatedness but may also involve difficulties with the development of a subjective self in the domain of intersubjective relatedness. The narcissistic personality disorder is a function of an abnormal outcome with the subjective self in the domain of intersubjective relatedness; neurosis would be a function of disorders of the verbal self in the domain of verbal relatedness, but any or all the senses of self could be involved.

Yet another important conclusion Stern arrives at from his infant development studies is one that dovetails with the work of Langs (1988b), namely, that *perception of reality*, rather than fantasy or drives, is the deepest and most forceful component of the unconscious. This conclusion suggests, first of all, that Freud was more correct than we had thought regarding his first theory of psychoanalysis, that of the censorship of traumatic memory. Second, it suggests that there needs to be a shift in our conception of the relative importance of *reality* and *imagination* as etiological factors in mental illness. Thus, traumatic reality experience may be primary, and our capacity for imagination (primary process) may have been instituted in order to regulate it through the production of fantasies.

I would add, however, that the production of fantasies originates not only within the infant but also occurs as a joint enterprise with the myth-fostering mother in her act of protective bonding. I further propose that the infant is born with phylogenetically honed "hardware" (DNA) programming that consists of inherent archetypes (Jung 1934, Samuels 1983), preconceptions (Bion 1962, 1963, 1965, 1970, 1977, 1979), and/or preperceptions (Grotstein 1989c) that are selectively released by experience. These primordial image-precursors are preternatural and uncanny. Fantasies and illusions (personal mythifications) seek to attentuate the absoluteness of these images. Jung (1934) put it very well when he said that it was the purpose of good mothering to discredit the projection of bad archetypes. I propose that the archetypal preconceptions and preperceptions released by traumatic circumstances would be of the prey–predator variety and would include a lexicon of all the possible horrors of our primeval past. Ostow (1986) discusses apocalyptic dreams and fantasies of schizophrenics and borderlines from the archetypal perspective.

GENERALIZED SCENARIO FOR THE DEVELOPMENT OF A PRIMITIVE MENTAL DISORDER

Patients in this category are characteristically unusually vulnerable to internal and external events. Whereas neurotic patients seem to have become secondarily sensitized to specific experiences in their past, the former patients may, in addition to having experienced specific traumata (deficiency and/or impingement) like the neurotics (but perhaps more general and more severe), also have been presensitized to experience by *unusual threshold sensitivities* inherent in their constitutional endowment either from heredity or from the womb environment and, furthermore, *in an atmosphere of mismatch with either mother, father, or the family system altogether* (Chess and Thomas 1986, Grotstein 1989c, Thomas and Chess 1977). The heightened vulnerability of the infant to experience poses a challenge in the first place to his capacity to undergo successful attachment to his primary object *and* a challenge conversely to his caretaker to bond with him, thereby doubly jeopardizing the continuing achievement of attunement. Failures in attunement precipitate a series of secondary disregulatory phenomena that may herald an *infantile catastrophe* (Bion 1959, Tustin 1981a,b, 1986) of objectlessness—and therefore of subjectlessness by default. In animal studies Hofer (1973a,b,c, 1975a,b, 1976, Hofer and Shair 1978, 1980, 1982) found that *noradrenergic* and *dopaminergic hyperactivity* (protest behavior) may occur, which, after a critical time of object absence or frustration, becomes permanently ingrained into the personality. Once released by experience, it seems to be unalterable, according to Hofer and Hofer and Shair. Another released phenomenon is that of *conservation-withdrawal* (Engel and Schmale 1967), which they postulate is an adaptive consequence of the need to survive with the anticipation of objectlessness. The former posture seems to correspond to anxiety, panic, and agitation (and protest), whereas the latter seems to correspond to clinical depression with its characteristic surrender to the inevitable.

NOTES ON TECHNIQUE

Patients with primitive personality disorders often conform to what Giovacchini (1987b) pithily describes as the "impossible patient," impossible because their demands for relief seem to be impossible to meet, to interpret, and so forth. These patients seem to be affect and impulse disregulated and dominated to a marked degree and therefore sorely try the patience of therapists. The debate between conflict or deficiency is trivial with these patients, because their massive and generalized deficits render them all the more vulnerable to experiencing conflicts.

The application of classical and/or Kleinian psychoanalytic technique to these patients has advantages and drawbacks (see Grotstein et al. 1987). The laying down of a firm therapeutic frame is of enormous value in helping these patients to develop a model for secure boundaries in which they can feel "contained" and therefore secure. The interpretation of their primitive mental mechanisms (e.g., splitting, projective identification, idealization, magic omnipotent denial) and of their derailed and fixated part–object functions is generally very helpful. One of the putatively negative points about classical and Kleinian technique is the possibility of "experience-distance" in the interventions. Self psychologists who have explored the treatment of borderlines prefer the empathic technique, which implies "experience-near" interventions. Conversely, one of the dangers of the so-called empathic mode is the possibility of collusion with a pathological split-off self that may dominate the personality of the patient and use empathy for tacit approval of its madness.

I should like to reconcile the two modes of intervention in the following way: the empathic mode is, I believe, a continuation of Winnicott's (1956) conception of primary maternal preoccupation, the purpose of which is to affirm the development of a cohesive "being" self (Winnicott 1963). This aspect of relatedness corresponds to the development of attachment and bonding (Bowlby 1969, 1973, 1980). The development of the separating self (Winnicott's "doing" self) depends on secure bonding and attachment as a prerequisite.

I therefore envision a dual track in which "bonding" and "weaning" can be thought of as metaphors for the strategies of intervention by therapists depending on where the patient is at any given moment. Further, one must pay very careful attention to the transitional needs of these patients. They experience separations as discontinuities of being; therefore, they despair of "going-on-being" in the therapist's absence. Interventions about their needs for transitional objects and phenomena can therefore be very helpful (see Giovacchini 1987a). Soothing, in other words, would take priority to confrontation—at the beginning of treatment, at least, according to this protocol.

Many authors have noted the importance of the occurrence of countertransference in the treatment of these patients. It constitutes both a treatment contamination and facilitation depending on the therapist's ability to access its benefits. Giovacchini (1975, 1979, 1987b), Searles (1979), and Boyer (1986, 1987) have each written in depth about both aspects. Ultimately, the prevalence of countertransference (and/or projective counteridentification) by the therapist is both a statement of the intensity and primitiveness of the regressed relationship (bilaterally) *and* of the nature of primitive emotional communication. Bion (1962) states that primitive mental disorders behave as if they as infants never had sufficient access to being able to employ projective identification into containing mothers. Countertransference may very well be the result of their attempts to develop this technique satisfactorily.

The employment of medication in primitive mental disorders is becoming less and less problematic in this country due to the relative cooperation between psychoanalysis and neurobiology in psychiatric training institutions. It must be remembered that medication, if employed at all, is appropriate for severe disruptive *states*; personality *traits* are transformable only through psychoanalysis and psychotherapy. Medication may be helpful generally in terms of arousal thresholds of excitability and, if used discreetly, may facilitate psychoanalysis or psychotherapy with these patients.

BRIEF CLINICAL VIGNETTES

Case A.

A 39-year-old physician who had been in analysis with me for depressive illness once revealed an early memory to me in which one of his worst fears occurred when he would dare look into and down the laundry chute in the second floor of his family home. He remembered experiencing a strong pull from within and believed that demons lived inside. He called that chute his "black hole." When he entered analysis he seemed to have a combination of a relatively normal or, at worst, neurotic personality *and* a very regressive, traumatized personality alongside it (Bion 1957). The second self (alter ego) was not psychotic per se but did appear to function on the borderline level as the analysis developed. First, he developed a series of phobic inhibitions, the most prominent of which were fears of high places, claustrophobia, and agoraphobia. Analytic gaps became unbearable as he would report terrifying feelings, persecutory phenomena, and a generalized sense of uneasiness.

I was able to make a series of interpretations that addressed his experience of the gap as follows: "You experience me as the instigator and manipulator of the analysis, the one who starts the conveyor belt of feelings to roll relentlessly and inexorably—but without my being there with you in the absences." (At these moments I would often have countertransference-projective counteridentification experiences of the Pietà, in which I was Mary, feeling guilty about bringing my Christ-child-patient into the world of suffering without adequate protection and a sense of safety.) He would associate to this kind of interpretation by informing me of how frightened of life he had always been, how he felt unprotected by his parents, particularly by his mother, and how he never really felt truly close (bonding and attachment) to either parent, although he had felt close to his sister. Gap dream imagery ranged from terrifying animals (prey–predator anxiety) to earthquakes.

I at first interpreted this apocalyptic imagery as the projective-introjective transformations of his hostility toward me, thereby causing me to become internalized as a demonic figure who persecuted him, either as a predatory animal or as a disintegrating background figure. The latter interpretation was more successful in reducing his anxiety. I then altered the former in the following way: I interpreted to him that I was as yet unable to accompany him in the gaps because he was as yet too frightened to allow for an internal space within him for me, so closed-off and bound was he to his fear and his pain. Moreover, the predatory animal was not only a transformed me but also represented his basic view of his own *un*transformed, needy, frightened self. Moreover, it represented him and all the preconceived terrors imaginable, all wrapped up in a single image, which were released into his awareness when I was not there to hold him and to contain his fears. They were my rivals and his worst fears, which were summoned or mobilized in order to prepare him for an even worse terror, that of fragmenting into nothingness and meaninglessnes, as forewarned by his growing feelings of chaos.

Eventually, we were able to see that his "persecutory anxiety" over the breaks in the analysis were unconscious imagery structures that were released by his clutching terror. Eventually, I was allowed entry into his dreams as myself, which heralded a transformation into transitionalness and ultimately into a working alliance. Throughout the analysis, however, it became apparent that I had to deal with two distinctly different types of transference phenomena, one with me as the background presence of primary identification (holding environment or subject mother) and the other with me as the container of his feelings. In the first, I was pictured as being behind him metaphorically and literally, whereas in the second I was a transference image in front—the object of his neediness.

Case B.

A male actor revealed that every time he left my office or, for that matter, any place he had to leave, he experienced an almost vertiginous collapse of self as if he were falling into a crack in the earth. He would then "space out" and be in an altered state of virtual disembodiment for hours, after which he would slowly and painfully recover—for the moment. In the course of his analysis it became suggestively apparent that he had never felt attachment with nor bonding from either of his parents and had lived a veritably alienated existence in which he always feared change, relationships, and sensuality. This fear abated as he became able to accept me as his "background object," but not before considerable enactments had taken place in the analysis, including self-mutilation, drug abuse, many prolonged absences from sessions, and so forth. My "take" on the absences was that it was his unconscious way of giving me (communicating) the experience of his having never felt important to his family. He responded positively to this interpretation and was then able to develop a closer working alliance with me. The denouement of the self-mutilations and suicide attempts, however, seemed to involve the appearance of second selves or alter egos. The more progress he would make in treatment, the more there would be a tendency for his more primitive personality(-ies) to present themselves, as if to say, "Don't forget about me! Don't leave me behind!" or, "Don't desert us for Dr. Grotstein. I'm your best friend; he's your enemy. I was with you through all the bad times. Who knows you better and who's closer to you?" It was in these "dialogues" that I was able to glean the deep sense of adhesive loyalty and bonding that this patient felt toward the personification of his illness, which had become a second self. A confrontation of this phenomenon, together with empathy for the point of view of the second self, enabled the patient to release himself from it.

Case C.

This young female schizotypal patient presented a dream toward the beginning of her analysis in which she was all alone on a desert. There was a mound or rise on the desert landscape on top of which was a round stone fortress. A hidden doorway revealed itself. As she entered, she became aware that there was a deep hole inside and no floor whatsoever to cover it. She felt an almost irresistible pull into the hole. She also looked around at the walls and was horrified to see a ring of torture instruments surrounding the hole. She ran away in horror and woke up. She had this dream again on several occasions but was able to have me join her for exploration as well as for protection. In some of the dreams we both fell into the hole and were suspended there. In one particular dream she fell into the hole, which became a birth canal, and she wound up at first in a torrential river flowing into infinity, but it then suddenly changed into a tightly enclosed cage (claustrum), where she felt trapped.

Her associations to these dreams went in many directions. The torture instruments were associated to her constant and severe self-mutilation rituals, which she would institute whenever she felt panicky, depressed, or suicidal. They were experienced as self-regulatory and would prevent her from experiencing uncontrollable regression. It then emerged that she had practiced anal masturbation since childhood, and she believed that, in fantasy, she lived in the rectum in a kind of encapsulated state in order to protect herself from her mother's and father's craziness and invasiveness. Much of her adult identity was not only a false self but also a screen identity to disavow more basic and frightening identifications (concordant, complementary, and oppositional) with each of them, phenomena that repeated themselves serially in the transference. She also demonstrated severe separation anxiety and stranger anxiety, and it became apparent that the image of the eerie and menacing stranger would intrude itself into the separation gaps of the treatment. Finally, the stranger emerged as a weird, nonhuman, bizarre object, part hallucination, part illusion. This bizarre object became understood—and finally resolved—when she and I realized that it was both the container for and the expression of massive regression.

CONCLUSION

In this chapter I have sought to explicate some of the invariant phenomenology that occurs in primitive mental disorders. The list includes:

1. Pathological or absent bonding and attachment, leading to heightened separation anxiety.
2. Heightened stranger anxiety ("prey–predator"—persecutory anxiety).
3. Pathological identifications (concordant, complementary, and/or oppositional) with the formation of complex alter egos.
4. The development of either a sharp "me/not me" interface or its opposite, a sense of boundarylessness as ego boundary and between self and other. In either case there is a low threshold (defective "rheostat") to internal and external experiential stimuli and an intolerance of change because of the inability to undergo the *transition* between mental states.
5. Defective primal and secondary repression with the consequences of heightened arousal and sensitivity as well as a failure to transform basic preaffective emotional enactments into affect representations (signals).

6. A frequent history of child abuse, which can now be more broadly understood as being either external or internal, but in either case frequently leading to a posttraumatic stress syndrome.

7. A failure to develop either a special, unique sense of self *or* to tolerate being an ordinary, needy, desiring, human self as well as being unable to achieve a balance between them.

8. The precocious development of a permanent dissociation between a sense of a "true self" and a "false self," the consequence of which is the development of multiple alter egos operating with separate personality agendas.

9. An inability to self-regulate, to receive, encode, and process the data of emotional experience they are subjected to, and an inability to transform these data into representable thoughts and feelings.

10. An aversion to or an inability to experience *and* express gratitude toward their caretaking objects, thereby interfering with their ability to achieve *memory*; that is, they are unable to furnish their minds with needed structures or representations of objects that constitute the necessary scaffolding and bridges for transition across changing states.

11. An alexithymic disposition, which includes anhedonia, faulty autosensualism, inability to recognize affect signals, and abnormal qualities of attentiveness or consciousness. Included in this category is the probability of abnormal primary process.

12. A profound and stigmatizing experience of shame and fatalism. They behave as if they are fate's prisoners, who are deprived of their souls in the grimy, humiliating struggle for survival, "knowing" all the while that they are "cursed" rather than "blessed."

13. A state of trance toward their meaningful objects, which is the state of consciousness of submission of a prey to a predator in the animal kingdom, and which constitutes an interactional regulator of group and kinship structure in terms of hierarchies of rank.

14. The interpenetrating presence of primary and/or secondary neurobiological factors, which may be specific or generalized in the form of low threshold, and so on.

15. A sense of being imprinted by one's early environment, especially when it is pathological, thereby depriving one of permission to leave it. This belief in not having a veritable passport leads to the negative therapeutic reaction in analytic treatment.

16. Neophobia because of a failure to achieve transitionalism.

17. An all-abiding obsession with safety and self-regulation, forfeiting pleasure.
18. A predisposition toward relationships characterized by *folie à deux,* in which they seem to need to be taken over by the energy and vital force of the other.

REFERENCES

Apprey, M. (1987). Projective identification and maternal misperception in disturbed mothers. *British Journal of Psychotherapy* 4:5-22.

Balint, M. (1968). *The Basic Fault.* London: Tavistock.

Bergman, P., and Escalona, S. (1949). Unusual sensitivities in very young children. *Psychoanalytic Study of the Child* 3:333-352.

Bick, E. (1968). The experience of skin in early object relations. *International Journal of Psycho-Analysis* 49:484-486.

Bion, W. R. (1957). Differentiation of the psychotic from the nonpsychotic personalities. *International Journal of Psycho-Analysis* 38:266-275.

—— (1962). *Learning from Experience.* London: Heinemann.

—— (1963). *Elements of Psycho-Analysis.* London: Heinemann.

—— (1965). *Transformations.* London: Heinemann.

—— (1970). *Attention and Interpretation.* London: Tavistock.

—— (1975). *A Memoir of the Future. Book One: The Dream.* Rio de Janeiro: Imago.

—— (1977). *A Memoir of the Future. Book Two: The Past Presented.* Rio de Janeiro: Imago.

—— (1979). *A Memoir of the Future. Book Three: The Dawn of Oblivion.* Perthshire: Clunie.

Bollas, C. (1987). *The Shadow of the Object: Psychoanalysis of the Unthought Known.* London: Free Associations.

Bowlby, J. (1958). The nature of the child's tie to his mother. *International Journal of Psycho-Analysis* 39:350-373.

—— (1969). *Attachment and Loss. Vol. I: Attachment.* New York: Basic Books.

—— (1973). *Attachment and Loss. Vol. II: Separation: Anxiety and Anger.* New York: Basic Books.

—— (1980). *Attachment and Loss. Vol. III: Loss: Sadness and Depression.* New York: Basic Books.

Boyer, L. B. (1956). On maternal overstipulation and ego defects. *Psychoanalytic Study of the Child* 11:236-256.

—— (1971). Interactions among stimulus barrier, maternal protective barrier, innate drive tensions, and maternal overstipulation. *Adolescent Psychiatry* 1:363-378.

—— (1983). *The Regressed Patient.* New York: Jason Aronson.

—— (1986). Technical aspects of treating the regressed patient. *Contemporary Psychoanalysis* 22:25–44.

—— (1987). Psychoanalytic treatment of the borderline disorders today. *Contemporary Psychoanalysis* 23:314–328.

Chess S., and Thomas, A., eds. (1986). *Temperament in Clinical Practice*. New York: Guilford Press.

Engel, G. L., and Schmale, A. H. (1972). Conservation-withdrawal: a primary regulatory process for organismic homeostasis. In *Physiology, Emotion, and Psychosomatic Illness*, pp. 57–85. Amsterdam: Elsevier. CIBA Foundation Symposium VIII.

Fairbairn, W. R. D. (1952). *Psychoanalytic Studies of the Personality*. London, Henley, England and Boston: Routledge and Kegan Paul.

Giovacchini, P. L. (1979). *Treatment of Primitive Mental States*. New York: Jason Aronson.

—— (1987a). The borderline state, the transitional state, and the psychoanalytic paradox. In *The Borderline Patient: Emerging Concepts in Diagnosis, Psychodynamics, and Treatment*, vol. 1, ed. J. Grotstein, M. Solomon, and J. Lang, pp. 181–204. Hillsdale, NJ: The Analytic Press.

—— (1987b). The "unreasonable patient" and the psychotic transference. In *The Borderline Patient: Emerging Concepts in Diagnosis, Psychodynamics, and Treatment*, vol. 2, ed. J. Grotstein, M. Solomon, and J. Lang, pp. 59–68. Hillsdale, NJ: The Analytic Press.

Giovacchini, P. L., Flarsheim, A., and Boyer, L. B., eds. (1975). *Tactics and Techniques in Psychoanalytic Therapy. Vol. II: Countertransference*. New York: Jason Aronson.

Gleick, J. (1987). *Chaos*. New York: Viking Press.

Greenson, R. (1958). On screen defenses, screen hunger and screen identity. *Journal of the American Psychoanalytic Association* 6:242–262.

Grinberg, L. (1962). On a specific aspect of countertransference due to the patient's projective identification. *International Journal of Psycho-Analysis* 43:436–440.

—— (1979). Countertransference and projective counteridentification. *Contemporary Psychoanalysis* 15:226–247.

Grotstein, J. (1977a). The psychoanalytic concept of schizophrenia: I. the dilemma. *International Journal of Psycho-Analysis* 58:403–425.

—— (1977b). The psychoanalytic concept of schizophrenia: II. reconciliation. *International Journal of Psycho-Analysis* 58:427–452.

—— (1978). Inner space: its dimensions and its coordinates. *International Journal of Psycho-Analysis* 59:55–61.

—— (1980). A proposed revision of the psychoanalytic concept of primitive mental states: I. an introduction to a newer psychoanalytic metapsychology. *Contemporary Psychoanalysis* 16:479–546.

—— (1983a). A proposed revision of the psychoanalytic concept of primitive mental states: II. the borderline syndrome—section 1: disorders of autistic safety and symbiotic relatedness. *Contemporary Psychoanalysis* 19:570–604.

—— (1983b). A proposed revision of the psychoanalytic concept of primitive mental states: II. the borderline syndrome—section 2: the phenomenology of the borderline syndrome. *Contemporary Psychoanalysis* 20:77–119.

—— (1983c). Some perspectives on self psychology. In *The Future of Psychoanalysis*, ed. A. Goldberg, pp. 165–203. New York: International Universities Press.

—— (1985). The Schreber case revisited: schizophrenia as a disorder of self-regulation and interactional regulation. *Yale Journal of Biology and Medicine* 58:299–314.

—— (1986). The psychology of powerlessness: disorders of self-regulation and interactional regulation as a newer paradigm for psychopathology. *Psychoanalytic Inquiry* 6:93–118.

—— (1987). Borderline as a disorder of self-regulation. In *The Borderline Patient: Emerging Concepts in Diagnosis, Psychodynamics, and Treatment*, vol. 1, ed. J. S. Grotstein, M. Solomon, and J. Lang, pp. 347–388. Hillsdale, NJ: Analytic Press.

—— (1989a). The "black hole" as the basic psychotic experience: some newer psychoanalytic and neuroscience perspectives on psychosis. *Journal of the American Academy of Psychoanalysis*. In press.

—— (1989b). A revised psychoanalytic conception of schizophrenia: an interdisciplinary update. Accepted for publication by the *Journal of Psychoanalytic Psychology*.

—— (1989c). *Meaning, Meaninglessness, and the "Black Hole": Self- and Interactional Regulation as a New Model for Psychoanalysis and Neuroscience.* Accepted for publication by Plenum Press.

Grotstein, J., Lang, J., and Solomon, M. (1987). Convergence and controversy: II. treatment of the borderline. In *The Borderline Patient: Emerging Concepts in Diagnosis, Psychodynamics, and Treatment*, vol. 2, ed. J. Grotstein, M. Solomon, and J. Lang, pp. 261–310. Hillsdale, NJ: Analytic Press.

Hofer, M. A. (1973a). The role of nutrition in the physiological and behavioral effects of early maternal separation in infant rats. *Psychosomatic Medicine* 35:350–359.

—— (1973b). The effects of brief maternal separations on behavior and heart rate of 2-week-old rat pups. *Physiology and Behavior* 10:423–427.

—— (1973c). Maternal separation affects infant rats' behavior. *Behavioral Biology* 9:629–633.

—— (1975a). Studies on how early maternal separation produces behavioral changes in young rats. *Psychosomatic Medicine* 37:245–264.

—— (1975b). Survival and recovery of physiological functions after early maternal separation in rats. *Physiology and Behavior* 15:475–480.

—— (1976). The organization of sleep and wakefulness after maternal separation in young rats. *Developmental Psychobiology* 9:189–206.

—— (1980). Effects of reserpine and amphetamine on the development of hyperactivity in maternally deprived rat pups. *Psychosomatic Medicine* 42:513–520.

―――― (1982). Seeing is believing: a personal perspective on research strategy in developmental psychobiology. *Developmental Psychobiology* 15:339-408.

―――― (1983). On the relationship between attachment and separation processes in infancy. In *Emotion: Theory, Research, and Experience. Volume 2: Early Development*, ed. R. Plutchik, pp. 199-219. New York: Academic Press.

―――― (1984). Relationships as regulators: a psychobiologic perspective on bereavement. *Psychosomatic Medicine* 46:183-197.

―――― (1987). Early social relationships: a psychobiologist's view. *Journal of Child Development* 58:633-647.

Hofer, M. A., and Shair, H. (1978). Ultrasonic vocalizations during social interaction and isolation in 2-week-old rats. *Developmental Psychobiology* 11:495-504.

―――― (1980). Sensory processes in the control of isolation-induced ultrasonic vocalization in 2-week-old rats. *Journal of Comparative and Physiological Psychology* 94:271-279.

―――― (1982). Control of sleep/wake states in the infant rat by features of the mother-infant relationship. *Developmental Psychobiology* 15:229-244.

Jones, J. (1988). The somatic substrate of the stranger anxiety syndrome. Unpublished manuscript.

Jung, C. J. (1934). *Archetypes and the Collective Unconscious. Collected Works,* vol. 9, trans. R. F. C. Hull. New York: Bollingen Series XX, 1959.

Kernberg, O. F. (1975). *Borderline Conditions and Pathological Narcissism.* New York: Jason Aronson.

Klein, M. (1940). Mourning and its relation to manic-depressive states. In *Contributions to Psycho-Analysis, 1921-1945*, pp. 311-338. London: Hogarth and Institute of Psycho-Analysis, 1950.

Kohut, H. (1971). *The Analysis of the Self.* New York: International Universities Press.

―――― (1977). *The Restoration of the Self.* New York: International Universities Press.

Krystal, H. (1977). The self-representation and the capacity for self-care. *The Annual of Psychoanalysis* 6:209-246.

―――― (1982). Alexithymia and the affectiveness of psychoanalytic treatment. *International Journal of Psychoanalytic Psychotherapy* 9:353-378.

Langs, R. (1988a). Psychotherapy and mathematical models: mathematics for psychoanalysis. *British Journal of Psychotherapy* 5:204-212.

―――― (1988b). *Decoding Your Dreams.* New York: Henry Holt.

Mahler, M. S. (1968). *On Human Symbiosis and the Vicissitudes of Individuation.* New York: International Universities Press.

McDougall, J. (1974). The psychosoma and the psychoanalytic process. *International Review of Psycho-Analysis* 1:437-459.

―――― (1980a). A child is being eaten, I: psychosomatic states, anxiety neurosis, and hysteria—a theoretical approach; II: the abysmal mother and the cork child—a clinical illustration. *Contemporary Psychoanalysis* 16:416-459.

—— (1980b). *Plea for a Measure of Abnormality*. New York: International Universities Press.

—— (1982). Alexithymia: a psychoanalytic viewpoint. *Psychotherapy and Psychosomatics* 38:81–90.

Ogden, T. (1986). *The Matrix of the Mind*. Northvale, NJ: Jason Aronson.

Ostow, M. (1986). Archetypes of apocalypse in dreams and fantasies, and in religious scripture. *American Imago* 43:307–334.

Pagels, H. (1985). *Perfect Symmetry: The Search for the Beginning of Time*. New York: Simon and Schuster.

Racker, H. (1968). *Transference and Countertransference*. London: Hogarth and the Institute of Psycho-Analysis.

Rapaport, D., Gill, M., and Schafer, R. (1946). The thematic apperception test. In *Diagnostic Psychological Testing*, vol. 2. Chicago: Yearbook Medical Publishers.

Rickles, W. H. (1981). Biofeedback and transitional phenomenon. *Psychiatric Annals* 11:23–41.

—— (1983). Personality characteristics of psychosomatic patients. In *Biofeedback and Family Practice Medicine*, ed. W. H. Rickles, J. H. Sandweiss, D. W. Jacobs, et al., pp. 155–174. New York: Plenum.

—— (1986). Self psychology and somatization: an integration with alexithymia. In *Progress in Self Psychology*, vol. 2, ed. A. Goldberg, pp. 212–226. New York: Guilford.

Rosenfeld, H. (1965). *Psychotic States*. New York: Basic Books.

Rosenfeld, R. (1987). *Impasse and Interpretation*. London: Tavistock and the Institute of Psycho-Analysis.

Samuels, A. (1983). The theory of archetypes in Jungian and post-Jungian analytical psychology. *The International Review of Psycho-Analysis* 10:429–444.

Sandler, J. (1960). The background of safety. *International Journal of Psycho-Analysis* 41:352–356.

Searles, H. F. (1979). *Countertransference and Related Subjects*. New York: International Universities Press.

—— (1986). *My Work with Borderline Patients*. Northvale, NJ: Jason Aronson.

—— (1987). The development in the patient of an internalized image of the therapist. In *The Borderline Patient: Emerging Concepts in Diagnosis, Psychodynamics, and Treatment*, vol. 2, ed. J. S. Grotstein, M. F. Solomon, and J. A. Lang, pp. 25–40. Northvale, NJ: Jason Aronson.

Stern, D. (1985). *The Interpersonal World of the Infant*. New York: Basic Books.

Stone, M. (1988). Toward a psychobiological theory of borderline personality disorder: is irritability the red thread that runs through borderline conditions? *Dissociation* 1:2–15.

Taylor, G. (1977). Alexithymia and the counter-transference. *Psychotherapy and Psychosomatics* 28:141–147.

Thomas, A., and Chess, S. (1977). *Temperament and Development*. New York: Breuner/Mazel.

Trevarthen, C. (1983). Development of the cerebral mechanisms of language. In *Neuropsychology of Language, Reading, and Spelling*, ed. V. Kirk, pp. 45–80. New York: Academic Press.

Tustin, F. (1981a). Psychological birth and psychological catastrophe. In *Do I Dare Disturb the Universe? A Memorial to Wilfred R. Bion*, ed. J. Grotstein, pp. 181–196. Beverly Hills, CA: Caesura Press.

—— (1981b). *Autistic States in Children*. London: Routledge and Kegan Paul.

—— (1986). *Autistic Barriers in Neurotic Patients*. New Haven: Yale University Press.

—— (1988). The "black hole"—a significant development in autism. *Free Associations* 11:35–50.

Wheeler, J. A. (1968). As quoted in Pagels (1985).

Winnicott, D. W. (1951). Transitional objects and transitional phenomenon. In *Collected Papers: Through Paediatrics to Psycho-Analysis*, pp. 229–242. New York: Basic Books, 1958.

—— (1952). Psychoses and child care. In *Collected Papers: Through Paediatrics to Psycho-Analysis*, pp. 219–228. New York: Basic Books, 1958.

—— (1956). Primary maternal preoccupation. In *Collected Papers: Through Paediatrics to Psycho-Analysis*, pp. 300–305. New York: Basic Books, 1958.

—— (1960). The theory of the parent–infant relationship. In *The Maturational Processes and the Facilitating Environment*, pp. 37–55. New York: International Universities Press, 1965.

—— (1963). Communicating and not communicating leading to a study of certain opposites. In *The Maturational Processes and the Facilitating Environment*, pp. 179–192.

—— (1971). *Playing and Reality*. London: Tavistock.

—— (1973). Fear of breakdown. *International Review of Psycho-Analysis* 1:103–107.

6

DAVID ROSENFELD, M.D.

Psychotic Body Image

Learn this, Thomas,
And thou shalt prove a shelter to thy friends,
A hoop of gold to bind thy brothers in
That the united vessel of their blood . . .
> W. Shakespeare, *King Henry IV, Part II*
> Act IV, Scene 4

This chapter is a theoretical conceptualization of the body image, based on psychoanalytic psychotherapy with psychotic patients going through acute crises as well as some psychosomatic disturbances.[1] I will try to define and describe, from a clinical point of view, a new concept of psychotic body image and neurotic body image.

When Freud (1914) speaks of the body, he refers to the projection of the ego onto the body's surface and describes the organization of the libido in the body. He also deals with the development of the erogenous zones, the way in which they are represented, and their importance in the formation of the body ego. The development of sexual libido takes place in major concentration zones that are in contact with the external world. Hence the paramount importance attached to orifices and their relationship with the external world; the relationship of each of them with the outer world prevails in the different developmental stages.

Anzieu (1974, 1987) points out that Freud did not confine the so-called oral phase to experiences related solely to the buccal-pharyngeal zone and the pleasure of sucking. He stresses the importance of the subsequent

---

[1] I wish to thank Noemi Rosenblatt and Dr. L. Bryce Boyer for assistance with the translation from the Spanish.

pleasure derived from feeling full inside. Anzieu also adds that just as the mouth provides the first experience of a differentiating contact and of an incorporation, feeling full inside, though usually neglected in the literature, would provide the infant with a more pervasive and lasting experience: the perception of a central mass, fullness, a center of gravity. Anzieu uses the term *moi-peau* (ego-skin) to describe an image used by the child's thinking during the early developmental phases to represent himself as self, on the basis of his experience of the body's surface. This corresponds to the period in which the "psychic ego" becomes differentiated from the "body ego" from an operational point of view but remains fused with it on a figurative level.

Bick (1968, 1986) has presented a wealth of clinical material to describe the development and growth of a mental perception of a skin and its relationship with introjection and projective identification.

I have discussed previously thoughts about the body image and its relationship to the patient's conceptualization of the skin (Rosenfeld 1975). In that presentation I described how a patient who suffered from a skin disorder acted out in his relationship with me the period of his infancy in which the skin disturbances had their origin. Additionally, in his sessions he repeated one of the aspects of the fairy tale *"Peau d'Âne"* ("The Skin of the Ass"). This patient felt he had lost his skin, comparing his experience to that of a crab that has lost its shell, and he was afraid of becoming an amoeba or a slug without any external envelope or endoskeleton. When I discussed this case with E. Bick, we were able to detect the mechanisms the patient employed to enable him to believe he could penetrate into the object in order to live parasitically inside somebody else's skin (Rosenfeld 1984, 1985, 1986a, 1988).

I would like to draw a distinction between these cases and those I shall now discuss: patients in whom the conceptualization of a skin has been lost. Rather than attempting to explain the disturbances in the notion of a skin, I will try to describe a certain type of body image where that notion does not exist. Another new concept is the notion of liquids as the nucleus of the psychotic body image and their possible transformation into solid or semi-solid substances as an indication of a change in connection with the body image, that is, a more integrated ego nucleus, which shows a different type of structuralization of the self and the body image. This may be seen, for instance, in the material of a patient, Agnes, when she dreams for the first time of something semi-solid, chewing gum, in her mouth.

By *psychotic body image* I mean the most primitive notion of the body image to be observed in certain patients whose work begins while they are already regressed or who regress during their treatment. In my view, the extreme notion of what can be conceived of as psychotic body image is the thought that the body contains only liquid, one or another derivative of blood, and that it is coated by an arterial or venous wall or walls. These vascular sheaths take over the functions that normally are fulfilled psychologically by the actual skin, the muscles, and the skeleton. There is only a vague notion of a wall that contains blood or vital liquids.

In turn, as can be seen mainly in crises associated with acute psychosis, this membrane containing the blood may be perceived to have broken or to have been damaged otherwise and to result in a loss of bodily contents, leaving the body empty, without either internal or external containment and/or support. Sometimes, the experience of becoming empty is expressed linguistically through a sudden and incessant verbal flow: The patient cannot stop talking.

The notion of a psychotic body image is not limited to clinical cases who are phenomenologically psychotic. It may be present in personalities that are neurotically adjusted to reality; I would even say that the psychotic body image prevails in personalities that may be very well adjusted to reality, for example, some psychosomatic cases. This psychotic conception of the body breaks through and invades what up to that moment was a different kind of mental functioning, and this may be expressed either through words or averbally through body language, in the psychosomatic disturbances. Additionally, the regression to the concept of the psychotic body image occurs at times during periods of personal crisis, as I have observed in patients following cardiovascular surgery.

We can speak of a *neurotic body image* (closer to the notion of normality) when there is an unconscious mental representation of the skin that warmly covers and contains the body image. The most normal psychological notion of skin is that representing the parents who warmly hold and contain the child's body (Bick 1968, 1986, Tustin 1986).

PART 1

I have been able to observe in various clinical disturbances that the idea of the protective membrane or skin sometimes disappears, especially when there is object loss or destructuration. These are patients who retain the idea that their bodies remain continuous with their mothers'; when she leaves, the child feels she takes parts of its body with her. Such patients are left without a skin every time there is a separation or a relationship is lost. Thus, in periods of crisis, of mourning, and due to object loss, they react as follows: The blood vessels function as a self-containment membrane in the patient's response to feeling empty. Bick has suggested the concept of a second skin as a substitute for the psychological notion of an external skin; this second skin is sometimes achieved through muscular hyperactivity. In neurotics there may be hypochondriac ideas related to the psychotic body image, as of suffering from leukemia or hemophilia. Clinically, under these circumstances a psychotic body image prevails. Every hypochondriac disturbance expressed through the psychotic body image should alert us to the possibility of a suicidal attempt or some accident of a suicidal nature. The likelihood of suicidal risk should also be taken into account in cases of drug addiction in which a psychotic body image prevails, for instance, intravenous self-administration of drugs, or when the patient has hypochondriac fantasies concerning the possibility of a blood infection. As an example, a patient may inject himself intravenously with antibiotics on the basis of such a hypochondriac fantasy (Santamaría 1978, Bucahi 1980).

The notion of becoming empty of blood has its origin in the earliest infantile relationships and in experiences based on body object relationships; every psychic activity is based on a biological function. For instance, the notion of projective identification does not arise in a child as an abstract theoretical conception; rather, it stems from body experiences and object relationships, for instance, putting out the tongue in search for the nipple without being able to find it. According to Tustin (1977), the baby then feels that he falls into a vacuum, and this becomes a model of becoming empty through projective identification. The hand of a baby who tries to get hold of the breast and cannot find it is a similar model. The hand and the attempt to grasp the breast allow me to express my own "model" related to the psychotic body image. When a child tries to grasp the breast with his hand and cannot find it, he may, in a second step, try to contain himself by pressing his fingers hard against the palm of his hand, even to the point of hurting himself with his nails. But when this self-containment system fails and there is no other, the idea is present that the arteries and veins begin to function like the palm of the hand in order to achieve self-containment: They close up or contract in the person's desperate effort to achieve self-containment, but at the level of the psychotic body image. The idea of a skin is displaced to a notion of vascular walls. The normal concept that the baby or regressed patient can derive from its primary relationship with the breast is that of a mouth with a nipple that has a warm skin, accompanied by a familiar smell and voice, as described by Bick. But when a relationship is based on the psychotic body image, the relationship with the breast seems to become established without the notion of a nipple covered with skin. A liquid merges with another liquid: milk, saliva, blood—a cocktail of liquids. This is particularly true when a child loses its mother or is separated from her; being abandoned by the maternal object is not experienced by the infant as losing the nipple from inside its mouth but as if it were being skinned and as if the mother takes with her the external surface or skin of its body covering when she leaves. Due to the infant's experiencing his skin as continuous with the mother's and the equation skin = vascular wall, the psychotic body image arises.

It is my belief that this notion of psychological self-containment provided by a wall or by arteries or veins may be at the root of certain psychosomatic disturbances.

The notion of liquids that spill often emerges in schizophrenic patients when they express their feeling of emptiness at the level of the psychotic body image. I have observed that, after many years of treatment, and if the patient improves, instead of the loss of liquids or blood, he sometimes begins to express fantasies of becoming empty of more solid substances, for instance, through dreams in which the car "loses" oil, and later of even more solid substances, like feces. I believe it is only here that the ideas of holding the object at the anal retentive level begin to manifest themselves. As an example, after six years of treatment a schizophrenic patient no longer dreams before the holidays that he becomes empty of liquids or blood; instead he dreams of losing solid feces, and this is accompanied by a period of anal masturbation. On the other hand, in the psychotic body image the notions about becoming empty correspond to a more narcissistic level, and the patient does not become empty through an erogenous zone but through his pores.

I think it is only after this stage that anal masturbation, as described by Meltzer (1966), can be analyzed. I suspect that when the psychotic body image prevails, the function of the rectum, of the anus, and of anal masturbation lacks the structuralization it has when it is based on the neurotic body image.[2]

Avenburg (1975) made us aware of the great similarity between what I am describing here and the concept of libido stagnation formulated by Freud, who spoke as if what became stagnated was a liquid. It is then a process of fluidization, of loss of quality, of dedifferentiation, similar to what happens when one liquid becomes mixed with another in the psychotic body image, in which self-discrimination is lost. According to Avenburg, the German word *Staung* used by Freud refers specifically to stopping the flow of a liquid.

----

[2]This formulation is important, in that it implies the need for technical approaches to anal masturbation, involving sensitive timing and different levels of interpretation.

On the basis of my experience with regressed patients, I am currently more convinced of the possible relation between hypertension and the conception of the psychotic body image. Through dreams and fantasies brought systematically into the analytic material, a patient revealed that he conceived of himself as possessing neither skin nor muscles, but instead he imagined that his sensations of movement were produced solely by contractions and other movements of arteries. The following two examples come from patients under supervision.

> The first patient develops hypochondria and imagines she has hypertension; she takes her blood pressure five or six times daily in an effort to corroborate her fantasy. What is of special interest is that she conceives of her body as a bag of fluids or blood, which empties out. The imaginary hypertension defends her against the feeling of emptiness, and the hypertension is conceived to result from being full of blood.
>
> The hypertension of a second woman has developed into a psychosomatic illness. The onset of her high blood pressure had coincided with her acting out by abandoning her psychoanalysis a month before the summer holidays; she required medical treatment. When she resumed treatment, her hypertension disappeared, and did not reappear. This patient also functions with a psychotic body image. Not being in a position to contribute a physiological or other medical explanation for this observation, I resort to citing the words of an eminent hypertension researcher, even though they are not original with her. "Hypertension is a riddle wrapped in a mystery inside an enigma" (Page and Durstan 1962, p. 433).

Models, Philosophy of Science, and Methodology

The concepts described constitute, from the methodological point of view, an explanatory model. Many of the hypotheses we formulate result from what in the field of methodology is known as *inductive generalization*. But if I make an hypothesis or model as an explanatory model, albeit empirically based, there is no reason why it should be of a very low level of abstraction; on the contrary, it may attain a high explanatory level, even as a model.

For example, the atomic theory was not formulated on the basis of direct observation but of an explanatory model (Meadows 1969).

Every model is a pattern of symbols, rules, and proposals that are regarded, partly or wholly, as consistent with the set of existing postulates.

Thus, every model postulates its correspondence with reality, the possibility of establishing its usefulness in the structure of reality. It should be noted that the construction of a model is an inner logical creation and, as such, sometimes a function of the cultural model. As was the case with Niels Bohr, the model is invented. In psychoanalytic practice one may sometimes find examples like the ones I shall present, and that is why the psychotic body scheme is a useful explanatory model for a variety of clinical cases. This model helps me to incorporate into a single idea developmental genetic and transferential concepts that apply to schizophrenic and psychosomatic patients and others when regressed. When we invent a model, we find it useful first for one particular patient but then for other patients as well. If I add to it, provided it is consistent, a developmental-genetic theory of infantile bonds that may be empirically demonstrated in the transference with the therapist, I may say it is already a hypothesis of a high level of abstraction and I may even develop a sound theory (if it passes the philosopher Karl Popper's test).

The psychotic body scheme is a nonobservable entity, but, when we invent the model, it becomes powerful from the explanatory point of view. This does not mean that the model represents the ultimate truth, but only that it is a useful model for the time being.

Perhaps the origin of this scientific model may be best described through clinical observations.

(1) Two of my schizophrenic patients showed their fingernails or their hands to me and stated they were losing blood and were "bleeding out"; (2) my experience with postsurgery cardiac patients, who very often have delusions in the course of which they say, for instance, that nothing is left in them except veins and arteries; (3) another psychotic patient who kept talking about his low blood pressure, but eventually said to me, "I don't want to have a corn removed because, if I do, they will realize I am hollow and with no blood inside." That is, I had to create a new and different explanatory model: When this psychotic patient speaks of his "low blood pressure," he really means that he is bleeding or that there is no blood left in his body. Then the observation was completed with the psychosomatic patients, and the model acquired paramount importance (see the case of Agnes below).

In other words, the model began to evolve and to show its usefulness for various psychopathological cases, and then became a more comprehensive model. If I then add a hypothesis about its genetic-historical origin, its evolution, and how it is shown in the transference, it becomes a fairly comprehensive and acceptable theory, if corroborated by clinical observations. The model began to be used for all these "psychopathological cases" and I found it useful from an explanatory point of view. When applied, for instance, to a severe psychosomatic case (Part 3, Agnes), it modified not only the theory but also the interpretive approach and, thus, the chances for survival in a seriously ill psychosomatic patient. The clinical evolution and the predictions that emerged may be quite novel.

Pierre, another patient, had a delusional episode after the removal of a (benign) brain tumor and, in the course of a session said, "I'm afraid of having leukemia. . . . I have begun to despair . . . to worry."

At that moment I asked him, "Why did you think of leukemia?"

And the patient answered immediately, "Because of the destruction of the red cells by the tumor. As if I were afraid of becoming empty . . . emptied of blood . . . as if I were soft all over. . . ."

Then I asked him, "Soft?"

He replied, "Yes, everything soft . . . like a sack full of blood. . . . I'm afraid of having a hemorrhage, and that everything . . . will come out. . . ."

The accuracy with which he expresses his fantasies concerning his body image is remarkable. The conception of the body as a sack full of vital fluids or blood (primitive psychotic body scheme) is clearly formulated here on a verbal level. The patient can express it with words, whereas Agnes acts it out through body behaviors, hemorrhages through the skin, because she cannot symbolize it verbally.

I also found this model quite useful for other psychosomatic pictures, like ulcerative colitis, that is, patients with diarrhea and loss of blood through the bowels. We have postulated that this illness may be explained on the basis of the primitive psychotic body scheme model, and invite validation. In several patients with ulcerative colitis, I have observed the fantasy was more closely related to bleeding than to the anal level. These patients let a part of their bowels express the most regressive and primitive levels of their self, and it is on this level that they express their emotions, persecutions, sorrows, and aggressions.

Blood is lost through some kind of skin—in this case, the bowels (Agnes, in Part 3, does so through the oral mucosa and the skin of her hands and feet). The patient with ulcerative colitis bleeds out or loses vital fluids but through another type of skin. Both are similar as regards the infantile models of object relationship. Therefore, I would like to insist once again that the conceptions of vital fluid and blood constitute a *different* "observational model" that provides another approach to patients with ulcerative colitis, who used to be understood only in connection with the anal stage.

These patients conceive of their body image in a different way, and this is a new model for further research.

Another example is H., a 30-year-old woman, who, before the summer holidays, dreamed that she had lost her scalp, part of the right side of the skull, and also the brain, and saw, in the dream, only an artery on the right side, a large brain artery. This artery, containing blood, had lost part of the wall on the upper right side. She was afraid of having a hemorrhage through this open side of the artery. It was her way of expressing her feelings in connection with my abandonment. But exactly a year after, that is, before the holidays, she had the same dream, with the only but fundamental difference that the artery was whole and no longer open. Not all patients are capable of expressing such regressive and deep transference feelings through body images. It may be that this theory is valid only for those patients who can express it in this way. I do believe that this model or hypothesis will help many analysts to be more on the alert and will provide them with a methodological framework better suited for an accurate understanding of these clinical observations.

Methodologically, many loose and unconnected clinical observations may be put together by means of a hypothesis designed to explain a larger number of observational facts in psychoanalytic practice.

The primitive body scheme model, for instance, also helped me to create new hypotheses concerning a type of hypochondriasis that have different origin and dynamics (Rosenfeld 1985).

PART 2

Now, lords, if God doth give successful end
To this debate that bleedeth at our doors,
We will our youth lead on to higher fields.
W. Shakespeare, *King Henry IV, Part II,*
Act IV, Scene 4

In order to show how a psychotic patient may express himself at the level of the body image, I will present two brief clinical illustrations in order to show how these patients express, through visual or corporal images, the most primitive notions of their self, which we call *corporal scheme* or *body image*. In this section, I first present case material pertaining to John, a 19-year-old patient of a supervisee, and then fragments of clinical material pertaining to Pierre, a patient treated by me. We will be able to observe the way in which I intervene and interpret the transference in a postoperative psychosis rooted mainly in fantasies about the psychotic primitive corporal scheme (P. C. S.).

John started treatment in July 1972 when, after a trip, he was hospitalized in an acute psychotic crisis.[3] He said, early in the first interview, "Every time I meet a girl, I surrender, I fall in love, and I bleed in her." He also said repeatedly, "I want to kill myself; there is no love in return, I bleed in her." He fixed his eyes on the therapist's eyes and told her something that he would repeat several times in the course of his treatment, "Your eyes give me life."[4] In the first session he verbalized another fantasy of the emptying that occurs in the presence of the psychotic body image, "I came into the world to bleed myself because of my love for all human beings. I am paying for my guilt over my sins." Later on he added, "I masturbate and people see it on my face." This material, that is, that people in the outside world see something specific on his face, seems to be an attempt at restitution through a self-reference delusion. He told a dream: "I was going to school. I came across Miriam but, Doctor, even if I wanted to I couldn't love her more. Are you going to watch Monzón's fight today?"[5] Apparently this is taken up again in the following session: "Suffering prevents me from loving." The understanding of this concept is essential for our comprehension of the suffering of a psychotic patient. Next he described another fantasy of the emptying existent in the primitive or psychotic body image, talking about cows that kill the butcher who is about to slaughter them. At that moment we understood this material as a retaliatory fantasy in which a breast-cow becomes revengeful.

Another possible meaning is that the attempt to bleed his mother's breast very soon turns into his own bleeding, showing the prevalence of the psychotic body image. Such material reappeared a week later, after he had been afraid that he would faint if he went to a party. It is interesting to distinguish between the different diagnoses: the fear to "feel sick or have low blood pressure" in a case of hysteria or anxiety hysteria, where the body may express sickness directly and, at a schizophrenic level, when a patient speaks of feeling sick or of having low blood pressure he is likely to have felt bled empty in the previous sessions. The same may hold true in distinguishing

---

[3] I wish to thank Dr. Delia Pistol for permission to use this material. See also Rosenfeld and Pistol (1986).

[4] It is usual during this type of acute episode for the patient to rivet his eyes to the therapist's eyes, as a baby looks at his mother's eyes during nursing.

[5] We may see here that dreams and waking life material are mixed in the description of the dream, which points to a dream-like mental state.

the material of patients who speak of "having a low blood pressure" or of "feeling empty or weak inside." It is important to make a differential diagnosis between a depressive patient who expresses his sadness by saying his blood pressure is low and a schizophrenic patient who, in the course of his treatment, spoke about having low blood pressure, which we could understand to represent a fantasy of his having been emptied. Some months later he said that his body was hollow; that is, he then experienced the psychotic body image. Another time, when he had to have a wart removed, he felt panicky because, "If that wart or corn was removed, they would know that I am hollow inside." That is, although phenomenologically the words are the same as a depressive neurotic would use, this psychotic patient expressed through them his experience of emptying out the inside of his body and the presence or prevalence of the psychotic body image.

But let us go back to John, our patient. In December 1972, he had another fragmentation episode, this time expressed through projective identification as his being in many pieces, in the form of thousands of cards that he distributed. But how did he return in March from Argentina, after the summer holidays? He no longer spoke of the cards he had distributed. Instead, he regressed, saying he was empty and hollow. That is, he was functioning at the level of the psychotic body image. Such material persisted until July. In March 1973 there was another fantasy related to the emptying of the psychotic body image: The patient said his mother "takes away from me and leaves me empty." A week afterward he organized a delusion and produced material including a satyr-penis or persecutory satyr. In June of the same year he dreamed again about the regressed body image; he had nothing left except his skeleton, and no other support. Here the fantasy of being emptied of liquids and blood seemed to be a kind of retribution for the possibility of retaining the skeleton. In my experience the skeleton by itself in dreams or drawings, no matter how ill the patient may be, has always proved, in the long run, to indicate an identification with the father or the paternal role. Some patients hold that the penis provides the breast with firmness. It may also be the father who is capable of taking care of the nursing mother. I thought that John's compulsive masturbation was an attempt to prove, among other things, that since at least some liquid came out from inside his body, he was not completely empty, thus reducing the intolerable feeling of utter emptiness and hollowness that implied madness. This schizophrenic patient felt that sexual intercourse amounted to bleeding; an acute psychotic crisis was for him a way of expressing his becoming empty in coitus, while a

delusion was an attempt at restitution vis à vis what he experienced as
the bleeding of the body-self. During the 1974 (Argentinian) summer
holiday he was unable to retain an image of the therapist. Following
the loss of her intrapsychic representation as an object, in March he
experienced fusion with her as fluid in a vascular sheath. He brought a
restitutive delusional fantasy: He felt capable of finding God, with
whom he identified and whom he hallucinated. In May, the patient
described his fantasy of bleeding during coitus; before having intercourse he shot several cats, watching them bleed to death.[6] Later on he
expressed object losses at the level of the psychotic body image: "I am
afraid of being emptied of you and of losing you."

A year later, in June 1975, he expressed clearly for the first time that
becoming hollow was being emptied of something *good*; that is, a prior
introjection of the benevolent therapist had taken place. Expressing his
gratitude to his therapist, he said that in his loss of her "One is emptied
of what is good." In another psychotic area, of course, persisted the
belief that he was God and that the devil was in others. The fantasies
near the end of that year concerning parting from his therapist before
the holidays were expressed in terms of blood and of the psychotic body
image through a fantasy of anastomosis and fusion with the therapist
(Searles 1961). In December 1975 he said: "If my blood spills, after me
the others which will exist will spill too."

In March 1976, after the end of the holidays, he developed a
delusion, intensified by the fact that his sessions were reduced from five
to four times weekly. He tried to compensate for the object loss and
feeling of emptiness by hallucinating the body of a girl. We understood
this to mean that the search for the missing breast was carried out by
means of an identification with the breast and that he tried to come
close to the therapist on the basis of this feminine identification. Three
months later the patient tried to reestablish his relationship with the
therapist through an organizing delusion, something better than the
complete loss of the object. He then chose a singer, Sandro, with whom
he identified through a fantasied homosexual relationship. Here I would
like to point out something important: This is the first emergence of an
aesthetic hysterical level concerning blood or the psychotic body image.
Ordinarily, the object loss experienced due to the loss of a single session
meant to the patient the end of the world, and was expressed at the level

---

[6]To imagine that one bleeds during coitus is at the root of many cases of sexual
impotence that are hard to cure and derive from the psychotic body image.

of the psychotic body image as the loss of blood. This time he expressed his becoming empty of blood at an aesthetic level, as happens with certain patients who have reached the hysterical level. He spoke about condoms that were as red as blood and about others that were blue.

The emergence of red and blue expresses the emptying of blood or of the psychotic body image in some patients with their attempts to express it at an aesthetic-hysterical level. Garzoli (1979) reported that a female patient dreamed that "while on the stretcher she had a transparent vision of herself, in which thick blue veins and red arteries could be clearly seen." An example of this may be found in the film *All That Jazz*,[7] when the final ballet expresses the death anxiety of the main character, who dances with his veins and arteries drawn in blue and red all over his body.

Once John became empty of the liquids of the psychotic body image, he tried to compensate by developing a strict obsessive order in connection with timetables and the like. The obsessive level was new and provided very important clues that must be taken into account to understand how this patient then behaved in December 1976. For the first time his preseparation fantasies did not include bleeding. In July 1977 he could express at the verbal level the fantasies of emptying of his psychotic body image: "Before I became empty, I could throw you out by masturbating. Now I can't." On earlier occasions of psychotic crisis the loss of semen, liquids, or blood had been equated in his thinking, and caused total emptying. Additionally, the patient now expressed on an apparently genital sexual level how he tried to expel his persecutory objects. This is quite interesting from a clinical point of view; if he had remained fixed at the level of blood, the diagnosis could be different. For example, patients who have delusional persecutory objects (the mother, for instance) fixed at the level of their psychotic body image may attempt to cut their veins in order to get rid of the thousand persecutory objects that have gotten into their blood.

I want to make clear that when I speak of persecutory objects in very disturbed patients I mean that they are genuine delusions, sometimes not fully expressed on the verbal level. For instance, other patients take high doses of diuretics in order to expel, through their urine, persecutory objects that have become fixed in the body's liquids. To extend an earlier remark, I

---

[7]Bob Fosse film.

have come to the conclusion that every expulsion of persecutory objects through the body's liquids, like blood, urine, and so on should make us more alert to the patient's suicidal potential. For example, in the case of drug addicts who take amphetamines, it is interesting to observe that if the fantasy accompanying the introjection of the drug is believed to help them expel parts of the body such as urine or feces that prevent them from thinking, special attention should be paid to a possible hidden, suicidal fantasy or, which is the same, proneness to have a suicidal or drug-induced accident (Boyer 1982, 1983).

Coming back to John, there came a time when he expressed his emptiness at all possible levels. I would like to add something else: Becoming empty of the liquids or blood of the psychotic body image can be expressed verbally, but when it is expressed in the body without any kind of verbal symbolization, we are faced with some of the psychosomatic disturbances. It is a peculiar type of dissociation, described by Liberman (1972).

I will now present some fragments of clinical material concerning one of my patients.

According to Pierre's relatives, he underwent periods in which he lost control of reality. One psychiatrist who had seen him thought his increasing alcohol intake was an effort to be unaware of periods of mental disorganization. He had been treated in supportive psychotherapy for two years, and received medication.

Pierre's relatives brought him to his first appointment. He looked older than his 43 years, and appeared to be exhausted. He lived with his mother and two brothers. His father had died five years previously, from multiple myeloma.

During the first session the patient was oriented as to time and place but was confused and felt persecuted. Previously he had sought to escape from apparently delirious persecutory episodes by fleeing from his home while carrying firearms and/or drinking great quantities of alcohol.

Noting that he had certain speech problems and nystagmus, I referred him to a neurologist, who found a tumor to have spread across the optic chiasma; immediate neurosurgery was recommended.

Pierre was terrified and asked me to remain by his side every day that he was confined to the hospital and especially requested that I hold his hand when he was anesthetized. While firmly clasping my hand he said, "Dad, dad . . ."

The extension and complexity of the case prevent me from transcribing it in its entirety, so I will reveal only brief fragments corresponding to the immediate postoperative period. This material brings to light in a very clear way the most primitive images of the patient's corporal scheme, and at the same time shows my interpretations of the transference. I beg readers to interpret my brief account as an example of how a patient may express this model of the PCS (primitive corporal scheme).[8]

He underwent an immediate postoperative psychotic episode: a delirium in which he was convinced that vital fluids were being extracted from his body, encephalic-spinal liquid, blood, semen, and urine. The third night after the operation Pierre sought to verify that he had not been completely drained of liquids, and, for this purpose, he had sexual relations with his girlfriend in his hospital bed. His intention, according to his own words, was "to see if any liquid came out. . . ."

During the postoperative period, Pierre oscillated between confusional states and semi-clarity. At times he was convinced that he or I was his dead father.

I will now reproduce parts of the material corresponding to the first weeks after the operation. These fragments underscore fantasies regarding Pierre's bodily image or corporal scheme, and show the way in which I intervened when he identified with his dead father and believed that I was persecuting him.

1. During a session the first week after the operation, the patient said:

P.:   I want to urinate, it scares me, three times a day. I'm going to urinate.

R.:   You're afraid to go urinate. . . .

P.:   It scares me because . . . (he stutters) you know? I might get wet, right? . . . In reality I try not to urinate very much. I hold back.

R.:   What did you say? That you're afraid to urinate?

P.:   (In muddled language and stuttering). . . . yes, I'm afraid to urinate, I'm afraid to bleed . . . to have blood come out, you know? . . . That urinating blood might rush out and I could bleed to

---

[8]The encapsulated glioma was removed totally.

death. . . . I am afraid that the tumor is lodged in the bladder, prostate gland, testicles. . . . I think I have bone marrow metastasis.

In this and following material it became increasingly clear that the patient was convinced of the following: (1) that the tumor was not removed, (2) that he had malignant mestastases, (3) that he was his father with bone marrow cancer, (4) that I was deceiving him as his father was deceived.

In a session later in the week, the following interchange occurred:

P.:   Well . . . uh . . . last night I defecated and also urinated, right?
R.:   And did the fear remain?
P.:   Well, the fear seems . . . uh. . . . "What was the fecal material like?" . . . I told mom . . . because she was with me, it seems like I was afraid to go to the bathroom alone, right?
R.:   And what did you think?
P.:   Well, I thought I would bleed or something like that.
R.:   You thought lots of blood would come out?
P.:   Well, yes. . . . I think like an external hemorrhage. I made mom look at what came out.
R.:   Ah . . . and did you believe your mother when she looked at the feces, or did you have to look yourself?
P.:   No . . . I . . . uhh . . . yes, believed her, she said it is . . . (stutters) not very . . . hard, she said . . . it was a bit we could say mushy.
R.:   And did you believe it was blood, or did you have to look?
P.:   No . . . no . . . no . . . , I believed her that it was not blood . . . let me see . . . but I also looked . . . I also looked.
R.:   Ah, you looked just in case.
P.:   Yes, yes, yes . . . I also looked, yes . . .

2. In the third week after the operation we can observe my intervention in the delirious transference. I must make clear that the delirious transference with me increased every time that spinal-encephalic liquid was extracted from him for studies. I became someone who hurt him or took his vital fluids, a vampire. (He had been placed on anticonvulsive medication and was apprehensive, believing various personnel were seeking to harm him.)

During a session after he left the hospital, he said:

P.: Yes, I thought that the fact that you could not hurt me . . . that
you did not tell me the truth and did not solve my problem, you
know? . . . that is that I would not have . . . fear of going out on
the street, to walk . . . it seems that being confined here, it seems it
would be better . . . being like this in a daze taking the pills that
made me somewhat dizzy . . . and . . . like this in a daze, in a
dream, you know? It seems that I wouldn't like to think . . . the
reality of the operation, right? . . . It makes me shudder . . . it
seems it would make me afraid of the treatments I would have to
undergo, right? The puncture, the Epamin (anticonvulsive medication).

R.: But perhaps it is also me that you fear . . . you may believe that
everyone will hurt you . . . including me.

P.: That, that, that they hurt me (stutters), that they could not make
me overcome the tumor . . . that they did not love me, you know?
That everyone is lying to me as to a child, right? And me living
with mistrust and with . . . we could say on the verge of departure,
you know? . . . without stepping soundly, it would seem, isn't it
true? The earth could split at any moment . . . (silence) and I
would be ashamed of crying, you know? That is why it's as if rage
gripped me, it seems that I do that before crying in front of you
. . . of . . . (stuttering) today . . . I was crying in front of my
mother, right? This morning she made me have trust, you see? But
I started crying because she was explaining to me the case of
Pinky, a girl who had metastasis and a number of operations.

3. The following fragment, which occurred during the third week
after the operation, depicts my interpretation of the transference related
to the psychotic identification where the patient believes he is the father
with bone marrow cancer.

During the session, while he talked about his meals, Pierre said:

P.: It's as if this were . . . uh . . . the desire to gain weight, don't you
think?

R.: Are you afraid of losing weight?

P.: It would appear so. Dad lost weight when he had the myeloma.

R.: Do you realize this panic you have is because you think you are
your father?

P.:   It seems as though I were dad with all the same symptoms, right?
That I might limp, that the medication were destroying me as
dialysis seemed to destroy him, right? And it seems I'm afraid I
might have to undergo dialysis, right? It's as if I had the tumor . . .
and the tumor had invaded all of me, that the operation was too
late, you know? That you had lied in the diagnosis, when you read
me . . . how do you call it?

R.:   The (anatopathological)?

P.:   The (anatopathological), yes.

R.:   You speak as if you were convinced that you still have the disease—
bone marrow cancer—and they haven't solved anything. So now
you stopped being Pierre and turned into dad, you think you are
dad with the myeloma and make me take the place of Pierre who is
deceiving you, and you think you are dad. . . . Do you follow me?
And you believe I deceive you like they deceived your father with the
diagnosis . . . and you pretend or believe to be the deceived dad. . . .

The patient's gradual acceptance over a period of several days of
this interpretation relieved this particular psychotic regression. Interpretation was the regular means, throughout his treatment, of helping
him reverse psychotic regressions. Although the use of regression as a
defense was not emphasized in the given example, it was an almost
regular element of effective interpretations.

I shall discuss how the fantasy of bleeding is expressed in the actual
body through a severe illness where the patient really bleeds . . . she loses
blood through the skin.

PART 3

I am mad in the blood [words of a female patient, Agnes, in the
course of a session].

This material pertains to Agnes, a patient in whose functioning
the psychotic body image prevails, a fact that is expressed through a
body language in a psychosomatic illness. The patient,[9] a 26-year-old

---

[9]A patient of Dr. Gloria Hanoni, a supervisee, who graciously permitted me to
use this material. I supervised this case for nine years.

woman, said she became aware of her illness after she and her boyfriend broke off. She wanted to be treated because "I am depressed, I want to die." She said that her illness consisted of necrosed sores in various mucosal areas and the skin and that, according to the many doctors who had sought to diagnose and treat her, their origin was unknown. The physicians considered her case to be hopeless in view of the severity of her illness: When she underwent any emotional crisis, the vascular inflammation and necrosis of the mucosae of the mouth, larynx, and lips were indeed severe. On one such occasion, she was unable to speak or eat for six months and had to be fed intravenously. One acute crisis resulted in a coma that lasted three days. The patient added, "There is no longer a prognosis for my illness," and, "At this moment I don't have so many necrotic sores on my legs."

I briefly summarize a startling phenomenon. Each time Agnes was left, her transference reaction could be understood as giving evidence of the psychotic body image. When she felt abandoned, her ulcerations actually became more severe and her bleeding and oozing increased. When she began to improve, she had a physical defensive response, a vasoconstriction of the arterioles that reduced both the dermal and the mucosal necrosis.

This case is typical of the way in which the use and functioning of the psychotic body image becomes rigid. The reemergence in times of crisis of the old psychotic body image becomes chronic, and this takes place in cases of infantile or psychotic autism, where what was once primary normal autism becomes pathological later on (Tustin 1972, 1981, 1986).

Three years of treatment led to an understanding of the nature of the patient's transference and enabled us to study more thoroughly, almost microscopically, the origin of her bleeding sores and necrosis, which were correlated with specific stages in the analytic transference. In 1976 Agnes could say that she felt something *before* the appearance of her sores. This was the first step, a small one indeed. She began to perceive affects instead of expressing them concretely through her body. On the basis of the psychotic body image, menstruation meant for this patient that her body self was going to be completely emptied of blood. That same year she had to undergo plastic surgery in order to reshape her mouth and lips, distorted by the severe skin and mucosal necrosis. Here we can study in greater detail material associated with the relationship between the nipple and the mouth, that is, her transference relationship with her female therapist.

(1) Due to the lack of psychological boundaries between her body and the therapist's breast that she imagined sucking, every separation or loss meant to her that the nipple takes or tears away from her fragments of her own skin. The nipple decorticates her, depriving her of her body's outer boundaries. (2) There is a fantasied murderous attack on the objects that abandon her (in this period it became possible to understand the deeper reasons that triggered the organic disturbance in connection with the loss of her boyfriend). (3) The lost object takes away with it pieces of the membrane, and she bleeds through her pores. (4) The confusion of subject-object-lips-nipple leads to the attack on the object in a space within her nondifferentiated body; therefore, to attack the nipple implies an attack against her own lips. The lack of boundaries (fusion) (Mahler 1968, Searles 1979) is the reason why, by attacking the object that abandons her, she becomes identified with parts of her own body's surface. This explains how she can attack and destroy her own body's envelopment: She is left with venous or arterial walls containing blood as her only conception of a body image. In this case, *the arterial and venous walls take over the function that should be fulfilled by the normal skin.*

In 1977, in connection with the transference experiences, it was possible to detect, on the basis of childhood material, that the mother had become pregnant when the patient was not yet 12 months old. That is, she was precociously abandoned by her mother in connection with her affect needs and during the period of structuralization of the body image (Abraham 1945, Pichon Rivière 1964, Schilder 1935, Scott 1948). Before the 1976 holidays there was a new intensification of the feeling of becoming empty of blood, manifested mainly in bodily terms—sores and necrosis—during the therapist's absence.

I would like to stress that I deal here with the *psychological* experience of the notion of a protective skin that covers and protects the body. The same applies to the psychological notion that Agnes's body is a kind of large artery or vein about to be perforated, but in no way do I refer to the organic concrete body, or to its anatomy, such as can be studied in anatomy or histology.

In my view, the type of hypochondria centered on and expressed through the psychotic body image is different from all others, not only because it concerns the blood or the psychotic body image, but also because in my experience it implies the danger of "accidents" or suicidal attempts. I refer to more active methods than those implied by Marty and colleagues

(1963, p. 355) (see Oliner 1988). Everything concerning the psychotic body image corresponds to a more primitive and psychotic level. Here, as in the case of other patients, the fantasy of suffering from leukemia is an example of a hypochondriac disturbance centered on the psychotic body image. It may indicate anything from becoming empty of blood to a severe persecutory delusion in connection with monsters or organisms that eat away the blood or an attempt at achieving hypochondriac control. These delusions sometimes bring about suicidal attempts, such as cutting one's veins to expel and get rid of persecutory objects that have already invaded the psychotic body image. There may emerge transient hypochondriac fantasies concerning blood in every neurotic personality, and always when there is a reemergence of the body image based on the psychotic body image.

I will attempt to illustrate this point by presenting dream material obtained from Agnes. It should be noticed that in the case of severely disturbed patients nocturnal dreams may appear only after a long period of treatment. The first dream, six years after the beginning of treatment, concerns some chewing gum the patient has and keeps in her mouth. This is the first time there is a representation of something she keeps. Besides, it is semi-solid—different from the fluid that oozes out through all her pores—and, additionally, it is centered in a circumscribed erogenous zone: the mouth.

In 1978 there is a period in which she can symbolize her fantasies through her dreams, while the disturbances of the body image are expressed on the linguistic level in a very peculiar way; for instance, the orifices do not appear in her skin but in her speech, which begins to lose the normal linguistic structure, that is, the "social skin." At a linguistic level, speech disorganization may express destructuration of the body image (Liberman 1972). The loss of the body's surface or skin is now expressed as the loss of the structuring envelopment of speech, but without reaching the point of psychotic disintegration at a linguistic level. During this period that patient dreams of "a little woolen dress, knitted with holes and given as a present to a little girl": fragments of skin-dress that cover her incompletely. The fact that the dream material shows that the loss or emptiness is not related to liquid or blood and that more solid materials, which are easier to retain, begin to appear, for instance, solid feces, is a very important clue that marks the beginning—though only the beginning—of her functioning on the basis of the neurotic body image and shows that the psychotic body image is not so dominant. In the content of this dream the body is also emptied of its contents, but this time they are not only liquids or blood, but also feces that are hard and seen as a penis (Freud-Hawelka 1974). Besides being more solid, they are contained or introduced inside an orifice in her own body (vagina), which contains it. In connection with the psychotic body image, this is expressed at a different developmental level: The patient says in the course of a session, ". . . Oh! I remembered a dream. . . . I was in the waiting room, laughing to myself, when I remembered. Is the session over?" (She laughs.) "I took out a . . . I don't know what to call it . . . puf . . . ouch uf . . ." (She makes noises.) "I kept quiet to see the expression on your face." The therapist pointed out that she, unlike the patient, was *not* alarmed or frightened. Then the patient seemed to believe the therapist and continued: "Well, shit came out, a very long one. . . . My God! It wasn't sticky, it was not disintegrated . . . to put it into my vagina . . . what a masturbation fantasy!"

In November 1979 the patient brought a dream including material related to the loss of blood associated with menstruation, in which she showed that a towel was not stained with menstrual blood. But menstruation was not expressed as before, that is, when she believed it implied bleeding through all the pores (we are reminded here of her sores every month). It could now be seen that she denied the bloodstain on the towel, and this implied a denial of the loss of blood which was closer to containment than to becoming empty. It was the equivalent of what the patient had expressed before through vasoconstriction; now it had a symbolic manifestation in the fact that blood did not come out and did not stain. The important thing now was that she could dream of this and symbolize it. Before, she expressed through the psychotic body image her feeling empty and the vasoconstriction through her skin injuries. When an inner space may be created (Bick 1968), and also a mental space between the patient and the therapist (Anzieu 1974, 1987, Winnicott 1957), another stage has begun. In a patient with such a severe illness, this stage brings with it the hope that the struggle or the battle will cease to be expressed through the body and will reach mental transference levels.

We hope, as Shakespeare says, that

. . . if God doth give successful end to this debate that bleedeth at our doors, we will our youth lead on to higher fields. . . .
[*King Henry IV, Part II*, Act IV, Scene 4]

REFERENCES

Abraham, K. (1945). *Selected Papers on Psycho-Analysis.* London: Hogarth.

Anzieu, D. (1974). Le moi-peau. *Nouvelle Revue de Psychanalyse* 9:195-208.

Anzieu, D., Houzel, D., et al. (1987). *Les Enveloppes Psychiques.* Paris: Dunod.

Avenburg, R. (1975). *El Aparato Psíquico y la Realidad.* Buenos Aires: Nueva Visión.

Bick, E. (1968). The experience of the skin in early object relations. *International Journal of Psycho-Analysis* 49:484-486.

———— (1986). Further considerations on the skin in early relations. Findings from infant observations integrated into child and adult analysis. *British Journal of Psychotherapy* 2:292-299.

Bleger, J. (1967). *Simbiosis y Ambigüedad.* Buenos Aires: Paidós.

Boyer, L. B. (1982). Analytic experiences in work with regressed patients. In *Technical Factors in the Treatment of the Severely Disturbed Patient,* ed. P. L. Giovacchini and L. B. Boyer, pp. 65-106. New York: Jason Aronson.

———— (1983). *The Regressed Patient.* New York: Jason Aronson.

Bucahi, J. (1980). Personal communication.

Freud, S. (1914). On narcissism: an introduction. *Standard Edition* 14:73-102.

———— (1917). Mourning and melancholia. *Standard Edition* 14:237-258.

Freud, S., and Hawelka, E. (1974). *L'Homme aux Rats.* Paris: Presses Universitaires de France.

Garzoli, E. (1979). La interpretación y los sueños. Symposium of the Buenos Aires Psychoanalytic Association.

Klimovsky, G. (1980). Teorías científicas, estructura y validación. In *Métodos en Psicologia,* ed. C. Zizniesky, pp. 59-70. Buenos Aires: Nueva Visión.

Liberman, D. (1972). *Lingüística, Interacción Comunicativa y Proceso Psicoanalítico.* Buenos Aires: Nueva Visión.

Mahler, M. (1968). *On Human Symbiosis and the Vicissitudes of Individuation.* Vol. 1. New York: International Universities Press.

Marty, P., M'Uzan, M., and David, C. (1963). *L'Investigation Psychosomatique. Sept Observations Cliniques.* Paris: Presses Universitaires de France.

Meadows, P. (1969). *Módelos, Sistemas y Ciencia.* Buenos Aires: University of Buenos Aires Publications.

Meltzer, D. (1966). The relation of anal masturbation to projective identification. *International Journal of Psycho-Analysis* 47:335-343.

Oliner, M. M. (1988). *Cultivating Freud's Garden in France.* Northvale, NJ: Jason Aronson.

Page, I. H., and Durstan, H. (1962). Persistence of normal blood pressure after discontinuing treatment in hypertensive patients. *Circulation* 62:433-436.

Pichon-Rivière, E. (1964). *Del Psicoanálisis a la Psicología Social.* Buenos Aires: Galerna.

Rosenfeld, D. (1975). Trastornos en lo piel y el esquema corporal. Identificación proyectiva y el cuento infantil "Piel de Asno." *Revista de Psicoanálisis* 2:309–330.

—— (1976). *Clínica Psicoanalítica. Estudios Sobre Drogadicción, Psicosis y Narcissismo.* Buenos Aires: Galerna.

—— (1984). Hypochondriasis, somatic delusion and body scheme in psychoanalytic practice. *International Journal of Psycho-Analysis* 65:377–387.

—— (1985). Distorsions des actes. *Nouvelle Revue de Psychanalyse* 30:191–199.

—— (1986). Identification and its vicissitudes in relation to the Nazi phenomenon. *International Journal of Psycho-Analysis* 67:53–64.

—— (1988). *Group Psychoanalysis and Dialectic.* London: Karnac Books.

Rosenfeld, D., and Pistol, D. (1986). Episodio psicótico y su detección precoz en la transferencia. Paper presented at the XVIth Latinamerican Psychoanalytic Congress, Mexico City, July.

Santamaría, A. (1978). El paciente la enfermedad y la muerta en psicoanálisis. Paper presented at the XIIth Latinamerican Psychoanalytic Congress, Mexico City, July.

Schilder, P. (1935). The psycho-analysis of space. *International Journal of Psycho-Analysis* 16:274–295.

Scott, W. C. M. (1948). Embryological, neurological, and analytical implications of the body scheme. *International Journal of Psycho-Analysis* 29:141–155.

Searles, H. F. (1961). The sources of anxiety in paranoid schizophrenia. *British Journal of Medical Psychology* 34:129–141.

—— (1979). *Countertransference and Related Subjects.* New York: International Universities Press.

Tustin, F. (1972). *Autism and Child Psychosis.* London: Hogarth.

—— (1981). *Autistic States in Children.* London: Routledge and Kegan Paul.

—— (1986). *Autistic Barriers in Neurotic Patients.* London: Karnac.

Winnicott, D. (1957). *Collected Papers. Through Paediatrics to Psycho-Analysis.* London: Tavistock.

—— (1971). Le corp et le self. *Nouvelle Revue de Psychanalyse* 3:37–48.

7

JOYCE MCDOUGALL, D.Ed.

Identifications, Neoneeds, and Neosexualities

For some twenty years I have struggled to find a satisfactory definition, from a psychoanalytic viewpoint, of what might be judged symptomatic with regard to sexual acts and sexual object relationships. Homosexuality, for example: Is it to be regarded as a symptom, under all circumstances? Or under all circumstances, as merely another version of male or female sexuality? Analysts are sharply divided in their opinions on this question. Leavy (1985), Limentani (1977), and Isay (1985), for example, express ideas that differ from those of Socarides (1968, 1978).

In fact, most people experience their erotic acts and object choices as ego-syntonic, whether or not they are judged by others as "perverse." Thus a given patient's specific form of sexual preference becomes an analyzable problem only to the extent that he or she regards it as a source of suffering and conflict. For example, some of our homosexual analysands might come to discover that they are latent heterosexuals and would be happier in pursuing heterosexual relationships. Others definitely would not, and find it vitally important to maintain their homosexual identity. In view of what is at stake, one cannot but feel they are right.

Turning our attention to heterosexual acts and relationships, we find the clinical issues no clearer than with homosexual object choices. The polymorphous nature of adult heterosexual activity needs no emphasis. Our analysands describe an infinite variety of erotic scenarios, including cross-dressing, fetishistic objects and adornments, sadomasochistic games, and so on, which turn up as interludes in their lovemaking and cause no conflict, since they are not felt to be compulsive. Then there are those of our heterosexual patients who have nothing but fetishistic and sadomasochistic scenarios at their disposal in order to achieve a sexual relationship. As with our homosexual patients, we might wish that these analysands were a little less restricted and less subjected to such inexorable conditions in their sex lives, but if these erotic theater pieces are the *sole conditions* that allow access to sexual love relations, we would be wary of wishing them to lose them simply because we may regard these heterodox versions of the objects of desire as symptomatic. The analysands themselves rarely wish to lose their erotic solutions. A number of patients, under the impact of the analytic adventure, frequently develop richer sexual and love relations, but should this not occur, then to lose the only system of sexual survival they have been able to devise would be the equivalent of castration. And more than that. In many cases these intricate and ineluctable erotic scenarios serve not only to safeguard the feeling of sexual identity that accompanies sexual pleasure but frequently reveal themselves to be techniques of psychic survival in that they are required to preserve the feeling of *subjective identity* as well. To emphasize their innovative character and the intensity of investment involved, I refer to these inventions as *neosexualities*, following in this nomenclature the pattern of neorealities that fragile patients may create in an illusory or even delusional attempt to find a solution to overwhelming conflict (McDougall 1982).

The latter remarks also apply to a number of homosexual men and women. This brings up the question of the differences that undoubtedly exist between many neosexual inventors and homosexuals. Freud maintained a distinction by referring to homosexuality as *inversion* and the deviant behavior of fetishists, exhibitionists, and the like as *perversion*. This distinction appears to me to be valid in that frequently there are important differences of a structural and of a dynamic kind in spite of many similarities in the oedipal structure and in the economic role played by a sexuality that is often marked by urgency and compulsivity. On the whole, the majority of homosexuals are uninterested in neosexual inventions, and the heterosexual deviants are, in general, little interested in pursuing homosexual relations.

Nevertheless, the variations in psychosexual structure are so great that we are obliged to talk in the plural: of heterosexualities and homosexualities. To these we must also add the category of autoerotic sexualities, since many sadomasochistic, fetishistic, and transvestite practices are played out in strict solitude. These might therefore be considered as deviant forms of masturbation in that fantasy alone does not suffice; the condensed erotic fantasies must be put into action.

This leads me to the question of erotic fantasy as such. We must ask ourselves whether there is any such thing as a *perverse* fantasy—and if so, we must be prepared to define what might be meant by a *normal* erotic fantasy. One of the chief functions of conscious fantasies in the psychic economy is to accomplish in imagination that which is felt to be forbidden or impossible to accomplish in reality. Thus a restricted capacity to use fantasy, such as is manifested in many deviant sexualities, witnesses to some breakdown in the important introjections that take place in what Winnicott (1951) named *transitional phenomena,* with a consequent failure to be able freely to create an illusion in the space that separates one being from another and to use such illusion to support absence, frustration, and delay. I shall return to this important point later in discussing the notion of *addictive sexuality.* With regard to the question of perverse fantasy, it seems to me that the only aspect of a fantasy that might legitimately be described as perverse would be the attempt to force one's erotic fantasies on a nonconsenting or nonresponsible other. Perhaps in the last resort only *relationships* may aptly be termed perverse.

From this standpoint, therefore, the pertinent question is not which acts and which preferences are to be deemed deviant, but when deviancy is to be regarded as a simple variation or version of adult sexuality in the context of a significant object relationship, and when it is to be judged symptomatic. I would like to apply this question to heterosexualities, homosexualities, and autoerotic sexualities alike. The quality of a relationship cannot be assessed from purely external signs. There are qualitative as well as quantitative factors to be taken into account: qualitative aspects that concern dynamic psychosexual structure and quantitative factors that concern the role of sexual activity in the psychic economy.

Both the dynamic and the economic aspects pertain to the theme of identification insofar as sexual deviancy is concerned. Human sexual patterns, as Freud was the first to point out, are not inborn; they are created. The ego-syntonic quality of sexual choices and practices reveals that we are confronted with a system of powerful identifications—and counteridentifications—to introjected objects of a highly complex kind. These inner constellations give rise to significant differences. The introjective images reveal themselves slowly on the psychoanalytic stage like so many players in a theater. The parental discourse on sexuality that continued throughout childhood plays a cardinal role in every individual's psychic structure. But over and beyond our interpretations of our parents' communications, and beyond their resounding *silences,* I would suggest that our most powerful identifications and defensive operations are constructed in relation to what we have understood of our parents' unconscious sexual conflicts and erotic desires and of the role that we are called upon to play therein. The unconscious demands often run counter to what is consciously communicated, creating confusion and conflict in the child's mind. These same confusions and conflicts are later manifest in the analytic situation and may require some years of disentangling.

Nobody freely chooses the highly restricted and exigent conditions imposed by compulsive neosexual inventions, nor the solitude of a sexual life that is largely confined to autoerotic creations. Likewise, no man or woman has the impression of choosing to be homosexual in a predominantly heterosexual society. These so-called choices represent the best solution that the child of the past was able to find in the face of contradictory parental communications concerning core gender identity, masculinity and femininity, and sexual roles. And they come to the child or adolescent as *revelations* of what his or her sexuality is, along with the sometimes painful recognition that it is somehow different from that of others; there is no awareness of choice.

I shall now address two major theoretico-clinical issues concerning sexual deviancy. These are first, the etiological and qualitative considerations and second, the role of deviant sexuality in the psychic economy, that is, the quantitative aspects. Both are intimately concerned with the processes of internalization in deviant sexual organizations. Failure to integrate and harmonize the various incorporations and introjections that are being structured from birth onward is invariably present.

ETIOLOGICAL AND QUALITATIVE FACTORS IN DEVIANT SEXUALITY

Freud's (1905) early formulations presented perversions and inversions as vicissitudes in the sexual drives and fixations to early stages of libidinal development. But by the 1920s, he had already come to consider the mystery of their creation to be intimately connected with the internal oedipal organization and the fantasies of the primal scene (Freud 1915, 1922). There is no need to recapitulate the well-recognized significance of superego identifications in the psychosexual structures. These structures, largely created through language—verbal explanations, encouragements, and prohibitions promulgated throughout childhood—are in turn founded upon an archaic substructure that precedes the acquisition of language. While it is tempting to accept the facility of Freud's conceptual framework regarding the important (and clinically confirmed) role of the phallic oedipal phase in deviant sexuality, this necessary explanation is not, however, sufficient. It should be remembered that Freud himself came to question the adequacy of his theoretical conception.

In attempting to conceptualize the internalizations that take place in the earliest bodily sensorial exchanges between mother and infant, the terms *incorporation* and *introjection* are more appropriate than *identification*. At this stage of development the mother's unconscious fears and wishes play a predominant role. It is only as symbolic communication slowly takes the place of bodily contact between the child and its parents that sexual identifications and counteridentifications become a permanent part of each child's psychic capital.

It is, of course, the mother who first names for her children their erogenous zones, and at the same time, communicates in manifold ways the libidinal and narcissistic investment—or counterinvestment—that these zones and functions are to receive. Sometimes the very existence of certain organs and bodily functions is virtually denied. A mother may readily transmit to her offspring, because of her own inner distress about zonal investments and sexual prohibitions, a body image that is fragile, alienated, devoid of eroticism, or mutilated. Clinical observation has led me, on many occasions, to the deduction that those children who are destined to sexual deviance in adulthood have created their erotic theater as a protective attempt at self-cure, not only in the face of overwhelming castration anxiety stemming from oedipal conflicts, but also in an attempt to come to terms with the introjected sense of a *damaged body* and a frightening sense of *inner deadness*. These frequently give rise to fear of the loss of the body representation as a whole, and with it the terrifying loss of a cohesive sense of ego identity.

Much has been written, yet it still remains to be said, about the fundamental representation of the penis, which, according to its nature as an introjected object, determines the role and the organizing power of the *phallus as symbol*—that is, the erect penis, symbol of power, fertility, and desire. As such it belongs to neither sex, but organizes the introjective constellation and fundamental fantasies that determine adult sexual patterns. Divested of its symbolic value, the phallus runs the risk of becoming split into two distinct penis-images: a detached and persecuting part object that must be avoided, and an idealized and therefore unattainable object that must be relentlessly pursued. A mother, sometimes even before her baby's birth, may consciously or unconsciously regard her infant as a libidinal or narcissistic extension of herself, destined therefore to repair a sense of personal inner damage. This frequently leads to a wish to exclude the father in both his real and symbolic roles. If in addition the father chooses to accept this passive role, for fathers are just as liable to emotional disturbance as mothers, then archaic baby-like libidinal wishes and terrors may not be integrated into the sexual representation of the adult self, thus creating what might be called *symbolic havoc*.

THE PSYCHIC ECONOMY OF DEVIANT SEXUALITY

The economic role of sexual deviance cannot be overlooked. I wish, very briefly, to introduce the concept of *addictive sexuality* (McDougall 1982). Freud, in emphasizing that the objects of need are innate, whereas the objects of desire are created, proposed that the sexual instincts are anaclitically derived from self-conservation needs. They must therefore become detached from the original real object and then find autoerotic satisfaction before eventually arriving at object choice. In other words, the primordial sexual act is not suckling but thumb-sucking (Freud 1905). The point I wish to make is the following: So long as sexuality functions as an anaclitic activity, it is irrevocably tied to an external object that is detached from essential introjects, perhaps because these are missing or highly damaged or dangerous. This may render inoperative any attempt to maintain stable sexual relations linked to feelings of love. The incapacity to assure for oneself, through identification, both maternal and paternal functions, while it may not affect core gender identity, will frequently perturb oedipal identifications, since narcissistic needs and fears predominate. Sexuality then risks becoming deviated and addictive. Therefore, to the notion of neosexualities I would add that of *neoneeds*, in which the sexual object, part object, or practice is sought relentlessly in the manner of a drug. The result may well be recourse to inanimate erotic objects or to people treated as inanimate or interchangeable objects.

This dimension of human sexuality, whether in a heterosexual, homosexual, or autoerotic context, may be conceptualized as a breakdown in the internalization process in what Winnicott (1951) termed *transitional phenomena*. The transitional object represents the mother (more precisely, her maternal functions) on the way to becoming a stable introjective constellation; the individual may then identify with this helpful introject. Faulty development in the introjective processes at this stage can have catastrophic results, not only on the developing sense of sexual identity, but also on the developing sense of self. Sexuality frequently, in this eventuality, comes to represent a dramatic and compulsive way of keeping one's narcissistic *self-image* from disintegrating. In consequence, the sexual act will then be required also to deflect the forces of infantile rage from being turned back upon the self or being directed against the internalized parental representations. Thus the act becomes a drug intended to disperse feelings of violence, as well as a threatened loss of ego boundaries, and a feeling of inner death. Meanwhile the partner and the sexual scenario become containers for dangerous parts of the individual. These will subsequently be mastered, in illusory fashion, by gaining erotic control over the other or through a game of mastery within the sexual scenario.

In metapsychological terms, the dynamic and economic dimensions of deviant sexuality might be summarized as follows: *Those who have created a neoreality in terms of sexual acts and objects in the service of libidinal homeostasis, and neoneeds in the service of narcissistic homeostasis, have short-circuited the elaboration of phallic-oedipal castration anxiety and at the same time, through disavowing the problems of separateness and individuation* (Mahler 1968) *and of infantile sadism, by creating a wall of inner deadness against associated affects, have circumvented the elaboration of what Melanie Klein termed the depressive position.*

I trust these conceptualizations will become clearer in the clinical illustration that follows. This vignette is taken from the sixth year of a lengthy analysis.

Jason, a man in his early forties, came to analysis because of severe obsessional symptoms that handicapped his sexual and social life. His professional life seemed free from this symptomatology. He claimed a passionate interest in his work and in fact had achieved a considerable reputation in a highly specialized branch of surgery. Predominant among his obsessive ruminations was a constant preoccupation with minority groups, for whom he expressed a positive prejudice. "Am I as good as an Arab?" "Am I as good as a black?" "Am I as good as a Jew?" In our initial interview he already revealed that what he called his "racist problems" were also intimately connected with his sexual life. He said: "Many women offer themselves to me, and if they're Arab, Vietnamese, African, and so on I always accept and my obsessions are put to rest." He added cryptically, "When there's no mixture, there's no problem." He then went on to explain that everything was complicated with women who, like himself, did not belong to these ethnic groups. In his early twenties he had married a young French woman whom he desired because, so it seemed, she had once had a brief affair with a famous Jew. He said, "I tortured my wife for years every night to tell me further details about her former love affair with X. The interrogations would go on for hours. Then I would get her to put on split panties and tie her up and rape her. But the sex wasn't so good. The questioning took so long." During his marriage, which came to an end after ten years, he continued to have innumerable adventures directed by the same ethnic bias. Jason then talked of a second woman with whom he had a long-lasting relationship. She had had a nebulous affair with a world-famous celebrity who was a black. She too had to submit to endless interrogations before he was able to make love to her. It appeared that the women would end up avowing or inventing whatever he wanted to hear. Jason claimed that the torture was as great for him as for his lovers and that one day it would drive him mad.

During our initial interview I gained a glimpse into the underlying significance attached to ethnic differences when Jason came to talk briefly, at my request, about his early family life. "There were endless quarrels between my parents because my mother is British and my father French. He looks a little dark and a little Jewish but he's not." Jason then talked of his only sibling, his sister, four years older than he. Both had suffered throughout childhood from hearing their mother's constant denigrating remarks about their father. As a little boy Jason was humiliated by his mother's accent, her hatred for French people and for many aspects of French culture. Insults would fly across the table, and the father would say she was an ugly English bitch. Jason continued, "My mother talked openly about my father's infidelities in front of us both. I know he had daily adventures with his clients, especially women of other races." He then added, after a pause, "All I had was masturbation—perhaps that's why I masturbated many times a day during my adolescence. In fact, I still masturbate on an average of twice a day." He added that his mother's image of true virility was that of her own father, who had lost a leg on the field of battle.

From this first interview, I had already made the deduction that from childhood Jason had displaced onto the difference between his parents' nationalities his anxiety concerning the difference between their sexes. In addition, ethnic differences and constant sexual activity were manifestly endowed with phallic significance. The place of the woman was less clear. It was evident, however, that Jason's choice of a woman analyst with a marked English accent, who also lived among the French, was no accident. Even though he had to wait another year before our analytic work could begin, he refused all other referrals. I was destined to pay for all the shame and psychological damage for which Jason held his mother responsible.

Since this chapter is concerned with exploring the internal structures that give rise to neosexual inventions, I shall add a few details about Jason's childhood, insofar as they pertain to his deviant sexuality. In our preliminary interview Jason had revealed only those aspects of his sexual activity that caused his suffering. Later he came to tell me how he had begun cross-dressing, during latency, in his older sister's clothing, particularly her dance clothes, and would masturbate in front of the mirror in this attire.

Jason's deviant and dangerous masturbation ritual, practiced throughout adolescence, also deserves mention, since it is a limpid illustration of the double polarity of neosexual inventions, namely an attempt to find a way around the interdictions and castration anxieties of the phallic oedipal phase as well as a struggle to circumvent the difficulties encountered at a much earlier phase, with separation anxiety and infantile rage and terror: in other words, the warding-off of both neurotic and psychotic levels of anxiety. In his masturbation ritual, Jason would take the elevator to the top of the building in which his parents lived, and then send it down while he would climb up the steel wire until he reached the banister near the roof. Here he would cling, suspended over a void of some forty meters, while he masturbated with the cord of the elevator. This practice was fraught with danger from various points of view of which the dominant risk was the eroticized fear that, at the moment of ejaculation, he might loosen his grip and crash to the ground floor.

Perturbed identifications in his feeling of sexual identity, and a certain confusion between his and his partner's bodies, were revealed in his adult sexual scenarios. One important activity was to get his girlfriends to wear a dildo and thus attired, to penetrate him anally. At other times he would tie consenting partners up while whipping them and penetrating them anally with his finger and, if possible, his whole hand.

I shall come back to the complex representations, introjects, and identifications that lay behind these compulsive neosexual inventions.

During our second preliminary interview, Jason discussed what he described as his homosexuality. He said, "I went for years to partouze parties especially to watch what the men were doing. There's something phony about my relationship with women. Although I work wonderfully well in surgery with women patients, outside the hospital I probably hate them. In fact, I'm convinced I'm a homosexual, except that I've never wanted sex with men. All this has to do with my English bitch of a mother." He then added, "I suppose you wonder why I want to do my analysis with you?" "Perhaps because I'm a woman and an English bitch?" "It's true. Your accent reminds me of my mother, but there's something about you that's different. You make me feel I exist." And his eyes filled up with tears.

Although I was well aware of what awaited me in the transference relationship to come, I was nevertheless surprised by unsuspected transference manifestations. At the first session on the couch, Jason addressed me as Joyce (a quite unheard-of practice in France) and in addition used the familiar "tu" form, which in French is reserved for family, intimate friends, children, and dogs. I fell into all of these categories at one time or another. Throughout the analysis I always addressed my patient as "vous." As may be imagined, Jason's way of attacking the framework led to many an interpretation, such as his narcissistic fragility and need to be seductive. To add to the confusion, Jason frequently addressed me by his name and would use my name when referring to himself. "Yesterday after the session I was again seized with terror in your street; everyone was threatening me. But I said to myself, 'Now, Joyce, you know you're just lending these people your own violence. They mean you no harm'."

There were many thought-provoking dimensions to this analysis, but I shall concentrate mainly on my patient's neosexual inventions and their role in his psychic economy. However, it is pertinent to mention one detail from the overall picture of Jason's psychic world. It became clear, for example, that, as a child, Jason had suffered from certain psychotic manifestations and that these had lasted for about a year. He would hear voices commanding him to make insulting remarks to family friends, particularly women. This led to his being regularly thrashed by his father, the more so when the little boy protested that it was not he but the voices that obliged him to do this. I could only presume that at this period of his life, Jason managed to expel from his mind both his violently angry and his erotic thoughts concerning different introjected images of his mother, and that these returned in classical Schreber-like fashion in the form of auditory hallucinations. According to Jason, his father proclaimed that he would be thrashed until he stopped hearing voices. This finally appeared to be effective. Jason and I came to the conclusion that it was around this time that the hallucinatory phenomena were taken over by compulsive questioning of his mother and her friends, which could last for hours. The questions frequently concerned matters such as the comparative prices and utility of articles of female clothing, such as fur coats.

When similar questioning occurred in the analytic situation (and I admit it had the power to drive one crazy—I sometimes had the impression that *I* was hearing voices)—we were able to reconstruct Jason's obsessive concern during childhood with sexual differences and in particular the conformation and functioning of the female body.

My interpreting this concern in numerous contexts led Jason to remember in detail his mother's daily litany at the table, in which she would put his father through an interrogation as to how many women he had had intercourse with each day. Apparently she would spy on him and whenever she saw him talking in animated fashion to a woman, particularly someone of different ethnic origins from her own, she was convinced that a sexual relationship was to take place. In the early years of his analysis, Jason firmly believed that his father had intercourse with four or five women a day; as time wore on, and his *need* for this belief diminished, he was able to say with conviction, "You know, I realize now that my mother was pathologically jealous. I think she had homosexual problems. Also, I had forgotten that my father frequently protested that no man could engage in continual sexual activity such as my mother imputed to him."

As the analysis progressed, it became clear that Jason's violent complaints against his mother were not limited to her constant denigration of his father and his supposed sexual activities. These had engendered painful confusion in the small boy's mind, but in addition he experienced his mother as unable to understand any viewpoint other than her own. Some of the most dramatic and poignant moments of his analysis concerned his conviction that he did not truly exist in his mother's eyes. "I hammered on the walls of my mother's mind, and the only response I got back was an echo." When similar fears came up in the transference (for example, if I had been silent for some time), Jason would scream at me, asking if I were asleep or dead. He used to shout so loudly that sometimes I could hardly hear what he was saying. When I asked if he were trying to keep me awake and alive, he would say that he had to shout in order to *reach* me because, being English, I would never understand what he was communicating. We were able to interpret his extraordinary manner of speaking as a feeling that he could not "reach" his mother, could not make her understand his suffering as a child, as though he were not truly alive, or she were not alive to him.

Jason's complicated sexual practices and relationships were attempts not only to shore up an insecure sense of *sexual* identity but also to ward off the much graver danger of losing his sense of self and feeling of *subjective* identity. Some two years after the beginning of the analysis, Jason's obsession with ethnic differences and his complicated sexual practices began to lose part of their compulsivity, but he now found himself faced with a catastrophic form of anxiety of psychotic dimensions, which he described as an experience of nothingness, or inner deadness. He called these feelings "voids" (*"états de vide"*).

By this time Jason no longer shouted in a deafening way, and he rarely confused our two names, but he was frightened of losing his mind, losing his professional skills, or of perpetrating crazy acts in order to fill up the voids. These states of depersonalization lasted for close on two years, and were a period of constant interpretive activity on my part, as well as leading me to parameters such as finding extra sessions, permitting him to telephone on occasions, and agreeing to his taking psychiatric drugs on the understanding that this was a temporary measure.

We also analyzed this recourse to medication (which lasted a few months) as a way of seeking a transitional object to palliate the void in which he could not carry with him the introjected image of a caretaking mother. He behaved in a manner that Mahler (1968) describes as the practicing subphase, in which children must come back to home base before setting off once again, since the internalized mother-image is readily lost. Jason's incessant masturbation also increased during this time. We were able to reconstruct that first, this represented a way in which he could assure himself that the most dangerous of the maternal introjects had not destroyed his manhood, and second, that masturbation gave him the feeling that he existed and that his body had definite limits. The feeling of inner deadness would disappear momentarily (Limentani 1984). The game of being penetrated by an artificial penis procured the same impression.

The analysis of Jason's castration fears at all levels—phallic oedipal anxiety, narcissistic castration fears, and their primitive prototype in the form of anxiety about separation and annihilation—was intense during this period and contributed to our understanding of the strength of his sexual obsessions and their underlying fantasy content. A clinical fragment taken from the third year of our work together may exemplify this.

Jason: When I make love to a black woman whose own man is black, there's no problem, no obsessions, because I get his penis by taking his woman. So I feel like a man for a short while. The blacks, the Arabs, the Vietnamese, the Jews all have real cocks. But I still feel intense panic with my women friends who haven't had such relationships. The hours of interrogation have come back again. Why?

JM: If the woman hasn't had one of these powerful penises in her, then she's a castrate, just as you feel yourself to be. When you can force her to admit she's had such adventures, you are able to penetrate her, but then your envy and hatred of her have no bounds, as we have often seen.

Jason: Yes. That reminds me of the times when I whip women. It isn't to hurt them, it's to prove that they aren't hurt and aren't going to die. At these times I have a phony penis that can make the woman have an orgasm. So it's a great system.

JM: And when you don't have this whip-penis, then it's the woman who has to pass you the powerful penis she took from another man?

Jason: Why have I always longed to be a woman?

JM: Perhaps it's because women have the female sex-organ that attracts men and their penises.

Jason: I don't know why I've never wanted sex with men, but I am a homosexual (he begins shouting), now don't deny it!

JM: Why should I deny it?

Jason: Well, that asshole Dr. X (an analyst Jason had seen for a short time before coming to see me, and for whom he expressed little esteem), silly ass, he said that of course I wasn't a homosexual since I had never slept with men!

The fact was that Jason desperately needed to have his homosexual longings recognized, since he felt his need for masculine identification to be forbidden by his mother.

JM: There seem to be two of you there—one who is homosexual and wants to receive the gift of a man's penis in order to become a man, and another who is heterosexual and wants to make love to a woman with the fantasy of getting a man's penis through her. As though *she* must give you permission to possess your own penis.

Jason: All those little games with my girlfriends and the dildo—you once said this was my mother with my father's penis tied around her and she was letting me swallow it up anally. (There is a long pause before he speaks again.)

Jason: (shouting) My mother hated my father and she wouldn't let me be like him, wouldn't let me love him. All I could have was *her* father, the wonderful war hero with the missing leg! (At this point Jason burst into sobs.)

I have quoted the above session rather fully because it expresses the essential elements of Jason's childhood sexual theories, derived from his introjective constellation. His fundamental sexual fantasy was that in order to become a man he had literally to incorporate the male genital (in the form of the artificial penis) but at the same time he did not want the "incorporation" *from a man*, because it was equally essential that his mother give him access to the father's penis so that he could possess *her*.

In this respect, Jason was acting out a common fantasy of little children in which they lie between the two parents, during which time the father puts his strong penis into a little boy who then develops a strong penis that can go into his mother: a concrete version of internalization fantasies in their oral, anal, and phallic aspects. These object representations eventually become foci for stable, if deviant, identifications to the parental couple in the fantasied primal scene. All that Jason had achieved in the way of identification to his father's phallic qualities was the pursuit of innumerable sexual adventures—a superficial adhesive kind of identification, for which, we have seen, he had to pay dearly, and which was further complicated by the fact that phallic strength was symbolized for Jason by the pursuit of partners who were ethnically different from himself.

After some years, we were eventually able to sort out that Jason had introjected what he came to construct as a crazy part of his mother, which had given rise to two conflicting images of his father. These introjected part-objects referred on the one hand to an idealized, uncastrated phallus in constant erection, with no real man behind it, and on the other, to a dirty, dangerous, and denigrated phallic introject, equally detached from a truly masculine internalized object. The latter was felt to have left the mother empty, incomplete, and crazy. Jason, too, felt deprived of phallic enrichment as he believed his mother to have been. His basic erotic fantasy, like many neosexual creations, was constructed somewhat after the manner of a dream. As evidenced in the session quoted above, the women who excited Jason sexually were those who, in his fantasy, had incorporated a powerful penis which he in turn would absorb anally, thus rendering his own penis phallic and capable of penetration. This highly invested sexual game played the same role, in many respects, as the compulsive seeking of addictive substances such as alcohol or drugs. In the latter case the aim of the act is to take in a substitute for the soothing maternal functions of the primitive "breast-mother." Jason's compulsive sexual pursuits carried this meaning as well. Although the literal incorporation of the part-object substitutes is based on an unconscious wish to obtain or repair what is missing or damaged in the internal world, these acts, obviously, *are not the equivalent of the psychological processes of incorporation and introjection*. On the contrary, the felt need for external objects in the form of compulsive sexuality or substance abuse witnesses to the breakdown of the internalization processes. The acts do nothing to repair the damaged representation of penis or breast in their symbolic significance. They relieve anxiety only temporarily and therefore acquire an addictive quality in that they must be pursued continually (McDougall 1982).

To conclude, I shall quote a fragment from one of Jason's sessions that I noted rather fully in the sixth year of our work together. My notes read as follows: Over the past three years Jason has created a stable relationship with a professional woman with whom he has had two children. Although he still frequently needs to find the solitude of his own apartment and feels unable to face the strains of conjugal life, he is deeply attached to his lover and their two children. Jason seems to have given up entirely his sadomasochistic practices and no longer seeks to have his partner penetrate him with a dildo. He retains considerable erotic interest in anal intercourse as a variant. His endless questioning prior to intercourse has considerably lessened, as has his compulsive masturbation. He says his friends and colleagues hardly recognize him because he is "so much less crazy." He himself claims that he no longer confuses his reality with other people's. He reiterates that during this last year he has known true happiness for the first time in his life.

His associations in the following session demonstrate many of the vicissitudes of the internalization processes linked to his varied sexual deviancies and relationships, and also provide some insight into the significance of Jason's voids. This experience of nothingness has completely disappeared.

Jason: I watch the way you dress. Each elegant detail. But the important thing is that they now become *my* clothes. I feel good as I lie down. You've seen what lovely clothes I now permit myself to buy. (Jason used to look unusually shabby, in a way that was inconsistent with both his profession and his means.) But my scarf's very old and dirty—and I'm forbidden to wash it, because then it wouldn't be *me* any more. Like when I was a kid. I would scream when my mother insisted on buying me new clothes. Atrocious public scenes, but worse for *me* than for her. I knew she was trying to destroy me, and I was fighting for my life.

We see in this small vignette how fragile was Jason's sense of self and how he felt his *clothes* kept him together. He invested them rather like transitional objects, in lieu of an internalized mother-figure who could reassure him of his bodily integrity and psychic security.

Jason: That makes me think of my terror of those voids when I was staring into nothing and didn't know who I was.

Jason had used all the infantile magic at his disposal—in particular his inventive sexuality—to fill those meaningless or dead spaces in which he found no echoing reflection back from his mother to confirm his individual existence or his sexual identity. The void, at this level, signified also the terrifying female sex, a dangerous genital related to an introjected image of his mother as a limitless void. Since he had no internal representation of his father's penis as playing a beneficial role in his mother's sex life, this did not allow for an introjected primal scene in which the representation of his mother's genital could be envisaged as complementary to his father's. In addition, there was no representation of a father figure who would protect him from being absorbed and engulfed by his mother, and with whom he could therefore safely maintain a genital identification.

Jason: She wanted me to rip off my clothes so I'd have no defense; then she could just devour me. I had to hide everything from her in order to exist. I'm thinking of my masturbation rituals, hanging over that forty-meter drop.
JM: Another void?

This was the first time it had been possible to connect Jason's states of inner deadness, his voids, with his adolescent sexual practices. Earlier attempts to interpret his associations in this respect, whether attached to the transference or objects of the past, had led to Jason's feeling confused.

Jason: Ah yes, but that was a void that was exciting! It was the *real* danger of the situation that was so erotic and made me ejaculate. And of course the risk of getting caught!

We see here that Jason has understood how he managed to render tolerable, through eroticization, the psychic factors that were the cause of his greatest anxieties (McDougall 1978): first, the empty void of his mother's sex and then the concomitant fear that his father might catch him in an act that was the unconscious equivalent of incest. In addition, the parents' communications about sexuality had created a *gap in meaning* in the small boy's mind. Nothing made sense. Jason was obliged to invent a new primal scene, which was subsequently integrated into his neosexual creation. Over and beyond the threatening sexual factors lay the archaic fear of disappearing into a void in which he would lose not only his body limits but his ego boundaries as well. In his condensed sexual practice, Jason had been able to eroticize both his phallic castration anxieties and the primal castration fears of annihilation and death. He was, like many sexual deviants, *flirting with death* in his dangerous sexual games, trying to prove that, in spite of his aggressive impulses and sexual desire, and in spite of his conviction of nonexistence in his mother's eyes, neither she nor he would die. Not only would he triumph over death, but these very anxieties would be the cause of his greatest sexual pleasure.

JM: So you refused to be terrified of the experience of nothingness and of your fantasies about your mother's body.

Jason: Yes, and I refused what she wanted—that I should be sexless.

JM: Refused to be a void for her?

Jason: Eh voilá! I was never anything but an *adjective* for my parents.

JM: An adjective?

Jason: Yes . . . "you're a brilliant boy," "you're a dirty boy," "you're a crazy boy!" But no one, you understand, no one ever told me I was a *boy*!

There is a long pause and Jason begins to cry. After mastering his emotion, he continues:

Jason: How could I know I was a boy? Or even what it was to be a boy? And that it was good *just* to be a boy? I became a man by accident. I wasn't one really; I just looked like one, acted like one. Had to be better than the Arabs, the Jews, and the blacks! Had to lay more girls than they could. Always the adjective! The big fucker. I was still not a *male*. Just a phony. But now I've become one. Out of the void I've created a real cock! The work we're doing here, it's like a birth process. Do you remember my first session on the couch? I said that I was coming out from between your thighs. It's as though I were watching my own birth as a baby. Like a wish that I've never admitted to myself. Why did I not exist as a boy for my mother? (Suddenly shouting) Joyce! Are you listening? Nom de Dieu, say something!

JM: Afraid that you do not exist as a boy for me?

Jason: It's worse than that, it's as though you don't exist either.

JM: So you've turned me into a void? As though you've eaten me up
           again?

(I make reference here to material from a recent session in which Jason
had expressed this fear that he had used up all my ideas, and was afraid
of being too heavy a load for me to bear.)

Jason: Yes, I see it now. I devoured my mother and the big danger was
           to empty *her* out, turn *her* into a void. She was always telling
           me what a voracious baby I was, how she had to pinch my nose
           to make me give up the nipple . . . and how much she always
           did for me through childhood—tore her guts out for me, she
           did! See, even as a baby I was only an adjective—bad baby!"
           (He laughs in a somewhat discordant way; I feel his anxiety
           acutely and search for the underlying incorporative fantasies
           that are seeking expression.)

JM: You make it seem that your mother might have been afraid of
           being devoured by you.

Jason: But she was, and she made me feel dangerous. Why was she
           so afraid? I know—that's called projection. I was afraid of
           devouring her, and she was afraid of her wish to eat me!
           I'm thinking of my grandfather's missing leg. I used to ask
           questions for hours on end about where it was. Another
           void!

JM: As though you imagined she had eaten it?

Jason: Yes! But that was a void I had to admire, whereas my father,
           who had two legs, wasn't worth a damn. (He begins to shout.) I
           could hobble about on one leg, but from my father I wasn't
           allowed to take anything! Nothing at all!

JM: Except for the "constant seducer." Even if it were an adjective,
           it was something you took from your father.

Jason: Tiens! I sure did! Without that I'd have been psychotic. I was
           crazy, you know—just like that boy Sammy you wrote about.
           We were very alike. When I first came here I was a closet
           psychotic!

JM: But the adjectives helped you to survive.

Jason: Yes, and my father was proud of my intelligence, used to say I
           was going to become a world-famous professor. Oh yes, I
           became a surgeon for all of them—to repair my grandfather's

leg, to fulfill my father's ambition. For years, I've repaired the whole world—while I stayed empty and damaged. Like you once said: "a psychic hemorrhage."

I hope this analytic vignette provides a glimpse into the intricate play of introjected objects, incorporative fantasies, and counteridentifications, to unconscious parental fears and wishes, that contribute to the construction of neosexualities. In the psychic theater, anxiety is the mother of invention. Although much analytical work remained to be done at this point in Jason's analysis, perhaps I have been able to convey, through Jason's desperate attempts to come to terms with the difficulties of living, some of the ways in which fears of castration and annihilation, and feelings of confused sexual identity, infantile rage, and inner death may be transformed into an eroticized, if inexorable, game.

Neosexualities serve not only to repair rifts in the feelings of sexual and subjective identity, but also, in unconscious fantasy, preserve the introjected objects from the subject's hatred and destructiveness. These arise in part from the relatively unmitigated oral and anal impulses that characterize infantile love. These problems could, potentially, give rise to more serious outcomes of a psychotic or psychopathic order.

With the miraculous discovery of the neosexual game, in place of meaninglessness there is now meaning, and in place of inner death, a feeling of vitality. In spite of the exigent conditions, the compulsivity, and the anguish that so often accompany deviant sexual creations, by means of their self-curative and reparative aims, Thanatos is shackled and Eros triumphs over death.

CONCLUSION

With regard to perversions, the pertinent question is not which acts and which object-preferences are to be deemed deviant, but when is deviance to be regarded as a simple variation of adult sexuality and when is it to be judged symptomatic. This chapter proposes that only relationships may aptly be termed perverse.

The term *neosexualities* is chosen to emphasize the innovative and somewhat unreal character of deviant sexual acts and relationships. These are a response to incoherent communications and unconscious problems on the part of the parents. The concept of *addictive sexuality* and *neoneeds* is also introduced in reference to the compulsivity that invariably accompanies perverse sexuality.

Its dynamic and economic aspects are summarized as follows: Those who have created a neoreality in terms of sexual acts and objects in the service of libidinal homeostasis, and neoneeds in the service of narcissistic homeostasis, have short-circuited the elaboration of phallic-oedipal castration anxiety and at the same time, through disavowing the problems of separateness and of infantile sadism, have also circumvented what Klein termed the elaboration of the depressive position.

A clinical vignette is given to illustrate the above theoretical propositions.

REFERENCES

Freud, S. (1905). Three essays on the theory of sexuality. *Standard Edition* 7:130–243.
——— (1915). Instincts and their vicissitudes. *Standard Edition* 14:103–140.
——— (1922). Some neurotic mechanisms in jealousy, paranoia, and homosexuality. *Standard Edition* 18:221–234.
Isay, R. (1985). Homosexuality in homosexual and heterosexual men. In *Psychology of Men: New Psychoanalytic Perspectives*. New York: Basic Books.
Leavy, S. (1985). Male homosexuality reconsidered. *International Journal of Psychoanalytic Psychotherapy* 11:155–174.
Limentani, A. (1977). The differential diagnosis of homosexuality. *British Journal of Medical Psychology* 50:209–216.
——— (1984). Toward a unified conception of the origins of sexual and social deviancy in young persons. *International Journal of Psychoanalytic Psychotherapy* 10:383–401.
Mahler, M. (1968). *On Human Symbiosis and the Vicissitudes of Individuation.* Vol. 1. New York: International Universities Press.
McDougall, J. (1978). *Plea for a Measure of Abnormality.* New York: International Universities Press, 1980.
——— (1982). *Theaters of the Mind: Illusion and Truth on the Psychoanalytic Stage.* New York: Basic Books.
Socarides, C. (1968). *The Overt Homosexual.* New York: Grune & Stratton.
——— (1978). *Homosexuality.* New York: Jason Aronson.
Winnicott, D. W. (1951). Transitional objects and transitional phenomena. In *Playing and Reality*, pp. 1–25. New York: Basic Books, 1971.

PART II

MASTER CLINICIANS ON THE THERAPIST-PATIENT INTERACTION

8

HAROLD F. SEARLES, M.D.

Unconscious Identification

My main purpose in this chapter is to convey a generous variety of clinical vignettes wherein one can detect unconscious identifications ramifying beneath or behind a relatively simple and obvious conscious one, something like a sea plant can be discovered to be flourishing far beyond and beneath the few leaves that can be seen on the water's surface. I have found these vignettes instructive in my own work with patients. Before presenting them, I shall spend a few minutes in spelling out my orientation to the work of psychoanalytic therapy (and psychoanalysis).

In my view, in the conducting of this kind of treatment, an intensive, open-ended procedure not limited at the outset to, say, ten sessions or one year of treatment, every patient proves to be difficult somewhere along the way. Every patient in intensive, time-unlimited psychoanalytic therapy calls upon the utmost, the full depths, of the therapist's emotional resources. Favorable personality change—maturation—is not permanent, not once-and-for-all achieved. Rather, regression can bring essentially all one's psychopathology back, and it does tend to do so not only in patients but in one's own work as their therapist or analyst.

One's largely unwanted identifications with parent figures, for example, are not permanently resolved or integrated during one's training analysis. These tend to become again less integrated, existing more as introjects once again, in the course of difficult work with a patient. A patient's transference to me as being a stern parent, for example, tends to undo hard, personal-analytic work on an unwanted identification with a perceivedly stern mother or father, and I may react to such developing transference by behaving (without consciously intending to do so) like a disarmingly lovable incompetent in the course of the session.

Regression in the service of the ego, a concept first enunciated in 1952 by Ernst Kris (Kris 1952) goes much deeper than we commonly have acknowledged. Although the therapist strives to maintain an observing ego, part of his ego necessarily regresses, so that there is a reactivation of the myriad introjects that initially had coalesced into his ego-identity (Searles 1984).

The borderline patient's transference reactions and attitudes are so powerful in their effect, over the long course of the therapy, as to mold the therapist's actual feelings and behavior during the sessions into conformity with those transference images (Searles 1979). Transference of this intensity, particularly when focused upon an area of a never-well-integrated introject in the therapist's actual personality functioning, is particularly stressful upon the therapist's ego-integration.

Parenthetically, a book that I read as an Army psychiatrist in 1945 entitled *Men Under Stress*, by Grinker and Spiegel, describing mental breakdowns in soldiers who have been subjected to appallingly stressful combat experiences, helped me to realize that such regressions need not be regarded as inherently shameful, when one can come to understand the nature and severity of the stresses that have brought them about. Although the stresses upon the therapist scarcely deserve comparison with those upon the combat soldier, the former are at times formidable indeed. The therapist finds that intrapsychic battles, which he or she had thought were favorably settled long ago, have become reopened—battles with largely unwanted identifications with part-aspects of his parents and other parent figures. In my previously mentioned paper in 1979 (Searles 1979), for example, I reported that one of the sources for my persistent hatred of one borderline patient was that his intense transference to me as being his highly obsessive mother exerted such a powerful pull upon me toward going back to my earlier, much more obsessive, only partially outgrown self, that I hated him for this.

In the relatedness between the largely regressed patient and the therapist who also is regressed to a very significant degree, there is much more of back-and-forth projection and introjection than we have comprehended, as judged by most of the literature concerning such topics as countertransference and projective identification. It is not merely, for example, that the borderline patient manifests the unconscious defense of projective identification, but that the therapist does also.

In 1949, as a recently arrived psychiatric resident at Chestnut Lodge, I had an experience that alerted me to the phenomenon of the therapist's projecting his own unconscious contents into the patient. While serving as doctor on call, I had to spend nearly an hour in the middle of the night on the male locked ward, alone and unaided in a room with a murderously furious, threatening, powerfully built manic man, while his favorite male attendant, an approximately 300-pound giant of a man, was being called from home to the sanitarium to cope with him. Meanwhile I sat, filled with feelings of helpless fear and with a crystal-clear awareness of the importance of my presenting to him a picture of limp and passive unthreateningness, while he was shaking a finger in my face and shouting furiously at me.

When the male aide finally arrived and I went back downstairs to the doctor-on-call quarters, I found myself suddenly filled with murderous fury at the patient. After I had vented this for many moments in intensely felt fantasies of killing him, I became mystified with the question of where these feelings of mine had been only a few minutes before, while I had been closeted with him upstairs. I then realized, with full and lasting conviction, that I had been projecting these into him—that he had been expressing not only his own murderous feelings but my unconscious ones as well.

Since then I have seen that very frequently the therapist projects into the patient his or her own various sorts of feelings, so that in the patient's giving expression, in session after session, to such feelings as rage, defiance, fear, lust, grief, deeply dependent feelings, and so on, he is expressing not only his own feelings but, fused with these, the therapist's projected feelings of that variety. This phenomenon is an important part of the basis of many stalemates in therapy. The therapist, meanwhile, senses that the bond with the patient is so precarious that he, the therapist, cannot afford the luxury of experiencing any full gamut of intense feelings toward the patient. Just as I had sensed, during the time of being incarcerated with the manic patient, that I could not afford the luxury of conscious anger at him, let alone murderous retaliatory fury, lest he lose control entirely and physically attack me, a therapist may be cowed by chronic threats lest the so-precarious bond with the patient be severed irretrievably, and the patient become suicidal or hopelessly psychotic or leave treatment permanently.

I shall not attempt to categorize the clinical vignettes that follow, but only say that some examples reveal that the patient unconsciously perceives the therapist as being involved in what we would call "as-if" (Deutsch 1942) psychodynamics; others reveal the patient's unconscious perception of a parent's behavior during the patient's childhood; in others, some of the patient's heretofore unconscious identifications with the therapist become clear to both patient and therapist; others are relevant to the patient's acting out; others have to do with premature interpretations; others reveal that the patient unconsciously perceives the therapist as being what we would call narcissistic or autistic; others reveal the patient's unconscious perceptions of his own self—reveal, that is, heretofore unconscious aspects of his own identity.

In the first of the clinical vignettes that form the core of this chapter, I had been working for more than seven years with an elderly woman, the mother of two daughters, who had initially sought treatment from me to help her cope with her chronically schizophrenic older daughter, then in her late 40s. For many years before and after starting with me, she had been estranged from her younger daughter, who was herself nearly 50 at the time of this incident. I was seeing her at a frequency of once a week. She had had a number of previous therapists.

During this session she referred to—among other things, as usual—a letter she had received recently from her younger daughter. I knew that she had not seen this daughter for many years, and that it had been some years since she had heard from her; I knew also that the daughter had had much psychoanalysis years ago.

My patient mentioned, resentfully, that one time she had asked me to read a letter she had gotten from her daughter and that I had spoken of my embarrassment in doing so. I did not recall having done so, and told her as much, but made plain that I did not doubt the accuracy of her memory.

This time, late in the session, I asked her if she wanted to give me another try, and she took the letter out of her purse and gave it to me to read. In reading it, I privately thought that it was very much like a love letter and showed, also, her daughter's unawareness of the negative feeling toward her mother that she was expressing in the letter. I did not attempt at all to analyze the daughter's letter.

I told the patient that I felt that part of what she was conveying in giving me the letter to read was to ask me, in essence, how *I* would reply to this letter if *I* were in *her* position. She agreed, confirming this; she had told me, before giving me the letter, "I don't know how to reply to it."

I then went on, "I do feel a sense of not actually being you, and therefore, I feel uncomfortable as to how I might respond to it." Actually, for me, the most memorable aspect of this interaction is that, in the moment before reaching out to accept the letter, I felt a very strong sense that it was not right for me to read the letter, since *I* was not the person to whom the letter was addressed; the force of this inhibition was striking to me, in light of her obvious wish that I read it.

It then occurred to me, as I went on talking, and I said, "But I wonder if *you* feel that *you*, likewise, are not the person to whom that letter is addressed." To this, she reacted in a strongly confirmatory fashion, saying that she had gotten a great deal of therapy over the years since she had been involved in the kind of thing that this letter was expressing. In essence, she strongly confirmed that my sense of not in actuality being the intended recipient of the letter had a counterpart in her strongly feeling, likewise, that she was not the person to whom the letter was addressed. Her confirmation, here, was expressed in sufficiently pent-up feeling as to let me know that she had needed this interpretation from me to enable her to know and express these feelings so clearly.

In this example, behind my conscious identification with her in my reading of this letter that had been addressed to her, was my unconscious identification with her own at least partially unconscious, previously unexpressed feeling that this letter was addressed to someone other than the person she now was.

A borderline man said that he couldn't remember which day I had said (last time) I would not be here and, as I remained silent, he soliloquized about whether his having forgotten was an example of his being controlling—that is, by requiring me to tell him again. His need to control was a long-familiar theme in our work together; I had spoken of it many times. Then he asked, "Am I just parroting what I think you're going to say?" I sensed here that the word "say" had an unconscious meaning of "parrot." That is, I sensed that he unconsciously had raised the question whether his parroting—of which he did much—was based on identification with my own parroting. I realized that such a perception of me, on his part, would have a world of validity in it, for there was much of a mechanical, parroting quality about my demeanor and verbal communications in my work with this highly controlling man.

A number of patients whom I have treated, or whose treatment I have supervised for extended periods, have spoken of their own "playing therapist," with an obvious, conscious meaning that they are playing at being the therapist, but with an unconscious meaning that they perceive therapists themselves as "playing therapist."

With a number of demanding, coercive, confrontational patients I have treated, and several more about whom I have heard in supervision, I have seen that the patient's saying to the therapist, "Now it's *your* turn to talk. It doesn't matter what you say; just say *something*. It soothes me to hear you talk," is a patient who has unconsciously identified with the therapist, whom he perceives not as being attentive and encouraging of his—the patient's —speaking, but, instead, demanding it in an infantile-dependent fashion.

Similarly, in working with a series of patients over the years who routinely ask me, on coming into my office, "How are you?," I have found it illuminating to realize that my own private, unverbalized feelings in response to this greeting are largely introjected from the patient or, to put it in a different way, projected by him or her into me. That is, in response to the patient's "How are you?" as he walks by me toward the couch or his chair, I often feel—particularly if the question has been put with a demeanor of warmth and caring—that I would dearly love to be able to unburden myself, and tell him in voluminous and basically endless detail of the myriad aspects of how I am feeling today; but, knowing how impossible this is, in light of our true situation here, I react mainly with bitterly ironic amusement, saying, "Just grand," or merely nodding. I am left feeling, more than anything else, tantalized. Then it occurs to me—and the first time it does so, with any one of these patients, it comes to me as an important denouement—that the patient himself is carrying within him (in his unconscious) the burden of very much these same kinds of feelings.

That is, he is entering a situation, each time he comes to my office, which implicitly asks him—although I do not myself explicitly do so— "How are you?" But he tends to feel that our time together is so fleeting that he could not make more than a pathetic beginning at unburdening his heart and his mind, before the time would be up. Even more impossible than the time limitations is the fact that *he* is supposed to be the one who is helping *me*, so that it would be inherently wrong for him to really pour out to me, in anything like fully felt detail, what he is feeling and needing. Here my paper "The Patient as Therapist to His Analyst" (Searles 1975) is relevant. In that paper I describe that, despite the outward trappings of the situation wherein the therapist is ostensibly treating the patient, and the earlier situation wherein the parent was ostensibly caring for the child, the patient (who once was that child) has a deep-seated (and well-founded, as regards his early years) conviction that the true situation, behind the outward trappings, is that it is the child who is responsible for being parent to the parent, and the patient who is responsible for providing therapy to the analyst or therapist.

In the series of patients I have mentioned, with regard to this greeting, "How are you?," I cannot say that when the denouement occurs to me, I am then able to make an interpretation that turns things around or opens things up in any revolutionary sense. But it nonetheless enables me, while remaining essentially silent, to foster an atmosphere wherein the patient can feel that he is being met with more of genuine patience and empathy than had been the case before.

Time and again, one sees (or hears about in supervision) a patient who recurrently acts out by absenting himself from work, or who recurrently threatens to quit the therapy and get a job in some other part of the country. In one instance after another, I find evidence that the patient is unconsciously identifying here with part-aspects of the therapist—a therapist who is being perceived, unconsciously, as not really working, not really doing a job, or who is recurrently and unpredictably quitting his job during the session and going off God knows where into what we might call autistic reverie. In my own work with such patients, it is comparatively rare for me to feel that I am genuinely and consistently present and am doing a valid job here. Instead, I have powerful, submerged urges to chuck this whole difficult and—so I often fear—basically undoable job, and go off into some other field far away. Hence the patient who acts out in a fashion that jeopardizes our collaborative effort is almost certainly doing so partly on the basis of identification with my own largely submerged urges to escape all this.

A female therapist, working with a severely borderline, hospitalized young woman, usually met with the patient in the therapist's office, and usually refrained from becoming involved with the administrative aspects of the patient's life on the ward. The patient, like the others in that hospital, was assigned an administrative psychiatrist as well as a therapist.

It was unusual, but by no means rare, for the therapy sessions to be held, for various reasons, in the patient's room. During one such session, the patient was bedridden with bronchitis. In the course of the session during which, as usual, there was a moderate amount of verbal communication back and forth, about various matters, the therapist said something relatively unusual for her: Concerned about the severity of the patient's cough, she suggested that it would be well for her to get an appointment with her (the patient's) internist. Although I knew the therapist's suggestion to be an expression of caring, I sensed that the patient could hear it as something of a command; she knew that the therapist herself served as an administrative psychiatrist for another ward in the hospital.

In response to the therapist's suggestion, the patient instantly jumped out of bed, pointed a reproving finger in the therapist's face, and screamed, "Don't you tell me what to do!"

I suggested to the therapist that the patient had tended to perceive her—the therapist—as having changed in her demeanor as suddenly and radically as, we agreed, the patient herself was now changed in her own behavior. That is, I surmised that the patient was identifying, here, with the suddenly changed therapist; the magnitude of the change in the therapist, as perceived by the patient, had been heightened greatly by projectional and transference factors.

This seemed to make sense to the therapist during the supervisory session. I have found it reliably true in my own work with patients over the years that, as I phrased it in a paper entitled, "Anxiety Concerning

Change, As Seen in the Psychotherapy of Schizophrenic Patients—with Particular Reference to the Sense of Personal Identity" (Searles 1961), ". . . the more deeply ill the patient, the more exclusively he experiences change as being an attribute of that which is outside himself, rather than as occurring within himself."

I am grateful to Teresita C. DiPinto, M.D., for permission to include the foregoing vignette from my supervisory work with her.

The specific example just described from my supervisory work reminded me of my own work with a chronically schizophrenic woman, who met with me in my office; our chairs were placed a foot or so away from the front of my desk, on which various personal memorabilia of mine are placed. In the course of one session with her, I asked her something, to which she made no verbal response but immediately—as if in response—reached far across my desk and picked up some personal item of mine and started examining it at close hand. I immediately sensed—with considerable shock at this new view of myself—how suddenly and aggressively intrusive and invasive she had tended to perceive my question as being. I phrase it in this stilted way because I doubted—and doubt still, long afterward—that she herself felt as much of the shock and the offensiveness of my question as I myself was given, by her physical response, to feel. I surmise that a relatively neurotic patient would have been able to feel and verbally express the sense of shock, and of being personally invaded, which this woman could convey to me only by this unconscious identification with my sudden invasiveness.

I mean to indicate here that a patient's unconsciously identifying with one of the therapist's introjects can be a cause of either acting in or acting out (as mentioned earlier here) on the part of the patient. Incidentally, to refresh your memory, the *Psychiatric Dictionary* by Hinsie and Campbell (1970) defines *acting in* as "A type of *acting out* that occurs during the therapy session; the patient discharges drive tension through action rather than through words."

In the instances of a number of patients who have begun keeping a diary in the course of my work with them—work that involved my taking (as they knew) relatively frequent notes, while they were reporting from the couch—it was apparent that one element in this acting-out behavior on the patient's part was an identification with my own writing of notes during the sessions. But the aspect of this that fascinated me in each instance was the evidence that the patient was perceiving me, unconsciously, as being—

while taking notes—psychologically as alone in the room as he was while writing in his diary. Moreover, he unconsciously perceived what I was writing as being as entirely a product of my own thoughts as was his diary a record of his own thoughts. Here again, there was being conveyed unconsciously, via the patient's diary-keeping acting-out behavior, an image of the therapist as strikingly narcissistically self-absorbed or autistic.

A number of fellow therapists, in treatment by me, have reported that they had "tried on" or "used on" some patient of theirs an interpretation that I had recently given to them, and have convincingly confirmed that this had served in part as a way of my analysand's getting rid of the interpretation that I had made to him or her. The aspect of this of interest to me here is that, in each instance, I found reason to believe that the therapist was not only consciously identifying with me in making the interpretation, but also unconsciously identifying with one of my unconscious motives in my making the interpretation to him or her: I myself had been trying to get rid of it by making it, prematurely, to my analysand before having tried it adequately upon myself, and before having accepted it as being true to a significant degree for myself. I had never applied the insight in question to myself in any deep, persistent, working-through fashion. I surmise that this kind of thing is among the determinants of premature interpretations in general.

Having written this, I am now reminded of how I used to feel, early in my own analysis, when I would leave my analyst's office and walk to the V. A. Mental Hygiene Clinic only a block away, returning to my work as a psychotherapist, where I would not uncommonly feel, sitting up and working with my patient, that I was somehow managing to keep myself propped up—so recently off the couch—and fending off the patient by making various interpretations that I had just heard from my analyst. Only now, nearly forty years later, does it occur to me that I had an unconscious image of my own analyst as being comparably infirmly propped up, and spouting interpretations at me primarily as an attempt to keep from being overwhelmed by my demands upon him—an unconscious image of him with which I was identifying unconsciously in my session with my own subsequent patient.

I can believe that any such image of my analyst on my own part was far indeed from fully accurate, but more striking to me is the fact that my relative idealization of him never permitted me, for nearly forty years, to entertain even fleetingly such an image of him. I am reminded now, too, of his uncharacteristic chatting with me, in a colleague-to-colleague fashion, at the end of one of the sessions, perhaps midway along in our work together, about a recently published article, entitled "Hate in the Countertransference," by Winnicott, that he had found to be of unusually lively interest to him. I listened politely, but experienced a vaguely troubled impression that perhaps he was trying to tell me something. Although he may never have felt anything like a propped-up puppet in his own work with his patients, he must at times have felt he was something less than fully his own person, or he would not have shown so essentially grateful a reaction to Winnicott's message as to the permissibility, inevitability, and therapeutic value of the analyst's being able consciously to hate the patient.

A few moments ago I touched upon the topic of premature interpretations, and I shall digress from my main theme to present a few ideas about the general topic of interpretations.

Kernberg, in his most recent book, *Severe Personality Disorders: Psychotherapeutic Strategies* (Kernberg 1984) states, in discussing the treatment of borderline personalities, "I have stressed the importance of maintaining an attitude of technical neutrality in order to be able to interpret the primitive transferences occurring in the patient-therapist interaction" (p. 122). He had explained earlier, "Technical neutrality means maintaining an equal distance from the forces determining the patient's intrapsychic conflicts . . ." (p. 103).

While I acknowledge that Kernberg makes a point here of fundamental importance in principle, to my way of thinking he carries it to a perfectionistic degree, such that in his book it comes to constitute a bit of the old classically psychoanalytic view of countertransference, which has no place, to my way of thinking, in this work with borderline and comparably ill patients. Again and again he stresses that it is important that when the therapist makes an interpretation, he make it from a position of technical neutrality.

Kernberg's book is written by one who seems convinced that he achieved full maturity decades ago, during his training analysis, and that his maintenance of this maturity has never been in appreciable doubt since then, no matter how disturbed the patients he is treating are. Such perfectionism tends to be intimidating to relatively young and inexperienced therapists and, taken as an ingredient of a role model, would be conducive to such a therapist's striving so diligently to maintain so thoroughgoing a neutrality, whenever he ventures to interpret, that he is all too likely to be projecting (unconsciously, of course) into the patient all sorts of far-from-neutral emotions, such as defiance, contempt, envy, lust, hatred, rage, fear, and so on.

To put this in a slightly different way, so rigorous a requirement for technical neutrality requires that the therapist endeavor to achieve and maintain an inherently unattainable self-concept as a therapist. This fosters his projection into the patient of feelings and attitudes that are not embrace-able within a "technically neutral position."

Also, this concept underestimates the patient's perceptiveness, a percep-tiveness that is fundamentally important to confirm as being a vastly impor-tant part of the patient's increasingly healthy ego-functioning. I have tried in a number of papers to show how important, in the therapist's perceptive-ness as to what is going on in the patient, it is for the therapist to notice the subtle affective tones in which the patient's verbal statements are made. The same principle holds true in the patient's registering of the therapist's verbal interpretations: The affective tones in which these statements are made are often more significant than their verbal content. The borderline (for exam-ple) patient's developing of a good sense of reality is at stake here.

The "technically neutral position" that Kernberg emphasizes that the therapist must be careful to occupy while making an interpretation is presumably rarely if ever fully neutral. I strongly surmise, further, that it is by affective (emotional) *departures from* strict neutrality—no matter how subtle these departures may be—that a significant degree of limit setting is done. That is, a hint of anger, anxiety, impatience, admiration, envy, excitement, and so forth in the therapist's voice in making the interpretation may convey to the patient that the therapist has reached the limit of his own emotional tolerance at this moment.

Last, with regard to interpretations, it is my impression that any nota-bly effective interpretation contains an element of the therapist's working through, in the making of the interpretation, a conflict within himself essentially like the patient's conflict upon which the interpretation is fo-cused. This degree of mutuality in the growth achieved in successful psy-choanalytic therapy—growth in the therapist as well as in the patient—assumes that working through is a lifelong process. Relevant here is a sentence from a long definition of *working through* in *A Glossary of Psychoanalytic Terms and Concepts*, edited by Moore and Fine (1968): ". . . Now considered a most important part of the analytic process, working through consists essentially of a repetition, extension, and deepening of the analysis of the resistances, which need to be overcome repetitively and progressively . . ." (p. 95).

I shall return now to the main theme of this paper, namely the presence of unconscious identifications behind or beneath conscious ones.

A woman was on the one hand receptive to my pointing out the evidence that some repetitive aspect of her behavior was based in part upon identification with her father, but the patient reacted with more than an expectable degree of embarrassment, also, at hearing this. I found reason to think that the embarrassment likewise was based upon identification with another aspect of him. I had formed long since the conviction that her father had been a chronically embarrassed individual. I chose not to interpret the embarrassment on this occasion. But I have found it useful, in many instances with many patients by now, to suggest to a patient that his or her discomfiture with the identificational personality trait in question may have had a counterpart in the parent himself (or herself)—the parent being portrayed now, in my work with the patient, as being someone other than a totally self-approving tyrant or whatnot, but rather a human being who was subject to internal conflicts and was striving to become as free as possible from his own dislikable personality attributes.

For many years I have found the following circumstance reliable. When I am in a session with a patient and I find myself experiencing some feeling or fantasy or both, and find it to be accompanied by a strongly not-me feeling component—a feeling that it is not like me to be having such a fantasy or feeling—I can feel reasonably sure that at least a significant degree of this experience is occurring by processes of introjection and projection—that I am introjecting, unconsciously, some of this from the patient's unconscious, and that he is projecting (unconsciously, of course) some of this into me. In recent years, as I understand it, the patient is said to be involved in a process of projective identification, and as a phase in this process, the therapist is identifying unconsciously with the patient's projections. But something that occurred to me only in recent years is that the not-me feeling accompaniment *also* is based in part on unconscious identification, on my part, with a comparable feeling at work in the patient's unconscious. Could he himself be aware, at this moment, of the kind of fantasy or feeling in which I have been finding myself immersed, he presumably would be quite overwhelmed with a not-me feeling reaction to it; that is, his sense of identity would be formidably disturbed.

The next vignette is from my work with a middle-aged woman who has an obsessive-compulsive personality, and who has many largely unconscious identifications with her deceased father, whom the patient had found, throughout her childhood, to be tyrannically controlling of her. She early established a transference to me as being this tyrannical father.

In one session I had ushered her in punctually from the waiting room as usual. Then, about one minute before the (not unusual) session was due to end, she introduced, in an apologetic, conflicted manner, a new topic, saying that it would take quite some time to tell this, and she indicated her awareness that the session was nearly over. When the end of the time did come a minute later, I clearly interrupted her narrative to call the end of the session. I did so with a powerful feeling of angry determination, though I felt this to be well controlled. My determination sprang from a keen and long awareness of how controlling she was, and from my self-righteous awareness that I had begun the session punctually.

Our next session, two days later, was scheduled for 9:00 A.M. on Saturday. I became involved at about 8:45 in trying to get my outgoing message on my telephone-answering device to sound less garbled. At 9:03 I realized that my session with her was not for 9:15, as for many years I had been used to starting the day on Saturday with other patients, but rather for 9:00. I had heard her come into the waiting room several minutes before this realization about the 9:00 starting time occurred to me.

I went quickly and got the session started, about seven minutes late, and apologized to her, at the beginning, for my lateness—explaining that I'd been used to starting on Saturdays at 9:15, and had just realized that our session was scheduled for 9:00. But within a very few minutes along in the session, I told her of my sense that I could not maintain the tyranically firm stance that I had been occupying at the end of the previous session. She had already spoken, in the present one—although in a not discernibly angry way—of her having been conscious that I had interrupted her at the end of the previous session.

For the purpose of this chapter, what I found of great interest was the idea that now occurred to me—that not only my subjectively tyrannical firmness, my determination, involved identification with her tyrannical-father introject, but *also* that my getting mixed up about the time, and thus undoing that firmly determined position, may have involved identification with an aspect of his feeling unable to go on providing her with the tyrannical strength that he felt she needed him to manifest. So do I have reason to feel that she needs for me to be able to endure the transference role of the tyrannical father with whom she was in a power struggle throughout her remembered relationship with him. I must be brief, here; but I can say that this realization threw a lastingly useful light upon the patient's own previously unconscious part in maintaining the father's tyranny, and upon the patient's previously unworked-through feelings of guilt and grief about the father's death from a long and debilitating physical illness.

Another woman was approaching the age of 35, the age at which her mother had died of cancer, when the girl had been 8 years of age. The patient, after detailing various physical signs and symptoms that she had been fantacizing to be precursors of cancer, said with both bitter irony and a kind of grim determination, "I'm planning to die of cancer at 35 as my mother did." This revealed not only a sense of identification with the mother with regard to the timing of the mother's death, but a previously unrevealed identification with the mother perceived as having been suicidally determined to arrange her (the mother's) own death by cancer.

Next I shall cite two examples from my personal experience.

For many years I have enjoyed washing dishes, and not rarely have had the feeling that this is the one thing in my life that I feel entirely comfortably capable of doing. I have always assumed that, in my washing of dishes, I was identifying with my mother, who routinely did them in my early childhood. But in recent years, since I have become increasingly interested in this chapter's title subject, it has occurred to me that I have been identifying with my mother not only in the form but also in my spirit of washing the dishes. I had not previously allowed myself to consider the possibility that she, too, may have felt so chronically overwhelmed, so chronically out beyond her depth in life, that this activity, this washing of dishes, was the one part of her life with which she felt fully equipped to cope comfortably.

In the second personal example, for nearly fifteen years, ending twenty-three years ago, I worked at Chestnut Lodge, a sanitarium owned and managed by Dexter M. Bullard, Sr., M.D., who lived with his wife and several children in a home on the grounds of the sanitarium. I noticed, as the years went on, that sporadically I privately felt, with pleasure, like a member of the Bullard family. These were on occasions when I felt my work with my patients to be going well, and I felt on good terms with both Dr. Bullard and Mrs. Bullard, who was the business manager there; I was never actually in their home any more often than the other staff members were. But within at most a few years of leaving there, I realized that there had been at least two levels of transference operating in me. Beneath the obvious level of transference from my parental Searles family to this Bullard family, there was, I ruefully realized now, the fact that I had felt, in childhood, only *like* a member of the Searles family—had felt, that is, that I never succeeded in becoming a full-fledged, bona fide member of it. Since then, I have come in my clinical work to find more and more examples of families wherein it is dubious whether any of the members feels securely to have made it, to have succeeded in this sense; instead (as I believe is true in the sicker families) each member uneasily feels himself or herself to be a relative impostor or hanger-on, among these other true, fully qualified family members.

Invariably, in writing a paper I learn things about myself. In writing this chapter, I have learned that the chronically overwhelmed feeling I have about my life—a feeling that I have had for decades—is and has been based in part upon a heretofore unconscious identification with such an attitude in my mother regarding her life. When I realized this, it occurred to me what a relief it is to realize that part of this is not one's own struggle—that one has been endeavoring, unconsciously, to accomplish someone else's task for that person. A life can be lived, I thought, if it is truly one's own life that one is living—if, that is, one is not having unconsciously to try to live various other persons' lives for them.

But I then reminded myself, and realized more deeply than I had before, one does not have an own self quite apart from and beyond such identifications. An individual, own self is like a symphony, and such identifications are among the indispensable notes that comprise the symphony; it could not exist without them.

CONCLUSION

I have presented a variety of clinical vignettes wherein one can detect, in either patient or therapist, unconscious identifications ramifying beneath or behind a relatively simple and obvious conscious one.

The therapist is threatened, at times, with the power of his own identifying with transference images of him on the part of the patient, transference images that coincide with only partially outgrown introjects within the therapist.

I have emphasized that in the relatedness between the largely regressed patient and the therapist, who necessarily is regressed to a degree greater than the literature generally acknowledges, there is much more of back-and-forth projection and introjection than we have comprehended heretofore. It is not merely, for example, that the patient manifests the unconscious defense of projective identification; so does the therapist.

I have explained that projective identification wherein the patient is identifying unconsciously with the therapist's projections is frequently a factor in various kinds of acting in or acting out on the part of the patient.

Some of these clinical examples reveal that the patient unconsciously, but with at least a significant degree of accuracy, perceives the therapist as being involved in "as-if" psychodynamics. In others, the patient unconsciously perceives the therapist as being what we would call narcissistic or autistic.

Other examples have to do with the therapist's making premature interpretations.

Others reveal the patient's unconscious perception of a parent's behavior during the patient's childhood. Some of these examples show how the discovery of previously unconscious identifications contributes to a developing image, in the conscious minds of patient and therapist, of the patient's parents as being or having been complex human beings who struggled with inner conflicts—who were struggling to deal with their own conflicting identifications.

I have endeavored to portray, throughout this chapter, that maturation is an ever ebbing-and-flowing process, rather than a permanent state achieved once-and-for-all, and that the maturational discovery of heretofore unconscious identifications is a process that tends to continue throughout one's life.

REFERENCES

Deutsch, H. (1942). Some forms of emotional disturbance and their relationship to schizophrenia. *Psychoanalytic Quarterly* 11:301–321.

Grinker, R. R., and Spiegel, J. P. (1945). *Men Under Stress*. Philadelphia: Blakiston.

Hinsie, L. E., and Campbell, R. J. (1970). *Psychiatric Dictionary—Fourth Edition*. New York: Oxford University Press.

Kernberg, O. F. (1984). *Severe Personality Disorders: Psychotherapeutic Strategies*. New Haven: Yale University Press.

Kris, E. (1952). *Psychoanalytic Explorations in Art*. New York: International Universities Press, p. 177.

Moore, B. E., and Fine, B. D. (1968). *A Glossary of Psychoanalytic Terms and Concepts*. New York: The American Psychoanalytic Association.

Searles, H. F. (1961). Anxiety concerning change, as seen in the psychotherapy of schizophrenic patients—with particular reference to the sense of personal identity. *International Journal of Psycho-Analysis* 42:74–85.

——— (1975). The patient as therapist to his analyst. In *Tactics and Techniques in Psychoanalytic Therapy, Volume II: Countertransference*, ed. P. L. Giovacchini, pp. 95–151. New York: Jason Aronson.

——— (1979). The countertransference in psychoanalytic therapy with borderline patients. In *Advances in Psychotherapy of the Borderline Patient*, ed. J. LeBoit and A. Capponi, pp. 309–346. New York: Jason Aronson.

——— (1984). Transference-responses in borderline patients. *Psychiatry* 47:37–49.

.9

RENATA GADDINI, M.D.

Regression and Its Uses in Treatment

Very cogently Greenacre (1968) noted:

> With extraordinary intuition Freud gradually fashioned the methods for psychoanalytic therapy after the principles of growth. This was the more remarkable in that the new method of treatment involved the undoing of strictures of the past which impeded and distorted normal psychic development, so that the latter might emerge and proceed by itself. This was in contrast with the most advanced theories of the day which depended largely, but often unofficially, on support, suggestion and direction in the current situation against a background of neurologizing hypotheses without much consideration for the individual's historical background.
>
> Free association, one of the cornerstones of the psychoanalytic method, is somewhat comparable to the fluttering, seemingly random activity of the child before he reaches a new stage. It also resembles the pondering rumination which goes on in the preconscious dreamy states of the creative individual when he is in the process of arriving at some new idea, formulation or discovery. In the analysand it naturally finds its way back to the sources of his difficulties in the past as well as his disappointments of the present and his hopes for the future. Since he is already caught in an inner nexus of binds, he might arrive at a state of unproductive brooding with obsessional repetition or rationalization if he were left entirely to himself. The analyst having travelled these or similar pathways in himself and with others recognizes the road signs and at appropriate times may point out the significances of the patient's being drawn to the familiar path even though in the past it

has led to pain and frustration. He may even indicate the presence of paths which have been previously bypassed. Gradually then courage for new development emerges. [p. 214]

REGRESSION AND GROWTH

The regression of the analyst to pregnancy and infancy, through his or her reverie with the patient, should be mentioned. It could be mentioned also that pregnant patients regress to their embryonic beginning through their primary maternal preoccupation with the baby conceived but not yet born. In patients of pregnant analysts we expect even more regression to primary, even envious, states through projective identification with the baby in utero. This is, at least, what a number of authors have implied. Interesting examples of regression in the course of pregnancy have been described by Conforto (1984) and, in four cases of women who became pregnant while in analysis, by Lester (1988). On the other hand, patients of pregnant women analysts have been observed to undergo regression (Fenster et al. 1988).

Notably, regression is often observed in our patients when they feel the approach of termination. In a dream of a protagonist of an attempt at premature termination in "The Timing of Termination" (Novick 1988), the analyst "has come to represent the degraded, discarded, devalued part of the patient's self representation. In other words, there has been a regression from a differentiated to an externalizing transference" (p. 310).

Facilitating regression as a way to progression has been an innovation in technique that has recently interested many analysts. We owe the little we know about technique to the study of the fusional states of early development in the natural growth process (R. Gaddini 1987, Mahler 1968) and to our attempts at using them in treatment, mostly connected with looking and with the mother's eyes. Looking, in Ballesteros's (1977) view, is like grabbing at the mother's eyes as if they were a breast, a part object. In Eissler's (1978) view, also, *looking* establishes a concrete continuity. E. Gaddini (1986) has described a very sensorial quality of looking in early stages, a sensorial quality which is not yet a perception. The question is: Has a self been built or not? In the latter case, subject and object are still the same. Looking, in this case, has more to do with touching and tactile contact than with the perception of the image.

From severely disturbed patients we have, in fact, learned that what these patients need is a very complex situation in which they can regress and in which the psychoanalyst can help them to make use of regression to dependence. These patients return emotionally to a very early state of development in which the analyst finds himself in the place of an early mother figure, that is, one that is prior to the patient's objectively perceived mother. There is no longer a differentiated transference. It is a time—that of the subjective object—when sense data, mostly connected with looking and with mother's eyes (Ballesteros 1977, Eissler 1978) are the basis for frustration.[1] The infant, at this time, experiences frustration that may be expressed in feelings of being overwhelmed and annihilated. When the mind develops, mental pain takes the place of these "primary agonies" (Winnicott 1974). Ideas and thoughts do not give the same sort of frustration. As E. Gaddini (1982) pointed out, the mind may well be seen, therefore, as a rescuer of the body, a way of saving the growing child from the fears of self loss.

THE LESSON COMING FROM "TOO SICK PATIENTS"

In a previous well-received work, Winnicott (1974), with his "Fragment of an Analysis," gave us an intimate glimpse into his technique of handling a seriously emotionally regressed patient.

Another example of working with a temporarily regressed patient, and of handling regression and progression, sharing both with anxious yet very collaborative parents, may be seen in the moving case of "Piggle," the 28-month-old child, who, at the age of 21 months when a sister was born, began to have fears of the black mummy (black for her meant "hate") and suffered serious anxieties on the basis of disillusionment (Winnicott 1977).

A major contribution toward a better understanding of the work with regressed patients may be found further in Winnicott's letters (Rodman 1987). The topic of regression and of treating the regressed patient comes up repeatedly in these letters, mostly in a stimulating and clarifying way. No doubt he is the author who, most of all, got close to the understanding of regression in a comprehensive way, and who gave value to this process. In this view, the transitional object, which is made of early sensations to which later developing affects and symbolic meaning are attached, is typical of regression no less than it is of creative reparation. In Winnicott's (1954) view, the gradual construction of the capacity to feel guilty and of the capacity for concern (Winnicott's *capacity for concern* is his term for Klein's

---

[1]Quoting Eissler's essay, Harrison (1988) notes on the matter: "Eissler did not raise the possibility that Freud's work may have been an antidote for the kind of gaze that destroys. While Freud was conscientiously at work, he was spared the critical scorn of Brucke's terrible blue eyes. Also, his own eyes were doing no harm" (p. 370).

depressive position) has, for him, its corollary in the way regression appears as a necessary condition to rescue basic data and feelings that are, originally, stored as part of the individual's growth. Capacity for concern and regression to dependence will influence heavily the whole growth process.

When I say that Winnicott gave value to regression, I mean to regression in the psychoanalytic process, that is, in the treatment of the regressed patient. Like Freud, who "vigorously repudiated the idealization of regression towards oneness with the universe, just as he did other mystical and religious beliefs" (Harrison 1988), he was keen in discovering pathology and in understanding the fears of breakdown that were at the basis of these surceases.

FROM WINNICOTT'S LETTERS (RODMAN 1987)

In a letter of March 1953 to Clifford Scott "recapturing some of his remarks to a paper presented the previous night,"[2] Winnicott mentions that "regression was not a simple return to infancy, but contained the element of withdrawal and a rather paranoid state needing a specialized protective environment." "I do believe, however," he added, "that this can be said to be normal in a theoretical way, if one refers to a very early stage of emotional development, something which is passed over and hardly noticed at the beginning, if all goes well (p. 49).

And, further on:

> In regard to the duration of regression, I could not, of course, predict its length. I had indications, however, which perhaps are rather subtle, and I might have been absolutely wrong. I took as my main platform the relatively normal first two years, and following this, the way in which it started at the age of two by using the mother and by his technique of living in a slightly withdrawn state. In regard to this particular point I am now very much strengthened by my experience of having allowed a psychoanalytic patient to regress as far as was necessary. It really happened that there was a bottom to the regression and no indication whatever of a need to return following the experience of having reached the bottom. [p. 49]

There is a postscript to this letter:

---

[2] "The management of a case of compulsive thieving."

In ordinary analysis one tries to make it unnecessary for regression to have to take place, and one succeeds in the ordinary neurotic case. I do believe, however, that the experience of a few regressing cases enables one to see clearly what to interpret. As an example I would say that since experiencing regression I more often interpret to the patient in terms of need and less often in terms of wish. In many cases it seems to me sufficient that one says, for instance: "At this point you need me to see you this weekend," the implication being that from any point of view I can benefit from the weekend, which indirectly helps the patient, but from the patient's point of view at that particular moment there is nothing but harm from the existence of a gap in continuity of the treatment. If, at such a moment, one says, "You would like me to give up my weekend," one is on the wrong track and one is in fact wrong." [pp. 49–50]

Regression to persecution is taken up in another letter to Esther Bick (June 11, 1953), who had used the expression in her paper, "Anxiety underlying phobia of sexual intercourse in a woman":

Your term *regression to persecution* means nothing at all as it stands, I expect you would agree with me that this was some kind of shorthand that you have evolved and that you had not time to say what you were meaning. . . . I suppose you are referring to Melanie Klein's concept of a paranoid position in emotional development, which I consider to be one of her less worked out theories, but in any case your term regression to persecution would not be able to convey any meaning to most of the people listening. [p. 51]

The discussion on technique goes on, with Clifford Scott (February 26, 1954), referring to Winnicott's Regression paper:

There is progress and regression and . . . for regression there has to be a rather complicated ego organization. I suggest that the word reversal is not so bad when applied to the word progress, whereas I agree that it is not sensible when applied to the word process.
     . . . Regression is an attempt to use previous types of behaviour normal or abnormal as a defence against present conflict.
     . . . Reversal should be kept for attempts on the part of the patient to reverse something, for instance, growth. When you compare impulses and wishes with needs you are stating the change of outlook that I am asking for. It seems difficult to get analysts to look at early infancy except in terms of impulses and wishes. Betty Joseph . . . takes wishes as the beginning of everything. I can agree

. . . that a bad breast is a fantasy of the infant; even when using judgment we can see a mother is failing. . . . Rage and depression refer to defensive techniques which also belong to a later stage of development. There is no state of frustration, because the individual has not yet become able to stay frustrated. The failure situation as I am referring to it results in a massive reaction to impingement; at the same time something that could have become the individual becomes hidden away; hidden where I cannot say, but separated off and protected from further impingement by the developing false self which is reactive as a main feature. . . . Difficulties in the classification of psychological disorders in young children and indeed in infants is due to the fact that we have not yet made full use of this concept of the false self developing reactively and more hiding the true impulsive self which might under more favourable circumstances have been gathering strength through experience on a non-reactive basis. [p. 59]

In another letter of April 1954 to Betty Joseph, still referring to his presentation of his paper on regression, Winnicott goes into the problem of the infant's fantasy of a bad breast and a bad mothering technique. He wonders, with Scott:

Cannot any bad experience be made worse by the patient's fantasy? . . . It is not the fantasy of a good or bad breast I am trying to draw attention to in the very early stages, quite apart from the fantasy . . . I find it difficult to get people to leave for a moment the infant fantasy of a bad breast and to go to a *stage further back*, to the effect of a bad mothering technique, such as for instance rigidity (mother's defence against hate) or muddle (expression of mother's chaotic state). [p. 59]

And further on:

What happens to the bad breast in the good state of regression? I think I dealt with this in my first letter when I was saying that I was trying to get to something earlier than the presentation of what can be felt by the infant as a bad or good breast. . . . The bad mothering technique comes out with extreme clearness in the sort of treatment that I was describing. . . . I want to emphasize . . . that the bad mothering is an essential thing in the sequence in the technique that I described . . . after a good experience which corrects the bad one the next thing is that the patient uses one's failures and in this way brings into the present each original mothering technique inadequacy. [pp. 59–60]

Special attention is given to "regression to sleep," a point which has been touched by Clifford Scott in a presentation to the British Society (January 27, 1954) in a way that "the little bit of truth which was in . . . [this] reference gets lost." Winnicott wonders whether sleep is the "right word" to be used for both.

> . . . the sort of sleep that most of us have at night, in which any dissociation between sleeping and waking is very markedly lessened by the dream that we, more or less, remember on waking, even if only for a second. . . . The sort of sleep that you are referring to seems to me to be more of the nature of a depersonalisation or an extreme dissociation or something awfully near to the unconsciousness belonging to a fit. [p. 56]

Here Winnicott takes the example of a patient "who is dangerous just after expressing genuine love. In this case the oscillation between love and hate seemed to have been almost measurable, but what is more important, they were painful to the patient. I could give other examples, and the one I think of immediately is that of children who are helped rather than hindered by being told that they fear madness, the madness they fear being the oscillation between love and hate" (p. 57).

A patient of mine, an anorexic girl of 14, who had become mute and totally negativistic shortly after beginning treatment, became aggressive and dangerous, first to the analyst's person and afterwards to her properties, when the girl began to feel attachment to her analyst.

I, too, felt that she wanted to be certified and surely my understanding and telling her that she was suffering because of her oscillations between love and hate, and that her fears of a catastrophe were fears of madness helped her in establishing a relationship.

The outcome of regression is mentioned in a letter written by Winnicott to Guntrip (August 13, 1954), where the element of hate in regression is put forward:

> In regard to the future of your woman patient, I certainly think that you are on the right road but there are difficulties ahead. For instance, you have been able to follow the patient's regression to dependence and to be in the place of an early mother figure, that is to say one that is prior to the patient's objectively perceived

mother. I would think that there may be very great hate of you because of this position that you have taken, as the patient emerges from the regression and therefore becomes aware of the dependence. If one is not expecting this one may be puzzled at the tremendous hate which turns up within the love relationship in these regressed states. [Rodman 1987, p. 79]

The theory that underlies regression is strongly stated in a letter to Joan Rivière (February 3, 1956): "Unless she [mother] can identify very closely with her infant at the beginning, she cannot 'have a good breast' because just *having* the thing means nothing whatever to the infant. The theme can be developed, and I have frequently developed it, because I know of its great importance not only to mothers with infants, but also to analysts who are dealing with patients who have for a moment or over longer phases been deeply regressed" (p. 96), and in one to Thomas Mann (February 25, 1957), who, at the Cassel Hospital, was offering opportunities to patients to regress while the analyst was actively adapting to needs. ". . . This work of yours is of importance to psycho-analysis. It may be that psycho-analysis can contribute to your understanding of the problem and that some of the analytic contributions you have not absorbed. . . . The fact remains, however, that your collecting together all the fragments of nursing reactions adds up to a real contribution to psycho-analysis" (p. 112). And, further on: ". . . The characteristic of this kind of patients is that hope forces them to bang on the door of all therapies which might be the answer. They cannot rest from this; as you know so well their technique for mobilizing activity is terrific in its efficiency." (We can see here Winnicott's capacity of recognizing hope as an important element for construction and reconstruction of self in regressed patients on the basis of trust, the way he had been able to do with delinquents.)

. . . These patients make us try hard because they have hope and because it is the hope which makes them so clever; yet at the same time, the fact that we cannot provide what is needed produces disaster. In other words, it is only contributing a little if one can show that what these patients need is a very complex situation in which they can regress and in which the psycho-analyst can help them to make use of regression. Whatever can be done here must be only a small bit of what would have to be done to neutralize the destructive potential of this group of people. Indeed I would like to say that the more psycho-analysts become able to do this kind of work with a few patients the more patients there are who will begin to have hope and therefore will begin to bash around in a ruthless search for a life that feels real. I do consider therefore that if psycho-analysts ignore the problem . . . they are ignoring a group of forces that could destroy psycho-analysis and in practice could account for the deaths of analysts and psychiatric nursing staff, and the breakup of the better type of mental institution. [p. 114]

With Masud Khan, the theme of integration is mentioned in connection with regression (June 26, 1961):

The word *integration* describes the developmental tendency and the achievement in the healthy individual in which he or she becomes an integer. Thus, integration acquires a time dimension (depressive position). The state prior to integration I call unintegration. . . . Unintegration seems to me to describe a primitive state that is associated clinically with regression to dependence. Dissociation (like disintegration and splitting) seems to be a defence organization. . . . [p. 132]

As it is known, for Winnicott the original environment is reproduced by the psychoanalytic treatment in which the analyst is concerned with the patient's state of mind, and it becomes especially important when the patient is regressed. As Rodman (1987) puts it:

Starting from this early area of pleasure-in-illusion, human experience expands to include play, creativity, and cultural life in general. These categories of experience all provide a resting place where strict definition of self and others is not only not required, but is a hindrance to fulfillment. They all occur in the area of overlap between what comes from within and what is given from without . . . [in] the regression to dependence severely disturbed patients return emotionally to a very early state of development of which one feature is their absolute dependence on a caretaking person. [p. xxxi]

This brings to mind a patient of mine—a psychotic woman almost 40 years old—who after a profound withdrawal in childhood and adolescence oscillated between catatonia and intense motor excitement, manic testing out, bulimia, and delusions of various nature. She came to analysis after a number of psychiatric admissions, which unconsciously she had promoted. Her defiant attitude to failures and/or rejection, which had been heavily experienced in early life, as well as her search for a need-satisfying process that she had missed, was expressed in soiling, involving neighbors and extended mothering functions besides the analyst.

In Rodman's already quoted letter (January 10, 1969), where technique is discussed, Winnicott points to the dangers analysts run with regressed patients:

> . . . the relief that comes from not having to be so artificially adaptive, quite beyond that what I will do in private life, is so great that I begin to swallow the bait the patient offers and find myself talking about things in general and acting as if the patient had suddenly become well. This is a very great danger area in the treatment of borderline cases where regression to dependence is a prominent feature. Perhaps you would agree on this. On the other hand, I do not want to say that even this kind of mistake is quite useless, if the case survives the experience. Undoubtedly it does show the patient to what an extent one was under strain. The awful thing when a patient commits suicide at this stage is that this leaves the analyst forever holding the strain and never able to misbehave just a little. I think that is an inherent part of the revenge that suicide of this kind contains, and I must say that the analyst always deserves what he gets here. I say this having just lost a patient through being ill. I could not help being ill, but if I am going to be ill then I must not take on this kind of patient. It is almost mechanistic when we think how things work in this area. [p. 182]

MATERNAL CARE, SEDUCTION, AND COUNTERTRANSFERENCE

Freud never abandoned the seduction theory, as Masson (1984) claims in his notorious volume *Assault on Truth: Suppression of the Seduction Theory*. In fact, he gradually modified it and integrated it on the basis of both his discovery of infants' sexuality and of the potential phylogenetic meaning that the same had on adults' neuroses and psychoses. In his *Assault*, Masson quotes only a part of Freud's (1905) formulation of the role played by external and internal reality on the etiology of neurosis, and, in so doing, alters its meaning. Freud's (1905) formulation indeed stresses the fact that

> . . . The reappearance of sexual activity is determined by internal causes and external contingencies, both of which can be guessed in cases of neurotic illness from the form taken by their symptoms and can be discovered with certainty by psycho-analytic investigation. I shall have to speak presently of the internal causes; great

and lasting importance attaches to the accidental external contingencies at this period. In the foreground we find the effects of seduction, which treats the child as a sexual object prematurely and teaches him, in highly emotional circumstances, how to obtain satisfaction from his genital zones, a satisfaction which he is then usually obliged to repeat again and again by masturbation. An influence of this kind may originate either from adults or from other children. I cannot admit that in my paper on The Aetiology of Hysteria (Freud 1896) I exaggerated the frequency or importance of that influence, though I did not then know that persons who remain normal may have had the same experiences in their childhood, and though I consequently overrated the importance of seduction in comparison with the factors of sexual constitution and development. Obviously seduction is not required in order to arouse a child's sexual life; that can also come about spontaneously from internal causes. [p. 190–191]

On the other hand, when Freud abandoned Breuer's theory on hypnosis, he turned his eyes on new facts. A new theory generates new techniques, even within its own ambit, and these, in turn, lead to new discoveries. In the unconscious, Freud had put into evidence the identity between internal and external space. After fifty years, Winnicott was thus able to speak of an intermediate space comprised between the "boundaries" of the inner and outer world, a space where the sense of self begins. It is in this space, a space to relax and to get strength, that regression takes place, in my view. With regression to early care, however, seduction comes in, as a possible inducer.

MATERNAL SEDUCTIVE CONFIGURATION

As Winnicott wrote in a letter to P. D. Scott on the theme of delinquency, on May 11, 1950 (Rodman 1987), ". . . any kind of sentimentality is worse than useless . . . it is a sort of weakness to be guarded against" (Rodman 1987, p. xxiv). Winnicott's view was that aggression, which is intrinsic to human nature, must be given its due outlet. "A sentimental idea is one that does not leave room for hate or, at least, for aggression. To elucidate this point, I may say that any type of sentimentality must be looked upon, in my opinion, as a disturbing, seductive element, whether same appears in maternal care or in analysis; it is an element to be carefully watched" (Rodman 1987, p. xxiv).

In another letter (to V. Smirnoff, November 19, 1958) commenting on a proposed translation of his work on transitional objects into French, Winnicott writes, ". . . The word 'tender' is rather good but it emphasizes an absence of aggression and destruction, whereas the word 'affectionate' neither emphasizes nor denies it. One could imagine a hug, for instance, being affectionate and yet far from tender. . . ." (Rodman 1987, p. 121).

The asserted seduction of Melitta on the part of her mother (Rodman 1987) made me think of a patient of mine—seriously borderline—now in her seventh year of analysis.

> She "remembered" her breast feeding, which lasted until she was seven months, as a forced feeding, particularly during the last months. ". . . My mother forced me to take her breast and I felt like vomiting . . ." This feeling of "disgust" and "nausea" arose in this patient every time she was confronted with a certain kind of emotion—for instance, when she discovered that her younger brother was a homosexual.
>
> She spoke of "milk" in her stomach as something inconsistent, and not as though she had eaten and satisfied her hunger. "I often have this feeling when I drink milk. . . . I mix it with baby food, the Mellin powdered food, for example . . . too much milk must have given me this feeling of inconsistency. Nausea is something much easier to deal with. . . . You can solve the problem by vomiting. . . . This feeling of being swollen . . . of floating . . . you can't do away with it by provoking vomit. . . . It is something that must be absorbed . . . (one thinks of merging). It is a sensation that I seek, no matter what. After dinner I take my milk with these things in it. . . .

In countertransference, I often felt that this fear of merging with mother had its counterpart in her fear of being manipulated and in her tendency not to accept interpretations at the time they were offered.

> Later in life, she was to force her own son—the last after two daughters—to the point of abuse. She forced her breast into him, and then forced him to let go by squeezing his nose to the point of suffocation. The son is now a seriously ill asthmatic, with difficulties in relating to reality. Twenty-two years old, without girlfriends, he is often in my patient's dreams, in incestuous situations, his head resting in his mother's lap, and she feels guilty. "So grown up . . ." she tells herself in the dream. When interpreting, I made her notice how she, 47 years old, felt too grown up to rest her head on the analyst's lap, complacently and without the strength to oppose her analyst. She

speaks of the correspondence between Marcel Proust and his mother, and how the mother called him "Mon petit loup." Then she goes on speaking of her own son: "Last night I surprised myself, telling him, 'Take this, darling.' The soup was on the table, and I was not sure he wanted it. I insisted, 'Will you have this soup, love?' as though he were a child. . . . He gladly plays along with these tender attitudes. On many occasions, as I was sitting on the sofa, speaking of his two sisters, he would come and rest his head on my lap and ask that I caress his hair.

"I recall a dream, A. and F. (mother and son) are there . . . a tender and seductive relationship between them. . . . Anna has always tended to Federico's bodily care until he was nine. . . . I tried to oppose harshness and indifference to the tenderness and affection that I felt for Giuseppe. . . . I was afraid of spoiling him . . . I tried to protect myself . . . the wrong way . . . through compensation. . . . I wanted him to be autonomous. . . . I had mistreated him in all sorts of ways when he was small . . . and . . . I carried with me the image of myself as a six-months baby seduced into taking mother's milk, when there were all sorts of things out there which I could have perceived. . . . It was humiliating, it was like being cut off from new things . . . everything was filtered through my mother, a caged-in, unnatural way, undirect, manipulative. . . ."

Once again I found myself feeling that as with a patient's seduction one gets a negative therapeutic reaction, so does one have—with the seduction of a child on the part of the mother—an interference in basic trust and, one could say, a negative reaction to life and to relations with others.

The patient continues: ". . . There are attitudes I see in others and, above all, in myself, that have something to do with seduction . . . childish attitudes . . . wanting to be seduced . . . not to break the fusional state . . . often my reaction is abrupt, of a forced estrangement . . . or it may be tender and seductive . . . two extremes. . . ."

Many times I thought how difficult it has been for her to deal with all that she was bringing up, in her transference, these passing years. In time, I have come to understand that seduction, for her, meant intrusion, "impingement" in Winnicott's sense, the tendency that certain mothers have to thrust themselves in the going-on-being of their children, above all during the first months of their child's life, when the formation of a sense of self is taking place. Thus their natural development is hindered. As we have mentioned above, Winnicott believed in the real object as an influencing factor of growth, and so do I. We have discussed it, and while we both have made ours Freud's revolutionary concept that it is the unconscious that organizes and shapes our perception of the external world, and have learned that babies are self-propelling beings in respect to their mothers, we have never accepted entirely the concept that excluded external reality from any determining value in the construction of the basic mental organization (E. Gaddini 1982) nor in early mental processes. This holds particularly true for the "concrete subject matter" of which Freud (1923) told us apropos of early sensations. Thus, clinical experience has taught us that, as analysts, we are never to "intrude" on our patients, particularly on the very sick ones, who seem more needy and dependent, lest we should interfere with their possibility of regressing, which we have learned to be beneficial in certain stages of the analytic process.

The respect and trust that I have come to place in the natural developmental process, which should manifest itself in an authentic way in every individual, interwoven as it is with instinctual development and early care, and opposing itself to every type of seduction, may be found in this 1952 letter of Winnicott to M. Klein: ". . . if he were growing a daffodil [referring to a colleague] he would think that he was making the daffodil out of a bulb, instead of enabling the bulb to develop into a daffodil by good enough nurture. . . ." (Rodman 1987, p. 35) and, in another letter, written to a correspondent in Tanzania, "We cannot even teach children to walk . . . but their innate tendency to walk at a certain age needs us as supporting figures" (Rodman 1987, p. 186). The image of parents as "supporting figures" who facilitate walking recalls the earlier attitude or inclination of the mother to be aware of the needs of her baby, and of the analyst to those of his patient. They exclude every form of intrusion and manipulation that provide narcissistic gratification to the mother and to the analyst. In this view, anything that goes beyond active adaptation, that is, letting oneself be used according to need, in the patient's search of mental sense and of an emotional color of his life's vicissitudes, is already seduction and brings with it, almost inevitably, in life and in therapy, a negative reaction. The patient feels trapped; basic trust is at stake.

Within this context, on the topic of regression, another example comes to mind. It is a case reported by Limentani (1987) in his introduction to "Perversions, Treatable and Untreatable":

> A patient had brought him a dream: "Tim (her homosexual companion) menstruated at the same time I did. He said, 'Well, now we can make love.'" The analyst reminded her that only the day before she had

told him that she could not even think of making love to a woman. If she had, she was afraid she would lose her sense of identity. The patient, restless, answered him, "Even you would be afraid to lose your sense of identity if you had spent your childhood with my mother. My mother was erotic with me, you know, because I've observed her with small children. Even now she's seductive, until my brother enters the room. I never let anyone touch me until I was two and a half years old. I can't forget those first years." The analyst said it was certainly because she seemed to have a compulsive need to reenact the same situation, which was that of coming into contact with someone, of getting excited and, at the same time, going towards frustration in the hope of maybe freeing herself. Much to his surprise, the patient said yes, that was possible, but how could she free herself? [p. 428]

We can, therefore, conclude, on the basis of what I have reported in these pages, that the true nature of the relationship, in other words, whether it is based on true availability or on seduction, depends more on the quality and not the quantity of maternal care, or of the analyst's care. The possibility of regression derives from it. I hope the case of my patient, who lived as an abuse of her prolonged breast feeding, has served to illustrate my concepts.

The theme of seduction as inducer of regression as well as of fear to grow is a topical subject in today's culture as well as in the most recent studies of psychoanalytic techniques.

Seduction is of such great interest today because we are living in times of great losses and deprivations of primary needs and consequently of fragility of basic mental organization (E. Gaddini 1982), with resulting distortions of early mental processes necessary for autonomy and for a mature identity (E. Gaddini 1984). Our young people, who, instead of having received good enough early maternal care, have suffered all forms of intrusion and impingement, are afraid to grow, and do not want to be autonomous: they want to remain puppies. A stepmother—consumerism— has too often replaced adequate maternal care and, therefore, also a true culture of infancy and childhood.

From the repetition compulsion Freud arrived at the concept of the death instinct. With his studies in imitation, E. Gaddini (1969) has made us see early compulsion to repeat as an attempt to relive and reenact endlessly the sensory experiences of early *being*. If seduction was part of this primary bonding that is being for the infant (seduction that always "serves to compensate," as one of my patients said), we cannot but find ourselves faced by cases of intrapsychic seduction, which paves the way for the many idols of today's youth. The underlying fear is self-loss.

REFERENCES

Ballesteros, G. R. (1977). El ojo de la madre como objeto parcial. *Revista de la Sociedad Colombiana de Psicoanálisis* 2:27–51.

Bick, E. (1953). Anxiety underlying phobia of sexual intercourse in a woman. Presented at the British Psychoanalytic Society on June 10. Unpublished.

Conforto, C. (1988). Note sul trattamento piscoanalitico di una donna in gravidanza. *Patologia e Clinica Ostetrica e Ginecologica* (in press).

Eissler, K. (1978). Creativity and adolescence. *Psychoanalytic Study of the Child* 33:461–517.

Fenster, S., Philips, S., and Rapoport, E. (1988). *The Therapist's Pregnancy: Intrusion in the Analytic Space.* Hillsdale, NJ: Analytic Press.

Freud, S. (1896). The aetiology of hysteria. *Standard Edition* 3:197–224.

——— (1900). A note in the prehistory of psychoanalytic technique. *Standard Edition* 18:213–265.

——— (1905). Three essays on sexuality. *Standard Edition* 7:123–143.

——— (1923). The ego and the id. *Standard Edition* 19:3–68.

Gaddini, E. (1969). On imitation. *International Journal of Psycho-Analysis* 50:475–484.

——— (1982). Early defensive fantasies and the analytic process. *International Journal of Psycho-Analysis* 63:379–388.

——— (1984). Changes in psychoanalytic patients up to the present days. *International Psycho-Analytic Association Monograph Series* No. 4.

——— (1986). La maschera e il cerchio. *Rivista Italiana di Psicoanalisi* 2:172–186.

——— (1987). Notes on the body-mind question. *International Journal of Psycho-Analysis* 68:315–329.

Gaddini, R. (1987). Early care and the roots of internalization. *International Review of Psycho-Analysis* 14:321–333.

Greenacre, P. (1968). The psychoanalytical process: transference and acting out. *International Journal of Psycho-Analysis* 49:211–218.

Harrison, I. (1988). Further implications of a dream of Freud: a subjective influence on his theory formation. *International Review of Psycho-Analysis* 15:365–373.

Lester, E. (1988). Towards a profile of maternal functions (panel). Second Delphi International Psycho-Analytic Symposium, New York, July 1988.

Limentani, A. (1987). Perversions, treatable and untreatable. *Contemporary Psychoanalysis* 23:415–437.

Masson, J. M. (1984). *Freud's Assault on Truth: Suppression of the Seduction Theory.* Boston: Farrar & Farrar, p. 308.

Novick, J. (1988). The timing of termination. *International Review of Psycho-Analysis* 15:307–318.

Rodman, R. F. (1987). *The Spontaneous Gesture. Selected Letters of D. W. Winnicott.* Cambridge: Harvard University Press.

Scott, W. C. M. (1954). Regression to sleep. Unpublished.

Winnicott, D. W. (1954). Withdrawal and regression. In *Collected Papers. Through Paediatrics to Psycho-Analysis*, pp. 255-261. New York: Basic Books, 1958.
—— (1974). Fragment of an analysis. In *Tactics and Techniques in Psychoanalytic Therapy*, ed. P. Giovacchini, pp. 455-493. Annotated by A. Flarsheim. New York: Science House.
—— (1977). *The Piggle. An Account of the Psychoanalytic Treatment of a Little Girl*. New York: International Universities Press.

10

Vamik D. Volkan, m.d.

The Psychoanalytic Psychotherapy of Schizophrenia

This chapter deals with the psychoanalytic psychotherapy of severely regressed adult schizophrenics who have been markedly deficient in their reality testing, who have manifested disorganization in other ego functions, and whose transference responses in treatment at least initially constitute what must be described as transference psychosis rather than the usual transference neurosis. I came to realize in my work with such patients that the psychoanalyst treating an adult schizophrenic patient by psychoanalytic psychotherapy has something in common with colleagues who treat children in analysis. Anna Freud (1936) noted that not only does the child's analyst become affected with libido or aggression, he also becomes a target of externalization, his person coming to represent some part of the child's personality structure. With our current grasp of how the child's self- and internalized object representations evolve, we come to understand more about the process involved in externalizing self- and object representations. Although the adult schizophrenic's self- and object representations are at the core undifferentiated, there are present differentiated but unstable ones as well; influenced by aggressive or libidinal drive derivates, they are split into the "good" and the "bad." Unlike the patient with borderline personality organization, however, the schizophrenic cannot maintain splitting as an effective continuing defense (Volkan and Akhtar 1979, Volkan 1987). "Good" self- and object representations may become "bad" at a moment's notice. Moreover, the schizophrenic individual experiences fragmentation and tension within the clusters of his "good" self- and object images as well as within clusters of "bad" ones. To complicate matters, the split opposite self- and object representations are then involved in continuous introjective-projective relationships.

I use the term *introjective-projective* in a general way in the belief that it provides graphic demonstration of the dynamic flow into and out of the patient's representation. (See Volkan 1982 for descriptions of the many concepts related to the state indicated by this general term.) *Introjective-projective* seems semantically correct in the situation in which the patient can differentiate the self-representation from that of the object. The term *fusion* refers to the loss of a boundary dividing the two representations.

Introjection-projection and/or fusion-defusion not only dominate the schizophrenic patient's mental state and his relationships, they also serve as defensive functions, however primitive they may be. The schizophrenic has an unremitting need to find a repository for unintegrated and disturbing aspects of self and objects in order to keep what is within cohesive. Whatever defenses are present basically serve the maintenance of a sense of self, and what is projected on behalf of inner cohesion is taken in (introjected) without modification; little or nothing that is new comes in to change the situation, so the patient must project again, only to introject in a cyclic way what has been rejected.

In this chapter I focus on how the therapist interferes with this cycle in order to bring about change. I report on the ways in which these patients first include the representation of their therapist in their introjective-projective cycle and then internalize and assimilate (identify with) certain of his functions at different phases of the treatment. I indicate how such identification helps them pull together their fragmented psychic structures and avoid regression to or maintenance of an undifferentiated core. I also describe later evolution of the whole treatment process.

NATURE VERSUS NURTURE

Mahler's (1968) suggestion that both nature and nurture play a role in the etiology of schizophrenia is not a new notion for psychoanalysis. In reference to neurosis Freud stated in 1914 that "disposition and experience . . . are linked up in an indissoluble etiological unity" (p. 18), and biological research into the mysteries of schizophrenia is now highly sophisticated. Nonetheless, biological theories about schizophrenia are "devoid of psychological content" and "increasingly suffer from reductionism" (Cancro 1986, p. 106). Contemporary research into the mental functions of infants (Emde 1988a,b, Stern 1982, 1985) is relevant also, since it is believed that in schizophrenia there occurs severe regression to the earliest stages of mentation. Biologically prepared motivational structures appear in early infancy and are used in the early relationship of the child and his caregiver. Eventually they evolve into the more complex motivational structures of adult life. Although research of the kind being conducted now will shed much light on early mentation and supplement and/or modify our conceptualizations, it does not now include observation of the dynamic unconscious. Apprey (1984) points to the absence of synchrony between routine research findings and clinical findings, and maintains that proactive observations in neonate research fall short of agreement with those retrospective observations in clinical practice that remain persuasive. Observation of an infant's biopsychological potential will not yield understanding of such phenomena as projected aggression in the mother–child dyad, a mother's unconscious fantasies about her child and the latter's corresponding unconscious fantasies, or the mother's deposit onto her child of fully formed mental representations of another person, such as those of a sibling who died before the child's arrival (Volkan 1987).

In summary, one might say that biological research informs us about brain functions; research into infancy tells us more about biological motivational structures, but it will take clinical psychoanalysis to give meaning to a patient's symptoms as they reflect developmental and unconscious human processes. That is not to say, however, that our psychological theories give us all the answers we seek and the only—or true—insight into how schizophrenia develops. Nonetheless, we do have clinical evidence that psychotherapy based on what we now know about mental conflict—particularly that of object relations—and on an appropriate transference in therapy is efficacious in treating schizophrenia. In psychoanalytic psychotherapy the patient gives evidence of changes in the mental structure, which becomes organized at a higher level than before.

At present, we can speak of the nature–nurture issues in rather general terms. It would seem that a child may be susceptible to schizophrenia if a biological weakness disturbs his memory, thought, and affect so as to render him unable to tolerate anxiety, to integrate, and to repress. Yet our clinical observations demonstrate that a constitutionally sturdy child who has had devastating and repeated trauma during his developmental years without a "background of safety" (Sandler 1960) may also be prone to schizophrenia.

The way in which a child experiences interaction with his environment and assimilates his experiences into his developing mind is as important as objectively "real" environmental circumstances are in determining outcome. Although the child's ability to introject and identify appropriately with the functions of others depends on his constitutional potential, it must be remembered that a child cannot "take in" more than is available in the environment. It is clear that some highly successful adults were as children exposed to bad environmental influences. We simply do not at present know very much from the point of view of biology or psychology about what makes some persons more creatively adaptable than others.

A child's ego-identifications (Hendrick 1951) are the foundation of his developing psychic structure. A constitutionally "normal" child with an unnurturing mother will accumulate a "bad" foundation through experiences that are real and later may be fantasized. I (Volkan 1976) have reported two cases of schizophrenic men who had had to identify with mothers who obliged them to break with reality as a way of defense—and a life-style.

The first man had had his finger chopped off when he was a boy, and his mother had kept the severed finger in a bottle as long as she lived. After her death the son, by then grown, continued to keep it in his bedroom. This practice affected the pattern of his life, becoming a model for his primitive defenses. For her own reasons his mother had conveyed to him that the grisly object was "alive," a detachable body part. This was the child's "reality" as he assimilated it.

The mother of the second schizophrenic man had given her son a golden ring on each of his birthdays, in spite of the fact that he had a deformed hand and the rings were too big for him to wear. The child identified with a mother unable to test reality. I do not explore here what other meanings were superimposed on either mother's strange behavior, but focus on her child's perception of it, and their identification with women who failed to test reality within the important area of interaction with their sons. Neither mother was psychotic in a global sense; although the first was dead by the time her son became my patient, I was able to interview the other. Each, however, had a focal break with reality in specific kinds of interaction with her son. I have described in detail (Volkan 1987) the case of a patient I call Pattie, who was also a psychosis-prone individual and whose case also manifested identification with a mother faulty in reality-testing in focal areas.

A child born with certain peculiar genes or a physical deficiency such as blindness, for example, may also collect and assimilate defective experiences; in spite of a "normal" mother, such a person may ultimately have a weak foundation. Both children may become schizophrenic, particularly if the "bad" experiences are collected and assimilated very early, during the first year of life.

Psychoanalytic tradition and clinical observation support the formulation that a mental illness such as schizophrenia has antecedent experience in infancy and/or the developmental years. I have been able in my clinical work with adult schizophrenics to identify *in every case* childhood structural defects and/or precursors of subsequent difficulty. My formulations concerning them helped me understand *the meaning* of their symptoms and the nature of their relatedness to the world. They were less useful, however, in disclosing why these patients were schizophrenic while other people with like backgrounds were not. Also, I am not sure that biological theorists would agree with the traditional psychoanalytic belief that vulnerability develops in infancy or childhood except in the case of the individual with marked psychic maturity who is assaulted by unbearable trauma he cannot be expected to handle without losing ground.

Adult schizophrenic patients give many clues supporting the notion of a "core deficiency" (Mahler 1968) or "basic experiential disturbance" (Pao 1979) in the developmental years. In treatment such patients sooner or later verbalize their perception of deficient childhood self-representations: "My middle part is missing"; "I am like a doughnut—without a core"; "I am made of plaster of paris—if you scratch the surface, you find nothing solid." Other schizophrenics speak of "decomposition products" (Glover 1950) of the unintegrated and/or fragmented self-representations and ego nuclei. They may speak of having many "souls" (Abse 1955) or "sides" or "frames of mind" (Volkan 1964). What they communicate of their inner drama is not altogether symbolic; their descriptions of souls, frames, and the like not only stand for other representations but indicate something the patient has *become*.

Such patients are fixated in an ongoing attempt to protect their sense of self and to build a core, and to a chronically ineffective attempt to integrate a core. In this way they are unlike the child sufficiently effective in following the same protocol to move on to more complex tasks. Through repeated experiences the child introjects ego functions, or their precursors, and makes them the building blocks of his core by identifying with what he introjects. Disturbing introjects are externalized in this process, so what is kept inside becomes more cohesive. The ability to establish externality and retain within what is comforting (Tähkä 1987, Volkan 1986, 1988) is necessary, along with the ability to introject and retain. Although he does have some mature functions, the adult schizophrenic is basically in a perpetual state of introjecting and projecting, but he is deficient in the collection and assimilation of sturdy building blocks and in effective externalization. Suslick (1963) has compared the schizophrenic's introjective-projective activity to the alimentary habits of an earthworm.

Using the term *mutual cuing*, Mahler (1968) wrote of the need of a "fit" or congruence between the infant and his caretaker. Mutual cuing is the essential psychological ingredient for the development of a feeling of being safe, and of a solid psychic foundation. Recent research into infant development (Emde 1988a,b, Lichtenberg 1983, Stern 1982, 1985) indicates that the infant is more stimulus-seeking than previously thought. The child reaches the stimulus barrier from his side and has innate equipment with which to regulate stimuli, so mutual cuing is influenced by both members of the dyad.

Lichtenberg (1986) observed that some babies seem discoordinated when approached by the mother or her surrogate, and seem less alert and less well physically coordinated than usual. He explained this unexpected response by noting that some neonates cannot use stimuli to learn about the environment because their immature nervous systems are overtaxed by them. Lichtenberg's data, dependent on observations of split-screen photography of infant–mother interactions during twenty-four hours, show that the effect on the mother of her infant's negative response may be profound.

> Rather than feeling the competence of their babies and their accomplishments with them, they become confused and frustrated. Here we have a biological factor turning into an environmental trauma, affecting the concrete experience of both partners. [Lichtenberg 1986, p. 91]

In the absence of mutual cuing the child is exposed to "basic experiential disturbances," and developmental deficiencies in ego functioning and in the formation of a sense of self-continuity.

PAO'S FIVE STEPS

Pao's (1979) theory about the formation of schizophrenia takes into account some involved processes taking place between basic experiential disturbances and the eventual crystallization of the schizophrenic illness. He describes *five* steps.

The first. The schizophrenia-prone person is burdened by the same kinds of conflicts others experience. A life event arouses repressed conflict in which erotic or aggressive impulses are an issue.

The second. In such a person conflict does not lead to ordinary anxiety but to *organismic panic*. Pao deliberately used a term like Mahler's (1968) "organismic distress," which is defined as that physiologic state of high tension experienced by the infant for which there is no relief without depending on the mothering person. Pao stresses that organismic panic is of relatively short duration.

The third. Organismic panic evokes a reaction like shock during the occurrence of which the ego's integrating function is temporarily paralyzed and most other ego functions are suspended. Pao stresses that the patient after recovering from this shock may recall it as a dreamlike experience; others have observed this also. Giovacchini (1983) noted it and stated that it is without psychic content. Grotstein (1983) called the phenomenon *nonpsychotic schizophrenia* dominated by "a psychosomatic state" of the central nervous system.

The fourth. After the shock the integrative function recovers from organismic panic. "As it recovers, regression in perceptual-cognitive-motor processes makes its appearance. Along with the reactivation of more primitive structures and defense mechanisms, self-experience will also be regressed" (Pao 1979, pp. 221–222).

The end result is a drastic change in the individual's personality that Pao implies is necessary to justify the diagnosis of schizophrenia.

The fifth. The symptoms of the illness crystallize according to "a best possible solution" (Sandler and Joffe 1969). Pao agrees with Sandler and Joffe that adaptation to the external environment is but one aspect of adaptation, others being concerned with inner drives, wishes, and standards (superego). The best possible solution available to the psychic apparatus will depend on the given circumstances and resources. Adaptation to reality and the reality principle can be regarded as a secondary consequence of the operation of the primary regulatory principle. Symptoms such as delusions, hallucinations, the practice of rituals, peculiar language, and so on, help buffer and protect the new self-continuity.

INTROJECTIVE-PROJECTIVE RELATEDNESS AND/OR FUSION OR DEFUSION

I am basically in agreement with Pao's findings, but I would like amplification, or at least greater emphasis on certain areas. Although in his major work on this issue (Pao 1979) he takes into account the sense of self in schizophrenia, I think he pays too little attention to his patients' internalized object relations. The schizophrenic develops a new pathological self and tries through symptom formation to avoid having another experience with organismic panic, but he is also involved with introjective-projective activity with objects and their mental representations designed to protect and maintain his new pathological self. Pao briefly mentioned in 1977 that this process is another of the maintenance mechanisms to be resorted to when one is experiencing or anticipating the experience of organismic panic.

Since adult schizophrenics have some higher-level structures and functions, they are able to use their existent introjective-projective relatedness, and even fusion–defusion activities, to contain the tension of object–relations conflicts and primitive defenses against them.

> Some fusions are libidinally determined; the patient fuses his "good" representational units with other "good" or idealized units to arrive at an ecstatic condition. Other fusions may be directed according to aggression, in which case the patient may fuse with a terrifying object representation in order to "kill" it so the terror will disappear, but then the terror is felt within because of the fusion. No satisfactory solution is achieved. Externalization of the terrifying units may follow, and the cycle will start all over again. [Volkan and Akhtar 1979]

In fusion, then, self is surrendered in order to make it a part of a larger support system, or to protect its cohesion against threatening objects.

> The young man whose mother had marked his birthdays during his childhood by the gift of golden rings became clinically schizophrenic when a female fellow student in high school remarked that his voice had changed. He took this to mean that he had visibly become a man, and that because of his deformed fingers it would be expected that his penis was abnormal. According to Pao (1979), this would not be an unusual conflict, but it began the disorganization of his existing sense of self, and ultimately led to the development of a core psychotic self.
>
> His new self was that of a gambler from the Old West. He wore a Stetson hat, a pocket watch on a chain, black trousers, and boots, keeping his body still as though it were altogether an erect penis. Thus in a psychotic way he altered reality, repaired his damaged finger/penis, and denied reality by using the method of his mother, with whom he identified.
>
> Even before his schizophrenia crystallized he lost himself in reading about Nazi Germany, fantasizing himself to be Goebbels, Hitler's "right arm." Becoming schizophrenic, he identified with Goebbels in his delusional state, and submitted to his tyrannical mother as he thought Goebbels had submitted to Hitler.

During his third hour with me he suddenly fell silent; he seemed relaxed, and began making sucking movements with his lips in a gesture of oral introjection. He said he was drinking German wine. He then explained that on approaching my office he had concluded that the name thereon showed me to be German. This conclusion was supported by his knowing because of my accent that I am a foreigner in America. He saw me "as strong as Hitler" and projected the Hitlerian image of his archaic mother on me. He was ridding himself of the external bad-object image by introjection, but with introjection he seemed terrified; he was then experiencing the bad object within. He was the sort of patient who, at that time, would be doomed to repeat an introjective-projective related-ness with its accompanying but ineffective defensive properties.

WHICH SCHIZOPHRENICS ARE TREATABLE IN PSYCHOANALYTIC PSYCHOTHERAPY?

It is a complicated matter to select those schizophrenic patients who would be suitable for psychoanalytic psychotherapy in four or five weekly sessions based on a psychoanalytic understanding of their illness. Suitability can be determined by the balance of biological and psychological factors initiating and/or maintaining their illness. In theory we can assume that when psychological factors dominate, the patient is a candidate for psychotherapy, but this is a simplistic assumption, since it is very hard to assess impact from the environment as apart from that of the disposition. They are in fact intertwined. Meaningful psychological relationships may modify the influence of biology. We see this as true in the clinical setting, although we do not yet have sufficient understanding to account for it.

I select patients for treatment according to my formulations about the meaning of the symptoms presented, and the communications the prospective patient offers during a diagnostic interview. I feel better if I can mentally map out during these interviews the patient's existing fragmented self- and object representations, and if the history of his childhood explains their nature. I always try to get an adequate history from a schizophrenic patient, even if it is available to me only as a melange of actual recollection and delusion. My ability to make an initial map of the patient's mind reflects my capacity for empathy with that particular individual. This is a clue to guide me—more emotionally than intellectually—in accepting a patient.

A 19-year-old male schizophrenic often cut himself gently and then examined the blood. Since he thought that its color was different at different times, he thought of himself as being different persons from time to time, and sought the "true blood." He had been adopted in early life, and his adoptive parents had always related to him with great ambivalence. His schizophrenia began when he learned of his adoption, and when as a teenager he tried unsuccessfully to locate his real parents. Soon these efforts gave way to a belief that he was related to this or that person. He became interested in blood chemistry in high school, and won praise and good grades from his teachers before his preoccupation with the subject became bizarre.

I thought during his diagnostic interviews that his interest in his blood and his search for "true blood" had something to do with his having been adopted and having been sometimes treated as though he came from a good bloodline and sometimes as though the opposite were the case. He was searching for his bloodline in a concrete way. With this knowledge I could understand some things about him at the outset. *He* could not conceptualize any symbolic meaning of his inspecting his blood. He had an appealing quality in his relationship with me, and he asked about the possibility of my having noble ancestry. I was included at once in his psychotic world—and I felt comfortable with it.

THE PSYCHOLOGY OF THERAPISTS AND COUNTERTRANSFERENCE

Psychoanalytic psychotherapy that brings about structural change in a schizophrenic patient is difficult, requiring a commitment to work with the patient three to five times a week for many years. It also demands that therapists be able to tolerate the primitive, intense negative and positive emotional reactions that their schizophrenic patients awaken in them (Volkan 1981a). They must be able to sustain their therapeutic posture, have empathy, and interpret their patients' demands but not gratify them. Since therapists must sometimes be an active auxiliary ego for the psychotic patient who lacks fully developed ego functions, they will find this kind of patient more taxing than a neurotic one. Accordingly, the psychology of therapists undertaking intense work with a schizophrenic needs consideration; for example, their ability "to regress in the service of the other" (Olinick 1980) is crucial. The tolerance and *therapeutic* utilization of countertransference in treating psychotic patients (Boyer 1983, Giovacchini 1988, Searles 1979) require that the therapist "meet" the patient in his regressed state, and validate (Loewald 1982) the patient's regression, in a sense seeing that he is not left alone. This conduct helps to change the patient's chaotic regression into therapeutic regression.

Because of their own psychological makeup, some therapists may be better equipped than others in using their personal responses to the patient's very primitive activities therapeutically. The therapist's *training* is also important; most psychoanalytic institutes do not provide the necessary training.

HOW NOT TO BE A MANAGER

Severely regressed and/or undeveloped patients may not be able to come regularly to the therapist's office because of their break with reality, their inability to control their impulses, or for other reasons due to their general condition. Such patients may need "managers," whether or not they are hospital inpatients. One of the first things therapists must consider is *not* to be seduced into "managing" patients' lives since it is likely that if they are, therapeutic relationships that lead to new structure formation will not take place. Boyer (1967, 1983), who has had wide experience in analysis with adult schizophrenic patients, refused to begin treatment in the absence of an available manager other than himself. Schulz and Kilgalen (1969) offer a list of twenty-four requirements a hospital staff should have in order to manage the hospitalized schizophrenic patient. This list, with some modifications, can be used by managers outside a hospital when dealing with an outpatient; it is useful in creating an atmosphere attuned to the patient's needs.

THE OVERALL TREATMENT PROCESS

Taking Pao's five steps into consideration, I see the aim of psychoanalytic psychotherapy as the initiation of a reverse process followed by progressive development. The schizophrenic patient must be helped to feel secure enough to try giving up his pathological self. This will take him to a point in treatment at which he will "revisit" organismic panic, although by then he will have enough observing and "work" ego (Olinick et al. 1973); when he is finished with "revisiting" he will form a new, healthier self-representation. The therapist's task does not stop there, however; since the healthier self-representation is very fragile, it needs to be solidified with more psychotherapeutic work.

I now turn to consider *selected* specific maneuvers such as: (1) those used in the initial phase, which may take years, during which the patient still adheres to his psychotic core; (2) those used when the patient gets ready to relinquish it; (3) those used when he establishes a healthier self-representation; and (4) those appropriate for the termination phase.

1. Therapeutic Maneuvers to Use When the Patient Adheres to His Psychotic Core

The therapist's images in the introjective-projective cycle. The individual functioning at an archaic level can be expected to have many difficulties. If his frail psychic structure is nourished therapeutically, however, it may evolve and organize itself at higher levels, much as a child's would in the course of normal development. We can see an analogy in an underdeveloped tree with a trunk that is still flexible. If the tree is fertilized and its trunk is given support, it will grow straight and tall as the trunk hardens. Cameron (1961) noted that it is possible for the regressed patient ". . . to introject massively with archaic completeness in adulthood and then be able to assimilate the new introject as an infant might, so that it disappears as such but some of its properties do not" (p. 93). A similar view was expressed by Loewald (1960) and Volkan (1976, 1982).

Psychoanalytic psychotherapy of schizophrenic patients begins with steady but gentle confrontations about distortions, contradictions, and other abandonments of reality, along with interpretations of defensive functions of the products of psychotic thinking (Boyer 1967). It should be remembered, however, that the patient may not "hear" these interpretations. What is important is the therapist's emphatic response and attempts to communicate without being intrusive, disagreeable, or seductive. The therapist has no choice but to use, besides involuntary nonverbal communication, logical sentences when addressing a schizophrenic, the dominant part of whose mind may not be able to comprehend such speech. However, the therapist must start somewhere, and brief, emphatic statements may, through repetition, become precursors of logical thought to which the patient will again learn to respond. From the outset the schizophrenic patient will involve the therapist in an introjective-projective relationship, so there is contact which must be made meaningful and therapeutic.

The patient takes in nothing new as long as his image of the therapist is contaminated with himself. Images of the therapist are not initially "taken in" as what Loewald (1960) termed a "new object" and Giovacchini (1969) called an "analytic introject," so they do not give the patient an analytical attitude for him to employ. It is up to analysts to differentiate themselves at the outset, *in piecemeal fashion*, from the archaic objects, so as to help their patients alter the nature of their archaic introjects (Boyer 1967, 1971). The differentiated images of the therapist can be used by the patient for identification, which may be a focus for the mending and grafting of fragmented self- and object representations. In dealing with such patients the therapist must be able to remain for a long time in a therapeutic symbiotic or psychotic transference with the patient (Searles 1965), while keeping an observing ego and protecting the patient's ego, however fragile that may be. After experiencing such therapeutic symbiotic relatedness the patient can start moving toward a more differentiated existence.

Since his primitive relatedness to objects naturally leads the patient to introject his therapist, any deliberate maneuver of the latter to offer him- or herself as a model is usually a seductive intrusion that will bring anxiety, and reduce the possibility of ego-building. It should be noted that internalization occurring in the transference may, in contrast to its use in ego-building, indicate an effort on the part of the patient to retain his primitive defenses as well as his primitive model of relationship, since any move he may make to individuate makes him fear the loss of his existing sense of self, however psychotic it may be. At times, the patient may perceive any attempt of the therapist's to promote the internalization process as the analyst's insistence on the continuation of this primitive mode of relating. Searles (1951) indicated that the "incorporative processes" within the transference-countertransference relationship may account for many long-standing stalemates in psychoanalytic therapy when they are used to defend against anxiety. Therapists would be forcing the internalization of themselves as models were they to give unnecessary personal information and convey the way they handle their own lives. Their basic tool in providing differentiation for their representation from patients' archaic object images is interpretation, along with clarification and nonseductive suggestions that patients may not "hear" at first, but subsequently will take in. This gives patients an environment in which therapists provide explanation and protection. There should be no lengthy speeches, but time should be made for patients to assimilate what has been said.

Reality base. There is, however, a way to give the patient restricted information about the therapist in a specific therapeutic interaction at the very beginning of treatment. I have used a technique that I call "the establishment of a reality base" (Volkan 1976). With neurotics we try to avoid interfering with the developing transference neurosis, but with the psychotic person it may be helpful to establish a reality base before the transference psychosis is fully developed. This will give him something to fall back on as he tries to work through the differentiation of his therapist's representation from his archaic self- and object representations. With the neurotic, a built-in reality base can be assumed by the very fact that the patient knows that the analyst is paid by him, and clearly has a role other than a parent's. The transference neurosis is built on this base of reality. In contrast, the schizophrenic patient, who may not differentiate the therapist from the representation of his parents, must be helped to develop a reality base and to take it into account in relating to him. Such help may also initiate the patient's observing ego and become its focal point.

Let us recall the young man who tried in the third hour of our work together to take me in as German wine, as an introject invested with the Hitlerian image. My response to him was the simple declaration that I am Turkish. In response to his question as to what kind of wine Turkey produces, I commented that Turkey produces *both* sweet and sour wines, as does Germany. I thus gave him "good" as well as "bad" targets for his projections. Had he been neurotic, I would not have interrupted his fantasies about me and my homeland; with him I interfered in order to establish the reality base. The clarification of my national origin arose naturally *within* this situation; my differentiation of my image from the archaic object images did not include providing the gratification of gaining detailed information about me.

Timely interpretation of externalizations and projections. The therapist must absorb the patient's externalizations of self- and object images and projections of unacceptable ideas long enough to make the necessary connections with the intrapsychic aspects, and long enough for the patient to take in a like tolerance when he reinternalizes the therapist's image. A quality so acquired may be retained. Although Giovacchini (1967) suggested in reference to character disorders that at the start of treatment interpretations may not have much specific content, the patient makes externalizations and projections, some quite obvious and others subtle, from the initial interview. By constantly interpreting the externalizations and projections, one causes an internalization of conflict. The therapist's purpose is to focus on the intrapsychic; when the patient succeeds in doing likewise, he gains considerable security.

Humanizing "deep material". What lies on the surface of the patient's relatedness to his therapist (such as cannibalistic fantasies primitively symbolizing introjection) manifests what we would call in the case of the neurotic patient *deep material*. The therapist should not shy away from interpreting such manifestations (Volkan 1968), since it helps the patient to have his uncanny fantasies and experiences named and designated as events in a developmental process rather than to have to regard them as something grotesque and outside human experience. This interpretation also helps him tame his aggressive impulses.

One of my patients, knowing that I am Turkish, felt panic lest his indulgence in a turkey dinner cost me my life. He was comforted to learn that his cannibalistic fantasies showed a wish to relate to me, and in his fantasy my destruction would mean his own. He perceived me as a "needed object," but relating to me would spell disaster. Clarification of his "need–fear dilemma" (Burnham 1969) proved most helpful.

Depressive material and paranoid ideation. Boyer (1967, 1983) suggests, and my experience confirms, that the therapist should not concentrate at first on material arising from libidinal drives per se unless an eroticized transference threatens and seems likely to become unwieldy and to restrict his interpretation of the aggressive aspects of what is being presented. Aggressive and libidinal materials are both examined in time. Boyer also chooses, as I do, to focus initially on depressive material rather than to pursue paranoid ideation. He believes that ego introjects cannot be altered efficiently unless simultaneous changes take place in the superego introjects in the direction of reducing the archaic, sadistic nature of that psychic structure. (Some writers today would refer to superego introjects or their precursors as "bad" object representations in the case of schizophrenia when superego integration has not been reached or maintained.) The idea is to deal first with the patient's reactions to the internalization of bad objects rather than to their externalization. Again, in time, reactions to both directions of the introjective-projective relatedness are examined.

Linking interpretations. Giovacchini (1969) described as linking interpretation a therapeutic maneuver in which the therapist tries to link events in the outside world to intrapsychic phenomena to promote the establishment of contact with reality. *Linking interpretations* are used during the initial phase of treatment of a schizophrenic patient; they not only make the patient more alert in testing reality but promote psychological-mindedness by nurturing an observing ego.

Giovacchini recalls Freud's (1900) concept of the day residue of dreams. Day residue, an extrapsychic stimulus—some seemingly irrelevant event—fuses with id content, which it stimulates.

"An interpretation may make a causal connection by referring to the day residue which may be the stimulus for the flow of the patient's associations or for some otherwise unexplainable behavior" (Giovacchini 1969, p. 180). A schizophrenic who had a stomachache after seeing a policeman while on the way to my office is an example. I interpret the link between the sight of the policeman and the pain in his stomach, saying that he had perceived the officer as too bad to be stomached. Note that emphasis at this point is on the introjection of the bad object (depressive direction). I do not focus on the externalization of his own aggressive aspects onto the policeman (paranoid direction).

2. Therapeutic Maneuvers to Use When the Patient Gets Ready to Relinquish His Psychotic Core

Progressive use of transitional relatedness. During the initial work with a schizophrenic I do not forbid him to bring to our sessions such objects or phenomena as he may use as a reactivated transitional object (Winnicott 1953). These items may be simply a piece of cloth, a tape recorder, a turtle—or a snatch of song, a saying, a way of twisting hair in magical ways. I explain that I understand such phenomena to be like a lantern with both opaque and transparent sides; when the patient feels comfortable with me, he turns the transparent side toward me, illuminating me. His transitional object helps him to get to know me. When he feels discomfort in my presence, he turns the opaque side of the lantern in my direction and wipes me out of existence. I make clear that the magical object or activity in question has both progressive and regressive aspects (Modell 1968). I demonstrate that I can be either reached or obliterated through its use, and that I can tolerate the latter fate. I make clear my understanding that the magical item or activity is under the patient's control, suggesting that as he gets to know me better he will use the progressive side more often and will eventually give up the need of magic in loving or hating me.

With the passage of years and as the schizophrenic more and more differentiates my image from that of himself and others, he will tend to use the progressive aspect of the transitional item or activity more often. He will eventually try relating to me without it. This move usually requires courage in the patient, and needs the therapist's attention. Since the patient may perceive the surrender of his magical item as a fearful task, he should not be unduly urged to give it up. The better technique is to encourage him to wonder what will happen when the magical defense between himself and his therapist is no longer there.

The surrender of the transitional object or behavioral quirk indicates that differentiation between self- and object representations is crystallized.

Emotional flooding (a revisiting of organismic panic). Progress paradoxically leads to a form of regression that is therapeutic. If there is no interference from the environment, and the therapist commits no major technical errors, the patient will visit his organismic panic and emerge from it in a progressive development. This "revisiting" reflects a turning point in treatment and initiates the start of new, nonpsychotic self-development. This experience, which I call *emotional flooding* (Volkan 1976), corresponds in many ways to Pao's (1979) description of temporary shock.

While the original organismic panic, followed by shock, induces personality change and the appearance of the psychotic self, emotional flooding helps in a reverse move to remove the psychotic self, and initiates the establishment of one that is more healthy. I have written of the first manifestations of emotional flooding (Volkan 1976). It occurs when a patient presents an accumulation of memories and fantasies (flooding in the ideational field) that support the same emotion. The patient may scream, seeming to have lost his human identity. The gesture or verbalization of "no" appears as a massive defense against the anxiety of giving up whatever self-continuity there is.

> Patients capable of reporting their experiences of emotional flooding after the event usually indicate that strange perceptual changes took place. They underwent a "metamorphosis" during the experience. . . . In this state, the representation of the affect becomes the patient's perceived self. [Volkan 1976, p. 183]

The ability to tolerate emotional flooding leads to greater tolerance for the experience of anxiety. Anxiety is no longer overwhelming; it becomes a signal affect and does not lead to organismic panic. While experiencing anxiety the patient begins to maintain an observing ego.

One young woman suddenly understood after visiting her organismic panic during the third year of treatment why she had always thought that pictures of her before the age of ten were those of someone else. At that age she had been very badly treated by her family, and had suffered a form of organismic panic, with consequent personality change. She then "visited" this distressing condition with horrible affects that she could not have tolerated previously. "I feel that I am starting all over from a burned-out situation!" she declared. "I don't need to use my old survival tactics now!"

3. Therapeutic Maneuvers to Use When the Patient Establishes a Healthier Self-representation

Sad affect and "mutual cuing" in therapy. Patients are not aware that tolerance of their emotional flooding marks the start of a healthier self. During the flooding the self is experienced as the representation of the affect, as if it were a sponge soaked in emotion, or a balloon swollen with it. Patients call themselves "swollen monsters" when they are overwhelmed with aggressive affect, but they soon indicate symbolically the development of a new and healthier self.

After tolerating an emotional flooding episode, one man went to Philadelphia to see the Liberty Bell, which symbolically represented his recent liberation. Another patient dreamed of a flower opening, and still another feverishly rearranged the furniture in her home, representing the new arrangement she felt within herself.

The prognosis is good when sad affect accompanies such activity; it indicates that the ties maintained for so long to the earlier, psychotic personality are being loosened, and that a form of the mourning process is under way. Genuine mourning does not appear in the repertoire of a schizophrenic until there is a healthy change in his core. Searles (1986) held that this is also true in the case of borderline patients. Once the patient is able to mourn, the therapist more and more often experiences pleasant emotions when in contact with him. He may laugh spontaneously at his patient's humor. He is like a happy mother playing with her child. "Mutual cuing" between the two parties increases.

I do not mean to say that once a patient is beginning to make progress after emotional flooding he will always maintain a forward movement. It would be ideal if this were true, but since the dyad does not exist in a vacuum, many reasons may account for the patient's return to old ways. With therapeutic intervention, however, he will progress, probably with ups and downs on the road to crystallization of a healthier self-representation.

Using the couch. My technique has the patient lie on the couch whenever I think this will make our therapeutic relationship more workable. Some schizophrenic patients have used the couch before making drastic changes in their psychotic cores, but I have found that lying on the couch provides a degree of organization in the chaotic lives of these psychotic individuals. I certainly have my patient lie on the couch after coming to tolerate emotional flooding.

Higher-level identifications. As the patient continues to progress, his attempts at identification with the representations of the therapist change descriptively and functionally. His introjection of and identification with the therapist's representation are different at different phases of the treatment (Tähkä 1984a). In the initial phase such attempts are accompanied by incorporative fantasies that refer to introjection in a gross, exaggerated way featuring personified part–object representations such as those of the therapist's penis, nipples, voice, or face. If early identifications are effective, they primarily center around the assimilation of the therapist's integrative functions, helping the patient to weld together what is fragmented and split in his self-representation and internalized object world.

Once a new and healthier core evolves, gross cannibalistic fantasies start to disappear. In his efforts to assimilate certain of the therapist's representations, the patient becomes involved in "therapeutic stories" (Volkan 1984), which are sustained from session to session. When some specific area in the child's interaction and experience with important mothering persons has been neglected, it is in this phase that the patient can develop an ego formation that will enable him to deal effectively with that area. Thus when we speak of identification with the therapist's representation at this time as being curative, we refer to one or many different representations of the therapist dealing with one or multiple specific issues.

It should be remembered that when the patient identifies with his therapist's representations they will compete within his mind (Abse and Ewing 1960) with archaic self- and object representations. The therapist should not encourage the patient prematurely to prefer his representation over the archaic ones, but should acknowledge the existence of competition and the patient's anxiety over losing the archaic representations with which he had been so familiar for so long.

The main focus in the analysis of a neurotic patient is on interpretation of unresolved mental structural conflicts as they relate to drive derivatives and the defenses against them that appear in the transference neurosis. Behind the central endeavor a "constant sense of micro-identifications" (Rangell 1979) with the analyst's analyzing function will come about. However, in the treatment of a schizophrenic, especially prior to his developing a relationship with the therapist that resembles a transference neurosis, the process of identification with various representations of the therapist is prominent. Indeed, this phenomenon is a critical aspect of the "cure."

Neutralization of aggression. As the patient identifies with different functions of the therapist, a neutralization of aggression comes about (Hartmann 1950), removing the need of fragmentation and splitting in the self- and object representations. Tähkä (1988) has told how this process takes place during normal child development. He states that with the gradually increasing ability to change passivity into activity (A. Freud 1936), the child starts to do for himself what his mother has previously done for him. According to Tähkä: "As a function-specific frustration gives rise to a function-specific (functionally selective) identification, the result will be the emergence of a corresponding functional capacity in the self with corresponding changes in the representations of self and object" (p. 127). Formerly the mother's failure in a particular function would lead to frustration and the reactivation of aggression but . . . "After an established identification, failures of the mother in that particular function no longer lead to frustrations since the arousal of the signal need will now activate the child's own, newly acquired function" (p. 127). A similar process takes place during the psychoanalytic psychotherapy of an adult schizophrenic. With this process comes a lessening of frustration, and activation of aggression. This change is usually referred to as the *neutralization of aggression*. According to Tähkä, ". . . no changes in the energy itself are postulated here, while that which is energized has undergone a structural alteration" (p. 127).

Effective externalization. At the age of between 6 and 36 months, a child is expected to complete the mending of his fragmented self- and object representation, but his process is, strictly speaking, never totally completed, since some unmended "good" and "bad" objects remain. They are thus a potential source of object relations conflict in the child at a later time. In normal development, the ego represses some of them (van der Waals 1952), but some are externalized under the guidance of the mothering person onto certain cultural amplifiers (Mack 1984) such as ethnic or nationalistic symbols. Since such amplifiers and symbols are common to all members of the child's group, they can effectively absorb his externalizations and projections, and help support his inner cohesion. I have referred to such amplifiers and symbols as *suitable targets of externalization* (Volkan 1986, 1988). There are those that absorb the child's negative unmended aspects, and those that absorb his good and idealized unmended self- and object representations. For example, the sauna might be a good suitable target of externalization for a Finnish child.

Because of difficulties of her own, or her child's, the mother of a child who will become schizophrenic characteristically fails to sponsor adequate targets of externalization. Adult patients identify with certain of the therapist's functions, and also, at a certain point in treatment, spontaneously perceive him as the provider of suitable targets of externalization. It is unusual for any of my schizophrenic patients to display interest in my Turkish origin at first, but interest will in time turn from my real or fantasied "good" and "bad" extensions "out there" toward his own religiously or culturally sanctioned "good" and "bad" issues.

For example, one Jewish patient read extensively about Istanbul, and played on her piano what she thought of as Turkish music. But then she started collecting Jewish folksongs, and made her first friends at the synagogue. This advance led her to explore wider horizons of the culture, and, eventually, of the world.

Upward-evolving transference. I agree with Boyer (1971, 1983) that once a patient's ego organization matures and he forms a cohesive self-representation and an integrated internalized object world, an upward-evolving transference relationship will appear. A more mature object relationship with the therapist will come about in a transference neurosis, and introjective-projective relatedness will fall into the background of this relationship. However, I monitor introjective-projective relationships throughout the treatment.

The patient's transference neurosis is like a child's passage through the oedipal years. Since before his illness the patient was not altogether "normal," and as a schizophrenic had an unintegrated, undeveloped, and undifferentiated sense of self, his experiences of oedipal issues at this time are new to him. He faces them for the first time with a cohesive self-representation. Rather than analyzing away oedipal conflicts, the therapist pays attention to the psychological obstacles that keep the patient from moving up the developmental ladder. Regressive moves and the appearance of object–relations conflicts are interpreted. It is a good prognostic sign when stories about old object–relations conflicts and representations of old psychotic symptoms appear in the patient's dreams without waking him or causing anxiety. The therapist may perceive him as depositing his memories of his psychosis in his unconscious, and repressing them. In his daily living the patient will now use repression and other sophisticated defense mechanisms effectively.

4. Therapeutic Maneuvers to Use When the Patient Is in the Termination Phase

The length of the termination phase. I plan for this phase to take a long time. It is not unusual for me to decide with the patient who has been schizophrenic that he will terminate in about a year, even in cases where it has taken many years to come to this point.

When he came to treatment, the patient displayed great difficulty in object relations and used primitive, magical ways of dealing with separation. Even after treatment has given him experience in grieving and letting go, he will need patience and time to face up to the highly significant separation of leaving his therapist. In this phase, the repression and other higher-level defensive and adaptive mechanisms previously developed are from time to time partly given up. Thus he returns to old ways of controlling anxiety, and he may even fear the reappearance of another organismic panic. Introjective-projective relatedness may reappear, but the experienced therapist does not become anxious. The technique is to let the patient see that he is reacting to termination, and to let him use his own insight to reorganize.

Searching for a magical object. Often during the termination phase a patient will activate a primitive magical method as a bridge to his psychosis and/or as a way to keep his therapist part of himself. This must be analyzed.

One patient had a painting that he had once used as a receptacle for his "bad" self- and object images. In his termination phase it became once more psychologically compelling. He wanted to give it to the therapist as a farewell gift; if the gift was accepted, he would thus keep a bridge to his early ways of functioning. While it would be possible for the painting to be an effective receptacle outside the patient's own environment, it would also be possible for him not to truly *own* his externalizations and projections. Because of this second possibility, this magical gift—and any gift can be magical—was not accepted; its psychological contents were, however, analyzed.

Mourning. We have noted the adult schizophrenic's initial lack of the ability to mourn, since the core of his self- and object representations is undifferentiated and he lacks stable object constancy. To mourn effectively in an adult fashion one must have a cohesive, stable self-representation that is differentiated from a similarly cohesive and stable object representation. Mourning of the adult type requires the ability to examine in a piecemeal way, consciously and unconsciously, the mental representation of the departed, and to reach a "remembrance formation." Tähkä (1984b) describes this in reference to the mental process through which someone previously experienced as existing in the outer world becomes a remembrance of a lost object. "In this process, the nature of the object representation alters, as an object belonging to the present and to the outside world changes into one belonging to the past and to the realm of memories" (pp. 17–18).

It must also be remembered that the mature mourning process finds the mourner once more selectively identifying with aspects of the one he has lost (Volkan 1981b). The first time a schizophrenic can be said to mourn is after the loosening of ties to the psychotic core. However, only in the termination phase is he expected to mourn genuinely as an adult, in leaving his therapist. The ability to so mourn is an indication of his treatment's success and a good indication that he will stay healthy. With most former schizophrenics, mourning continues silently for many years after treatment terminates; it is part of the growth process of learning to function better in an adult world. The therapist will do well to prepare his patient for the possibility of a protracted period of mourning.

The therapist should not conceal his own grief at letting the patient go. The patient's last important identification is with the representation of a therapist able to let go, grieve, and permit the true independence of the one leaving him. In turn, the patient learns how to grieve while letting his therapist take up his life without the object to which he had devoted so considerable a period of his affective life.

REFERENCES

Abse, D. W. (1955). Early phases of ego-structure adumbrated in the regressive ego states of schizophrenic psychosis, and elucidated in intensive psychotherapy. *Psychoanalytic Review* 42:228–238.

Abse, D. W., and Ewing, J. (1960). Some problems in psychotherapy with schizophrenic patients. *American Journal of Psychotherapy* 14:505–519.

Apprey, M. (1984). Review of *Psychoanalysis and Infant Research* by J. D. Lichtenberg. *Review of Psychoanalytic Books* 3:451–457.

Boyer, L. B. (1967). Office treatment of schizophrenic patients: the use of psychoanalytic therapy with few parameters. In *Psychoanalytic Treatment of Characterological and Schizophrenic Disorders*, ed. L. B. Boyer and P. L. Giovacchini, pp. 143–188. New York: Science House.

—— (1971). Psychoanalytic techniques in the treatment of certain characterological and schizophrenic disorders. *International Journal of Psycho-Analysis* 52:67–86.

—— (1983). *The Regressed Patient*. New York: Jason Aronson.

Burnham, D. L. (1969). Schizophrenia and object relations. In *Schizophrenia and the Need-Fear Dilemma*, ed. D. L. Burnham, A. I. Gladstone, and R. W. Gibson, pp. 15–41. New York: International Universities Press.

Cameron, N. (1961). Introjection, reprojection, and hallucination in the interaction between schizophrenic patient and therapist. *International Journal of Psycho-Analysis* 42:86–96.

Cancro, R. (1986). General considerations relating to theory in the schizophrenic disorders. In *Towards a Comprehensive Model for Schizophrenic Disorders*, ed. D. B. Feinsilver. New York: Analytic Press.

Emde, R. (1988a). Development terminable and interminable. I. Innate and motivational factors from infancy. *International Journal of Psycho-Analysis* 69: 23–41.

—— (1988b). Development terminable and interminable. II. recent psychoanalytic theory and therapeutic considerations. *International Journal of Psycho-Analysis* 69:283–296.

Freud, A. (1936). *The Ego and the Mechanisms of Defense.* New York: International Universities Press.

Freud, S. (1900). *The Interpretation of Dreams. Standard Edition* 4 and 5.

—— (1914). On the history of the psycho-analytic movement. *Standard Edition* 14:7–71.

Giovacchini, P. L. (1967). Psychoanalytic treatment of character disorders. In *Psychoanalytic Treatment of Characterological and Schizophrenic Disorders,* ed. L. B. Boyer and P. L. Giovacchini, pp. 208–234. New York: Science House.

—— (1969). The influence of interpretation upon schizophrenic patients. *International Journal of Psycho-Analysis* 50:179–186.

—— (1983). The persistent psychosis-schizophrenia: with special reference to *Schizophrenic Disorders* by Ping-Nie Pao. *Psychoanalytic Inquiry* 3:9–36.

—— (1988). *Countertransference Triumphs and Catastrophes.* Northvale, NJ: Jason Aronson.

Glover, E. (1950). *On the Early Development of Mind.* New York: International Universities Press, 1956.

Grotstein, J. (1983). Deciphering the schizophrenic experience. *Psychoanalytic Inquiry* 3:37–70.

Hartmann, H. (1950). Comment on the psychoanalytic theory of the ego. *The Psychoanalytic Study of the Child* 5:74–96. New York: International Universities Press.

Hendrick, I. (1951). Early development of the ego: identification in infancy. *Psychoanalytic Quarterly* 20:44–61.

Lichtenberg, J. (1983). *Psychoanalysis and Infant Research.* Hillsdale, NJ: Analytic Press.

—— (1986). Pao's theory: origins and future directions. In *Towards a Comprehensive Model for Schizophrenic Disorders,* ed. D. B. Feinsilver, pp. 75–96. Hillsdale, NJ: Analytic Press.

Loewald, H. W. (1960). On the therapeutic action of psychoanalysis. *International Journal of Psycho-Analysis* 41:16–33.

—— (1982). Regression: some general considerations. In *Technical Factors in the Treatment of the Severely Disturbed Patient,* ed. P. L. Giovacchini and L. B. Boyer, pp. 107–130. New York: Jason Aronson.

Mack, J. E. (1984). Paper presented at the Committee on International Affairs at the Fall Meeting of the Group for the Advancement of Psychiatry, November 10–12.

Mahler, M. S. (1968). *On Human Symbiosis and the Vicissitudes of Individuation.* New York: International Universities Press.

Modell, A. H. (1968). *Object Love and Reality: An Introduction to a Psychoanalytic Theory of Object Relations.* New York: International Universities Press.

Olinick, S. L. (1980). *The Psychotherapeutic Instrument.* New York: Jason Aronson.

Olinick, S. L., Poland, W. S., Grigg, K. A., et al. (1973). The psycho-analytic work ego: process and interpretation. *International Journal of Psycho-Analysis* 54:143–151.

Pao, P.-N. (1977). On the formation of schizophrenic symptoms. *International Review of Psycho-Analysis* 58:389–401.

—— (1979). *Schizophrenic Disorders.* New York: International Universities Press.

Rangell, L. (1979). Countertransference issues in the theory of therapy. *Journal of the American Psychoanalytic Association (Supplement)* 27:81–112.

Sandler, J. (1960). The background of safety. *International Journal of Psycho-Analysis* 41:352–365.

Sandler, J., and Joffe, W. G. (1969). Towards a basic psychoanalytic model. *International Journal of Psycho-Analysis* 50:79–90.

Schulz, C., and Kilgalen, R. K. (1969). *Case Studies in Schizophrenia.* New York: Basic Books.

Searles, H. F. (1951). Data concerning certain manifestations of incorporation. *Psychiatry* 14:397–413.

—— (1965). *Collected Papers on Schizophrenia and Related Subjects.* New York: International Universities Press.

—— (1979). *Countertransference and Related Subjects: Selected Papers.* New York: International Universities Press.

—— (1986). *My Work with Borderline Patients.* New York: Jason Aronson.

Stern, D. N. (1982). Implications of infancy research for psychoanalytic theory and practice. *Psychoanalytic Update* 2:8–21.

—— (1985). *The Interpersonal World of the Infant.* New York: Basic Books.

Suslick, A. (1961). Pathology of identity as related to the borderline ego. *Archives of General Psychiatry* 8:252–262.

Tähkä, V. (1984a). Psychoanalytic treatment as a developmental continuum: consideration of disturbed structuralization and its phase-specific encounter. *Scandinavian Psychoanalytic Review* 7:133–159.

—— (1984b). Dealing with object loss. *Scandinavian Psychoanalytic Review* 7:13–33.

—— (1987). On the early formation of the mind. I: differentiation. *International Journal of Psycho-Analysis* 68:229–250.

—— (1988). On the early formation of the mind. II. from differentiation to self and object constancy. *Psychoanalytic Study of the Child* 43:101–134. New Haven: Yale University Press.

van der Waals, H. G. (1952). Discussion of "The Mutual Influences in the Development of Ego and Id." *The Psychoanalytic Study of the Child* 7:66–68. New York: International Universities Press.

Volkan, V. D. (1964). The observation and topographic study of the changing ego states of a schizophrenic patient. *British Journal of Medical Psychology* 37:239–255.

—— (1968). The introjection of and identification with the therapist as an ego-building aspect in the treatment of schizophrenia. *British Journal of Medical Psychology* 41:369–380.

—— (1976). *Primitive Internalized Object Relations. A Clinical Study of Schizophrenic, Borderline, and Narcissistic Patients.* New York: International Universities Press.

—— (1981a). Transference and countertransference: an examination from the point of view of internalized object relations. In *Object and Self: A Developmental Approach,* ed. S. Tuttman, C. Kaye, and M. Zimmerman, pp. 429-451. New York: International Universities Press.

—— (1981b). *Linking Objects and Linking Phenomena.* New York: International Universities Press.

—— (1982). Identification and related psychic events: their appearance in therapy and their curative values. In *Curative Factors in Dynamic Psychotherapy,* ed. S. Slipp, pp. 153-170. New York: McGraw-Hill.

—— (1984). *What Do You Get When You Cross a Dandelion with a Rose? The True Story of a Psychoanalysis.* New York: Jason Aronson.

—— (1986). Suitable targets of externalization and schizophrenia. In *Towards a Comprehensive Model for Schizophrenic Disorders,* ed. D. B. Feinsilver, pp. 125-153. Hillsdale, NJ: Analytic Press.

—— (1987). *Six Steps in the Treatment of Borderline Personality Organization.* Northvale, NJ: Jason Aronson.

—— (1988). *The Need to Have Enemies and Allies. From Clinical Practice to International Relationships.* Northvale, NJ: Jason Aronson.

Volkan, V. D., and Akhtar, S. (1979). The symptoms of schizophrenia: contributions of the structural theory and object relations theory. In *Integrating Ego Psychology and Object Relations,* ed. L. Saretsky, G. D. Goldman, and D. S. Milman, pp. 270-285. Dubuque, IA: Kendall/Hunt.

Winnicott, D. W. (1953). Transitional objects and transitional phenomena. *International Journal of Psycho-Analysis* 34:89-97.

11

PETER GOLDBERG, Ph.D.

Actively Seeking
the Holding Environment

ABSENCE OF A BASIS FOR COMMUNICATION

It is a widely accepted belief that a specific and carefully evolved technique is indispensable to therapeutic practice with those patients deemed amenable to psychotherapy. There are, nevertheless, those patients who defy our technique and our method. Among the variety of patients who do not appear to be amenable to the existing evolved technique, who do not "fit in" to the therapeutic setting or framework, are those who seem unable to communicate or enter into a dialogue with the therapist. In these cases, it is difficult for the verbal-symbolic method to get off the ground, because of a basic incongruity between the therapist's framework (which we assume to be essentially verbal-symbolic in character) and the patient's framework (which may, for example, be founded upon perverse, somatic, narcissistic, or hallucinatory modes of containment and meaning-creation).

THE PATIENT'S ATTACKS AS A POINT OF CONTACT

In addressing the challenge of the patient who does not fit the basic psychoanalytic situation, I draw particular attention to the inevitable point of attack by these patients on the therapist's framework. Paradoxically, it is precisely here, at the point of attack, that initial meaningful contact may begin between therapist and patient: For if the incongruity between therapist's and patient's frameworks was based entirely on indifference, constituting a disinterested alienation, a passing of ships in the night, then it is quite

271

probable that no therapeutic work would be possible. Indeed, the patient who cannot fit the verbal-symbolic mode, for whom experience and meaning are registered in some alternative code, is also always acting against the therapeutic framework, so that this framework is in one way or another attacked, rejected, corrupted, or foreclosed. But a tentative bridging between frameworks is not likely to occur without the *therapist's active search for a certain posture or position* that, in a sense, makes the patient's linking attack possible and comprehensible by both.

ACTIVE SEEKING RATHER THAN PASSIVE CONTAINMENT

This line of argument leads to two conclusions, or assertions: First, the environmental provision or "holding" revealed to us by Winnicott (1965) in practice involves, quite commonly, much more than a passive state of empathy. Indeed, the holding environment must sometimes be *actively* sought and created—or discovered—within the therapist, a process that may involve the therapist in a great deal of internal activity and struggle. This observation would, I am sure, come as no surprise to parents, who all know that their child's distress and incapacity to communicate frequently requires innovative and experimental responses. The parent tries one thing, then another and another before the solution is found.

Second, it will, I hope, become clear that the active seeking of a holding position by the therapist is not exactly the same as what has been described as the containing or processing or metabolizing of projective identifications. While the latter processes are indeed active in the treatment of difficult patients, the challenge of the patient who does not fit the setting may nevertheless require, first and foremost, a bringing together of frameworks.

In speaking of the active search for a holding environment, I wish to reiterate and clarify that what is being proposed here is not any greater *observable* activity on the part of the therapist, not necessarily any external activity at all, but rather a certain internal activity or experimentation with internal mental states that may not, and perhaps should not, be observable from the outside. Hence, I am not in any way advocating the abandonment of therapeutic neutrality, insofar as I believe that the therapist should continue to refrain from moral judgment, persuasion, self-revelation, or prejudicial selection of the patient's material. On the other hand, one may call into question whether the principle of maintaining "evenly hovering attention" (Freud 1913) can be upheld to any worthwhile degree under circumstances of the therapist's active internal search for a suitable holding position.

THE MEANING OF THE FRAME CONCEPTION

It will be necessary to turn our attention to a brief consideration of the frame conception, which is difficult to grasp and define because it refers to the particular area of mental functioning that is never represented. The relation of mental representations or internal objects to the frame may be likened, in a very partial sense, to the relation in Gestalt terminology of *figure* to *ground*: The ground can never in and of itself by depicted or represented, existing as it does only to frame the figure. We are aware of the frame or the ground only by inference, for it is unknowable in its own right.

To take a somewhat different metaphorical tack, allow me to employ for a moment the analogy of the painter's canvas,[1] which must be still and secured in order for the painting to be made, or the background of silence against which a symphony is played, or the curtain or prop that marks off and signifies the area where a play takes place. A similar background function is provided not simply by the therapeutic setting and ground rules, but much more importantly by the mental framework that every therapist brings to his or her work.

Jose Bleger (1967), first to formally describe the frame conception, defined the frame as an essential "nonprocess," the silent bulwark or backdrop against which psychological activity and meaning can be perceived and comprehended. The frame therefore functions, according to Bleger, as a containment for the psychotic part of the personality, securing a *nonprocess* so that a discernible psychological *process* can come into existence—just as the canvas is secured so that a painting can come into existence.[2] Grotstein (1981), from a Kleinian point of view, encompasses the elements of the frame conception in his concept of the background object of primary identifica-

---

[1]Marion Milner (1952) first introduced the term by describing the role of the actual frame of the painting as an analogy to the frame of the therapeutic situation. But Lewin's (1946) earlier concept of the dream screen seems to comprehend the same phenomenon, that of a mental framework. Winnicott's (1965) ideas concerning the "environmental provision" and Bion's (1977) theory of the "container and the contained" are also obvious forerunners of the frame concept.

tion. Andre Green (1980), clearly articulating the spirit of Winnicott's discoveries concerning the internalization of the environmental mother's "hold," describes the transformation of the primary maternal (fused) object into a "framing structure" which then serves as a "container of representative space" (p. 166). He continues:

> The space which is thus framed constitutes the receptacle of the ego; it surrounds an empty field, so to speak, which will be occupied by erotic and aggressive cathexes, in the form of object representations. This emptiness is never perceived by the subject, because the libido has cathected the psychical space. Thus it plays the role of primordial matrix of the cathexes to come. [p. 166]

Thomas Ogden (1986), employing the term *matrix* in preference to *frame*, investigates the complex conditions necessary for the establishment of a viable mental framework, in which a self-reflective sense of I-ness or subjectivity is achieved by means of the internalization of the maternal matrix or holding environment. In elaborating upon the importance of entering into what Melanie Klein described as depressive position functioning, Ogden reveals how this self-reflective form of subjectivity relies upon a capacity for dialectical experiencing of fantasy and reality. This dialectical capacity in turn relies upon the establishment of a viable internal matrix, or mental framework.

The point of view taken here is that the nature of the mental framework that is assumed in psychoanalysis (and ultimately in all cultural institutions), and the accompanying code used to construct meaning, is verbal-

---

[2]It is perhaps worth noting explictly how the frame concept differs most fundamentally from the concepts of ego and self: The latter are, theoretically speaking, knowable processes, capable of representation, whereas the frame is not. Kohut (1977), in his description of the incorporation of maternal caretaking functions by means of what he calls "transmuting internalisation," clearly views these caretaking functions as part of the evolving structure of the self. In my view, a theoretical distinction should be maintained between on the one hand the self, so many facets of which reflect the vicissitudes of the drives and of object relationships, and on the other hand something like the frame, which always lies behind or beyond representation and which, by definition, exists only outside of the domain of the drives, its nature being to attempt to contain the area of the drives. The frame cannot be cathected, and is born out of a nonobject relationship. This distinction between a representational product and a containing or facilitating function is maintained by Winnicott and blurred by Kohut.

symbolic in character. This point of view has been most comprehensively grasped in Lacan's (1977) exposition of what he calls the *symbolic order of language* in its role as the vehicle of the constitution of all human subjectivity. This is, in turn, an extension of Freud's theory of the constitution of human identity in the matrix of the Oedipus complex. In short, psychoanalysis in this view assumes that human subjectivity and identity can be satisfactorily arrived at only through the intervention of language (and its imposition of a cultural order) in the deep intrapsychic life, interrupting and forcing into repression other prevailing modes of psychic meaning-construction—for example, the "imaginary" mode (Lacan 1977), or the hallucinatory mode (the wish fulfillment of infancy), as well as all the infantile omnipotent modes of experience that eschew consensual codes of meaning construction and, hence, refuse the repressive but self-constituting role of symbolic words in the mediation of the inner life.

THE VERBAL-SYMBOLIC FRAME AND CODE AND SOME ALTERNATIVES

The verbal-symbolic framework provides culturally given symbols for the mediation and transformation of the elements of subjective experience, so that the individual can enter the world of consensual meaning and escape the area of exclusively privately created meanings. The analytic psychotherapist implicitly promotes the verbal-symbolic framework, or at least aspires to, but the patient might employ a quite different framework, built upon a more idiosyncratic code of transformation of experience, a more peculiarly personal mode of overcoming chaos and securing the indispensable backdrop or frame of psychical existence. These alternative modes include the perverse code, which deploys sexualization for the purpose both of denying gender and generational distinctions (Chasseguet-Smirgel 1985) and of establishing stable meaning (what Joyce McDougall [1986] has called *neosexualities* and *neorealities*); the narcissistic code, which serves to mask envy, fearfulness, and dependent needs by stripping objects of their realistic value and claiming absolute self-sufficiency; the delusional code, whereby mental space is prevented from collapsing by means of hallucinated bizarre objects rather than symbols (what Bion [1965] called *transformations in hallucinosis*); the paranoid code, which removes the site of danger from inside to outside, and in so doing denies symbols of their essential function, namely to superimpose inner and outer without prejudice; the somatic phenomena, which McDougall has described in terms of foreclosure of symbolization and psychological experience; and the autistic mode (Tustin 1981), wherein autistic objects and phenomena serve to preclude the development of subjective identity.

THE ROLE OF BOTH RESISTANCE AND TRANSFERENCE SHOULD BE REEVALUATED

A further two questions are examined, directly and implicitly throughout this chapter, with regard to the challenge of the noncommunicating patient:

1. The Question of Transference

The estrangement that exists between the patient's mental framework and the verbal-symbolic framework assumed in the psychoanalytic situation creates difficulties in psychotherapy that may be described as more essentially *interpersonal* than *intrapsychic*, because the most important source of the distortions that arise between patient and therapist is not the (intrapsychically founded) transference of mental contents, but is rather the *actual* incongruity existing between patients' and therapists' frameworks. There exists in these cases not an imagined or fantasied antagonism but an *actual interactive struggle over the way meaning is to be established and appropriated between therapist and patient.* To the extent that noncommunication is a manifestation of incongruent frameworks, it is a sign of a fundamental alienation between therapist and patient, a divergence between the basic psychical processes and hence the kind of psychical reality available to each of them. It follows, then, that the task of establishing a common or consensual framework between therapist and patient would, from this perspective, necessarily take precedence over the uncovering of the unconscious or the analysis of the self, the ego defenses, or the transference and resistance.

It would, however, be inaccurate to hold the position that transference has no role in this standoff, this opposition of frameworks. In fact, the incongruence of frameworks is undoubtedly a transference phenomenon in itself, but of a very different kind to the conventional transference of internal psychical contents or processes. The type of transference active here, in the struggle between frameworks, is the transference of a failure of the holding environment, a failure that has left in its wake an incapacity on the part of the individual to utilize the consensual framework of symbols, and the individual's reliance instead on an idiosyncratic mode of mental functioning, as I have already described. What is being transferred here, from the past and from the patient's internal psychical world, is the alienation between child and parents, and between child and the societal world at large. The patient's idiosyncratic mental framework is testimony to the failure in childhood to internalize, by way of the parent's own internalized functions, the verbal-symbolic code of cultural identity; the idiosyncratic framework, then, is a form of transference, not of the libidinal or aggressively cathected figure of childhood, but of the failed environment of childhood.

2. The Question of Resistance

I begin from the standpoint of recognizing the historical specificity of Freud's analytic setting, a setting that has always assumed for its purpose a certain type of subject, one more or less neurotic in character. I will offer a particular view of the challenge posed by the noncommunicative (who is also usually a nonneurotic) patient, suggesting how *opposition* to the framework of the analytic setting differs from *resistance* as it is conventionally understood.

This may be an opportune moment to clarify what I mean by *noncommunication*, for by this I do not simply mean silence. Silence does not by any means necessarily signify noncommunication, and speech does not automatically produce communication; schizophrenic speech, for example, is often antithetical to communication. I will take the position that both intrapsychic and interpersonal communication depend for their existence upon symbolic thought and the use of a symbolizing medium. Where the symbolic use of language and symbolic mediation of experience is absent, we encounter noncommunication.[3]

Following this line of reasoning, I will apply the term *resistance* only to those obstructions of understanding that take the form of compromise formations, and therefore are in themselves communications that may ultimately be decoded, revealing the hidden meaning (although, of course, for any given resistance this may not be feasible). In contrast to resistance, the

---

[3]It would become necessary to modify this exceedingly clear-cut definition of what constitutes communication if I were to be persuaded that some other form of communication is possible *between subjects*. Of course there exists rich communication of a nonsymbolic nature between a subject and object, such as in the case of projective identification. Ogden (1987) highlights the importance of what he refers to as autistic-contiguous types of communication, such as imitation, as distinct from both paranoid-schizoid and depressive modes of being and communicating. But I am not convinced that these very important autistic-contiguous phenomena constitute what I am referring to as communication—namely, the exchanging or sharing of experiences within a consensual framework of meaning.

activity arising from the noncommunicating patient's alienated framework opposes the therapeutic frame more fundamentally, short-circuiting the use of symbols and the construction of compromise formations.

RESISTANCE VERSUS NONCOMMUNICATION

The nature of noncommunication arising from incongruent frameworks, in contrast to resistance, deserves some further comment. The conventional concept of resistance takes for granted the existence of a formal communicative capacity. It is assumed that what stands in the way of clear communication, preventing clear access to meaning and understanding, is some strongly warded-off content that has invited defensive activity on the part of the ego. Resistance to acknowledgment of these unconscious contents and defensive processes puts a brake on communication. Eventually, we assume, some symptomatic expression can be identified which, once recognized, would allow us to account for the patient's inability to enter smoothly into the therapeutic dialogue.

The concept of incongruent frameworks reveals a different understanding of the problem of noncommunication. If resistance is analogous to speaking in different tongues, then incongruence of frameworks produces a situation that would be closer to the contrast of spoken language to the "language" of the computer. Different tongues require only translation (which always involves some interpretation) for the obscure to become intelligible. Translation between spoken tongues is analogous, in this point of view, to psychoanalytic interpretation of resistances, defenses, and other unconscious contents and processes. By contrast, spoken language cannot be similarly translated into the "language" of the computer; it can only be transposed into a fundamentally different mode of registration, by being encoded into bits of information, without any meaning waiting to be revealed.

To put the dilemma in another way: We can speak *about* patients who employ alternative frameworks, but we may find it very difficult or impossible really to speak *to* them, even when aided by translation (interpretation).

COMPREHENSION IS POSSIBLE AND MAY BE HELPFUL OR MAY OBSTRUCT THE BRIDGING OF FRAMEWORKS

The objection may be raised that the distinction being drawn here between noncommunication on the one hand and resistant communication on the other is too neat, perhaps a caricature of what in reality is a complex gradation of communicative capacities, or worse, that this distinction is wrong because even the hallucinating, paranoid, or somatic patient can, after all, be understood and communicated with by the therapist. I would be powerless to rebut such objections, but I will introduce two statements at this point for the purposes of clarification: First, I am not asserting that noncommunicating patients are beyond comprehension. Understanding may be possible, and the use of understanding in communication may be feasible. There is no doubt that the nonsymbolic or presymbolic experience of disturbed individuals can be symbolically comprehended in the interpretations of therapists with great beneficial effect (cf. Boyer 1983). I am addressing myself instead in this chapter to the practical clinical dilemma posed in those instances where comprehension is absent or is useless. Second, it seems to be especially true of patients who are alienated from the verbal-symbolic code and framework that the therapist's knowledge, if it is cultivated in the absence of any common ground between the parties, will lend itself to further alienation. Premature knowing can be the enemy of meeting the patient, because without a shared framework the patient's sense of alienation is simply confirmed by the therapist's form of knowledge; and because the therapist might well use knowledge to remain fixed rather than discover a new therapeutic position through subjective experimentation, which involves a suspension of comprehension.

REPETITION: CONFIRMATION OF THE CONTAINING FUNCTION OF THE "PATHOLOGICAL" FRAME

At this juncture one may justifiably ask, given an actual situation of noncommunication between therapist and patient, how this alienation between frameworks is overcome. Where can we begin to forge a common ground if the patient's system of making meanings and registering experience is not only idiosyncratic and different from ours, but also, as I shall illustrate, basically at odds with and antagonistic to our own? The object relations theory of Melanie Klein and her followers has given us an indispensable tool in dealing with preverbal psychical phenomena, namely the theory of projective identification. But I am not convinced that, in the case of noncommunicating patients, a constructive or therapeutic form of projective identification alone can be understood to provide a means of bridging the gap between frameworks. Let me clarify this briefly by drawing attention to the heart of the argument being developed here, namely the contention that our more difficult patients do indeed possess their own idiosyncratic psychical frameworks: For the most part, they do not simply seek what Bion (1977) referred to as containment of the presymbolic bits of experience (beta elements) by projection of these elements into the therapist. Perhaps above all, I believe they also seek to *confirm and reestablish their own form of self-containment that they carry within them.* It seems to me that certain therapeutic steps might have to be taken before the therapist can really begin to be used as a therapeutic container for the presymbolic bit-projections, because the patient's own mode of containment and meaning-creation must to a significant degree first be relinquished if verbal or preverbal therapeutic communication is to take place.

MOVING INTO THE LINE OF FIRE: BUILDING A CONSENSUAL FRAMEWORK AT THE POINT OF ATTACK

I will propose, through the presentation of case material, that the point at which some contact can begin between patient and therapist, where the gap between frameworks can initially be bridged, arises from an observable need on the part of the patient to attack, transform, or invalidate the therapeutic frame: If the therapist can, as it were, find a way to place himself or herself successfully in the path of such an attack, in such a way that some mutual appreciation of the event can be registered, then perhaps a beginning can be made. Why it is that the point of attack on the therapist's framework proves to offer this opportunity remains to be adequately understood and explained. This is not, as would be conventionally understood, essentially an attack in the transference. It is not the expression of an object relationship, but is rather a repudiation of the therapist's entire way of being, which is based on verbal-symbolic modes of transformation.

FORECLOSURE OF THE THERAPIST'S FORM OF EXISTENCE

In the light of these considerations, it may be argued that inasmuch as an individual brings to the therapeutic setting a framework at odds with the verbal-symbolic framework of psychoanalysis, this individual also implicitly negates the subjectivity (objective existence) of the therapist. A common form of this negation of the therapist's humanity may be observed in a preponderant self–object (as opposed to symbolic object) use of the therapist and setting. The patient's frame, in these instances, constitutes a nonprocess of a particular kind—one that promotes the active processing of experience exclusively in terms of subjective, literal phenomena; the therapist is exploited literally, for gratification of basic psychical needs, that is, as a subjective object or self-object. Winnicott undoubtedly was referring to another aspect of this same phenomenon when, in emphasizing the importance of the therapy environment, he wrote that whereas for the neurotic "the couch may be symbolical of the mother's love," for the psychotic the "couch *is* the analyst's lap or womb" (1947, p. 199). Searles (1968) offers another type of description of the patient's investment in his or her own idiosyncratic method of creating psychic reality, stressing the central role of omnipotence:

> The patient unconsciously splits up psychological processes which belong together, and fuses processes which need to become differentiated from one another. One of the reasons for this is that he is struggling unconsciously to become a fully human individual without relinquishing his subjective omnipotence, omnipotence which would include his nondifferentiating from either the human or nonhuman surrounding environment. [p. 30]

The utility of the frame concept may make itself felt at this point, insofar as it is possible to view the patient's closed-off, subjective domination of the person of the therapist and of the setting, as well as his repudiation of the therapist's discourse, not primarily in terms of developmental arrest or regression to be analyzed through transference and resistance, but rather as the *essential valid functioning of the patient's framework*, which has evolved over time, developing its own particular functional integrity. As I have suggested, foreclosure of the therapist's mode of meaning construction produces a fundamental alienation, giving rise to a specific form of conflict in the therapeutic encounter: not primarily intra-agency or drive-derived conflict manifested in the transference, but an actual conflict between modes of establishing psychic reality.

In order to clarify the nature of this type of conflict, which entails a refusal of the therapist's mode existence, I will briefly recapitulate a fundamental distinction arising from Winnicott's theory of the environmental provision, the distinction between an "environmental mother" (never the object of the instincts) and the mother-as-object (source of transferences).

FAILURE OF ENVIRONMENTAL PROVISION
AND ALIENATION OF FRAMEWORKS

Winnicott asserts that the environmental provision (the "hold"), which I view as the prototype of the frame, is never represented consciously or unconsciously (for it cannot attract the interest of the instincts), and hence cannot become part of the material for analysis. Never having being repressed, it cannot be recalled or reconstructed. It is not the environment—the framework or backdrop of experience—that becomes analytic material, but the objects within that environment. On the other hand, where the holding environment has failed, the consequences of this failure do assume representation, and hence are registered in the unconscious. Thus can we understand fixed ideas, addictive activities, fetishes and delusions, and dependencies as petrified expressions—visible foreground elements of what should have been the invisible backdrop or framework, established upon an alienated but functional framework—of the parents' unique failure to provide an adequate psychological environment. Indeed, except in cases of acute chaotic fragmentation, there remains always some version of a secure backdrop to experience, a "silent" framework forged from experience and providing the context of meaning for all experience.

I wish to extrapolate this line of reasoning in order to clarify the nature of the alienated (nonneurotic) framework. The nonneurotic individual is remarkable not so much for the intensity or the quality of the *transferences* he brings to the therapeutic situation, but for the non-process (frame) he silently establishes as a fundamental challenge to the verbal-symbolic structure that underlies and adorns the psychoanalytic process. What the psychoanalyst assumes to be secure and silent and still in order to exist and do his work is not necessarily the same as what the nonneurotic patient assumes must be secure and silent and still in order for *him*—the patient—to exist. The analyst's hold is not the patient's hold.

The source of the patient's alienation from the analytic framework, his inability to accept the "hold" that engenders verbal-symbolic modes of experience, must be assumed to be in the original failure of the environmental provision in infancy. But the patient's individual solution to this failure lies precisely in the "hold," the particular form of containment, that he has evolved. If this frame, born of an original failure and invariably at odds with the frame assumed by psychoanalysis, is not somehow changed, no therapeutic change can reasonably be expected.

RECOGNIZING AND IDENTIFYING
THE ALIENATED FRAMEWORK

The difficulty of communicating with a psychotic patient impresses itself readily on therapists, and the different framework of these patients is, for the most part, implicitly taken for granted, particularly when the patient is actively hallucinating or is extremely withdrawn or assaultive. What is far less obvious is the frame incongruity in the case of those patients who can and do enter into manifestly verbal communication, but who destroy the possibility of *symbolic* communication and experience in the therapeutic situation, often in quite subtle ways. These patients may speak, but cannot sustain "illusion" (in the sense defined by Winnicott [1951], Milner [1952], and Khan [1971], and hence manifest an impaired metaphorical quality in their speech (cf. Rosolato 1978).

Even more commonly encountered are those patients who move in and out of symbolic discourse, who oscillate between acceptance and abandonment of the therapeutic frame (Goldberg 1987). Of course, the objection can readily be made that even the healthiest individuals oscillate between less and more fruitful levels of discourse and experience in the therapeutic encounter; however, with such patients, we properly account for these shifts not in terms of a fundamental incongruity of mental framework, but in terms of resistance and defense arising primarily in the intrapsychic sphere of conflict. Those individuals who truly oscillate between frameworks are, I believe, both numerous and difficult to identify, requiring the kind of active approach to securing a therapeutic frame that I am advocating here.

UNCONSCIOUS NONVERBAL COMMUNICATION:
A CLINICAL ILLUSTRATION

The patient, a young homosexual man whom I shall call Roy, presented himself in a most tenaciously provocative, seductive manner, embarking from the very first moment upon a series of maneuvers aimed at disrupting the therapeutic setting and ground rules. Very handsome and narcissistic, Roy was both charming and compliant, but all the same never ceased in his quest to corrupt and befriend and degrade the therapist, and to receive special attention and treatment. He wished to leave his bill unpaid, to arrange unusual appointment times, to tape-record sessions, to change the venue and length of meetings, and so on, seemingly without end.

Roy's disrupting sorties were always full of guile, creativity, unpredictability, and above all, hostility, all of which contrasted markedly with his verbal discourse, which was repetitive, contrived, and often quite meaningless. With the aid of his good looks and enterprising manner, Roy had evidently achieved a joyless existence consisting in the repetition of futile, short-lived liaisons, each of which followed a pattern of seduction, corruption, rejection, and withering criticism. This pattern characterized not only his sexual relationships but his employment and schooling situations as well. His repeated failures in every aspect of his life, his insecurity, loneliness, and lack of prospects, and his pitiful need for recognition and attention, altogether fueled a defensive propensity in this patient toward idealization, grandiosity, and self-inflation.

One was challenged by this patient in two ways: first, in how to deal with his hostile, disruptive actions, and second, in how to facilitate some metaphorical quality in the therapeutic discourse. I came to recognize that the disruptive actions, despite their controlling and often sadistic quality, at least provided some potential point of contact, but not as yet a useful contact.

The problem of the patient's rarified, almost vacuous discourse, on the other hand, seemed intractable. Typically, he would begin talking in a vague, long-winded, grandiloquent fashion. Left to carry on in this way, he could easily consume the entire session with rambling, pseudophilosophical descriptions of his daily activities or past experiences, without betraying a single hidden meaning, wish, or fear. No significant object relationship could be inferred from the content of his discourse, and hence it seemed impossible to discern transference meanings. He did not talk about himself, but created instead an *image* of his life—not truly an imaginative image but a contrivance, something with the two-dimensionality of a screen image, which the therapist was forced not only simply to witness and admire but actually to submit to (or, in other words, partially merge with).

All attempts at providing perspective or insight through verbal intervention seemed meaningless and ineffective. Inactive empathic mirroring (Kohut 1977) and/or inactive "holding" (Winnicott 1965) as deliberate approaches to the patient could not be usefully sustained (as is unfortunately too often the case) because the patient succeeded in casting the therapist so completely in the role of the excluded, totally demobilized, and utterly controlled self-object. Where the therapist and the verbal-symbolic framework are disenfranchised to

this degree, inactivity on the part of the therapist often serves to per-
petuate the impasse; the therapist's framework (the definer of his subjective existence) might remain omnipotently foreclosed indefinitely.
In searching for an *active* means of intervention with Roy (i.e., some
means of *interrupting* the cocoon of his narcissistic discourse), I was
able to discover, in this case without any conscious awareness at all, a
subjective posture or position of potential responsiveness that, if deployed at an optimal moment during a session, appeared to prevent the
session from deteriorating into a spiraling vacuum of meaningless
words, beyond intervention. This unexpected turn of events came about
as follows.

Comments and questions of a supportive nature were taken for
granted by the patient, automatically conscripted into his discourse
with an air of mild contempt, fleeting gratification, and finally indifference. On the other hand, *explorative* and *interpretive* verbal interruption of the patient's monologue proved to be both futile and risky, due
to his particularly sensitive tendency to feel rebuffed, insulted, or
wounded. Such interruption would lead inevitably to heightened grandiosity and increasingly rarified and depersonalized speech. When this
happened, Roy, inevitably feeling terribly attacked, would fall into an
abstract mode of speaking in which, commonly, all reference to persons
would be obliterated, and even the first person subject would apparently disappear. Thus, for example, he might report his own thoughts
by saying: "It is considered that the idea of muscle perfection is a good
one"; or "Thoughts of writing and making movies have been appear-
ing again and are exciting." Feeling wounded by routine psychotherapeutic words, he would typically withdraw into grandiose specula-
tion—for example, by describing at length a movie project in which he
would write the script, direct, act, do the cinematography, and so on. Or
he might decide to become a famous poet or artist.

I was startled to note a break in the impasse after about six months
of treatment, during which time the sessions had conformed by and
large to the pattern I have described above. Increasingly, and inexplicably, the sessions were now turning in a more fruitful direction. Pres-
ently I discovered, to my surprise, that in place of my attempts at verbal
intervention ("frame interpretations" intended to link the patient's
defensive acting-in the setting with the underlying existence-anxiety), I
had unwittingly substituted a *nonverbal* communication. Having obviously become sensitive to the fateful defensive withdrawal into impenetrable, grandiose isolation in the patient's discourse, caused by my

verbal interventions or simply by his own heightened anxiety, I found myself at these critical moments making an inquiring gesture with my head and hands, a gesture itself so subtle that only after several months did I become fully aware of what I was doing. The patient, however, was increasingly responsive to this gesture. He would stop his monologue abruptly, even in mid-sentence, and make a visible effort to backtrack, find what it was that he had initially been trying to say, and then try again in a more meaningful way. In response to my barely perceptible nonverbal intervention, it became possible for Roy to attempt to examine his disruptive actions and to begin to reflect upon his emotional states and anxieties, much along the lines suggested in my attempted verbal interpretations. It is worth noting that I only became cognizant of my own physical gestures, and of their communicative function, as I began to observe these occasions where he tentatively entered upon a form of self-reflection that clearly represented a far greater degree of verbal-symbolic functioning.

I came to understand that, in the rhythm of the sessions, Roy's direct (through action) and indirect (through impenetrable speech) attacks upon the therapeutic setting would be aggravated, as a rule, by my verbal interventions. My words would simply register as a destructive attack on the patient's way of being. By contrast, my unwitting nonverbal gesture did succeed in allowing the patient to see and reflect upon what he was doing and what was happening to him psychologically, and also allowed the patient to remain in communication with the therapist and accept the therapeutic task of self-examination through words.

With regard to the use of nonverbal communication in this case, I would like to make the following observations and deductions:

1. The nonverbal gestures depended for their meaning and efficacy entirely upon what had previously been verbally articulated. What I want particularly to point out here is the way in which a nonverbal gesture came to stand for (to be signified by) the type of verbal intervention (frame interpretation) that I had been formulating in each session; and, in addition, how the patient was able to make better use of the nonverbal communication than he was of the signifying verbal intervention itself.

2. The efficacy of the nonverbal communication, it seems to me, must be ascribed at least partially to its *nonmanipulative* character and use. I was not consciously employing the gesture, as one might a

manipulation.[4] Indeed, by the time I became aware of it, the patient was to some degree able to perceive his own propensity toward narcissistic withdrawal (which entailed a refusal or foreclosure of the verbal-symbolic medium) and was partially able to contain his own anxieties in this regard (an instance, I believe, of the internalization of the therapeutic frame or hold). In other words, once I had become aware of the nonverbal artifice, it had become redundant, and the patient and I were able to discuss it with simple clarity. The conscious use of such an artifice, as a deliberate technical tool, would be more problematic, for the manipulative intent would undoubtedly become apparent, reinforcing the patient's sense of mistrust.

3. This nonverbal form of communication had a role only during the phase of establishing a therapeutic frame, after which time its utility and justification ceased to exist, being replaced by the use of words. This development can be understood in light of the fact that, initially, Roy had little use for or trust in the symbolic value of thoughts or words; he experienced verbal interpretations as threatening *things* from the outside world, impingements to be warded off or controlled. In order to neutralize my verbal interpretation he would select a part of it and ignore the rest, using the part to merely punctuate his monologue rather than enter into a dialogue. In this way, he routinely stripped my words of their interpretive, metaphoric dimension, and thereby negated the therapeutic framework in which a symbolic interchange might take place. If this neutralizing strategy did not succeed, he would become more urgently grandiose and unreachable, as I have described.

The nonverbal gesture, on the other hand, was more tolerable, and Roy was able to find a connoted meaning or meta-message in the gesture: namely, that there existed some other potential means of containing his terrible fear and anxiety arising from his fragile self-esteem—a means of self-caretaking provided by verbal-symbolic self-reflection and self-understanding. To this extent, therefore, it was possible for Roy to abandon the pathological narcissistic means of defense against his sense of insignificance and infant-like weakness. The fact that this new verbal-symbolic, self-reflective means of cop-

---

[4]The question of an unconscious manipulation is more difficult to judge, but the gesture lacked the specificity of meaning to qualify as a bribe (as compared, say, to a smile or a look of approval). Indeed, if the gesture had any independent meaning, it was to signify an explorative questioning, that is to say a nonmanipulative enquiry.

ing with fearful affects became possible only through the active symbolizing functions (here manifested in a nonverbal gesture) provided by another human being—in other words, the fact of Roy's *dependency* on another—could be appreciated only later and after much working through in the treatment.

4. Clearly, then, the patient's inability to make use of words or symbolize his experience should not automatically be treated as manifestations of resistance, but should rather be viewed as an incapacity to enter the verbal-symbolic medium of psychotherapy, an incapacity reflecting the existence of what I have referred to as *incongruent frameworks*. Hence, as I have suggested, we may say that, in the case of Roy, the nonverbal gesture facilitated the internalization by the patient of a *function* or formal capacity, comparable to what Bion (1977) termed alpha function, which engenders a capacity for symbolic thought and experience, self-reflection, and the intrapsychic containment of psychotic anxiety. This internalization of a formal containing function (analogous to Winnicott's environmental hold) is perhaps the major element in establishing a therapeutic frame, that is, overcoming the frame incongruity that more disturbed patients inevitably bring to the therapeutic situation in one form or another.

5. I wish to stress the activity necessary on the part of the therapist in discovering—albeit quite inadvertently, in this case—a subjective posture that facilitates some communicative common ground; I searched actively for a subjective state of responsiveness that would meet the need of the patient. This entailed, first and foremost, the formulation of interpretations, but something in addition as well, a rather active yet undirected search for an adequate *form* or state of mind.[5]

6. An initial promise of tangible engagement was evident in Roy's disruptive activities and attacks upon the therapeutic situation, as I have already mentioned. But these attacks in fact provided little

---

[5]G. de Racker (1961) describes beautifully the way in which the therapist might inadvertently be provided by the patient with a particular way of uttering an interpretation, such that the patient can receive and use it. Her case illustrations emphasize the nonconscious or unintentional conveying of a useful element from patient to therapist, and the equally unwitting use of the element by the therapist in delivering the interpretation. She does not particularly emphasize what I refer to as active seeking of an adequate subjective state on the part of the therapist. Her interest is to show that the helpful element garnered from the patient and introduced by the therapist into the interpretation represents the hidden, secret role of the good object in the patient's psychic life.

opportunity for therapeutic insight, because of the peculiar nature of the therapeutic impasse: Roy's attack was not *primarily* upon the representative of a figure transferred from the past (I stress "primarily," because the object-related, transferential element is, of course, also inevitably part of the picture). He was, rather, I believe, above all asserting the valid functioning of his own mental framework, which consisted in a grandiose, narcissistic system of self-management and caretaking, quite at odds with the verbal-symbolic mode. In such cases, the therapist's functioning must be attacked not primarily because of who the therapist is in the mind of the patient, but because the therapist's functioning is hostile to the patient's functioning, insofar as the therapist invariably intends to bring about a change in (i.e., destruction of) the patient's mode of functioning. Thus there exists an actual, rather than a fantasied, struggle over the construction of meaning and of reality. Only once this struggle had to some extent been resolved—once a consensual communication had been established—did Roy's attacks on the therapeutic frame become therapeutically useful points of engagement, throwing light upon specific transference figures and object relationships. I could then interpret his attacks in terms of transference and defense in the context of symbolic meanings and self-reflectivity, whereas previously the attacks reflected a struggle over the axioms of meaning construction, a refusal of symbolic meanings and verbal mediation.

CASE ILLUSTRATION OF THE FREE USE OF THE THERAPIST'S IMAGINATION IN STORYTELLING

The patient, a 13-year-old boy from an economically disadvantaged area and a depriving family situation, very tall for his age and always wearing a baseball cap and a sarcastic smile, was brought into the psychotherapy clinic after becoming explosively angry and potentially violent on several occasions at school. After compliantly mumbling answers to my questions in the first couple of meetings, he fell completely silent. But for the exchange of pleasantries at the outset of a session, he would simply drape his long limbs comfortably over the arms of his chair, stare out of the window with the ever-present smile, and say nothing at all. My most persistent efforts to win a response might, at most, produce a condescending glance and a grunt.

My difficulties were compounded by an extraordinarily powerful soporific quality that I experienced in the presence of this patient. Not simply the silence—for silence can be a fertile medium for reverie or can be charged with tension—but a stifling, languid heaviness in the atmosphere made it literally impossible to remain awake. I imagined that it was a matter of some amusement for him to watch me slipping unavoidably into a stupor.

Having exhausted my options, including vigorous interpretation of his behavior, educative comments, friendly conversation, and eventually veiled threats to terminate the sessions (which, incidentally, he attended regularly without coercion), and barely able to face another session fighting off the almost narcotic effect, I decided to experiment with a variation of friendly conversation, remembering a comment by Andre Green (1975) to the effect that in some cases the therapist has to provide all of the symbolization, in lieu of the patient's incapacity to do so. My decision was to attempt the telling of another story (I had already told stories with both education and friendly conversation in mind), but now I determined to do this without purpose or forethought—in essence, to allow myself to freely associate. The initial story that emerged took the following approximate form:

> A wanderer, a guy who went from village to village, looking for a place to work and live, was always very excited as he came over the hill and saw the village below in the valley, bustling with people going about their business. Eagerly he would make his way into town, but upon arriving there he would find everybody asleep, taking their siesta.

Variations on this tale followed, each story elaborating a little on the previous one. The patient remained steadfastly distinterested and unresponsive, but I continued telling stories because now, for the first time, I was alert and not troubled by sleepiness. After several sessions of this storytelling, answered only by increasingly frequent looks of disbelieving curiosity from the patient, the theme of my tale had developed to roughly this version:

> He could pitch an excellent fast ball, and was going from one town to another looking for a ball club that could use him. The managers were always impressed with his arm and wanted him to pitch on their team. But the same thing happened each time: He'd get up on the mound, wind up to throw the first ball, and the batter would be passed out, asleep at the plate. Everyone would be asleep, and he'd have to move on to the next town.

It was during the relating of this particular version that the patient uttered his first protest: He declared my story "bullshit!" and set about analyzing the shortcomings of the story both if it were taken as realistic and if it were treated as an allegorical tale. At first he seemed somewhat concerned at the possibility that I meant him to believe literally in the truth of the story, but soon he showed relief at realizing that we could treat it as allegorical. Shortly he began telling me stories.

The active seeking of a useful position vis-à-vis the patient was quite obvious in this case. The particular strategy of creating stories by allowing myself maximal imaginative freedom, with no intentional goal in mind, produced an instantaneous change in my own experience in the therapeutic situation. Eventually, in turn, the patient was able to establish communication with me (although one cannot be absolutely sure that the storytelling definitely led to the creation of a dialogue). At the very least, the storytelling allowed me to persist—and in fact aided my participation—in the psychotherapy.

One might make the case that the patient's silence simply reflected a fearful paralysis, something along the lines of a fear of the destructiveness of words or fear of embarrassing speech—in other words, that his silence was essentially a resistance in the transference situation. The patient's state of mind during the period of his silence remains a mystery. Two observations suggest, however, that this apparent resistance was in fact a manifestation of a more fundamental alienation, an opposition of frameworks: First, the incapacitating assault on my verbal-symbolic functioning mounted by the patient, an instance no doubt of a powerful projective identification of his rage-inhibiting, depressed self, but I think more importantly a total rejection of my therapeutic way of being and an assertion of his framework. Second, his concern over whether or not I was insisting on the literal truth of the stories provides a clue—namely that the metaphorical dimension that we take so much for granted in the verbal-symbolic framework was still a matter of uncertainty for him. His argumentative entry into communication with me revealed a mistrust of metaphor, of the symbolic ambiguity that characterizes the verbal-symbolic framework. I was left with the impression that his criticisms of the story constituted a coming to terms with the verbal-symbolic framework that he had previously rejected in favor of a framework incapable of using verbal mediation. In contrast to the previous attacks on the therapeutic framework, attacks which foreclosed any symbolic type of understanding, these criticisms also provided a useful point of engagement, a hostility that could be comprehended in transferential terms in the context of a shared verbal framework.

CLINICAL ILLUSTRATION: CASE OF TED

Ted was 11 years old when he entered treatment, apparently without friends, barely managing to stay in school, and anatagonistic in the home almost to the point of physical violence. In the sessions he would busy himself fiddling with toys, clay, and other objects without actually making anything or playing any game. The only words he ever uttered were occasional esoteric phrases taken from comic books or television shows. No communication was addressed to me, and any attempt on my part to speak to him was met inevitably by a single syllable response which seemed phonetically to be located at a point equidistant between yes and no. This response perfectly sabotaged any attempt at starting a meaningful interchange.

This stalemate persisted for some months, during which time I tried out different approaches, for the most part motivated by a persistent boredom and sense of purposelessness and even hopelessness in the case. In retrospect, I was able to discern three separate approaches in these initial months, which I believe constituted three different experimental subjective states.

Phase 1. After futile initial enquiries and attempts to communicate through play, I resorted to a rather forceful use of interpretation, speculatively based on certain theoretical notions of what I thought must be going on inside the boy's mind. On more than one occasion, this "interpretive" activity became so insistent that I was able to perceive an unmistakable sadistic quality in what I was doing. Consequently I gave up this approach, there having been not the slightest change in the impasse already described.

Phase 2. Interpretation, confrontation, and friendly enquiry all having proved useless, and somewhat dismayed at the sense of almost violent intrusiveness in my interventions, I opted for a silent presence, hoping to provide the much-talked-about "holding enivornment," but this showed itself immediately to be most difficult. The pervasive boredom I felt, and at times an apparently complete absence of recognition by the patient of my human presence, made it seem impossible for me to avoid drifting off into daydreams in a rather compulsive way. For his part, Ted busied himself with various spurious activities that were in fact nonactivities. Not a session passed when I did not undertake to terminate the treatment, and I think that one reason that kept me from doing so was the belief that my own discomfort and despondency were, in large part, induced by means of a projective identification, which therefore gave some potential therapeutic meaning to the miserable unpleasantness of the situation.

Phase 3. Reacting to the powerful, forced sense of alienation and noncommunication, and finding no clues in the content of my daydreams, I deliberately chose a new strategy, namely to devote my full attention to Ted, focusing all my faculties on his presence, while at the same time resisting any temptation and refraining from any attempt to understand or speculate about what was going on inside him. This was by no means easy, but I soon felt rewarded by observing that Ted seemed engaged in a concentrated activity—albeit with his back turned to me—namely, making rather intricate and highly artistic figures out of plasticine. I would be allowed occasional glimpses of the creations during the sessions, but he would destroy the pieces at session's end. I felt acutely disappointed and even attacked when he did this, and the frustration engendered by his tantalizing behavior during this period made me aware of his sadistic capacities. Nevertheless, there no longer seemed to be a hopeless void between us, and I was no longer bored or despondent. His sadistic treatment of me felt like a point of contact.

This contact, of sorts, that now existed between us gradually developed to the point where Ted no longer destroyed his sculptures, but would leave them on the shelf until the next session, at which time he would enter and immediately destroy the piece before setting about creating another. The pieces all had aggressive, warring motifs, but were totemic rather than simply grotesque. New variations were introduced into our interaction, at first with a ball game requiring careful cooperation in which we would bounce a light foam ball in the air for as long as possible without letting it touch the floor. War games with army men followed, and gradually Ted began to talk in short phrases, revealing tidbits about school and new friends, but warning me off any sustained discussions of a psychological nature.

That this fledgling form of communication between us was fragile was brought home to me when I committed an impulsive error at the beginning of a session during the period when he had developed the capacity to allow the sculptures to be preserved until the start of the following meetings. The incident occurred one day when, as he strode toward the shelf to retrieve his sculpture, I playfully snatched it away, no doubt indulging my continuing frustration and disappointment at his habit of destroying the pieces. This lapse on my part had the immediate and dramatic consequence of Ted returning to the previous mute attitude of noncommunication, which only gave way after some weeks to a renewed trust and resumption of communication.

PROJECTIVE IDENTIFICATION AND THE BRIDGING OF FRAMEWORKS

With regard to this case material, only a few summary points need be made. While the patient's "resistance" was starkly obvious from the outset, and his defensive use of projective identification could be detected in the interaction, no headway could be made by offering verbal interpretations of these facts. Indeed, the interpretations themselves could not escape at all from the cycle of projections, and were experienced by the patient as sadistic attacks. I think it is important to note here that the presence of projective identifications, which have often been referred to as a primitive form of communication, did not necessarily offer in and of themselves the possibility of therapeutic communication. The latter requires some reconciliation of the basic frameworks of the patient and therapist, and it is within this common framework that projective identifications may be used and modified in a therapeutic direction. Nevertheless, as was illustrated above, an awareness of the effects of projective identifications can be indispensable in the therapist's efforts to understand his or her own experience where communication has not yet been established, even if the actual interpretation of the projective identification is quite futile or even harmful.

THE ACTIVE SEARCH FOR A HOLDING POSITION

The task of providing a setting in which the patient can begin to enter into the verbal-symbolic order of experience, and gradually give up his own framework, is a very specific task indeed. Winnicott's "holding environment" and Bion's "containing" function are the obvious theoretical conceptions applicable to this specific kind of activity, but as the clinical material above suggests, the therapist may be called upon to pursue a very active internal search for this holding or containing position vis-à-vis the particular patient. Unfortunately, no specific technical approach exists, to my knowledge, that might dependably guide us in our approach to the alienated patient. Perhaps, in undertaking the psychotherapy of frameworks, the nature of the difficulties that arise are such that each solution will necessarily be discovered in a surprising way, so that concrete technical proposals would be found to be applicable. Certain more general technical statements are, however, most helpful and are pertinent to the discussion of what might aid us in the active search for a holding position. Describing a deliberate variation in the therapist's subjective state, L. Bryce Boyer (1986) writes:

> Although most of my thinking during analytic sessions with regressed patients continues to be directed and dominated by secondary process, I have become progressively more able to let my attention wander simultaneously, permitting the development of a split-off, slightly altered ego state in myself, and then to become aware of more of the nuances and symbolism implied by the patient's manifest productions. [p. 8]

In another variation on the therapist's subjective state, Marion Milner (1969), addressing herself to the problem of establishing a therapeutic communication, emphasized the importance of the therapist's achieving at least a partial state of nondifferentiation: "I needed to achieve, knowingly, a partially undifferentiated, indeterminate state, to hold a blankness, an empty circle, empty of ideas, not always pushing myself to make an interpretation" (p. 253).

CONSENSUS SYMBOLIZATION ARISING AT THE POINT OF ATTACK

The necessity of actively seeking a holding position in the treatment of alienated patients arises, as I have said, from the fact that these individuals bring their own hold, their own containing function, to the therapeutic setting; and that a way must be found to introduce the verbal-symbolic framework as a viable form of containment. Where a discrepancy exists between the two forms or types of framework, the therapist's hold or containment is not only unacceptable to the patient, but is disdained and sabotaged. It is, I have claimed, precisely at the juncture of the patient's attack upon the verbal-symbolic framework that the therapist can offer to meet the patient's experience (and, thereby, fulfill the patient's invariable hope for a new beginning). But what distinguishes an alienated and therefore therapeutically useless attack from an attack that marks a point of engagement, of potential consensus (in the basis of meaning-creation), between patient and therapist?

In the case of Ted, one may correctly say that the attack upon the verbal-symbolic framework was in evidence from the start, but it seems to me that this attack took on a more symbolically mediated and relational form only at the point where his concerted sculpturing of figurines began. This in turn occurred, according to my observation, only when I consciously assumed a new posture, combining attentiveness on my part with a deliberate effort to avoid any attempt to understand his inner feelings or thoughts. I wish to propose, then, that my eventual discovery of a particular posture—in this case a nonintrusive, attentive, nonverbal attitude—made it possible for the patient to bring his attacks into a playful relation to me, giving rise not only to a sense of engagement, but leading directly to other forms of communication, most notably to the use of words. In his tantalizing and sadistic hiding, showing, and destruction of the figurines, Ted was engaging me on common ground, in a game of hopeful pleasure, disappointment, and punishment—a game of his own making that involved a communication of feelings and the use of a symbolic, creative medium (the sculpturing).

Similar conclusions may be drawn in the case of Roy: Disruption and disparaging of the therapeutic situation were prominent from the outset, but this took place in the context of a complete repudiation of the therapist's independent (verbal-symbolic) functioning. A new context was eventually provided in which the patient's attacks became opportunities for a mutual (verbal-symbolic) discovery of meaning—but this new context could arise only as a result of a concerted effort on my part to find a responsive subjective position vis-à-vis the patient (which in this case found expression in an unwitting nonverbal communication, a physical gesture that apparently allowed the patient to reflect upon, rather than deny and disperse, his anxieties and fears).

What I wish to emphasize here is that as a result of the therapist's active search for a holding or containing posture, the alienated attacks by noncommunicating patients on the verbal-symbolic framework can potentially be transformed into attacks that can be understood *within* a common symbolic framework, and the analysis of defense, resistance, and transference can proceed from there.

The crucial therapeutic activity, then, in this beginning phase of "frame analysis" (the psychotherapy of alienated frameworks) is not necessarily the conventional analysis of transference or of resistance, nor should we retain exclusively the interpretive approach which stresses understanding; it is, rather, the conscious, nonverbal attempt by the therapist to find a psychological and emotional position that would allow the patient to enter a common ground of potential experience, one in which symbols provide not only the means of communication between individuals but the means of intrapsychic communication as well.

CONCLUDING COMMENTS ON THE VALUE OF SUBJECTIVE EXPERIMENTATION

Finally, it must be admitted that no clear and firm guidelines can be offered to the practitioner engaged in the difficult task of building a therapeutic frame. The means by which a therapist might more assuredly discover the posture or internal attitude that may facilitate the entry of a particular patient into the verbal-symbolic mode of experience and communication appears to depend upon subjective repositioning of the therapist, in the style of trial and error rather than by means of conforming to a prescribed technical approach.

Until such time as we witness the formulation of a rigorous, unified technical approach to the problems encountered in the building of a therapeutic frame, we will in all likelihood have to rely upon these rather vague and paltry guidelines: namely, that the therapist should attempt to maintain maximum imaginative flexibility within the context of therapeutic neutrality, or, more specifically, should be prepared to actively experiment with different subjective states of mind in relation to the patient. Furthermore, it should be kept in mind that the patient's disruptive and degrading attacks on the therapeutic framework and the therapist might potentially provide a point of meaningful contact in the midst of fundamental estrangement and noncommunication between therapist and patient.

CONCLUSION

The patient who does not "fit" the verbal-symbolic framework of the therapeutic setting poses a particular challenge to our therapeutic technique. Where communication is very difficult or impossible, we encounter the fact that the patient employs a framework of experience and a code of meaning construction that is not only fundamentally different from ours, but is also indispensable to the patient. In these cases, the actual alienation between therapist and patient is substantial and real, and the expressions of this alienation are therefore not usefully understood in terms of transference or resistance. By suspending understanding and experimenting with different internal subjective states of mind, the therapist might discover a position that allows common ground to develop with the patient. It is at the inevitable point of attack by the patient on the therapist's framework and mode of being that the bridging of frameworks is most likely to occur.

REFERENCES

Bion, W. R. (1977). *Seven Servants*. New York: Jason Aronson.
Bleger, J. (1967). Psycho-analysis of the psycho-analytic frame. *International Journal of Psycho-Analysis* 48:511–519.
Boyer, L. B. (1983). *The Regressed Patient*. New York: Jason Aronson.
——— (1986). Technical aspects of treating the regressed patient. *Contemporary Psychoanalysis* 22:25–44.
Chasseguet-Smirgel, J. (1985). *The Ego Ideal*. New York: Norton.
de Racker, G. T. (1961). On the formulation of the interpretation. *International Journal of Psycho-Analysis* 42:49–54.
Freud, S. (1913). Recommendations for physicians on the psychoanalytic method of treatment. In *Collected Papers, Standard Edition* 12:109–120.
Goldberg, P. L. (1987). The role of distractions in the maintenance of dissociative mental states. *International Journal of Psycho-Analysis* 68:511–524.
Green, A. (1980). The dead mother. In *On Private Madness*, pp. 142–173. Madison, CT: International Universities Press, 1986.
Grotstein, J. S. (1981). *Splitting and Projective Identification*. New York: Jason Aronson.
Khan, M. M. R. (1971). The role of illusion in the analytic space and process. In *The Privacy of the Self*, pp. 251–269. New York: International Universities Press, 1974.
Klein, M. (1930). The importance of symbol formation in the development of the ego. In *Contributions to Psycho-Analysis 1921–1945*, pp. 236–250. New York: McGraw-Hill.
Kohut, H. (1977). *The Restoration of the Self*. New York: International Universities Press.
Lacan, J. (1976). *Écrits: A Selection*. London: Tavistock.
Langs, R. (1978). Validation and the framework of the therapeutic situation. In *Technique in Transition*, pp. 381–412. New York: Jason Aronson, 1978.
Lewin, B. (1946). Sleep, the mouth, and the dream screen. *Psychoanalytic Quarterly* 15:419–436.
McDougall, J. (1985). *Theaters of the Mind*. New York: Basic Books.
——— (1986). Identifications, neoneeds and neosexualities. *International Journal of Psycho-Analysis* 67:19–31.
Milner, M. (1952). Aspects of symbolism in the comprehension of the not-self. *International Journal of Psycho-Analysis* 33:181–195.

—— (1969). *The Hands of the Living God*. London: Hogarth.

Ogden, T. (1986). *The Matrix of the Mind*. New York: Jason Aronson.

—— (1987). On the dialectical structure of experience. *Contemporary Psycho-analysis* 24:17–45.

Rosolato, G. (1978) Symbol formation. *International Journal of Psycho-Analysis* 59:303–319.

Searles, H. F. (1986). *My Work with Borderline Patients*. New York: Jason Aronson.

Tustin, F. (1981). *Autistic States in Children*. Boston: Routledge and Kegan Paul.

Winnicott, D. W. (1947). Hate in the countertransference. In *Through Paediatrics to Psycho-Analysis*, pp. 194–203. New York: Basic Books, 1975.

—— (1951). Transitional objects and transitional phenomena. In *Playing and Reality*, pp. 1–25. New York: Basic Books, 1971.

—— (1965). *The Maturational Processes and the Facilitating Environment*. New York: International Universities Press.

PART III

MASTER CLINICIANS ON THE THERAPIST

12

L. Bryce Boyer, m.d.

Countertransference and Technique

Almost thirty years ago I introduced into the North American literature a concept that to my knowledge was new, the idea that unresolved counter-transference constitutes a major impediment to the successful psychoana-lytic treatment of regressed patients (Boyer 1961).[1] I became aware later that such an idea had been implied earlier or contemporaneously in the writings of Searles (1953) and certain British and French authors and their followers in Latin America (Balint 1968, Garma 1962, Grunberger 1971, Heiman 1950, Khan 1964, Nacht 1963, Racker 1968, Winnicott 1947). Subsequently, that position has found much support, although it is not universally ac-cepted.[2]

Following my initial communications, I have written of the roles of other factors in the treatment of the regressed patient that are aimed at the resumption of ego development (Loewald 1979) and his becoming more alive as a subjective, historical being (Ogden 1986) who emerges from analysis as an empathic, effective, and creative person (Giovacchini 1986): (1) the establishment of the working or therapeutic alliance; (2) the holding or facilitating environment; (3) timely empathic interpretations; and (4) the analyst's internal security and optimism in the face of inevitable transfer-ence regressions.

---

[1] I even erroneously believed that I had introduced the term *countertransference neurosis*, a phrase used by Racker in 1953. So far as I am aware, my use of the term *countertransference psychosis* was original.

[2] Thus, Waldinger and Gunderson (1987), in their recent *Effective Psychother-apy with Borderline Patients*, scarcely mention countertransference.

In the introduction to this book, I discussed the advantages of the therapist's being selectively aggressive in his search for usable data in analysis and how interpretations based on his awareness of his own physical, emotional, and ideational responses to the patient's veiled messages can be effective in treatment (Boyer 1986). Analysts have become progressively aware of the potentially beneficial therapeutic uses of countertransference phenomena (Boyer 1983, Giovacchini 1989, Hann-Kende 1933, Little 1981, Racker 1968, Searles 1979). Yet Waldinger's (1987) recent overview of the work of North American psychoanalysts who treat borderline patients considers the role of countertransference but in passing.

In this chapter, I hope to demonstrate that interpretation facilitated by countertransference experiences constitutes an important agent of psychic structuring in the treatment of at least some regressed patients.

As illustrative material, I discuss the treatment of a group of patients whose use of projective identification appears to be excessive; it very heavily influences their relationships with others as well as their psychic equilibrium. Their principal conscious goal in therapy is to relieve themselves immediately of tension. Often they greatly fear that the experience of discomfort is intolerable and believe that failure to rid themselves of it will lead to physical or mental fragmentation or dissolution. Bion (1962, p. 114) holds that "excessive projective identification should be understood to apply not to the frequency only with which projective identification is employed but to excess of belief in omnipotence."

The principal data of this chapter consist of a precis of the psychoanalysis of a woman who, during a period of regression that was limited almost entirely to the consultation room, attempted to empty herself totally of mental contents and deposit them into me or into space. I believe that the data demonstrate that interpretation facilitated by countertransference experiences constituted in this case an important agent of psychic restructuring. I have treated three other similar patients who confirm to my satisfaction that interpretation thus facilitated proved to be equally beneficial.

COUNTERTRANSFERENCE

In my experience, both the most effective interpretations and the recovery of the most relevant repressed memories are based frequently on information gathered through transference-countertransference interactions. In working with regressed patients, many of those interactions depend on the patient's projective, and the analyst's introjective, identification. Searles (1976) found that effective interpretations also can be based on the analyst's projective and the patient's introjective identifications.[3]

Psychoanalytic impasses can be traced to the analyst's faulty use of his introjections, based on his idiosyncratic psychology (Grinberg 1979, Racker 1968). Especially during the patient's inevitable regressions, the analyst at times undergoes experiences that enable him to reach previously hidden material (Green 1975, Searles 1976). Freud (1912) recommended that the therapist "turn to his own unconscious like a receptive organ towards the transmitting unconscious of the patient . . . so that the doctor's unconscious is able to reconstruct the patient's unconscious" (pp. 115–116).

Analysts have long sought to understand what constitutes Reik's (1948) "listening with the third ear," or Isakower's (n. d.) "analyzing instrument" (Beres and Arlow 1974, Fleming and Benedek 1966). Spiegel (1975) noted that both analyst and analysand operate in similar states of mind (free-floating attention and free association, respectively) and noted that this results in a type of conversation that is unique to psychoanalysis. Balter and colleagues (1980) speak of the analyzing instrument as operating within a subsystem of the ego of the analyst who "is more likely to perceive connections between words, ideas and images which are products of the patient's primary process, because his subsystem is itself in part freed from the constraints of secondary process thinking, reality testing and so on" (pp. 490–491). They note that "the regression in the [ego] subsystem of the analyst is essentially of the same nature as that which obtains in the subsystem of the analysand" (p. 486).

Khan (1964) conceives of countertransference as an instrument of perception, and McDougall (1985) holds that she articulates her introjections of the patient's preverbal and presymbolic experiences. At times she becomes aware of the meanings of countertransference disturbances through analysis of her own dreams (McDougall 1978). Winnicott (1971) and Ogden (1985, 1986) have stressed the need of the analyst to be able to allow the existence of potential space in which creativity can occur, and Bion (1967), the need for the analyst to enter a "reverie" allowing a similar development.

Apparently it has become usual for some analysts to include quite consciously their countertransference reactions in their interpretations, particularly with regressed patients. (See also Loewald 1986.)

---

[3]It has been assumed for many years that countertransferences are determined largely by the analyst's introjections of qualities of the patient that come into contact with the therapist's unresolved infantile conflicts (Federn 1952, Fenichel 1945, Fliess 1953).

When working with neurotics, the analyst is frequently able to make significant interpretations from a position of technical neutrality, although Jacobs (1986) reminds us that "neutrality, too, may become involved with countertransference reactions" (p. 197). To judge from the literature and my own experience, mutative interpretations made to regressed patients often are made from a position tinged with the analyst's emotions. Searles (personal communication) reminds us that the "neutral" psychoanalyst "is all too likely to project into the patient all sorts of far-from-neutral emotions."

The range of experiences the analyst must be able to tolerate, understand, and interpret meaningfully extends from feeling like an excluded object (Giovacchini 1967, McDougall 1972) whose interventions, if acknowledged, are treated by the patient as evidence of the analyst's madness, to reacting to the patient's fusional regression and dependence as though the analyst is an extension of his mind and/or body, and to his sometimes startling somatic displays when on the couch.

Many regressed patients present psychosomatic syndromes that have been interpreted as masking symbolic thought or interfering with the patient's capacity to symbolize, through what McDougall (1985, 1989) has called *psychic shortcutting*. In order to reach the level of regression that will enable them to develop a new kind of object relations and experience transference in such a way that it can be interpreted profitably, some patients may require that the process of shortcutting through somatization, which more or less separates psyche and soma, be reduced. Reducing the shortcutting process may result in *symbolic formation* (Chiozza 1976, Demers-Desrosiers 1982, Fain 1966, Marty et al. 1963, Taylor 1984). With others, psychic shortcutting is accomplished through acting out. The analyst's tolerance may be taxed severely as he observes such developments in the course of analysis of patients who seemed relatively psychologically mature when treatment started; we know that many therapists refuse analysis to psychosomatic patients or to those who customarily deal with their problems through action.

CLINICAL DATA

The following information emerged in a highly fragmentary manner during the course of the analysand's treatment, because her conscious goal was to use each interview solely for the purpose of relieving herself of tension or "internal pressure." When she was very tense and felt such internal pressure, she panicked, and, for periods of varying length, believed quite literally that her mind would explode and her body would fragment. A major therapeutic task was to enable her to see the value of understanding internal conflicts.

Doing so involved my being, for me, unusually aggressive in insisting that she listen to, associate to, and think about what she and I had said, and her emotional and physical responses to our interactions.

Prior to our understanding of a rather spectacular regression and my reaction to it, no direct information had emerged pertaining to real events in her early life, information crucial to our comprehension of her intrapsychic problems and her resumption of more accelerated ego development.

Mrs. T. was a 39-year-old housewife with four children, all under 7 years of age. She was the baby of her family by five years, an "accident." She and her older siblings, two boys and two girls, were reared by maids and cooks, because her mother was so busy in pursuits pertaining to Zionism and Jewish social welfare. Her husband was physically unlike her father but his psychological twin. Both were physicians, passive, easy-going gastronomic bon vivants who were unperturbed by their domineering and shrewish wives' behavior and saw no necessity to help their children develop a capacity to control themselves and think of the rights of others. Mrs. T. established some contact with her mother by joining her from early childhood in her auxiliary religious activities and by serious involvement in Judaism. She studied eagerly for *bat mitzvah* and became fluent in Hebrew.

Undisciplined as a child, she easily ruled her parents with screaming, kicking, biting, and clawing temper tantrums. She had close relations only with her age-mates. Parents, caretakers, teachers, and siblings found her to be an intolerable brat.

During early childhood she was severely troubled with typical phobias. In her grammar school years, the phobias receded in intensity, being gradually replaced by almost continuous obsessive thinking related to problems of living and dying and forbidden sexuality. Beginning in preadolescence, those symptoms were replaced by discharging tension through immediate action and the development of asthma and a spastic colon. A teenage truant, she ran with a delinquent crowd, smoked marijuana, shoplifted, and was promiscuous. Before and following her period of rampant action, she resentfully followed her mother's dictum that she was to be pretty and popular and "hook a rich doctor."

The high school psychologist had recommended professional help, but upon her graduation she joined a kibbutz in Israel. Uncomfortable there, she soon left. She met and felt needed by a gentile "hippie" and lived happily with him as beggars in a commune in Jerusalem. For her, sex was "like nursing and being nursed." When she faced the obvious, that he was sleeping with several women, she returned home, entered psychotherapy, and attended college.

During the next five years she lived a passive, apparently almost catatonic-like existence at home. Aside from auxiliary religious activities and rather casual involvement with mundane craft productions, she masturbated more or less compulsively and daydreamed. The contents of her renewed phobias and obsessions symbolized simultaneously dyadic and triadic relationship anxieties.

At 30 she met her husband-to-be at a Jewish social function, immediately idealized and adored him largely as a good combined parental surrogate, and, after finding him to be the first man who could bring her to orgasm, married him within a few weeks. From the moment of marriage, however, she saw him as contemptible and inadequate, was furious that she was dependent on him for orgasms, and vowed to make his life as miserable as she had known her father's to have been at the hands of her mother.

She resumed seeking to identify with her mother in some roles, being more interested in the welfare of Jews as a group than of her nuclear family. It was easy for her, having felt emotionally starved, to adopt one of her mother's means of belittling and frustrating her gourmet husband. As her mother had refused to cook except for company, Mrs. T. ignored her husband's requests, got dinner solely after he arrived home at night, and served only raw vegetables and bland dishes she thought to be healthy for her children. She tried to establish a kosher home despite her husband's sharp objections, limited her extra-domestic activities to Jewish issues, and set out to have five children immediately.

Mrs. T. came for treatment reluctantly. She had been in therapy almost continuously for twenty years for a variety of complaints, for each of which she received transient mild relief. She chose me as her therapist because she had heard that I was a harsh disciplinarian and treated patients everyone else rejected. Her specific reason for seeking assistance was worry about what she called her "destructive, intrusive, uncontrollable anger." From the first interview she spoke about the presence from childhood of overt sexual fantasies involving her father. She said she supposed having them should have bothered her, but that they were useful to calm her and enable her to go to sleep. Apparently unconcernedly, she said her first reaction to me was to imagine sucking my penis. While the incest fantasies did not bother her consciously, she had been unable to touch her father or permit his touch from girlhood and it was over a year before she could allow her hand to touch mine as she gave me her check.

During the first few vis-à-vis interviews she seemed to enter a mild fugue state as she talked loudly and continuously. The manifest content belittled me although she acted also as though I were not in the room. In response to a question, she said she visualized her anger and words to be going either into space or into me; they were seen as enclosed in balloons emanating from mouths as in cartoons. During the fourth session she announced very angrily that she had decided to go to a "competent" Jewish female psychiatrist. My first interpretation dealt with the interpersonal aspects of projective identification and enabled her to enter psychoanalysis. I told her that she sought to establish safe links with me by believing she had put some of her anger into me and then by seeking to pick fights in which she imagined that I would help her to behave by dominating her and thereby reassure her that she could not hurt me. Vastly relieved, she introduced the subject of night terrors, and said that she often woke in the morning convinced that she had murdered her husband in her sleep.

I believe that if I had not subsequently forgotten my early conviction that her primary need was to empty herself into me, her treatment would have been less confusing and I would have been able to make synthesizing interpretations more often.

Her everyday life was chaotic. She displaced her need to be in control of her internal urges to a need to control her husband's and children's activities absolutely; much of her time was spent in rages because one or another of them had disobeyed some mandate.

She could not establish priorities. The house and her very existence were littered with projects enthusiastically begun and soon interrupted. She did all household repairs and improvements. Although she was terrified by thoughts of voyeurs, attacks, and rape, neither blinds nor curtains had covered the windows of the master bedroom or the bathroom for eight years. She followed her mother's custom of parading naked before husband and children, "to show them that I am not ashamed that I have breasts and no penis."

She took charge of family finances and transacted them solely by check. She did not record deposits or withdrawals and, since her husband used credit cards over her objections, threw his bills away. Each month she was surprised to discover that her finances were a shambles, detecting no contribution on her part. Yet she paid me accurately and on time although my patients are asked to keep track of their obligation to me and to pay me on the last interview of the month.

The same chaos characterized her behavior in treatment. Ordinarily she talked continuously and loudly, attaching equal emotional intensity to every utterance. Subjects shifted rapidly and there was no orderly time sequence. For months the predominant affect expressed was mixed aggrieved anger and suspiciousness. At times her paranoia was temporarily delusional. She perceived herself as being wronged and deprived by almost everyone and in every imaginable way. Nothing outside of her session relieved her tension for more than a few minutes, whether she thoughtlessly ate ravenously, masturbated frantically, engaged in orgies of insulting neighbors and hired help, or physically beat her husband or children. She was surprised to discover that she felt calmed in my presence, even while the suspiciousness and transitory persecutory delusions shifted over a period of months from the actions and motivations of people in her domestic environment to those of people near the consultation room and eventually to my behavior and secret intentions.

My most helpful intervention during the first year was to speak repeatedly of the defensive use of the regressive behavior. I suggested that the disordered presentation and failure to listen to herself or me were in the service of hiding connections from herself and internal conflicts that she sought to externalize. In order for me to get her attention, I sometimes had to command her forcefully to stop talking and listen to me or to try to remember what she had said during the previous few minutes and to seek to link the subjects. Her reactions to such actions on my part were complex. She was surprised to become aware that I did not read her mind and automatically understand what she meant even though she didn't, while she railed at me for hopeless stupidity and incompetency. She was grateful that anyone would discipline her, take the trouble to try to help her present herself in an orderly and understandable way, and assume that she had the capacity to learn.

By the end of the first year, she tolerated better the examining of her internal conflicts and had developed an interest in remembering her past and understanding her life and identity as a continuity. Her interview experiences were so much with her that her everyday life seemed to her to be superimposed upon what she called her "continuous dream," and my interpreting the initial interview material as day residue (Boyer 1988) was readily accepted by her. During the first year, as I have found to be beneficial with regressed patients in general, I focused my interpretations almost solely on her fears of, and defensive maneuvers against, aggression. In her case, the dominant defense consisted of projective identification or evacuation.

As her adolescent living in action and psychosomatic problems were followed by the reemergence of phobias and obsessions, they were recathected in analysis as she gave up much of her psychic shortcutting through action. Neither asthma nor spastic colitis reappeared although she did experience frightening episodes of tachycardia, tightening of the throat, and intolerable vulvar itching, which she not infrequently attempted to relieve by scratching her perineum during the interviews.

Part of the subject matter of her initial chaotic verbal productions had to do with fury because her husband both deprived her of sex by his passivity, which forced her to humiliate herself by seducing him, and had the capacity to bring her to orgasm by his special oral-genital techniques. Gradually she began to have anxiety attacks while driving to my office through a tunnel and had to drink water en route to relieve the hyperventilation-induced dryness in her throat. Her anxiety and the fluid intake forced her to begin to use the toilet provided for patients. She developed phobias with delusional intensity that black men lurked there to attack her and that other women would hold her helpless while the huge phallus penetrated her mouth, vagina, or urethra. Later her urinary pressure became vaginal excitement and she believed transiently that I had secret mirrors that enabled me to see her vaginal contractions and thereby gratify my voyeuristic wishes. She was sometimes certain that I was masturbating behind her and was simultaneously afraid that I would choke her with my phallus or that she would bite it off, and furious because I did not rape her.

Largely as a result of my consistently interpreting her reactions to me as transference displacements from earlier relations with her father and older brothers and suggesting reconstructions, we gradually understood her phobias and their attendant obsessive thinking largely in terms of her reactions to observations of her parents' bedroom activities. As a girl 3 to 5 years of age, she listened at their door or sneaked into the bedroom, observed their polymorphous activity, and was terrified by fantasies pertaining to combined lust and danger and confusion about who had what sexual organs and how they were used. At the same time, she shared their excitement and found herself able to get relief of tension through urination. As the highly eroticized transference abated, her life became quite calm. Her relationships with her husband, children, and parental nuclear family were unbelievably peaceful, and she stopped provoking her children's teachers and the neighbors. She cooked for and socialized with her husband and began to think of leaving treatment and having her fifth child.

This phase of her analysis occupied the first two years, and her rate of improvement left me uneasy. In my experience and that of some others (Ornstein and Ornstein 1975, Rosenfeld 1966, Volkan 1976), the mutative analysis of triadic relationship, oedipal material prior to the understanding of dyadic relationship material, is at best unusual in the treatment of regressed patients. In a sense, her involvement in the eroticized transference could be viewed as a flight into relative health from the basic problem of her need to empty her contents into others, which I understood to mean that her early relationship with her mother was defective and that her ego structure was grossly deficient. Nevertheless, the regression that followed both surprised and bewildered me because I was unaware of connections to be spelled out now, until I reviewed my extensive process notes while preparing this chapter.[4]

When patients begin analysis with me, I inform them that I shall be absent perhaps six times during the year and that I shall tell them the dates of my planned absences as soon as I know them. This practice helps people focus on issues pertaining to separation, an issue of consummate importance to regressed patients. Mrs. T. initially reacted to this information with ambivalence; she was relieved because she could save money and she was infuriated that I treated her like a "second-class citizen" by establishing rules. She forgot the dates of my first absences, and only dream material hinted that she was aware that they were imminent. Her forgetting and the absences themselves were of no conscious interest to her.

During the period when the eroticized transference was in the forefront, her jealousy was intense, and the manifest material of her dreams and interviews was concerned largely with rage at me and the woman or women I was gratifying while I was away. As her sexual reactions toward me were understood in transferential terms as reenacting triadic childhood relationships, they diminished greatly in intensity and my absences became once again of no apparent interest to her.

Although her life outside the consultation room continued to be peaceful, she began to behave periodically as she had during the first months of treatment. Having more leisure than previously to study the regressions during which she entered an altered ego state and sought to evacuate her mental and affectual components into me or into space, I observed that during those periods she concretized thoughts and feelings through somatization. As an example, her pleasure because of an intellectual achievement would be instantly converted into clitoral ex-

---

[4]As do Greenacre (1975) and others, I keep process notes during the interviews; I note not only the patient's verbal and nonverbal productions but also my comments and private fantasies, emotions, and physical sensations.

citement. Such excitement was unaccompanied by conscious thought, but was followed by feelings of abandonment and an altered ego state during which she was terrified of bodily and/or mental fragmentation. The somatization, thus, was a shortcutting of ideation. At times, we were later able to trace the sensation that she had been abandoned to feelings of guilt or shame. Only subsequently were ideas associated with the awareness of guilt or shame. Chiozza (1976) would designate such a somatization a presymbolic equation, used in the service of discharging tension without ideation, or in Kleinian, Bionian, or Grinbergian terminology, evacuation. Regaining awareness of me removed the feeling of abandonment. Then she was able once again to generate symbols and use them for purposes of communication, signaling her need to use me as a repository.

Review of my notes indicated that such regressive behavior followed by some days an announcement of a forthcoming absence that she had been reminded of by some life event, a connection of which I had been consciously unaware. I also forgot that during the early periods of regression she had mentioned off-handedly several times that she had dreams of, or read about, insects or larvae, and had fleeting thoughts of watching them or other small objects being torn apart. In my experience, insects and larvae most often symbolize small children and fetuses, often siblings. Thus, I missed the intense wrenching trauma to her of my leaving her, and her feeling torn from an imaginary continuum. I had recognized, but been unable to use effectively, that the regressive behavior was accompanied by, or followed, talk of some current event involving hostile relationships with various women. The women were not obvious transference figures but rather appeared to be vehicles to contain her anger and persecute her with it, but my interpretations scarcely warranted her notice.

The dominant theme of the interviews was the change of her view of me. Previously, for a long time, I had been her kind, good supporter, an ideal father. Now I became incompetent, physically ugly, truly beneath vilification. My attempts to interrupt her increasingly loud flow of imprecations were treated with contempt. Finally, for a period of a week, she spewed out hatred toward me; essentially nothing else occurred during the interviews. She seemed to enter a light trance state; gradually my efforts to interrupt her flow of words were less and less successful. I noted that while she consistently threatened to murder or castrate me, she dressed more attractively, was eager to come for her interviews, and said nothing about wanting to terminate treatment. Retrospectively, I gradually became more passive and periodically drowsy. Ultimately, I dozed. Suddenly she sat up, shouted that she would not tolerate such contempt of her, screamed that she was quitting, and ran to and opened the door. I had no doubt that our work was over if I did not respond appropriately and immediately, since she had quit treatment with other therapists suddenly and stormily four times previously. I commanded her to stop and to return for another interview to discuss what had happened and our future plans.

When she appeared for the next session, she was enraged and could scarcely sit, preferring to pace the room while making faces and threatening gestures. I told her that I recommended further analysis and would place her with another therapist, or, should she choose to continue with me, I would seek to handle privately the internal problem that had led to my falling asleep. She continued to fume. Then, to my total surprise, I heard myself saying that her having left me through her altered ego state and having treated me as though I were a worthless thing had made me feel lonely and that I wondered whether her behavior had been designed to do just that. Then, with remarkable clarity I silently remembered dreams and fantasies that had involved my having been left in many ways as a young child by a disturbed caretaker and also of having torn the wings off flies soon after the birth of my brother.

Her reaction startled me. For the first time during her treatment, she cried. She curled up in the chair like a little girl. She told me I must have been misunderstanding her although she had thought I knew, as she did, what was going on. She had to act as though she hated me and discharge her rage into me and the consultation room to keep from killing her husband and her older son, her husband because his passivity enraged her so and her son because she was unable to help him stop his temper tantrums. She adored me, I was her savior, her Abba Eban.

She had thought about why I had fallen asleep and decided that she had had to make me feel the loneliness and sense of being unwanted that she knew she had felt as a young girl and thought that she must have felt as an infant. She supposed the only way she could do that was to empty her feelings into me and she had thought I "was strong enough to contain them without being upset." She had "always known" but had never remembered while she was with me that her mother had been hospitalized for some months for postpartum depression after each of her children was born. Mrs. T. had had, during her first year, several different caretakers and probably had not seen her own mother during her first four or five months. After she spoke of such issues, she returned to the couch.

Thenceforth, her analysis proceeded calmly and dealt primarily with dyadic issues. I came to represent the mother of her early years. Concurrently, her need to provoke her husband and children practically disappeared. He came to "wear the pants" much of the time, the children's temper tantrums disappeared, and she became a gourmet cook. As her sexual relations with her husband improved, she stopped her compulsive masturbation. After a year, she decided to stop treatment precipitously "on a trial basis."

I did not then discover why or how she made her decision. In my experience, following the meaningful analysis of dyadic material in the treatment of regressed patients, analysis or reanalysis and working through of oedipal issues occurs. Because this had not happened and I did not understand her motives for her sudden decision, I was uneasy about her termination. I suggested that she allow a few months before a planned ending, but she was adamant.

Four years later she requested further analysis. She revealed that she had been pregnant when she terminated her treatment, wanting to savor her "feeling of oneness" with the baby inside her and the early years with her baby, who was a girl, without "analytic interference." She was still troubled by her inability to control her temper. However, she was much changed both in her life and in the consultation room. The most striking differences were that she was much better organized, no longer used projective identification and evacuation as dominant defensive operations, and had the capacity to experience depression. She cried readily. The principal problems that emerged were her identification with the dependent needs of her daughter and problems that ensued from her incapacity to help the little girl to control her impulses, whether libidinal or aggressive. The analysis of that dyadic relationship has now been satisfactorily completed and she has entered into a satisfactory analysis of her oedipal problems.

By chance, I learned from another source that her mother had in fact suffered the postpartum depressions that Mrs. T. remembered following the interpretation I made that was influenced so heavily by countertransference, and that Mrs. T. had had little if any contact with her mother during the first half year or so of her life. During the second period of her analysis, it became apparent that she had repressed knowledge of that trauma once again.

DISCUSSION

The most singular events of the analysis were her responses to two of my interventions. The circumstances were very similar. During the initial interviews, Mrs. T. entered a mild dissociative state, essentially excluding me from an interpersonal relationship with her, as she vilified me interminably. Finally, apparently afraid that I could not help her handle her unmodulated aggression, she threatened to stop and to go to a "competent" female Jewish psychiatrist for treatment, obviously a fantasied idealized mother surrogate who could tolerate Mrs. T.'s using her as a container. The second event occurred during a dramatic regression that lasted for over a week following episodes of like nature that had become more intense and frequent and had lasted longer, over a period of a year. Ultimately I responded to her having entered an altered ego state, during which she did almost nothing but scream obloquy, by withdrawing in my own way, eventually falling asleep. Again, she felt compelled to stop treatment, for the same reason, as I believe.

The first time, I made an interpretation I had formulated intellectually, one that I thought would enable her to reestablish relationships with me and use me as a container, rather than to continue to seek to evacuate her terrifying aggression "into space."

I rather viewed her then as an autistic child who sought to have relationships solely with something inhuman; I saw her space as an autistic object and sought to force her to pay attention to me rather than to the hypothesized space-autistic object. Tustin (1980, 1984) has found such separation of autistic child and autistic object to be mandatory before she could be used as a container.

The second time, I commanded her to return the next day, having quickly formulated a maneuver, again, as I believe, via secondary process thinking alone. I thought that what had happened had resulted from an emotional problem of my own, although I had no inkling about what it might have entailed.

That night I was insomniac but could not remember my dreams or hypnogogic or hypnopompic fantasies.

My unplanned interpretation to her was clearly the product of my repressed emotional reaction to her having left me during her altered ego states and having spoken of her having felt that she was ripped apart while being considered to be an unwelcome pest. It was an intolerable reminder of my own early life experiences and my responses to them. My defensive withdrawal had culminated in my falling asleep. She had forced me to return to a relationship with her with her furious threat actually to abandon me. Subsequently, I forced her back into a relationship with me by my command, offering her logical alternatives and then my interpretation.

As had been the case throughout the year during which she had undergone the increasingly severe regressions while in the consultation room, she had been able to think logically much of the time when alone at home. She had never thought to tell me that she had come to love me deeply and totally platonically and idealized me as incomparably wise, the savior of all the Jews, as extensions of her nuclear family. She assumed that, in my ascribed omniscience, I knew. She had been sure that I could contain for her the rage that she had sought to empty into me to avoid killing her husband and son, and remained certain that that judgment was correct. When at home, she had known that she expected me to serve the functions she had read in Winnicott's writings that a good mother served for her infant, including making possible the "existence of a potential space within which I can be creative."

During the interview while she sat, my interpretation that she had sought to make me feel lonely had gratified her greatly and set off a new line of thought. The night before, she had become aware that her rage because I had fallen asleep had served to keep several painful phenomena from her awareness. She knew retrospectively of an intense fear that I had abandoned her through death as did in fact a previous therapist, although several years after she had left him and even though she had "forgotten" him. Likewise, she became cognizant that she had felt acutely alone when I drowsed. Earlier periods of having felt abandoned, frightened, and lonely, returned from the repressed. When she had curled up in the chair, she had wanted to be held in my arms as a baby, and then she remembered for the first time in many years what she had "always known," namely that her mother had suffered from postpartum depressions requiring hospitalization after each child was born, and that she had been deprived of her actual mother throughout most of her early childhood.

H. A. Rosenfeld (1950) found that only precise interpretations were mutative in the psychoanalytic treatment of a man who suffered from confusional states. It will have been noted that the effective interpretations made to my patient were quite exact. In my experience, the potentially beneficial inexact interpretations of which Glover (1931) wrote are helpful more often in the treatment of neurotic than regressed patients.

It would seem that the interpretation made on the basis of my having become aware of the countertransferential reasons, both intra- and interpersonal, for my falling asleep was markedly mutative. However, it was the culminative event of an overlapping series of phenomena, and it cannot be separated from them. Following the interpretation, Mrs. T. was able to put aside using projective identification as a dominant defensive mechanism and to switch to more mature defensive operations. Bychowsky (1952) and

Bion (1957) would say that her nonpsychotic personality now remained in ascendancy. The first memory to emerge following the culminative interpretation was her having been abandoned in infancy as a result of her mother's psychotic regression. We could say that in her renunciation of projective identification, that is, her psychotic personality, she renounced an identification with her mother. It then became possible for her to identify further with some of my traits.

The progress of her treatment was very unusual (in my experience) in that some significant degree of meaningful analysis of oedipal material preceded that of preoedipal material, following consistent interpretation of her use of projective identification as a defensive and communicative mechanism. Perhaps this special transference unfolding resulted from her individual constellation of experience. Her lifelong tendency to go into action, modulated somewhat during the oedipal and latency periods by the development of phobias and obsessive thinking, can be ascribed to her having learned only insecurely to use symbols and language to mediate between her feelings and identity or between herself and others (Deri 1984). She could mediate essentially only through action and projective identification, and, when there was no adequate container for the projections, through evacuation. Her father's personality made it impossible for him to serve as a mediator between her and her mother and him, too, she apparently deemed incapable of serving as a container for her projections. At least, however, he was kind.

We remember that throughout her life she openly fantasied sexual intimacy with him. Her actual observations were that no physical intimacy existed between her parents except for the primal scene activities from which she appears not to have been excluded and which she found to be frightening, stimulating, and confusing. During her childhood she secretly idealized her father and ascribed omniscience to him, while pretending that she agreed with her mother's evaluation of him as contemptible and worthless. She believed that he could tame her mother's alternately overt and covert hostility through the use of his penis.

In the transference, at least after I helped her to develop the capacity to order her thoughts and to prioritize behavior, she consciously ascribed omniscience and omnipotence to me, which I would use in helping her subdue her rage. We cannot forget that I was secretly viewed as Abba Eban.

During the year of the analysis of triadic relationship material, fantasies of my helping her control her rage by subduing her with my phallus were succeeded by deeply felt, loving fantasies of sexual relationships involving mutual giving and caretaking. She was able to have them in actual life with her husband during the last year of analysis. Perhaps, then, the reason for the unusual unfolding of the transference stemmed in part from her past and in part from my demonstrating to her that I could help her to develop the capacity to mediate between impulses and identity.

It would be difficult to overstate the importance of the provision of a facilitating environment in the treatment of regressed patients. Its elements are provided largely by the capacities of the therapist. The patient's personal security must ensure that the therapist retain objectivity and equilibrium during the patient's regressions and tolerate modulated experiences that are similar to those of the patient during some of his or her regressions. My temporary incapacity to do so was the basis for the impasse that went on essentially for a year in the treatment of Mrs. T. although I did not recognize its presence. But other qualities of therapists are at least as important. They must be able above all to provide constancy and patience, to be able to abide, without more than transient despair, endlessly repetitive maladaptive behavior on the part of the patient, whose personality is being changed slowly while his actual object relationship development and transference experiences influence each other and are understood, as was discussed so well by Loewald (1960). The question often arises as to whether analysts can successfully treat someone they do not like. My work with patients whom I viewed initially as disagreeable, contemptible, or otherwise unsavory has been successful in general. I believe this results in part because I see their personalities as indicative of the best they have been able to do in adjusting to their lifelong stresses, internal and external. Additionally, I am convinced that the analytic experience has a good chance of helping them to become less self-oriented and to develop the capacity to behave automatically in ways that seriously consider the rights of others. At the end of his long analysis that had sometimes tried the patience of both of us, a particularly disagreeable man who had changed remarkably said, "While your interpretations were crucial, they would have been useless but for your constancy, patience, and optimism, which gave me self-worth." Therapeutic optimism, then, based on experience, I deem to be a most important element in working with regressed patients.

In the regressed patient's development of a personality structure that is often very different in certain ways than at the beginning of analysis, he reexperiences early childhood in modified form in a better environment. Identifications with pathological aspects of prior caretakers are rendered unnecessary and replaced by healthier identifications with qualities of the analyst, primarily as mother surrogate. Obviously, I have no intention of underplaying the importance of the analyst as the surrogate of other people who are important in the rearing of children; I speak here only of the needs of patients while they are regressed.

CONCLUSION

Some patients whose sole conscious goal in therapy is to relieve themselves of tension can be viewed as continuing to use projective identification as a dominant defensive and interpersonal communicative mechanism. During the inevitable regressions that occur during psychoanalysis, they lose contact with the therapist as a potential container who might be able to hold and process their frightening aggression and/or libido and seek to discharge their terrifying feelings and the mental representations of their impulses into space. At such times the psychotic part of the patient's personality is in the ascendancy, presumably in identification with aspects of the mothering figure(s) of his infancy.

Ordinarily, the analysis of the psychotic part of his personality must be accomplished before the patient will be able to deal adequately with other psychic defects and conflicts. To be effective, interpretations that will help him to renounce his identification with psychotic aspects of his mother's personality and his achieving perhaps for the first time some elements of psychic structure must be made in a facilitating environment. The dominant element of that environment is the therapist who must have the ability to remain calm, objective, and optimistic and, at times, to undergo experiences that are similar to those of the patient during his inevitable and necessary regressions. The analysand is provided with and identifies with aspects of his analyst's personality as he develops the capacity to use symbols and language to mediate between his chaotic emotions and his personal identity.

Not uncommonly, the most effective interpretations are found to be those that stemmed from the analyst's use of his countertransferential responses to the patient's productions.

Viewing and interpreting the analytic session as if it were a dream facilitates the analyst's comprehension of the analytic process and gives him or her greater objectivity and security. The usual day residue of the session-dream is the dominant unresolved transference issue of the preceding interview or interviews.

In working with regressed patients, the most effective interpretations are based frequently on information gathered through transference-countertransference interactions, interactions that often depend on the patient's projective and the analyst's introjective identification.

A group of regressed analytic patients seeks to rid themselves of tension predominantly by evacuating or projecting their unconscious fantasies into the analyst. A fragment of the analysis of such a patient illustrates how her fantasies could not be adequately contained by the analyst because they revived in him inadequately resolved conflicts from early childhood, conflicts that resembled closely those being relived by the patient. His reacting by falling asleep created an emergency that was resolved by his making an unplanned interpretation that proved to be significantly mutative, a "turning point."

REFERENCES

Balint, M. (1968). *The Basic Fault. Therapeutic Aspects of Regression.* New York: Brunner/Mazel, 1979.

Balter, L., Lothane, Z., and Spencer, J. H., Jr. (1980). On the analyzing instrument. *Psychoanalytic Quarterly*, 49:474–504.

Beres, D., and Arlow, J. A. (1974). Fantasy and identification in empathy. *Psychoanalytic Quarterly*, 43:26.

Bion, W. R. (1957). Differentiation of the psychotic and non-psychotic personalities. In *Second Thoughts. Selected Papers on Psycho-Analysis*, pp. 43–64. New York: Jason Aronson, 1967.

—— (1962). A theory of thinking. In *Second Thoughts. Selected Papers on Psycho-Analysis*, pp. 110–119. New York: Jason Aronson, 1967.

—— (1967). *Second Thoughts. Selected Papers on Psycho-Analysis.* New York: Jason Aronson.

Boyer, L. B. (1961). Provisional evaluation of psycho-analysis with few parameters in the treatment of schizophrenia. *International Journal of Psycho-Analysis* 42:389–403.

—— (1983). *The Regressed Patient.* New York: Jason Aronson.

—— (1986). Technical aspects of treating the regressed patient. *Contemporary Psychoanalysis* 22:25–44.

—— (1988). Thinking of the interview as if it were a dream. *Contemporary Psychoanalysis* 24:275–281.

Bychowsky, G. (1952). *Psychotherapy of Psychosis.* New York: Grune & Stratton.

Chiozza, L. A. (1976). *Cuerpo, Afecto y Lenguaje. Psicoanálisis y Enfermedad Somática.* Buenos Aires: Paidós.

Demers-Desrosiers, L. (1982). Influence of alexithymia on symbolic function. *Psychotherapy and Psychosomatics* 38:103–120.

Deri, S. K. (1984). *Symbolization and Creativity.* New York: International Universities Press.

Fain, M. (1966). Regression et psychosomatique. *Revue Française de Psychanalyse* 30:451–456.

Federn, P. (1952). *Ego Psychology and the Psychoses.* New York: Basic Books.

Fenichel, O. (1945). *The Psychoanalytic Theory of the Neuroses.* New York: Norton.

Fleming, J., and Benedek, T. F. (1966). *Psychoanalytic Supervision. A Method of Clinical Teaching*. New York: Grune & Stratton.

Fliess, R. (1953). Counter-transference and counter-identification. *Journal of the American Psychoanalytic Association* 1:268–284.

Freud, S. (1912). Recommendations to physicians practicing psycho-analysis. *Standard Edition* 112:109–112.

Garma, A. (1962). *El Psicoanálisis. Teoría, Clínica, y Técnica*. Buenos Aires: Paidós.

Giovacchini, P. L. (1967). The frozen introject. In *Psychoanalysis of Character Disorders*, pp. 29–40. New York: Jason Aronson.

—— (1986). *Structural Pathology. Transitional Space in Breakdown and Creative Development*. Northvale, NJ: Jason Aronson.

—— (1989). *Countertransference Triumphs and Catastrophes*. Northvale, NJ: Jason Aronson.

Glover, E. (1931). The therapeutic effect of inexact interpretation: a contribution to the theory of suggestion. *International Journal of Psycho-Analysis* 12:397–411.

Green, A. (1975). The analyst, symbolization and absence in the analytic setting (on changes in analytic practice and analytic experience). *International Journal of Psycho-Analysis* 50:1–22.

Greenacre, P. (1975). On reconstruction. *Journal of American Psychoanalytic Association* 23:693–712.

Grinberg, L. (1979). Countertransference and projective counteridentification. *Contemporary Psychoanalysis* 15:226–247.

Grunberger, B. (1971). *Le Narcissisme. Essais de Psychanalyse*. Paris: Payot.

Hann-Kende, F. (1933). On the role of transference and countertransference in psychoanalysis. In *Psychoanalysis and the Occult*, ed. G. Devereux, pp. 158–167. New York: International Universities Press.

Heiman, P. (1950). On counter-transference. *International Journal of Psycho-Analysis* 31:60–76.

Isakower, O. (n.d.) See Balter, Lothane, and Spencer.

Jacobs, T. J. (1986). On countertransference enactments. *Journal of American Psychoanalytic Association* 34:289–308.

Khan, M. M. R. (1964). Ego-distortion, cumulative trauma and the role of reconstruction in the analytic situation. In *The Privacy of the Self*, pp. 59–68. New York: International Universities Press, 1974.

—— (1974). *The Privacy of the Self*. New York: International Universities Press.

Little, M. (1981). *Transference and Countertransference*. New York: Jason Aronson.

Loewald, H. (1979). Reflections on the psychoanalytic process and its therapeutic potential. In *Papers on Psychoanalysis*, pp. 372–383. New Haven: Yale University Press, 1986.

—— (1986). Transference-countertransference. In *Papers on Psychoanalysis*, pp. 372–383. New Haven: Yale University Press.

Marty, P., M'Uzan, M. de, and David, C. (1963). *L'Investigation Psychosomatique. Sept Observations Cliniques*. Paris: Presses Universitaires de France.

McDougall, J. (1972). L'antianalysant en analyse. *Revue Française de France* 36:167–184.

——— (1978). Countertransference and primitive communication. In *Plea for a Measure of Abnormality*, pp. 247–298. New York: International Universities Press.

——— (1985). *Theaters of the Mind: Illusion and Truth on the Psychoanalytic Stage.* New York: Basic Books.

——— (1989). *Theaters of the Body. A Psychoanalytic Approach to Psychosomatic Illness.* New York: Norton.

Nacht, S. (1963). *La Presence du Psychanalyse.* Paris: Presses Universitaires de France.

Ogden, T. H. (1985). On potential space. *International Journal of Psycho-Analysis* 66:129–142.

——— (1986). *The Matrix of the Mind. Object Relations and the Psychoanalytic Dialogue.* Northvale, NJ: Jason Aronson.

Ornstein, A., and Ornstein, P. (1975). On the interpretive process in schizophrenia. *International Journal of Psychoanalytic Psychotherapy* 4:219–271.

Racker, H. (1953). A contribution to the problem of countertransference. *International Journal of Psycho-Analysis* 34:313–324.

——— (1968). *Transference and Countertransference.* New York: International Universities Press.

Reik, T. (1948). *Listening with the Third Ear. The Inner Experience of a Psychoanalyst.* New York: Farrar & Straus.

Rosenfeld, H. A. (1950). Note on the psychopathology of confusional states in chronic schizophrenia. *International Journal of Psycho-Analysis* 31:132–137.

——— (1966). Discussion of "Office Treatment of Schizophrenia" by L. Bryce Boyer. *Psychoanalytic Forum* 1:351–353.

Searles, H. F. (1953). Dependency processes in the psychotherapy of schizophrenia. *Journal of American Psychoanalytic Association* 3:19–66.

——— (1976). Transitional processes and therapeutic symbiosis. In *Countertransference and Related States. Selected Papers*, pp. 503–576. New York: International Universities Press, 1979.

——— (1979). *Countertransference and Related States. Selected Papers.* New York: International Universities Press.

Spiegel, L. A. (1975). The functions of free association in psychoanalysis: their relation to technique and therapy. *International Review of Psycho-Analysis* 2:379–388.

Taylor, G. J. (1984). Alexithymia: concept, measurement, and implications for treatment. *American Journal of Psychiatry* 141:725–732.

Tustin, F. (1980). Autistic objects. *International Review of Psycho-Analysis* 7:27–39.

——— (1984). Autistic shapes. *International Review of Psycho-Analysis* 11:280–288.

Volkan, V. D. (1976). *Primitive Internalized Object Relationships. A Clinical Study of Schizophrenic, Borderline and Narcissistic Patients.* New York: International Universities Press.

Waldinger, R. J. (1987). Intensive psychodynamic therapy with borderline patients: an overview. *American Journal of Psychiatry* 144:267–274.

Waldinger, R. J., and Gunderson, J. G. (1987). *Effective Psychotherapy with Borderline Patients. Case Studies.* New York: Macmillan.

Winnicott, D. W. (1947). Hate in the countertransference. In *Collected Papers*, pp. 194–203. New York: Basic Books, 1958.

—— (1971). *Playing and Reality.* New York: Basic Books.

13

HEITOR F. B. DE PAOLA, M.D.

Countertransference and Reparative Processes within the Analyst

I seek to investigate a specific aspect of countertransference phenomena, one related to reparative processes within the analyst.[1] First I discuss briefly the theoretical concept, then present case material pertaining to a regressed patient, emphasizing my sensations, feelings, and emotions during a period of her analysis, and finally some ideas derived not only from this experience but from the entirety of my practice. I suggest that this theme is of relevance to the investigation of psychoanalytic interventions in working with regressed patients.

THE CONCEPT OF COUNTERTRANSFERENCE

The concept of countertransference has been disputed since its formulation by Freud (1910). According to Strachey (1958), Freud referred rarely to countertransference because of his fear that future patients would diminish the effectiveness of their psychoanalyses through having come into contact with technical details and even suggested that the publication of technical papers should be restricted to literature available solely to analysts.

According to Segal (1950), countertransference was considered previously to be a neurotic disturbance on the part of the analyst as if its presence obviated an objective study of the patient. Segal believed that, as

[1] I wish to express my thanks to Eliahu Feldman for his discussions with me of the main points of this paper and to L. Bryce Boyer for his editorial assistance and help with my translation from the Portuguese into English.

psychoanalytic understanding progressed, countertransference had become recognized as a primary source of information about the patient and an important element of the interaction between analyst and analysand. Racker (1953) wrote of the countertransference neurosis. Nevertheless, many modern analysts continue to hold, as did Ferenczi (1919) and Stern (1924), that countertransferential responses stem solely from inadequately understood unconscious infantile conflicts within the analyst and require the reanalysis of the therapist.

This controversy is connected to the fact that what is understood as countertransference covers a wide range of phenomena that include both the analyst's conscious and unconscious reactions to the patient and his communications (Glover 1955, Little 1951, Orr 1954, Reich 1960). Obviously, the analyst is an individual with his own physical complexes, anxieties, and fears, and it is desirable that he undergo as thoroughgoing a psychoanalysis as possible. Thus, various questions present themselves, such as: Can an analyst's transference use of his patient be unrelated to the patient's transference to him? What is the relationship between the analyst's consciously perceived feelings and those unconscious situations that lead to psychoanalytic impasses, collusions, and actings-out?

I have no definitive answers to these questions but suggest that they open promising paths of investigation. All psychoanalytic "schools" are becoming progressively more interested in investigating the analyst's complex role in the analytic process.

For the purposes of the present chapter I shall use the concept formulated by Heimann (1950): "Counter-transference [covers] all the feelings which the analyst experiences toward his patient." These feelings "may serve as an instrument of research into the patient's unconscious" (p. 81).

As the development of the investigation of projective identification progressed, the psychic mechanisms that enable one person to experience the emotions aroused by others became clearer. If we understand the psychoanalytic process as an interplay of projective identifications, as I have expressed elsewhere (De Paola 1982), we can view all sensations and emotions experienced by the analyst to contain information about the patient's transference, communicated by unconscious paths, probably predominantly subliminal behavioral mechanisms. Although the feelings and emotions belong to the analyst himself, they are responses to specific communications emanating from the patient. When we deal with patients during their periods of regression, nonverbal may predominate over verbal means of communication. But we can understand such means of communication solely if we use our free-floating attention not only as an intellectual avenue of comprehension but also as a "special opening up of feelings, allowing our feelings and our mind to be affected by the patient in a way that is not expected in social relations" (Segal 1950, pp. 82–83). It is my viewpoint that, at the same time, the analyst's mental state remains close to that of scientific curiosity, although a special concern for the welfare of the patient remains, without the analyst's having become emotionally involved with the analysand's conflicts. In this state, the analyst may experience the patient's feelings and sensations and yet refrain from acting-out collusions, and rather use his experiences in the service of deepening his understanding (Money-Kyrle 1956, Segal 1950). Segal stressed the analyst's use of his "mothering parts" in this deepening of understanding.

In this chapter I shall limit myself to an attempt to demonstrate a specific aspect of countertransference: those feelings and emotions that stand in the psychoanalytic situation for the "radio interferences" cited by Bion (1974): "If we have this prejudice that there is something like the human mind that is worthwhile to investigate, we must be able to listen to psycho-analytic 'interferences' in the same way that somebody is listening to radio interferences, instead of the program. That [sic] is little chance of progress in these areas usually called psychotic or borderline if we don't listen to what is happening." Should the therapist lack this capacity, it will probably be impossible for him to comprehend the communications of the psychotic or borderline patient.

From another theoretical context, Boyer (1961) opines that major impediments to the success of the analysis of regressed patients are to be found in unresolved countertransferential problems and suggests that analysts turn to themselves and their own physical and emotional reactions connected with the patient's productions. More recently, while describing his developing technical changes in treating regressed patients, he considers his greatest change to result from his having become more aware of his physical and emotional sensations and to his private analysis of them together with related fantasies and dreams (Boyer 1986). He believes that such experiences are more likely to occur during altered ego states experienced by the analyst, a view I share.

In previous papers I have stressed the importance of getting into contact with the patient through the countertransference (De Paola 1982, 1984, 1986), as have other Brazilian colleagues (Pacheco 1978, 1980, Petrucci 1989, Zanin 1989).

Now I turn my attention to a point stressed by Money-Kyrle (1956).

I believe there is a fairly rapid oscillation between introjection and projection (in the analytic process). As the patient speaks, the analyst will, as it were, become introjectively identified with him,

and, having understood him inside, will reproject him and interpret. But what I think the analyst is most aware of is the projective
phase, that is to say, the phase in which the patient is the representative of a former or immature or ill part of himself, which he can
now understand and therefore treat by interpretation in the external world. [p. 361]

In my judgment, the analyst treats those parts in his internal world as well,
since the analytic function is a constant reparative process of the psychoanalyst's internal object relations.

I suggest that the analyst projects his own internal objects into the patient
and that they become identified with the objects that the patient is projecting
onto him. In this process the analyst has the unique opportunity to repair his
own objects internally and, at the same time, to help his patient to make his
own reparations. The objects that the latter projects onto the analyst are
extremely variable and change rapidly, which is why the analyst must have
acquired a great flexibility of his capacity to use his projective identification.
The use of projective identification by the person who is in a regressed state is
rigid, and this interferes with his capacity to use that psychic mechanism for
reparative functions. The analyst must have the ability to allow a certain
"fluctuation" of his internal objects in order to leave them free to entangle
with the patient's dominant projected object or objects of the moment.

So long as this entanglement of an object of the patient's is with an
internal object of the analyst that is adequately healthy, or (in the vocabulary of this chapter) has been repaired in the course of his life and personal
analysis, the work with the patient can proceed in a quiet atmosphere. If, to
the contrary, the internal object of the analyst that becomes entangled with
the projected internal object of the analysand has remained damaged, a
severe countertransferential problem is likely to arise. It is precisely the most
primitive internal objects of the patient that tend to stimulate their counter-
parts within the analyst. It is in these terms that I understand Boyer's (1961)
postulation that perhaps the major impediment to the psychoanalysis of the
regressed patient is to be found in unresolved countertransference problems.

CASE MATERIAL

The case material that follows derives from the analysis of a seriously
regressed female patient. The data will be used later to clarify further my
point of view. For reasons of confidentiality, certain details have been
suppressed and are represented by descriptions.

At the beginning of her treatment, the patient, a musician, was 19 years old and had a sister and a brother, aged 18 and 14. Their parents had divorced when she reached puberty, and each had remarried soon afterwards. Her psychotic symptoms had become manifest when she was 5, and she had been under constant psychiatric care of myriad forms, including two years of psychoanalysis. There had been twelve hospitalizations; all therapeutic efforts had been without effect. The dominant symptom was a mystical religious delusion that she had a mission to save mankind from sinners. She bitterly accused her various relatives as well as her foster parents of all sorts of sins.

She first came to see me in my office immediately following her discharge from a hospital. Although she was violent and believed herself to be dangerously persecuted, she came to my consultation room unescorted. She lived with her father, who paid for her psychoanalytic care. All arrangements were made between her and me, and I did not speak with her parents. Initially she was seen five times, although later there were periods when six or seven interviews transpired weekly.

The following material comes from the end of the first year of analysis. Prior to then she came alone, rarely missed an appointment, and used the couch most of the time. Although she was violent toward the people with whom she lived and frequently felt extremely persecuted, no hostility was expressed toward me. Usually it was very difficult to follow her discourse because she rarely completed a sentence or loudly sang Jewish folk songs, although she was not Jewish. During many interviews, she slept.

Just after the Christmas and New Year's breaks, a month before the planned summer vacation, she became very anxious and either failed to come to her sessions or came very late; she refused to lie down and violently attacked me verbally. She accused me of madness and claimed I sought to make her insane. She thought she should stop coming to see me because I was incapable of being a psychoanalyst and my interpretations were maddening. Eventually, I became fearful lest she assault me physically or, between sessions, commit suicide.

Two days prior to New Year she complained of intense pain in her back, looked at me suspiciously, and asked if I were well. I told her I understood her to be telling me that she was afraid that she was unwell and that she was fearful lest something very bad happen to her during the coming holiday and during my approaching vacation. After a period of silence, she sang so loudly I was concerned that the neighbors might complain. Suddenly she stopped singing and began to name bathroom fixtures. I told her she was using me as a toilet into which she was evacuating the terrible sensations inside herself that she was experiencing. She then walked about the room, silently menacing me with her fists. I said she was trying to make me fear that she would attack me.

In the next session she gestured that she was unable to speak. I said she felt guilty for her behavior during the previous interview. She agreed and said that she did not know how to talk to me, inasmuch as her feelings had got out of control during the previous session.

During the last interview before the holidays she said that she had felt overly "aggressive and violent." "I can't stand any longer that whore living with my father. She's always following me to criticize whatever I do. I left an unextinguished cigarette in an ashtray and she told my father about it and he got mad at me because of the risk of fire. She's a whore and a whore is only to fuck and screw and not to love." I interpreted that she was very angry with me, feeling that I was treating her as a whore I fucked and would then leave for four days of holidays without consideration of her feelings and that, even worse, I would soon leave her for the vacation period. I continued that she was accusing me of being unaware that her wish that I stay with her was harder to extinguish than a cigarette. As she stood staring at me for some minutes, her anxiety lessened. Then I said that all this rage during the holidays was directed at her father and stepmother because she could not use them as substitutes for me. Then she took a tourist advertisement leaflet from her purse, threw it on a nearby table, and said "I don't want it anymore; it's yours."

The following day she found the leaflet still lying on the table and said, "Is it still there? I'll leave it here with you. It stands for last month's payment." She had not brought the money; she was contemptuous and provocative. I interpreted the leaflet as an attempt to push her emotions into me in a concrete form.

She did not appear the next day and, without knowing why, I spent the entire session period reading the leaflet. At the end of the scheduled interview, I laughed when I realized I had spent the time that way because I had thought she had put the money in the leaflet. I then thought I had taken the leaflet for the patient herself.

During the next session she knew she had made me angry and was frequently sarcastic. Again she told me she would not pay, since the leaflet was enough. I did not tell her what I had in fact done with the leaflet but said I thought she had meant for me to look for the money in it and to become frustrated because no money was there. She then lay on the couch for the first time in several weeks, looked very sad, and produced no further sarcastic statements. I said that for the first time since our last interruption she had regained a good relationship with me and regretted having turned so much hostility toward me and her relatives. She then paid her account, and for several sessions she remained in a cooperative mood and progress was made.

Suddenly she resumed her hostile mood, opening a session saying, "Looking at your pictures in the waiting room made me think the only places you have been are to Europe and North America. The rest of the world is better, but you can't travel there because of your restricted budget. I know that because I pay you almost nothing!" I interpreted that she envied me because she had paid me not only with money but with her good feelings, which she felt I now possessed while she did not. I told her that that was why she usually gave me only her hostility, anger, and jealousy. I said that the "better-to-travel-with feelings," love, caring, and friendship, were more expensive. I spoke of the leaflet as a concrete means to show those beautiful places within her, of which I knew but little, although she had given me a glimpse during the past few sessions. She was sad again. At the end of the hour I said I believed this to be an important moment in her analysis in which she was moving toward experiencing loving feelings, which frightened her and against which she defended herself by feeling guilt and persecution.

I have now reached the point to which I want to call the reader's attention. The last-reported session occurred on a Friday. She missed her Monday appointment and did not reappear until Tuesday.

She entered my office complaining of pain in her back and walked with great difficulty. She said she had caught a bad cold. She lay on the couch but was silent beyond saying her cold prevented her from talking. After a time I began to feel drowsy and in the altered ego state turned to my own fantasies. I recalled a situation from my own remote past, one "forgotten" for many years, and felt very strongly the sadness I had experienced at that time. I then "came back" to the immediate session and recalled her sadness at the end of Friday's session and her having failed to appear on Monday. I interpreted, "You are trying now to push into my mind, in an effort to help me understand you better, all of the feelings of sadness you experienced during the past weekend and how much you missed me so differently this time than another weekend when you were filled with rage towards me." Previously her position on the couch had been rigid; now she let herself lie more comfortably and breathed more easily. After some time I enlarged the interpretation, saying that now, perhaps for the first time since the beginning of her work with me, she was experiencing feelings of love and friendship toward me and for that reason she was able to miss me as a good object she had lost, when we were separated; at the same time, she had been unable to come yesterday and could not speak because of her guilt for having felt rage toward me on so many other occasions. She continued her silence and resumed her rigidity and hard breathing. I felt anxious once again and simultaneously remembered that when I was a student working in a mental hospital I was forced to observe a colleague being hospitalized following his having destroyed a restaurant and a police car during an acute psychotic episode. I recalled my having felt sadness and fear, and I reexperienced those feelings. Then I told my patient that she was pushing into me her hatred and fear, which accompanied her having become aware of the better relationship with me of which I had spoken. "You hate me now because you feel it to be difficult to handle those feelings that I spoke about because they make you deal with your hostility toward me every time you have missed me during the last months."

She resumed her normal breathing once again and her comfortable position on the couch but remained silent until the end of the interview. At the end of the hour she smiled in a very friendly way and shook my hand.

The patient did not appear for the following two interviews. During the second one, I found myself worrying about a potential defect in my car, although I knew it to have been repaired previously.

When she reappeared the following Monday, she was euphoric and laughed without apparent reason. Seeing the leaflet, she mocked me once again: "You still have it here? Why didn't you take it with you? It's yours; I gave it to you with all my love." I interpreted that, having given me all her love, she felt loveless, which explained why she was being arrogant and ironical toward me today. I continued, saying that during the previous session she had pushed into me all her love and sadness and said that she was being ironical to deny her fear related to my absence during the approaching vacation; I said that these actions made her feel even more menaced, because she had no good feelings to protect her during my absence. She looked at me intently; then lay on the couch and was silent. After a time, I became drowsy once again and daydreamed about my forthcoming vacation, during which I planned to enjoy myself immensely with my wife and sons on a long-planned trip. I observed that she was smiling and remarked that she was still and smiling because she had recovered her loving feelings within herself because of what I had told her, and I suggested that for the first time she was looking forward with some pleasure to her own vacation. To my surprise, she agreed and spoke of her plans to travel to nearby places while we were apart. We shared a long silence, during which I was aware that I felt fond of her and was pleased to have her as a patient.

In the next session, the last before my vacation, she came with a friendly attitude, paid my fee for the previous month, looked at the leaflet and said: "Now I can take it with me. It's mine, isn't it? It always was!" I said she was reclaiming what had always been hers; but that she had to leave with me her feelings of love and friendship and her sadness. She lay on the couch and used her time telling me of her plans for the next month. At the end of the hour we parted in a warm atmosphere. When we met again four weeks later, the warm atmosphere persisted.

DISCUSSION

I am aware that my psychoanalytic technique as exposed in this chapter is unusual, particularly for North Americans. I used my personal recollections to interpret to the patient because I felt that they were accompanied by shared emotions that could be understood as belonging to our relationship. In the following pages I present more detailed information and discuss some theoretical issues.

I prefer to keep private the details pertaining to my first recollection. The second was related to one of the most difficult situations I faced during my professional career. The colleague to whom I referred was a dear friend, although I had recognized previously that he had certain psychotic traits. Under the Brazilian military dictatorship we were ideologically very close. Due to his idiosyncratic traits, he was ridiculed generally but not by me; this was the basis of his friendliness toward me. When I saw him treated as a violent maniac, I was astounded, and so involved that I could not use my psychiatric knowledge. I felt very guilty that I could not help him. Today, following my personal analysis and training, I can understand that my guilt was due to my personal shortcomings. I probably also felt guilt because he made me aware of my shortcomings and I was, therefore, angry with him.

My recollection during the session described above was the result, not only of my personal internal mental operations, but also of our interpersonal mental operations. In a state of drowsiness, that is, in an altered ego state such as that described by Boyer (1986), my internal objects were "fluctuating" in order to meet my patient's internal objects and become "entangled" with them. In that particular situation the entanglement was to be made with the patient's feelings of hatred because of the failures of her life. From a Kleinian viewpoint such failures began during her infancy because of her relations with her mother's breast. It is worthwhile to imagine that she had been unable to tolerate weaning and the intervals between feedings; then she probably felt hatred toward the breast that had disappeared and only rarely had she really missed it. From this theoretical stance, the absent breast was experienced as a bad object rather than an absent object that she could miss and feel sad about. By means of projective identification the patient made me experience her psychical situation through my own past experience of failure in a moment in which I had been unable to deal with a violent person psychoanalytically rather than merely psychiatrically. Obviously, concurrently I felt myself to be a failure with her, too, since I was experiencing great difficuly in understanding and dealing with her violence and her attacks on my mind. Clearly, I was trying to help her in a way in which I had been unable to help my friend.

I understand her giving me the tourist leaflet to constitute her concrete effort to help me travel within her mind, so that I would know more about her than she could know unassisted, in order that I could help her to understand herself better because of our mutual journey. I believe that in working with such regressed patients, psychoanalytic treatment depends on the possibility that the analyst can maintain a state that I should call *open-mindedness*, as expressed above. The capacity to freely associate during the patient's primitive regressions obviously depends on the tolerance of the analyst. When we can maintain such open-mindedness, we can receive a special kind of communication that comes from the unconscious and is perceived unconsciously; this communication is reached through our countertransference feelings, aroused by projective identification. Viewed thus, the most mutative interpretations will be achieved through the countertransference (see Chapter 12).

It is not my judgment that supernatural communication has transpired, such as telepathy or the literal transmission of thoughts as intrusive foreign bodies. Mutual entanglements of emotions and ideas frequently had occurred previously, at times, no doubt, on the basis of subliminal physical stimuli and their unconscious perception. I believe that as time passed, these points of identification were able to create in my unconscious an "entangled" person whom I could disentangle with interpretations.

To return to the first "patient," my friend, I believe that our psychotic parts were already entangled so that, being unanalyzed at that time, I could not deal with them objectively. The difference between the two situations expressed my own progress in dealing with those psychotic parts within myself, but it is my contention that, again, the fresh situation expressed new reparative processes in my own psyche. I think the patient felt a great relief that I could manage the situation better than she and that that in itself helped her deal better with her own internal conflicts. The sessions following the one of recollections show the modifications of her attitude toward me and toward herself, including her view of her own vacation and the possibility that she might enjoy it, as indeed she subsequently did.

CONCLUSION

I suggest that one of the main sources for understanding regressed patients is the proper use of countertransference feelings, and that this is one of the most important psychoanalytic tools when the psychoanalyst treats seriously regressed patients. I also suggest that one must remain aware that regressed areas, even psychotic islands, or what Bychowski (1952) called the *psychotic core,* are to be found in all patients who come to psychoanalysis. In my judgment, these countertransferential feelings are perceived through the mechanism described by Klein (1946) as *projective identification.* However, the use of the concept is not without risk. The analyst must remain aware that interpretations based on assumed countertransference are tentative formulations that must be validated by the patient's unconscious responses to them. Psychoanalysis cannot be an omnipotent means of pushing into the patient the analyst's hypotheses about himself. What I suggest here resembles, but has nothing in common with, other theories based on introspection as the only way of acquiring knowledge about other persons as suggested by Kohut (1959). The difference lies in that I strongly defend the need of reality testing of our hypotheses to avoid the danger that while thinking that we are grasping a fundamental aspect of the patient, we may be in fact grasping some object from our own history, without any relation with the patient's objects, to paraphrase Treurniet (1983).

Only the patient's response to our hypotheses (interpretations) is decisive. I believe I have demonstrated what I mean in the clinical material. The fact that the analyst makes reparations of his own internal objects, as I believe, does not indicate that I propose any change in the fundamental task of psychoanalysis, that is, to help the patient make his or her own reparations. What I want to convey is that this task is facilitated by the psychoanalyst's internal operations.

REFERENCES

Bion, W. (1974). *Clinical Seminars. Brasilia and São Paulo and Four Papers.* Abingdon, England: Fleetwood Press, 1987.

Boyer, L. B. (1961). Provisional evaluation of psychoanalysis with few parameters in the treatment of schizophrenia. In *The Regressed Patient,* pp. 68–88. New York: Jason Aronson, 1983.

—— (1986). Technical aspects of treating the regressed patient. *Contemporary Psychoanalysis* 22:25–44.

—— (1987). Countertransference and technique in working with the regressed patient: further remarks. Paper presented at the Boyer House Foundation Conference, The Regressed Patient, San Francisco, March. (See Chapter 12, this volume.)

Bychowski, G. (1952). *Psychotherapy of Psychosis.* New York: Grune & Stratton.

De Paola, H. F. B. (1982). Considerações sobre momentos de crise no processo analítico. *Revista Brasileira de Psicanálise* 16:63–81.

—— (1984). Transferência nas psicoses. *Brasileira de Psicanálise* 18:221–246.

—— (1986). Interpretação na análise de psicóticos. *Correio de Fepal. Anais do XVII Congresso Latino-Americano de Psicanálise.* São Paulo. Número Especial do Congresso, pp. 230–243.

Ferenczi, S. (1919). On the technique of psycho-analysis. iv. the control of the countertransference. In *Further Contributions to the Theory and Technique of Psycho-Analysis,* pp. 186–189. London: Hogarth, 1950.

Freud, S. (1910). The future prospects of psycho-analytic therapy. *Standard Edition* 11:139–157.

Glover, E. (1955). *The Technique of Psychoanalysis.* New York: International Universities Press.

Heimann, P. (1950). On countertransference. *International Journal of Psycho-Analysis* 31:81–84.

Klein, M. (1946). Notes on some schizoid mechanisms. *International Journal of Psycho-Analysis* 27:99–110.

Kohut, H. (1959). Introspection, empathy and psychoanalysis—an examination of the relationship between mode of operation and theory. In *The Search For the Self,* ed. P. Ornstein, pp. 205–232. New York: International Universities Press, 1980.

Little, M. (1951). Counter-transference and the patient's response to it. *International Journal of Psycho-Analysis* 32:32–40.

Money-Kyrle, R. E. (1956). Normal counter-transference and some of its deviations. *International Journal of Psycho-Analysis* 37:360–366.

—— (1968). Cognitive Development. *International Journal of Psycho-Analysis* 49:691–698.

Orr, D. W. (1954). Transference and countertransference: a historical survey. *Journal of the American Psychoanalytic Association* 2:621–670.

Pacheco, M. A. P. (1978). On the working through of the psychotic elements in the analytic process. *International Journal of Psycho-Analysis* 59:2-3.

——— (1980). On neurotic and psychotic transference. *International Review of Psycho-Analysis* 7:157-164.

Petrucci, J. C. (1989). Relações de objeto, mundo representacional e experiencias contratransferenciais: Idéias a respeito de um caso. Unpublished paper.

Racker, H. (1953). A contribution to the problem of counter-transference. *International Journal of Psycho-Analysis* 34:313-324.

Reich, A. (1960). Further remarks and counter-transference. *International Journal of Psycho-Analysis* 41:389-395.

Segal, H. (1950). Countertransference. In *The Work of Hanna Segal. A Kleinian Approach to Clinical Practice*, pp. 81-87. New York: Jason Aronson, 1981.

Stern, A. (1924). On the counter-transference in psychoanalysis. *Psychoanalytic Review* 11:165-174.

Strachey, J. (1958). Editor's introduction to "Papers on Technique," *Standard Edition* 12:85-88. London: Hogarth.

Treurniet, N. (1983). Psychoanalysis and self psychology: a metapsychological essay with a clinical illustration. *Journal of the American Psychoanalytic Association* 31:59-100.

Zanin, J. C. (1989). Teoria e técnica da análise de psicóticos. Unpublished paper.

.14

CHRISTOPHER BOLLAS, Ph.D.

Regression in the Countertransference

The psychoanalyst's use of countertransference in understanding the patient's transference and in processing the analysand's projective identifications is now a firmly established feature in the technique of many practicing psychoanalysts and psychotherapists. Indeed, it is difficult to distinguish the structural function of countertransference (as a processing of the patient's transference acts) from its hermeneutic yield, when the analyst transforms his or her inner psychic experience of the analysand into meaning. To process the analysand is to know him. To interpret one's situation, in the here and now, is both to transform slowly the structure of projection and to convey the meanings of the many transferences.

One of the results of this creative leap in psychoanalysis is the narrative account by psychoanalysts of their states of mind as they work with their patients. Readers of clinical literature now often look for clinical writing that includes an account of the analyst's ongoing inner state. My view (Bollas 1987) is that contemplation of the countertransference is a systematic reintegration into the psychoanalytical movement of an exiled function: that of self-analysis. Early on, psychoanalysts erred in thinking that Freud's self-analysis, instrumental in his processing of his patients, his inner evolution, and his imaginative creation and recreation of psychoanalysis was a biographic irregularity. He needed self-analysis because he had no analyst. When self-analysis was regarded as something engaged in for lack of analysis proper, a crucial feature of Freudianism was eliminated. The intense interest in countertransference is, in my view, the reintroduction into psychoanalysis of the self-analytic element, that factor in analysts that leaves them a continuous surprise to themselves, as they produce associations, daydream, fantasize, conjure exact ideas that have a surprisingly brief life, somatize existence periodically, and voyage through their situational moods. Analysts' inner experiencing of themselves and their application of mind to such inner experiencing is what I mean by the self-analytic element, to be distinguished from self-analysis proper, which is the informative outcome of the self-analytic element.

Is Freud's theory of the value of free association derived from his own inner free associating? When Dr. Freud had Sigmund on the couch, the analysand associating to his dreams, with Freud to gather this experience into interpretation, did Freud project his experience as analysand onto the patient? If so, then free association would be an inner association, an inner processing of unconscious knowledge that is precursor to any knowing of the latent meaning of a mental content. Countertransference experiencing, then, is the origin of free associative life, which was unwittingly projected onto the analysand. If I am correct in this understanding, then Freud's error made it possible for analysts who were so inclined to inherit and sustain this split, allowing them to believe in a relative neutrality, with the patient's associations held to be the primary place of manifest and latent texts. By splitting psychoanalytic analysand, by transferring the intrasubjective integrity of self-analysis to the interpersonal field, Freud passed on a psychoanalysis partly denuded of its rich subjective origin. Countertransference theory, however, has slowly become the effort of many psychoanalysts to recover the loss of the analyst's own inner free associating and to find different technical means to bring such information to its interpretive potential. If the analyst has an inner receptive space for the registration of the analysand's free associations and transference acts, a space biased by the ideal of evenly hovering attentiveness, such a space must simultaneously receive and register the analyst's free associations. We could think of a cinema screen, which represents a double projection in an intermediate space. It receives impressions from the patient and from the analyst, in a special internal holding environment that is the mental effect of psychoanalytical training. Among other things, analysts develop a part of their mind to act as an inner holding environment for the reception of intersubjective and intrasubjective impressions.

When psychoanalysts work with seriously disturbed analysands, they may find that they increasingly turn to responsive inner associations of their own rather than to the reception, per se, of the patient's associations, as such communications are often not conveyers of meaning but part-acts that are only sensible (and then of potential meaning) as they effect analysts' finding their completion in that category of signification that we term *object relations*.

I will now consider a period in the psychoanalysis of a hospitalized adolescent who suffered from paranoid schizophrenia. My aim here is confined to an examination of a particular type of clinical regression, which often is fundamentally experienced only by the psychoanalyst, who is compelled into regressive states of mind by the patient. Discovering what this regression is, why it is so, and how it can be managed is the object of this chapter. So now to Nick.

NICK

To convey my experience of Nick, I must consider that period before I met him, as it figures in the formation of my countertransference. Hospitalized some eight months prior to his acceptance at the open hospital where I was working, Nick was regarded as a more than potentially violent patient, who had, in fact, drawn a knife against his mother and chased her about their home in the fashionable suburbs of a midwestern town. He was 18, had dropped acid four or five times a week for five years, and had experimented with as many drugs as he could find (or manufacture), except heroin. He had discharged himself from the hospital against medical advice after pressuring his parents into taking him back home. In the course of his prior hospitalization he had had to be physically restrained on a few occasions, was too disruptive to be with other patients, and had to be in isolation to protect the patient population. The director of admissions at my hospital found him cooperative but extremely suspicious and monosyllabic. He appeared polite and formal in an eerily false manner. In the morning staff conference, there was a general consensus that this patient was likely to "blow," and the discussion fell into consideration of his medications. When it was announced that I was assigned to the patient, my colleagues smiled and jested in the way we all do when our amusement is a "Thank God it wasn't me" relief.

CONCEPTUALIZING THE PATIENT
FROM WHAT ONE HEARS

Before I introduce the patient, it is well to consider this particular phase of my countertransference. We form mental pictures of all of our analysands from what we hear. Whether a colleague refers a patient to us for our private practice, whether a patient telephones us of his own initiative, or whether a hospital assigns us a patient, we hear about them before we meet them. And of course, the patient imagines us even if he hasn't heard so much about us. Some analysands, and Nick is one of them, develop a reputation of some notoriety so that they enter the conceptual space rather disturbingly. Indeed, a Nick knows this and fosters a troubling reputation partly in order to enter the other's conceptual space on his own particular terms.

I value my peace of mind. I do not like it disturbed; part of the pleasure of analytic training and experience is to develop an inner area for the reception of disturbing patient communications, which nonetheless is sufficiently containable so as not to disturb the container itself. I enjoy just listening to a patient; it is pleasurable to be part of a structure (the analytic process), which has its laws (absence of socialization, economy of intervention), that enables me to freely associate and concentrate on certain interesting figurations of meaning that develop from time to time. Every analyst who works with the neurotic patient, particularly the good hysteric, knows what a pleasure it is simply to be the analyst who analyzes.

PHASE ONE: THE PSYCHOANALYST'S SPLITTING OF THE SELF

Then there are the Nicks. As this stocky, red-haired thick-forearmed young man sank into the chair opposite me on our very first meeting, I was instantly not my psychoanalyst self. At the time I did not know why this was so. In fact, I did not know that this *was* so. In hindsight I can say that I must have been uneasy carrying him inside me in that pregnant period from referring conception to delivery at the consulting room door. For here was a most strange, bizarre infant. He sat staring at me with a fixed gaze, a slightly mocking smirk playing across his face. After a long silence, I asked him how he found things here. He allowed this question to hang about long enough for both of us to feel the echo of its emptiness before he replied, "Fine." After a pause, I said, "What is fine?" and he said, "I am comfortable." No doubt struck by the sanguine paradox of his apparent ease juxtaposed to my unease, I replied, "What do you find comfortable?" to which he said, "Everything." After a seemingly endless session I managed to extract from him the news that he liked the hospital because it was an open unit and he had found the other patients "nice."

What I did not know during this session, although I was certainly a witness participant, was what was so disturbing to me about the patient. I was not aware that, although he stared at me, he did so at a precise, unvarying angle; not exactly out of the corner of his eyes, but at a slant. I was also aware only weeks later that every five minutes or so he would rotate his head to the left, to look to the window side of my office. It was not the action of a person looking outside the window to capture the view; it was more like the mechanical movement of a television monitor, scanning the space with intentless emptiness. I saw him do this and I wondered if he were hallucinating; I asked him if he had just had some thought, to which he replied, "No," after, as usual, leaving my comment to hang itself in silence. What I did not notice was the effect this bizarre rotation was having on me. And although I did note that Nick sat perfectly still for his sessions, I did not realize, in fact, that for the first weeks, he never moved in the chair. He never crossed his legs or changed his position in any way. He placed both hands on the armrests and never moved them. Never, that is, except for the moment in a session, after some twenty minutes, when he would reach into his left shirt pocket with his right hand to extract his pack of cigarettes and his lighter. With his left hand still holding the chair arm, he would remove a cigarette, bring it some twenty inches or so in front of his face, then horizontally bring it to his mouth, where it would sit for a few seconds before he lit it with his lighter. Then lighter and pack of cigarettes would go back into the same pocket. Both the rotation of his head and the lighting of the cigarette occurred without any sympathetic movement in his own body. On reflection I can say that his monosyllabic responses were simple, isolated vocalizations that were as detached from meaning as his movements were detached from his body.

During the first weeks with Nick, I worked very hard to engage him. As I did so, I was annoyed with myself for straying from the ordinary analytic position that I enjoy so much, and I was furious with myself for the many empty questions I put to him and for my sense of being deeply false with this patient. I was cross with myself for trying so hard to engage him, for simply trying to get along with him, to establish some rapport. All the work of the hour came from me as Nick would simply sit in utter silence if I did not initiate, sustain, and develop knowledge of him. Due to my false self I was able to extract details of his life history and to learn some of his experiences at the hospital. He said that his problems began when he changed schools at age 7. He had felt like an oddball at his old school, but his classmates had liked him, while at the new school, he had been an object of intense persecution, which he dealt with by increasing his oddness. He would stand in the playground, engaged in an isolated idiosyncratic sign language display, gazed upon by classmates who were meant to believe that this was the representation of some superior knowledge he possessed and expressed in this way. I tended to focus on how the move to our hospital must be like the move at 7, and how clearly determined he was to try to be liked. I tried to discuss his fears with him, but he insisted he felt fine, that I was a good therapist, that there was nothing to know about him other than the disturbing move at the age of 7.

As we know, each of our patients creates an environment within which we are meant to live a psychoanalytic lifetime together. This means that the analyst will undergo internal changes, and struggle to come to terms with his successional lives in this world. As I now look back on these first weeks with Nick, it is clear that of the two of us, it was I who was undergoing a psychic change. Nick remained his oddly inert and suspicious self, while I was progressively more irritated by my questions, or interpretations, which felt compliant on my part. I was ill at ease with the patient, struggling fruitlessly to get to that place I like to be when working as an analyst: the intermediate space, a rendezvous of the patient's thoughts and actions and my associations—all taking place in that wonderful concentrated stillness that characterizes analytic silence. But Nick had me out of that place. I felt displaced, removed from my analytic identity, alarmed by a seeming inability to arrest my progressive false self adaptation to the analysand. As I coaxed this patient to speak about his life, employing as many subtle interactive proddings as I could, I began to loathe the patient, and really to *hate* the content of my remarks, the sound of my voice, and the shallowness of my personality. In my view, I had regressed by splitting my personality, in which I was out of touch with my real self, taken over by a false self increasingly unable to be effective. The only real state of self I was aware of was my intense irritation with the situation and my role within it, although my hate— due to this regression—was of no use to me, or to my patient.

Transference–countertransference communicating may be considered a special type of object relating, an "informative" relating (Bollas 1989) as one subject alters the other subject's psychic structure through particular intersubjective actions. Faced with a lifeless, dismissive, yet bizarre other, I split my personality, adopting a false self to meet this bizarre other, splitting off my private inner reality, which I could not bring into the hour. Am I living through an early object relation that characterized Nick's life? Has he been there before me? Has he had to give up his sense of identity to put it outside the space of interrelating? Does he show me something of the personality of the object (or objects) that displaced his true self from its idiomatic use of the object world? We shall see.

PHASE TWO: FRIGHTENED FOR ONE'S LIFE

As the weeks passed into months, I had worked on myself sufficiently to diminish false self-adaptiveness on my part. I would greet
him at the door as he came into the room. He would sit down and then
a silence would descend upon us. It is not something I can describe. A
deep fear enveloped us, perhaps that fear that occurs in an ordinary
dream in the split second before it becomes a nightmare, or that fear
created out of the eyes of the other, so familiar to me in my youth in one
particular context, while body surfing, languishing about in small
waves, glancing up at friends on the shore whose looks were fixed to a
place far out to sea, a place beyond my situational vision, but the place
where all immense waves originate. It is the look that means I must
swim for my life, as fast and as powerfully as I can, not even taking the
time to look for the wave and its successors. You have to swim as far
toward it as you can; you can sense its movement toward you. You
inhale as much precious oxygen as you can, and then dive to the sands
below, where you grip the sand firmly, relaxing your body into a kelp-
like limberness, and wait for a sea-avalanche to pass over you, without
carrying you along with it. Maybe that kind of fear.

As the days pass, this fear intensifies in the sessions. When he
rotates his head, I say, "You are looking at something?"; he replies,
"No"; then a long silence follows. One day he says, "You hear it?"
"What?" I reply. "The fly." "What fly?" "*The fly*," he says. "Where?"
"Over there, by the window." I can see nothing, nor hear anything, and
haven't seen a fly since the early autumn. It is winter now, and there is
snow on the ground. Ten minutes of silence ensues. "It's still there."
"This fly on the wall?" I query. No reply. Another long silence. I make
an interpretation: "As we know, you often look to that side of the room,
where I think you feel there is a fly on the wall observing us, listening to
us, and troubling us. But I think I also trouble you, and you may feel
spied upon by my listening in to what you say." A long silence follows.
"No, I don't. You are a good therapist." Then the dense silence de-
scends again.

The chairs in the consulting room are large, soft leather chairs.
When you sit in them, they rather exhale. Noisy objects. If you move
about, the chair echoes the shift of the body. Yet Nick sits in the chair
and makes no noise. This noiselessness contributes to the ever-increas-
ing eerie fearfulness of this place, as if we must make no sound to
announce our existence. Looking back, I think I almost stopped breathing. I rarely moved.

Then an extraordinary event. Amid this fear-ridden silence Nick moved slightly in his chair, and the leather uttered a material shriek. Both the patient and the analyst jumped in a startled response. My heart was pounding with anxiety. But why? Over what? The sound of leather squeaking? I can recall thinking to myself, "All right, that's enough, God damn it! This is ridiculous." I was furious that "it" should come to this. Although I did not know what to say, I was determined to speak. "I want to try now to think out loud with you about what has just happened. When you moved—ever so slightly— your chair made a noise and we both jumped. Why? Why should this be so? Is it the case that you have no right to move, lest you scare yourself, or me? What is it that does not permit movement? No. What is it that does not permit your existence? It's as if you are hiding from a monster! And what is this monster? Where is it? Is it me? Am I a monster: a Bollas monster?" A disembodied laugh ricocheted off the wall. Nick had not laughed before, if that's what this "fit" of laughter could be called. The next day Nick, walking down the hallway, called out to me, "Hello there, monster!" That dreadful silence had ended.

What have the analyst and patient lived through? I think of it as a fight for survival, when one's very existence, very right to be alive, is challenged by the insidious yet indistinct presence of the other. I had regressed from an over-talkative false self to an endangered and frightened being. I had no psychosomatic aliveness to me. I was all bunched up inside, barely breathing, without body movement: a lifeless nonentity. Although this environment was promoted by the analysand, I was more aware of my inner madness, rather than the patient's frame of mind. His behavior, as I have said, was a constant. I had "lost" the integrity of the structure of the psychoanalytic process. I had no psychosomatic aliveness to speak of. I was living a marginal life, dominated by a nameless fear.

Nick and I did, however, share a common response to the world in which we lived. We were both startled. And when I became furious, I sensed that my anger, my protest, and my effort to speak were spoken for the two of us. It felt as if I were standing up to something, to speak from a soma of distress, to establish a right to speak my mind.

By fostering a deadly silence and killing off interrelating, the patient sponsored false self-adaptiveness in me not unlike a defense the patient had taken earlier in his life when presented with a similar killing of human intimacy, although Nick concealed his false self-adaptation by conjuring a negative identity (Erikson 1968). The intensity of my fear cannot, however, simply be occasioned by the bizarre behavior and hostility of the other toward me. As we know, it is the marriage of the actual happening and projected inner states that produces an emotional crisis. If we examine my fear, it was so compelling because, since I had become a false self, my hate was split off and projected into X. Not into the patient per se, but into the environment inhabited by the patient and myself. My fury over our startled response can be seen, therefore, as my partial recovery from this pathological process. Perhaps my hate would become useful.

PHASE THREE: THE WORRIED MOTHER IN ME

Nick emerged from this silence to become a comparatively more talkative patient, although not to the point where I could ever relax into the analyst's position. However, my troubles were by no means over. "By the way," Nick said, watching me intently, "I had some great pot last night." As he knew, this was decidedly against hospital rules, as was his consumption of booze, which he also told me about. Indeed, each session was now spiced by his announcement of one form or another of calculated provocation. "Sue and I were at Safeway the other day and stole a whole carton of M&Ms." "I went to the bar across the street and guess what? They served me!" "I found a whole stash of mushrooms. I'm going to fix them up." I was aware that his actings out were intended to offend me, but initially I was not certain what precise object relational meaning lay behind the acting out.

I was aware of a new kind of anxiety within me, characterized by an intrusive worry about what he was up to. Whenever Nick attended a session, I would have some difficulty listening to him because I would wonder if he had been the perpetrator of some of the misdemeanors reported at morning conference only a few hours earlier. This mood was matched by a knee-jerk response to lecture him about hospital rules, and so forth but I kept such responses to myself and instead said that I thought he was trying to worry me, which I think gave him pleasure. Soon he complained that he thought it was a drag that the hospital had so many rules. He wanted to be free, and taking drugs or boozing was his way of exercising his freedom. I disagreed and said that it seemed quite the opposite: He was provoking the hospital into noticing, monitoring, and eventually restricting his movements. He eventually likened some of the hospital staff's scrutiny of him to his mother's fretful and intrusive "eyeballing" of him. As far back as he could remember, she was always peering into his room. He had no latch on the door, and eventually he tried to rig up a warning system to alert him when she was opening the sliding door to glance into his room. In early adolescence he put towels on the floor against the door to prevent his mother from detecting whether his lights were on. While he complained about his mother's intrusiveness, it was clear that he had also developed a technique for provoking her by leaving evidence of his drug habits lying about the house for her to see. It was clear to me then that he was bringing out the worrying mother in me by informing me of his intended actions. I told him this, and for the first time there was a glimmer of recognition in him of the potential usefulness of psychoanalytic interpretation. Although it is true that he was provoking me to establish an alarmed and intrusive mother whom he could control, this feature of his transference was unconscious.

This period of my own regression in the countertransference, however, was characterized by my occupation of the mother's frame of mind, a fragmented position, littered with unintegrated islands of affection, interest, coldness, withdrawal, overconcern, indifference, and so forth. It so happened that Nick's mother wrote to the hospital to supply us with her personal history and details of Nick's early life. It was a deeply moving account of her early failing of her child. Some eighteen months after his birth, she became preoccupied by the terminal illness of a member of her family. Nick responded by clinging to her. She could barely have a moment to herself when she was at home. Her preoccupation with her relation's illness continued until, when Nick was 3½, she found herself feeling intensely cold toward him. She wrote of how she rejected him, and then how subsequently Nick detached himself from her, apparently killing off his feelings for her. As the years passed, she was haunted by what had happened, and when Nick began to take up drugs and act bizarrely, she could only be intrusive. In effect, she did not know how to love him effectively.

Nick's descriptions of his mother's personality seemed accurate enough for me to match them with my countertransference; now, with the mother's account of herself, I was quite sure that we had moved to a new level of object relating. But understanding an unconscious process and interpreting it to a patient, as we all know, does not necessarily add up to change, and Nick's actings out had now caught the attention of the nurses, the people within the activities center, therapists working in group sessions, and so on. I knew that the best way for me to work with Nick's enactments was not to react as the mother, but to interpret to him what he aimed to bring out in me, and the sadistic but organizing pleasure of this object relation. In so doing, I felt that we were slowly emerging from the illness of a child/mother relationship, and by managing to contain and process the mad mother he brought out in me, I was succeeding in working our way out of pathologically regressed object relations. But the hospital's understandable response both complicated and intensified the endeavor.

I found that at almost every morning conference, when the nurses read their reports of the day and night before, Nick figured prominently in the news. In his first weeks at the hospital, he was rarely mentioned. In the early days I had looked forward to the morning conference, as an occasion to sip coffee, listen to the *Under Milkwood*-like narrative of the many different patients' nighttime life: their nightmares, sexual adventures, political intrigues, and the like. I could greet different colleagues, gaze at one or another of the attractive nurses, catch up on local hospital news. It was a nice start to the day. When Nick's name was mentioned in connection with the disturbing pot, I was shocked out of my dormantly pleased state into an altogether different frame of mind. I was more a creature of my respiratory system, sponsored as I was by my anxieties, barely able to think what I was meant to say. I knew that eventually my colleagues would ask me if I could assist them in their understanding of what was happening. I knew they didn't want to do this, as this is an intrusion in the therapy, but it would happen. As the reports continued, with nurses now reporting rumors circulated by patients about Nick's misdemeanors, I found myself in another, very much more difficult struggle: the effort to prevent the patient from succeeding in his unconscious effort to become a behavioral object.

I think there is a struggle, common to most treatments of a psychotic patient, that is characterized by the analysand's unconscious effort to force the analyst into regarding him as a behavioral object, as a creature defined by his manifest behavior. By acting out against established hospital rules and routines, the patient coerces the environment into reacting to him as a phenomenon defined by his actions. Indeed, the patient becomes associated with acts: "Well, pot is around, so what was Nick doing last night?" "We have had a report from the police of a shoplift at a local store. Anyone know where Nick was yesterday afternoon at 4:00?" The environment's response is understandable and in a way, it should be, but the total situation may achieve the effect of rendering the patient into a thing.

To become a thing, an unreflected-upon source of reaction defined by manifest acts, is one of the unconscious aims of schizophrenic object relating. The schizophrenic aims to deaden the other's psychological empathy, just as he has deadened his own inner life. During this long spell in Nick's treatment, I emphasized how he was aiming to be viewed as a thing-creature-of-habit, to be that which the mother saw, and to bring about in the hospital a deadening hatred of him. Fortunately, he knew this to be so and assisted me in working this through with him. There were many times in the course of morning conferences when my colleagues and I were in a necessary conflict with one another: they to announce his transgressions and to consider courses of action, I to remind the group of the psychological meaning behind these actions. It felt at times as if the nursing report of his actions and the administrative response was pure beta element (what Bion means by *undigested facts*) and I was pure alpha: thoughtfulness working on the beta (Bion 1962). A good working group, such as the one at my hospital, allows for creative polarizations and I always felt an underlying support for my conflict with the behavioral view of the patient. Regrettably, many psychotic patients effectively get hospitals to see them as a behavioral thing and to treat them with a mixture of chemotherapy and a "supportive" psychotherapy that is somewhat like the way one treats a puppy.

Reflecting on this last period of work with Nick, I have come to see that he unconsciously aimed first to bring out a part of the mother's personality within me, a worried and intrusive mother; then he regressed me and the community to an earlier, deadlier mother, who regarded him as a thing.

PHASE FOUR: CONCLUSION

Before we discuss the issues latent to this case presentation, it is well to summarize the stages of regression and recovery within the analyst's countertransference. They were

1. The stage of a splitting of the analyst's personality into false self-adaptiveness, leading to a loss of a sense of personal reality in work with the analysand. This is partly due to the patient's presentations of deep maternal refusal (of interrelating), with the analyst experiencing the child-patient's loss of personal reality.
2. The stage of terror over survival, as the analyst is overcome by a dreadful silence that immobilizes his psyche-soma. This is understood as the patient's presentation of maternal hate, of death wishes against the aliveness of the child. The fear, however, is due to the child's responsive destruction, expressed by the analyst's countertransference. The analyst, having split his personality, has projected his hate into the environment, leaving him only a part analyst. The

analyst, shocked out of this by a moment within a session, mobilizes his fury into speech. Aggression is now a means of survival.

3. The stage of the worrying mother, in which the analyst takes on the mother's personality, as the patient now switches the analyst's subjective position from the child's place to the location of the mother. The analyst uses understanding and interpretation to recover from the regression into the mother's madness.

4. The stage of the desubjectification of the patient, in which the patient aims to coerce the analyst and community into regarding him as a behavioral object. To think or not to think about the meaning behind the patient's actions is the question, with the analyst working to transform the mother's deadening of meaning into meaningfulness.

DISCUSSION

To treat a severely disturbed patient means that each analyst will have to live within that environment (Bollas 1983) created by the analysand, a world that is disturbed and will be disturbing. Many analysts, but notably Searles (1965, 1979, 1986) and Giovacchini (1979), have written about their own mad internal states while being with a borderline or psychotic patient.

In such situations, the analyst may be the figure in the patient–therapist relationship who experiences *informative regression*. This is a regression unconsciously determined by the patient's projection of parts of the self and parental object world into the analyst's psyche, thus forming the analyst's inner experiences in order to communicate the patient's experience of being and relating. Some psychotic patients, such as Nick, preserve an unreal calm to their self, while the analyst, on the other hand, may be enduring quite disturbed states of mind. When this is true, the analyst must hold himself within these regressions, giving time to the other parts of his personality, so that the information being processed in the countertransference, an in-formative object relating that is part of the unthought known, can be worked upon by the parts of the analyst's personality that are still available to reflect on experience. All clinical situations are an *intermediated psychic reality*, and during work with the psychotic patient, the intermediate nature of an hour assumes a greater significance in the analyst's mind than it does with the neurotic analysand. Healthier patients produce meaning that can be reflected upon within the hour. Much of this work is already the outcome of the analysand's intrasubjective processings, but the most disturbed patient cannot do this, and the work of the hour takes place in the intermediate area of experiencing. The analyst, now bearing split-off portions of the patient's true self and its object experiences, is not sure at any moment who is carrying what and why at that time. This lack of boundaries is a condition for work in the intermediate area. As time passes (and it is interesting how time assumes a different and curative function in this situation), the analyst is able to transform an informative object relation into thought. When he can objectify his countertransference position, the analyst can then formulate it into an interpretation to be made available to the patient. And as some psychotic patients sponsor the regressions in the analyst, rather than within themselves, analysts will endure regressive episodes from which they recover through time, patience, and reflective work. When this is so, analytic insight and interpretation are in the first place curative for the analyst, who gets better first. Psychic change, in this instance, begins within the analyst. Only gradually, through interpretation, holding, and the passing of time, does the patient get better.

Finally, I think analysands unconsciously appreciate that inner experience endured by the analyst. They know that he or she is living through their inner object world and through their history. The analyst's tolerance of psychic pain, effort of thought, and somewhat aggressive delight in working through malignant regressions, is heartening for those patients who have been incarcerated in a world of seeming no-exits.

REFERENCES

Bion, W. C. (1962). Learning from experience. In *Seven Servants*. New York: Jason Aronson, 1977.

———— (1983). Expressive uses of the countertransference. In *The Shadow of the Object*, pp. 200–235. London: Free Association.

Bollas, C. (1987). Self-analysis and the countertransference. In *The Shadow of the Object: Psychoanalysis of the Unthought Known*, p. 236. London: Free Association.

———— (1989). *Forces of Destiny: Psychoanalysis and Human Idiom*. London: Free Association.

Erikson, E. (1968). *Identity: Youth and Crisis*, pp. 172–176. London: Faber.

Giovacchini, P. (1979). *Treatment of Primitive Mental States*. New York: Jason Aronson.

Searles, H. F. (1965). *Collected Papers on Schizophrenia and Related Subjects*. New York: International Universities Press.

———— (1979). *Countertransference and Related States: Selected Papers*. New York: International Universities Press.

———— (1989). *My Work with Borderline Patients*. New York: International Universities Press.

.15

PETER L. GIOVACCHINI, M.D.

Epilogue: Contemporary Perspectives on Technique

All the contributors to this book have chosen to write about clinical situations that involve patients suffering from fairly severe psychopathology. Though they cover many areas of patient–therapist interactions, they can still be loosely grouped in several categories. This is interesting because it demonstrates the directions toward which clinicians are moving as they attempt to reach the deeper recesses of the patient's mind in order to help alleviate primeval misery and terror.

Before enumerating specific orientations and exploratory perspectives, I wish to emphasize that this book, among others, represents another attempt to broaden our intrapsychic perspective. In view of recent trends to limit clinical interactions and understanding to phenomenological and behavioral frames, the authors serve an important function as they demonstrate a viewpoint that is dedicated to a thorough understanding of patients. They avoid mechanistic explanations as they seek to discover and restore the patient's basic humanity. Their efforts have led to increased insights and renewed attempts to engage primitive mental states in a therapeutic relationship as our technical understanding is augmented and as we develop a basic and awed respect for early mental processes that are instrumental to the emergence of later psychopathology.

In roughly placing these chapters in several categories that, of course, overlap, we are identifying topics that occupy clinicians who focus their research interests on the treatment interaction. I find it extremely interesting to discover that all of the authors have independently chosen to discuss how various aspects of the patient's character structure affect their therapeutic perspective. It is also fascinating to note how many prominent psychoanalysts, like those who write here, concentrate their efforts on the treatment of severely disturbed patients and on how their technical and theoretical concepts converge. It is further striking that so many independent thinkers do not clash with one another. If anything, various chapters complement and supplement one another, a welcome change from so many polemics that, in the past, have proved fruitless and potentially destructive for psychoanalysis in general.

Practically all the authors cover a wide gamut of the psychotherapeutic frame, but they tend to focus on certain particular aspects. For example, Searles, Ogden, and I concentrate on various structural deficits and how they become incorporated and affect the treatment interaction. They do not become embroiled in arguments about the controversy between deficits versus intrapsychic conflicts. Rather, they candidly reveal their experiences with patients, and it becomes obvious as the various introjective processes are experienced in the transference–countertransference dimension which ego distortions and primitive psychic mechanisms are operating.

Concerning early developmental phases, Gaddini, Grotstein, Ogden, and Tustin provide us with valuable insights. The emergent personality is considered from a much more sophisticated and useful viewpoint than that emphasized by the clashing forces and vectors that characterize the psychodynamic hypothesis and the stages of psychosexual development (Giovacchini 1987). Freud (1905, 1914), when outlining the various psychosexual stages, stressed those phases that dealt with external objects, that is, the oral, anal, and phallic phases and finally the Oedipus complex. He did, however, also refer to stages that preceded attachment to objects or related to very primitive forms of object relatedness and recognition. He wrote about autoerotic activities and primary and secondary narcissism, developmental processes associated with the earliest periods of the structuring of the psyche.

The authors here expand on the time periods that Freud was discussing when he outlined the progression between autoerotism and secondary narcissism. The latter he considered to be the beginning of and first form of object relations. Ogden, in particular, gives us what might be considered a macroscopic perspective of the psyche preceding the origin of mental life and then moves forward to the earliest types of psychic processes. These developmental occurrences are explored by all the authors in the context of traumatic impacts as they refer to pathological distortions of the course of emotional development. Very little attention is paid to the drives, per se, although needs and their frustration and gratification are placed in a developmental perspective.

Nevertheless, Freud has not been abandoned. Rather, his ideas have been extended by the ideas of such writers as Melanie Klein and Bion. De

Paola, Grotstein, and Rosenfeld rely heavily on the insights provided by Klein and Bion, but they are able to keep their feet in Freud's camp as well. They accept only what is consistent with observable clinical experiences and do not get lost in theoretical constructs that are not compatible with either the data derived from recent neonatological studies and experiments or from their relationships with patients as they revolve around the transference-countertransference axis.

Bollas, Boyer, De Paola, and Searles directly address countertransference issues. Boyer and Searles, in particular, have been using their countertransference reactions as barometers of the therapeutic climate, which has helped them understand their patients better, especially as to how psychopathological adaptations have had their impact on the treatment setting. They have measured the latter by their personal responses and feelings. In the United States, Boyer and Searles have been pioneers who, by monitoring their countertransference reactions, have contributed considerably to our knowledge about severely disturbed patients. They have helped us understand various psychic processes, such as projective identification, that determine the nature of the patient–therapist interaction and when it will be destructive or potentially constructive.

The study of the treatment process and technical innovations leads to further insights about psychic structure and its psychopathological deformations. To some extent, this is the antithesis of what occurs with the psychoneuroses. In that clinical area, the understanding of psychodynamic conflicts precedes and determines treatment strategy. With more severely disturbed patients, those suffering from defects in psychic structure, an understanding of basic problems, adaptive patterns, and ego structure often cannot be gained until later, when the patient's projections are felt and processed by the analyst. This constitutes a therapeutic diagnosis, a clinical judgment that is made when the therapist is able, in some measure, to experience the patient's anguish and misery, a countertransference response that facilitates the comprehension of pathologically distorted primitive mental functioning.

Bollas, Gaddini, McDougall, Rosenfeld, and Steiner give special attention to various areas of primitive mental functioning. At times, they seem to be writing about what could be considered the architecture of the personality. Bollas, in particular, demonstrates how his countertransference discomfort helped him discover the existence of infantile traumas and the impact they had on the developmental process and the structure of the ego. I believe he admirably illustrates how diagnostic evaluations cannot be simply so-called objective observations when clinicians are trying to make some sense of the confusing and defensive material the patient brings to the consultation room. Bollas found himself participating in the therapeutic regression before he was able to have a clear view of both the patient's psyche and what he, as a therapist, was doing.

Rosenfeld and Steiner also reach conclusions about psychic structure, and Rosenfeld emphasizes that distortions of the body image and a psychotic core are significant in determining how various ego subsystems will be deficient in coping with the exigencies of the external world.

As has been implicit in this perusal of the chapters in this book, the topics I have referred to are, to some degree, discussed by all the authors. Some concentrate more on a specific aspect of the treatment interaction, whereas others may focus in greater depth on structural considerations. In all instances, however, whatever the main approach, technical or theoretical, the authors are dedicated clinicians whose primary concern is to further the treatment of all patients who seek psychoanalytic treatment, and particularly those who, in the past, were not considered to be good candidates for an in-depth approach (Boyer and Giovacchini 1980, Giovacchini 1979, 1987).

Goldberg, Volkan, and I discuss technical issues from both a clinical and a theoretical perspective. I investigate the communicative aspects of interpretation as the patient is eventually able to integrate insights that lead to the expansion and acquisition of psychic structure. Goldberg and Volkan continue with a thoroughly clinical orientation. The treatment of borderline and psychotic patients causes us to reexamine our ideas concerning technical maneuvers, including those discussed by Freud (1911–1915) in his technical papers, which presumably were applicable to the treatment of better-structured patients.

Clinicians have reached a juncture in the development of psychoanalysis in which many traditional formulations are being challenged. True, revisions have been made gradually throughout the years; in the forefront of making modifications was Freud himself. With the recent interest in the borderline phenomenon, however, there has been an intensification of interest in the various elements of the treatment interaction, such as interpretation, transference, countertransference, and analytic neutrality. Standard approaches are also being challenged, such as the formal elements of analysis that include use of the couch, frequency of interviews, types of interpretations, and how the transference is handled.

Attempts to change or modify psychoanalytic technique are not new. Many years ago Ferenczi and Rank (1923) wrote a book that advocated extremely active participation by the therapist in order to undo the effects of early psychic trauma and deprivation. Their recommendations were so drastic that Freud, though he tried, was unable to accept them. They represented such extreme alterations of the treatment setting that they bore very little resemblance to a psychoanalytic interaction. Others, such as Alexander and French (1946) have also made recommendations that would have destroyed the analytic perspective. Briefly, these authors have changed the therapist's orientation from a nonjudgmental person dedicated to understanding how the patient's mind works to a participant in the patient's life who actively attempts to create an environment that will compensate for and rectify infantile trauma.

The contributing authors to this book do not advocate any basic change in the analyst's stance. They are still basically observers who remain predominantly within an intrapsychic frame of reference. Their purpose is to understand the patient who has never been understood. They respect intrapsychic processes, rather than turning their attention elsewhere and manipulating external reality or their role, so that the patient feels some degree of security. Usually such attempts have deleterious effects and often lead to unmanageable countertransference difficulties.

DEVELOPMENTAL FACTORS, THE ANALYTIC INTERACTION, AND INTERPRETATION

The tone of this book does not stress intrapsychic conflict as the outcome of clashing internal forces. Very little is written about the upsurge of id impulses as they assault a vulnerable ego that seeks protection by constructing defenses. To repeat, most of the authors deal with defects in psychic structure that characterize the psychopathology of severely disturbed patients, such as borderline and psychotic patients. Though the question has not been explicitly stated, clinicians often covertly ask: How can structural deficits or distortions be analyzed? Are these not primarily problems of management and care, as Winnicott has frequently stated?

With certain patients, management may be a primary approach or a necessary condition before treatment is possible, or in order to be able to continue therapy. The combination of psychotherapy or psychoanalysis and a supportive holding environment is, of course, an ideal situation in an inpatient hospital setting. Still, whatever the background, the therapeutic interaction has to be understood in terms of processes that include changes in psychic structure. With severely disturbed patients, the acquisition of psychic structure is an ultimate goal, and the methods involved in gaining structural accretions are equivalent to the working-through process in the analysis of psychoneurotic patients. Both working through and psychic processes that are responsible for reaching higher levels of psychic structure are poorly understood; they are subjects for further exploration.

Ogden, Gaddini, and Grotstein refer to the earliest phases of emotional development and how they are distorted by infantile traumas. They discuss the interplay between structure and function and demonstrate how primitive and pathological mental operations lead to structural changes such as splitting, and defensive maneuvers that are the outcome of psychic splitting. Predominant among these defenses is projective identification, which often characterizes the transference interactions and frequently leads to specific countertransference responses. It is in the area of the transference–countertransference axis that progressive character changes occur. Some of the authors of this volume believe that projective identification, a mechanism that determines the quality of the transference, can eventually lead to the patient acquiring self-esteem and a restructuring and cohesiveness of the self-representation. To understand these processes further, the earliest stages of emotional development have to be thoroughly explored, especially as to how they lead to interactions with caretakers and the surrounding infantile milieu.

I have referred to the first phase of emotional development as a *prementational phase*, which means that it antedates phases that are capable of psychological elaboration, that is, of mentation (Giovacchini 1979, 1986). Boyer discusses some aspects of this phase in his introduction. Some clinicians believe that the psychopathology of very severely disturbed patients may be the outcome of overwhelming trauma to and fixation on the prementational phase. This presents an obvious dilemma. If we are dealing with developmental phases that cannot be psychologically elaborated, which also means that they are incapable of structuring affects, then how can these patients be dealt with in an analytic context? Analysis involves transfer of feelings, thoughts, and fantasies, all products of higher developmental levels, of a psyche that is capable of mentation. The prementational phase would not even be able to sustain introjective-projective processes and defenses as primitive as splitting and projective identification.

Neonatologists (Klaus and Kennel 1982, Stern 1985) keep discovering that the duration of the prementational phase becomes increasingly shorter. The infant, even during the first days or weeks of life, is capable of some rather complex perceptions and discriminations. The reflexive mode of responding lasts only briefly as a dominant stimulus–response sequence. Nevertheless, early modes of relating do not entirely disappear and continue to exist side by side with later, more sophisticated adaptations that have psychological representation.

From a theoretical perspective, we can raise the further question as to whether psychic structure can form mental representations, or whether it is an intellectual construction that cannot be psychologically elaborated, but within whose frame certain mental operations can be understood. If we are dealing, for the most part, with abstractions, then are we concretizing a concept when we make formulations that refer to the acquisition of psychic structure or deal with structures in a psychoanalytic context? If we are, then it becomes even more difficult to understand how we can treat these patients psychoanalytically. Yet the authors here do not seem to doubt that they are participating in a psychoanalytic relationship.

Patients, especially at the beginning of treatment, do not usually reveal to their analysts ego states that are similar to those that are related to the traumatic infantile milieu. The latter come to the fore after a somewhat comfortable regression has been achieved. Initially patients use more secondary process-oriented adaptations to communicate and perhaps to protect themselves from anticipated attacks that are reminiscent of the disruptive experiences of their childhood. I emphasize, however, that defenses and adaptations associated with higher developmental levels are called into action to defend against traumas that occurred when the infant's mind had just begun to develop. Relatively sophisticated adaptations defend the patient against the vulnerability and terror of primitive ego states.

I am describing an unevenness of the personality, in that perceptions and responses do not stem from the same ego level or ego state. This causes the patient to appear fragmented, a fragmentation that must be distinguished from dissociation or splitting. Regardless of what might be considered a lopsided organization of the personality, it is this quality that permits seriously disturbed patients to communicate with their analysts and in many cases makes psychoanalytic treatment possible.

Eventually in many thoroughgoing analyses, the patient, through his regression, recapitulates the ego state—that is, the level of development where the deleterious effects of the infantile environment were most acutely felt. If the prementational phase represents the level of regression, this does not mean, however, that because of the lack of psychological elaboration, the patient is incapable of communicating or of reaching higher levels of comprehension. The regressed state is never an exact duplication of the corresponding developmental stage and point of fixation. The patient, though regressed, retains many later acquired functions. He can still walk, talk, and remain continent, activities that are not possible during the neonatal period. Consequently, though the ego state manifested during the treatment regression is the earliest one on the developmental pathway, the patient is still able to relate to the analyst and to describe primitive processes with sophisticated speech and feelings that did not yet exist during the prementational phase. This is analogous to the use of higher-level defenses against the disruption associated with ego states that, at the time, were not capable of structuralizing such relatively sophisticated adaptations.

Although there is much diversity as to what constitutes the various elements of the psychoanalytic process, there is near unanimity of opinion regarding the therapeutic significance of the interpretation of the transference. How fundamental such interpretations are for patients such as those described in this book must be investigated, because it is not self-evident that they are the most significant therapeutic factor.

As discussed, many functions acquired later are retained during the treatment regression. Nevertheless, as discussed in Chapter 1, there are patients who are able neither to project nor to introject when they experience such a regression, or whose ego defects manifest themselves sufficiently that they exhibit such deficiencies in their relations with the external world. Thus, it would seem we are faced with a problem, because if they cannot internalize, that is, introject transference interpretations, then how can any type of change occur, structural or otherwise? In their daily lives, these patients constantly reveal how they are unable to benefit from or incorporate potentially helpful experiences.

Some analysts have stressed that the treatment of primitively fixated patients must include some educative influences. Because of deficiencies in both the perceptual and ego executive systems, these patients simply do not have the techniques that enable them to deal with the exigencies of their current milieu. They do not know how to cope, a quality that I consider to be the essence of the borderline state and which was most eloquently stated by a patient who said that he had an arithmetic mentality but lived in a world of calculus complexity. Thus treatment somehow must set in motion once again an arrested and distorted developmental process, which is an educative experience for the patient.

Unfortunately, attempts to educate patients often take the form of managing their lives outside the treatment, and, as we have frequently seen, this can destroy the analytic interaction. The patient frequently believes that he has been promised omnipotent salvation, and he reacts with bitter disappointment, if not paranoid fury, when he realizes that the analyst's implicit promise cannot be fulfilled. Furthermore, clinicians have to be more explicit when they speak about educating patients and helping them acquire adaptive techniques that they are lacking. The problem is compounded if these patients are unable to internalize helpful experiences, as I have discussed.

To formulate the treatment interaction, we need to examine in greater detail the path from the prementational state to beginning object relations.

What are the psychological factors that permit the infant to progress from one stage to another? Certainly, physical maturation supplies the impetus for growth, but we have to consider the accompanying psychic mechanisms that contribute to emotional development and that eventually culminate in satisfying and rich object relations.

Similar psychic processes also occur within the treatment setting as patients achieve higher levels of ego integration and efficient adaptive techniques that permit them to enter the surrounding world as active participants. Therefore, as we are able to trace a developmental continuum, we may be learning something about therapeutic resolution for patients who suffer mainly from structural defects.

To facilitate such an investigation, I turn once again to the nurturing relationship. As discussed, I view it as containing two components, the nurturing interaction per se and the soothing environment that enables the infant to assimilate nutriment, which leads to growth in both physical and mental spheres. The child reaches higher levels of physical and psychic integration as the soma and mind further structuralize. Something equivalent occurs during treatment. As mentioned, interpretations can be equated with nutriment, and the background soothing that the mother provides constitutes the holding environment that the analyst creates.

Since the newborn has a paucity of, if any, mental mechanisms, we must inquire how psychic maturation occurs. Physical growth can occur without a corresponding psychic development for a short time, as emphasized by Spitz (1941) when he studied children who were physically nurtured but who were isolated from any human relationship. Eventually these children died after they had achieved a modicum of physical development.

The devoted mother feeds and protects her child. This enables the prementational infant to physically grow so that the central nervous system continues to develop and psychological integrations and configurations are formed. At this stage, the child is, in a sense, being held and supported to permit the maturational process that began in utero to continue. Nothing in particular is internalized in the prementational phase. The child is sufficiently neurologically immature that internalizing processes are not yet operating. They come into play later, but still, traumas during this period will affect how the psyche will develop.

Although the child is not able to perceive needs in a structured sense, he still requires ministrations from caretakers in order to survive. He has to be fed and protected. In this context, however, there must be some rudimentary interaction which must also involve the infant. Lately, a good deal has been said about bonding, and we think in terms of a mother–infant bonding. The mother's participation is clear enough, but something must also correspondingly occur in the child, although it is a much more primitive level of internalization. The child does not even have the equipment to permit any kind of structured internalization.

A woman patient in a fantasy or delusion (to this day I cannot distinguish) described what I believe was a primitive, psychologically distorted self-representation. She told me that she had given birth to a monster baby. It had an amorphous face without any features, no nose, mouth, or eyes. For arms it had the curlicued cords of a telephone. This child had no equipment that would enable it to achieve nurture or to internalize care-giving, helpful experiences. This child could not hug because of defective arms, could not be fed since it did not have a mouth, nor could it be admired or lovingly gazed at because it had no eyes. The child was just an amorphous blob incapable of feeling. To be fed it had to be put in a refrigerator where it absorbed the odors of the surrounding food by osmosis.

This monster could survive and be nurtured in the cold isolation of the refrigerator. There was no possibility of growth; it was simply being maintained. If it were removed from its cold enclosure and placed on a windowsill in the warm sunlight, small pieces of it would break off and crumble. The patient stated that it had leprosy.

The patient who is discussed in my chapter was unable to form and hold a mental representation without the actual presence of the external object; she had not developed the capacity for evocative memory (Fraiberg 1969). There were marked problems that were related to her inability to incorporate and internalize potentially helpful experiences. Her fantasy or delusion referred to how she perceived herself at the beginning of life. To some extent, she gave "birth" to this monster baby in order to expel it, a process that occupied her many years in treatment.

My patient's construction was the outcome and a reflection of her psychopathology but, as psychoanalysts know, much can be learned about nonpathological processes when we study the distorted exaggerations of emotional distortions. The monster was fed in a particular fashion because it lacked incorporative equipment or, in mental terms, psychic equipment that would permit it to be receptive within the context of a nurturing relationship.

During ordinary development, in a much less bizarre way, the child has a relative lack of internalizing capacities. Thus we can further ask: How does a physiologically oriented organism take in experiences that will set the stage for, or that are the forerunners of, mental processes? Perhaps our monster baby can be helpful. I am referring to it being nurtured by osmosis. Osmosis does not require mentation or elaborate receptor systems. It is a primitive incorporative technique.

I am, of course, indulging in whimsy when I seem to suggest that the neonate's behavior can be equated with a process that operates within an organism at a cellular level. The infant, however, is sensitive to external stimuli to the extent that he requires a protective environment, a protective shield (Reizschutz), as Freud (1920) discussed. With regard to the impingements of the external world, the child is extremely vulnerable. He has a thin skin, so to speak, and needs protection. This type of care represents an aspect of the soothing holding environment, which, when properly established, creates a setting that the nurturing interaction satisfies, relieves tension, and leads to growth. The mother, in essence, acts like a sieve or filter, protecting the child by deflecting harmful stimuli and permitting soothing and nurturing elements to be absorbed. Freud (1915) and Klein (1946) believed that this early maternal interaction established the polarities of good and bad. Freud described the forerunner of hate as the child's spitting out, that is, rejecting, bad-tasting food. In a more general fashion, I am describing a mother who filters out the bad and allows the good to be taken in.

Inasmuch as the infant has so little self-protection from noxious, disruptive stimuli, he can be viewed as permeable. The mother erects protective barriers at the somatic periphery of her child. From her viewpoint she is fused with him, although the child knows nothing about fusion. He presumably feels only states of tension or calm that can be physiologically translated as homeostatic imbalance or balance. Eventually, however, these states will be psychologically elaborated into sensations of pain and pleasure. As much as possible, with good mothering, pain will be avoided and pleasure will become part of a general response as the child is nurtured and soothed.

Because of the mother's protective filtering, she blocks out, as much as possible, painful and disruptive stimuli. True, many of these stimuli are created by the child's inner needs, such as hunger and other types of discomfort, but the child does not distinguish then between inside and outside.

Thus, the infant's permeability has its advantages and disadvantages. At a physiological level it permits the child to incorporate growth-promoting experiences and nutriments. On the other hand, it makes the child extremely vulnerable, because he is exposed to the disruptive influences of both the inner and outer world. He has a lower threshold. From a development viewpoint, we are faced with a paradox. The quality that promotes development, permeability, also causes the infant to feel helpless and vulnerable. That is where the mother enters the picture; she nourishes her baby and mitigates the noxious qualities of the early environment. She promotes development by providing a safe and secure setting, and whatever innate growth forces are operating can continue to unfold without the interference and disruption that are the essence of the deleterious effects of a traumatic milieu.

I am describing a duality that consists of circumstances and elements that direct the neonate toward integration and structure, a somatic and psychic continuation of what began in utero as the fetus developed from a zygote to a complex, but still immature organism. It also includes forces that work counter to progressive structuralization. There is a balance between integration and disintegration. In utero, the fetus is totally protected, whereas after birth, disintegrative factors are not completely excluded. Perhaps Freud (1920) elaborated this fundamental duality that recapitulates the sequence of need-satisfaction to the esoteric concepts of life and death instincts. Regardless of how we conceptualize this duality, I am referring to fundamental biological processes that demonstrate that there are opposing vectors in the living organism, one striving toward greater organization and the other running in the opposite direction. Satisfaction of a need such as hunger leads to both maintenance and structural accretions in the infant. The positive effects of metabolism affect both somatic and psychic systems. What is built up is eventually torn down, although the ratio between these antithetical processes varies depending on the life stage we are examining. Early in life the former dominates, making physical and emotional development possible.

Because the child is relatively unstructured and vulnerable, he is from one viewpoint resilient, which means that he is better able to incorporate helpful experiences. Research in child development has demonstrated that there are optimal times for learning certain skills, such as language. Langer (1942) writes about a chattering period occurring around the end of the first year of life. At this time, the child becomes involved in intense verbal communication and begins to incorporate verbal skills. This is the phase of life when language is acquired. If the child is not given verbal input then, he may never learn how to talk.

I am equating permeability with receptivity and distinguishing it from introjective processes. As others have done (Loewald 1960, Schafer 1968), I think of internalization in general terms, which simply means that something outside is moved to the inside. It is internalized. How this occurs varies; it may be assimilated, incorporated, or introjected, each of these processes being characterized by specific ego states, stages of emotional development and psychic processes. Permeability refers to a prementational type of internalization that, as development proceeds, allows the child to structure more sophisticated internalizing mechanisms such as introjection. There is a hierarchy of internalizing processes.

Simply assigning a word to designate how experiences and nurture are internalized does not, in itself, explain anything. In a sense, it represents a tautology, which can be expressed by the question, "What is the mechanism that permits the neonate to internalize?" The answer is permeability, but then we could further ask, "What is permeability?" The answer is that permeability is the mechanism by which the prementational phase is able to internalize. Unfortunately, many of our newer psychoanalytic concepts are based on tautologies and the use of complex, pedantic terms to explain relatively simple, mundane ideas. To elevate the word *permeability* to an explanatory and clinically useful concept requires that it be placed in a larger context that highlights how it differs from other internalizing processes.

Clearly, permeable, semi-permeable, osmosis, and other similar terms belong to the prementational frame and are processes connected to interchanges between cells. When we discuss the quality of permeability, the investigator is usually describing an attribute of the cell membrane. We are definitely dealing with the peripheral elements of a primitive organism which are not connected to any organized sensory or receptor systems. By contrast, introjection, for example, is associated with the oral phase of psychosexual development, in which part–object relationships are established and its prototype is oral incorporation. The mouth and gastrointestinal system constitute the receptor apparatus, receptor structures that the amorphous monster baby did not have.

To continue with the use of the concept and quality of permeability, which here, as is true of most psychoanalytic concepts, can be considered to be a metaphor, it differs from introjection in several respects, but I want to focus on its peripheral elements. As described, during the nurturing interchange, the mother and child are joined to each other at the outer skin boundary (see Bick 1986). The assimilation of nutriment that occurs by introjection, an oral process, occurs deeply within the organism. During the neonatal phase it is as if the mother and child blend with each other, and even though, in actuality, what is inside the mother, breast milk, is transported into the infant's stomach, the child presumably has no mental representation of that stomach. I conjecture that, because of the baby's physiological orientation, he experiences the nurturing relationship as constituting an exchange across peripheral (skin) boundaries. This, I believe, is not a discrete perception but a fundamental organic sensation that cannot be further organized at this early stage. Rosenfeld writes about something similar when he describes the role of the skin and internal regulatory mechanisms. I will not dwell further on the skin, per se, though I believe that future research will focus on its contribution to psychic development and the structure of the body image.

The relevance of peripheral versus deeper exchanges relates to the therapeutic process. These are not just simple theoretical abstractions. They can help us understand how analysts communicate with severely disturbed patients and how patients process what they receive from their therapists. Conceptualizing early communicative and nurturing patterns will eventually lead to insights about therapeutic technique and the various psychic mechanisms that are involved in the structure and internalization of interpretations as they create character changes. The mechanisms operating during early developmental phases, in some instances, are, in a modified form, recapitulated during psychoanalytic treatment and interpretative exchanges within the transference context.

Returning to the mother–infant bond, the child matures as homeostatic balance is maintained, an achievement that is facilitated by the modulation of external stimuli. When the mother functions as a protective shield against traumatic impingements, this does not mean that she blocks out all stimuli. As stated, she acts more as a filter than a shield. The infant has proved to be primarily stimulus-seeking, a factor that contributes to emotional and physical growth.

The organic substratum of perceptions, feelings, and thought processes is the central nervous system. Recently, there has been some very interesting research concerning the development of the brain (Aoki and Siekevitz 1988). These investigations conclude that the final wiring of the brain occurs after birth and is dependent on early experiences. They have identified a protein called MAP2 that is responsible for the molecular events that cause the brain to change, that is, to structuralize further. Their experiments were confined to the visual cortex of cats. By shutting out the vision of one of the kitten's eyes by suturing it shut during the first several months after birth, they discovered that the proportion of neurons responding to stimulation of the closed eye dropped markedly. After the animal had use of both eyes once again, it remained blind in the deprived eye for the rest of its life.

The protein MAP2, known as a *cytoskeletal protein*, helps dictate the shape of neurons and is involved in determining the morphology of dendrites, which are responsible for the transmission of nerve impulses. Dendrites represent the receptor elements of the neuron, as they receive impulses and react to neurotransmitters. There is considerable knowledge of the chemical changes associated with the activity of MAP2 and the specific morphological effects it has on dendritic systems. It is responsible for forming connecting bridges between dendrites.

The activation of MAP2 depends on external stimuli. The chain of reactions is complicated, but it has been documented. For our purposes it suffices to recognize that traumatic events such as the suturing of the kitten's eye and the absence of sensory input leads to developmental arrests and distortions, whereas the proper balance of input promotes development of the central nervous system, especially the sensory apparatus.

These findings can be easily transported to the mother–infant dyad in the context of emotional development. Abandonment, absence of stimuli, and trauma cause the psyche to develop improperly whereas good maternal care and well-modulated stimuli supply the impetus for psychic maturation. Scientists are beginning to understand the physical and chemical processes that represent the intermediary links between internal and external stimuli and elaboration of neurological structure. Psychoanalysts seek similar knowledge regarding the evolution of the mind.

At the beginning of life, relationships are not symmetrical. To repeat, the mother fuses with her child, an extrauterine continuation of her primary maternal preoccupation as described by Winnicott (1956), but the child does not have the mental mechanisms that could cause him to reciprocate at the same psychic level. The mother–child dyad resembles a cocoon, an external representation of the intrauterine relationship in which the womb surrounds the fetus, furnishes it with what it needs, and protects it from any noxious or disruptive influences. During pregnancy the child is actually inside the mother; after birth she fuses with him by incorporating him psychically. In the meantime, as in the psychic cocoon or formerly in the uterus, the baby continues to grow and structuralize.

Throughout the course of emotional development and as object relations are formed, the initial asymmetric relationship acquires some degree of symmetry. The ultimate symmetry occurs when whole object and intimate relations are achieved. By symmetry, I refer to an equal depth of involvement in an object relationship, and the interplay of similar psychic mechanisms. In the past (Giovacchini 1958), I have written of such relationships as being symbiotic in that two persons can fuse with each other but still retain their individual identities. The achievement of the status of an autonomous separate entity is particularly relevant, because it is a process that is vital for the treatment of primitively fixated personalities. How the psychic larva emerges from the cocoon is especially pertinent.

Many analysts, especially Mahler (1968), write about a hatching phase in which the child emerges from a symbiotic fusion; this represents the beginning of object relationships. This is difficult to understand, because it assumes that in a previous phase, the infant must have had some perception, even if dim, of an external object. Consequently, to some degree, he must have already reached a stage of object relatedness before he could emerge from a preobject phase, obviously a conceptual absurdity.

The cocoon analogy can be compared to the birth process. When the fetus leaves the womb, the mother has externalized part of herself, but she, at some level, continues to treat the baby as still belonging to her by fusing with him. Clearly the fetus-just-turned-infant does not fuse with the mother to maintain the status quo ante. Later, as the infant experiences satisfaction, which at the beginning simply means homeostatic balance, some degree of sensory integration is attained and perceptions become organized. The child perceives the external world, but he does not know it is an external world. He recognizes only himself as he is delighted at the discovery of various parts of his body. He literally plays with himself, the forerunner of masturbation and the establishment of the autoerotic phase Freud (1905) first described. When the mother enters his perceptual space, she is treated in the same playful and joyous way as he sucks his thumb or treats his toys. The baby has established a transitional area in which he believes that what he perceives is part of the self. I am adultomorphizing when I attribute recognition of the self and the infant's sense of possession. Still, it is not too difficult to believe that the child relates to others as if they are not separate, autonomous persons with needs of their own not related to their interaction.

This early perceptual area is known as the *transitional space*, and the objects in that space, including the mother, are *transitional objects*. Gradually, the infant learns that states of discomfort and comfort are related to activities with these objects, and they begin slowly to acquire an existence of their own. This applies even to parts of the self. Later in childhood this orientation persists and is manifested by the child's tendency to anthropomorphize.

Fusion, splitting and, introjective-projective mechanisms are psychic mechanisms that are constructed after some self- and object differentiation has occurred. The child begins to acknowledge that there is an external world and persons who exist outside the sphere of his transitional space. He recognizes that the source of nurture does not reside within the self, and he can be comfortably dependent on his caretakers. He accumulates a series of introjects as he attains higher levels of ego integrations.

There are parallels that can be drawn between self- and object differentiation, the acquisition of introjective-projective mechanisms and the treatment process. Money-Kyrle (1956) believes that the therapeutic relationship consists of introjections and projections by both patient and analyst. For example, the analyst introjects the patient's projections and then projects them back into the patient through the analyst's interpretations.

Throughout this book, the psychic mechanism known as *projective identification* is frequently mentioned. It is viewed as a process involved in transference–countertransference interactions and as a vehicle that can lead to cohesion of the self-representation. The analytic setting, according to some authors, is based on a relationship in which projective identification plays a dominant role.

In a sense, all object relations contain elements of projective identification. The way we perceive and relate to another person always involves some aspect of the self. The perceptual system is part of the self-representation which, to some degree, determines how we perceive. In turn, our mode of perceiving contributes to how we view ourselves as we consolidate our sense of identity. Consequently, we can never relate to others in a purely objective fashion, that is, without putting a part of ourselves in our perceptions, transactions, and communications.

Perceptions, in a sense, are examples of introjection inasmuch as a sensory registration occurs within the person who is perceiving. The object representation is shaped according to the recipient's psychic structure, meaning that it contains some elements of the self-representation. Thus, there is some degree of identification involved in introjective processes.

Furthermore, there is no absolute distinction between self- and object representations. Every object-representation is, to some extent, also a self-representation. Both introjections and projections contain elements of identification, meaning that projective identification is ubiquitous once object relations are established. Still, this mechanism can be conceptualized in quantitative terms, in that there are different degrees of identification contained in various introjections and projections.

In terms of a developmental sequence, Mahler's (1968) and other investigators' ideas about separation-individuation and object relations beginning after hatching from a symbiotic phase have to be revised for a reason other than the one just discussed that emphasized conceptual inconsistency. In this instance, rather than emerging from a fused state, beginning object relationships are formed and individuation develops as a fused state is achieved. *It is through fusion rather than dissolution of fusion that the child gains self-object discrimination.* Fusion is an important attribute of object relationships. Granted, as object relations reach higher levels of integration, there is less fusion involved, but this cannot be conceptualized as a quantitative sequence. In mature intimate relations there is considerable fusion alongside the recognition of the partner as a distinct, autonomous person. This is similar to the transitional space receding and expanding throughout life, and it is much involved with creative activity.

The more we learn about the treatment of severely disturbed patients, the more important early developmental phases become to our understanding of the treatment process. The psychic mechanisms that operate to establish individuation and early object relationships are also instrumental in the interpretive interaction between therapist and patient. In many treatment relationships, the patient resumes the pathway of emotional development in a modified form. The analyst, of course, is not the patient's mother, but the differential gradient between the therapist's and patient's psychic structure, as Loewald (1960) has also discussed, provides an opportunity in which the patient can gain higher levels of ego integration. The analytic interaction helps the patient enter the surrounding world as he emerges from a state of relatively autistic isolation and withdrawal.

I have on several occasions divided both the nurturing situation and the treatment process into two components, the foreground of nurturing and the background of soothing. In treatment the soothing interaction is an important feature of the holding environment. During the beginning phases of therapy with many primitively fixated patients the holding environment is of foremost importance.

There are striking parallels in the construction of the holding environment and the mother's first ministrations to her child as she establishes a bond with him. The patient begins to react to the calming influence the therapeutic setting exerts. There are many reasons why the relationship, by itself, can be soothing. Its constant reliability and nonjudgmental atmosphere are important elements that create trust and security, but the analyst's exclusive devotion to understanding how the patient's mind works, I believe, provides the patient with an experience he never has had before. No one has shown such an intense interest in him as a person or has demonstrated such respect for his mental processes. Perhaps some patients cannot recognize how they have become the recipients of such intense interest, but eventually, they may be able to sense and recognize how the treatment setting places them in a position of crucial importance, enhancing integrative narcissistic supplies and elevating self-esteem. More crucial, however, are the different levels of psychic integration between patient and analyst and the psychic mechanisms involved in their interaction.

Similar to mothers, analysts will relate with higher levels of adaptation than are available to their patients. The mother, as discussed, fuses with her infant, who, at the early stage of prementational organization, cannot, in turn, fuse with her. The patient–therapist relation is also asymmetrical, in that analysts, as they seek to gain empathic understanding, fuse with their patients. At first, the patient relates, again as the infant, at a peripheral level but, because of the analyst's fusing with him, he can experience a modicum of security in the analytic setting.

I emphasize that the analytic setting is especially appropriate and well-suited to providing security in primitively fixated patients. Freud (1911–1915) had a different viewpoint as he focused on the impact of the analytic procedure and interpretations on removing resistances and undoing repression so that conflicting drives could be dealt with at ego levels. He did not consider that the analytic orientation that is devoted to understanding rather than managing the patient could lead to the acquisition of further psychic structure.

When dealing with patients whose psychopathology stems from the prementational phase, I have often been reprimanded by some of them for trying to find something inside of them that simply does not exist. They have considered my interpretations to be too sophisticated for their simple orientation and outlook. They have further accused me of reading or putting things into them that are really not parts of their psyches. One patient remonstrated that I was seeking meaning where there was none, and another patient stated I was interpreting "upwards."

I gradually realized that I was viewing these patients as having psyches similar to mine with comparable ways of perceiving and adapting. Though I was trying to see the world through their eyes, I was really seeing it through mine.

My relationship to these patients could be considered to be based on the mechanism of projective identification. I was putting myself into the patient and then bringing it back into myself as I tried to process my feelings and observations. More important, I was fusing with the patient, although at that stage of treatment, these patients were not reciprocating.

My interpretations were, for the most part, wrong, since I was attributing elements of my mental apparatus to them. But they were not entirely wrong. They would have been correct if the patient had progressed a little further on the developmental pathway. Furthermore, my formulations represented the way I wanted to see the patient. Again, I am emphasizing my state of fusion, which was associated with some expectations I had, but which also suggested the direction I wanted to pursue.

When my patients confronted me, they were not particularly critical. They did not feel that I was being intrusive or that I was robbing them of their autonomy. They did not feel they had any autonomy to protect.

I am discussing a particular group of patients, since other patients would feel very much threatened and intruded upon if analysts had some need to view them according to their therapeutic expectations. Fusion may be an extremely frightening experience. With these patients, however, the analyst may eventually represent a protective filter, and later the patient may regard the analyst's fusion as a benign, potentially helpful endeavor.

It may seem paradoxical that patients who are initially terrified of the analyst's propensity to fuse are higher up on the developmental ladder than the group I have been discussing. They have progressed beyond the prementational phase to the stage of beginning object relations. Their attempts at fusion as they try to achieve self-object differentiation are conflictful and traumatic, because the fused state is experienced as catastrophic and destructive. The mother has used her child as a receptacle for her hatred and self-hatred. The child needs to fuse as he relinquishes control over transitional objects and moves toward the external world. The latter, however, is a destructive world, so the fused state itself represents a traumatic assault. The therapist is also felt to be an assaultive individual from whom the patient has to defend himself. Furthermore, these patients have to maintain absolute control to protect themselves from being swallowed up in a relationship.

As clinicians are keenly aware, there are very few patients who belong exclusively to a particular diagnostic category. Most of the patients we see are mixed types, which, in this instance, means that they display a combination of prementational features and traumatic early object orientations characterized by pathological fusion states.

The therapist's fusing with the patient may also contain psychopathological elements rather than representing a beginning treatment relationship that will eventually engage the patient in a benign and potentially helpful transference–countertransference exchange. Some fusions can be disastrous because they are motivated by idiosyncratic countertransference needs and reproduce the destructive maternal fusion of the patient's traumatic infantile past.

A middle-aged married woman illustrates how a therapeutically nonproductive fusion state operates. She had been seen for many years by an analyst who has retired from practice. During the course of her subsequent treatment with me, she reported that with her former therapist she did not see herself as a person in her own right. She was only a reflection of him, and believed that she was continually tied up in a relationship. For example, she felt that the two of them were connected to each other by taffy. When she left his office, this taffy would stretch and bend so that the two were always in contact with each other. This was not, however, a pleasant situation. She felt constricted, and as stated, she did not have an identity apart from him. For the most part, she considered herself an as-if character.

According to the patient, her analyst was not aware of the destructive aspects of their fusion even when he shared a fantasy with the patient that made it painfully obvious that he was experiencing destructive countertransference feelings. As I have reported elsewhere (Giovacchini 1986), he shared with her the belief that psychoanalysis was dead and added that in order to preserve it, they should stuff him, a psychoanalyst, put him in a case, and display him in a museum. Obviously he was a depressed character.

She replied that there is no such thing as a psychoanalyst without a patient. She should also be stuffed and placed on a couch, and the two of them, but really the unified entity, psychoanalysis, would be put on display. This type of fused relationship remained static and did not lead to any progressive changes. At best, it served to maintain the patient, but she did not feel particularly comfortable.

On the other hand, a fusion based primarily on a need to understand the patient can, similar to the nurturing and soothing mother, establish a certain degree of calm and security that will enable the patient to move up the developmental scale. The analyst may interpret upward and the patient may chide him for having missed the point, as discussed, but usually this occurs in a benign context. The patient is either overtly or covertly pleased that the analyst wants to understand, even if he or she attributes qualities to the patient's character that he has not yet achieved. In some instances, the patient feels flattered and gains some confidence in that another person finds something in him of value, even though he himself cannot see it.

All treatment interactions have their individual courses and variations, as there are detailed differences in traumatic infantile environments. I have been outlining a generally progressive course leading to the achievement of a psychologically minded outlook and external object relationships. In turn, these achievements would be the outcome of the acquisition of psychic structure and the further cohesion of the self-representation. Accompanying these therapeutic endeavors, however, may be considerable turmoil and conflict.

I have reported this patient elsewhere (Giovacchini 1979), but I believe he illustrates well many of the formulations and processes I have been discussing, so I will present him once again with the addition of some aspects of my countertransference feelings. The patient, a freshman college student, suffered what at first was diagnosed as an acute schizophrenic reaction but later was revised to an identity–diffusion syndrome (Erikson 1959). In any case, for the first six months of therapy, he said practically nothing. I had told him during our first interview, as he was exerting great effort to give monosyllabic responses, being unable to offer anything spontaneously, that perhaps he would be more comfortable lying down and relaxing on the couch. He could be alone with his thoughts, but if he wanted to share them, I would be nearby. He seemed comfortable with this arrangement.

The patient for the most part lay quietly and peacefully on the couch. I did not get the impression that he was withdrawing from me, nor did I feel compelled to do something. I found myself, however, wondering what he was thinking about and, if he had disturbing feelings, how I could help soothe him. He did not appear to need soothing while with me, but he gave me sufficient hints indicating that his life outside of treatment was hectic and filled with misery.

I ultimately concluded that he was not having any particular feelings in my presence, that he was fairly blank, in a void, and this was a sign of his inability to relate to people and to cope with the exigencies of the external world. I believe that I was gradually fusing with him and could sense his inner emptiness. Somewhat on cue, he began to make comments, or, to be more precise, to ask questions. He asked about how to conduct himself in the ordinary pedestrian affairs of everyday life, such as how to dress for certain occasions, how to get from one section of the city to another, even how to call a girl on the telephone to ask for a date. I had the distinct feeling that he really did not know how to get along in the world and consequently did not know who he was, as he acutely demonstrated when suffering the throes of the identity diffusion syndrome. I felt very much drawn to him, especially in view of his helplessness. I thought of him as having a defective and nonfunctional ego executive system.

I saw him as a crippled bird that I was protectively holding in the palm of my hand and covering. My hand was molding around the contours of his body as he blended into it. I do not believe he had any strong feelings toward me at the time, except that he was secure enough to be able to expose his helplessness and hope that I would respond to his neediness.

Ordinarily, I do not answer many questions. I believe that infantile needs cannot be directly gratified, and I prefer to analyze the motive for asking the question. With this patient, I felt entirely different; I wanted to fill him with my knowledge and help him move into the external world. Therefore, I answered all of his questions as best I could, feeling somewhat enthusiastic in my responses rather than experiencing him as intrusive, as I would have other patients. As I look back upon my reactions, I surmise that I was demonstrating something akin to maternal concern and preoccupation as I fused with him, and hoped that this would create a sufficient state of intrapsychic harmony that would further his emotional development and lead to the acquisition of adaptive techniques as the ego executive system expanded.

The patient was comfortable with our interchanges, although I did not believe he acknowledged me as a unique, distinct being. He needed me, and he felt safe in my office. At times, he was aware of warm, pleasant sensations bathing his body. He recognized it as a type of security and associated it to soaking comfortably in a soothing hot tub.

I am now aware of his peripheral reactions, whereas I often perceived him as being inside of me. I believe I had a gut relationship with him, whereas he was at the skin level. Boyer, in his chapter and introduction, notes how important these visceral and somatic reactions, as part of the countertransference, are when one is conducting the treatment of severely disturbed patients.

In retrospect, I note that he was using me to gain functional adaptations. I doubt that he had much feeling for me as a person, but apparently this did not matter. Regardless of what might have been his incapacity to acknowledge my importance to him, I nevertheless felt that I was serving a vital function. I believe that the different levels of our orientations were responsible for the asymmetrical qualities of our relationship. I was able to have more feeling for him as a person than he did for me or for himself. I was functioning at a higher level, but it was this differential, in my opinion, that was responsible for the establishment of a therapeutic relationship. As other patients have complained, I was seeing more in him than was there or than he was capable of perceiving. I was attributing higher integrative elements to his psyche through my projections and fusion.

After about eight months of treatment, he started telling me stories in addition to asking me questions. He talked about space travel, visiting distant planets, and going back in time with elaborate time machines. For the first time, he smiled and showed animation. I still did not feel, however, that he was actually relating to me; I felt he was using me as an audience, but this was not unpleasant.

He described moonlike landscapes studded with hills and caves. He lived in caves; at first, he crouched in them, as if he were hiding; then he would venture outside in the cold, dreary, empty expanses. He was aware of a pervasive sense of aloneless, but somehow, in telling me about these fantasied experiences, he felt better. I asked him several weeks later whether he were free of gravity. He chuckled and said he was, and then he saw himself as playfully happy and jumping large distances. He compared his actions to those of a person on a trampoline but with considerably more power. He could jump fifty to a hundred feet upward, and turn somersaults or glide. As he became more and more immersed in this fantasy, he felt exhilarated.

I was aware that my question about gravity caused him to elaborate his fantasy in a playful manner. I doubt that he would have done so without my intervention. True, as he talked about venturing outside the cave, his mood lifted, but he had not been able to let his imagination take him further. I introduced another element, that of the possibility of the lack of gravity, but it could harmoniously be integrated into his scenario. He did not view my suggestive question as intrusive; in fact, he did not perceive it as my contribution. It simply blended into the fantasy he was creating, and he believed, if he thought about it at all, that it belonged to the natural development of his "story." He never acknowledged that I had participated in his imaginative creations. I was there to listen to what had begun as a monologue.

I had a different outlook, as I did not feel that I was a passive, albeit an appreciative, spectator. It is easy to understand that I would have been appreciative, since I had sat next to him for many months when he was silent. Now, he was brightening the consultation room with his stories, a welcome change from the tomblike atmosphere he had created previously. I did not feel, however, as if I were or could remain a passive spectator. I did not enter the world of his stories, but I asked many questions and on more than one occasion, I subtly or not so subtly suggested the direction his adventure might take. As had become his habit, he accepted my suggestions but acted as if they were his own. I did not dispute ownership.

The months went by and, by and large, we were both satisfied with our arrangement. The plots he elaborated became increasingly complex as he left the isolated, barren landscape that represented his first world where he emerged from various caves. Now he visited other planets that were heavily populated and had highly advanced civilizations. Often he felt bewildered, and, on occasion, he turned to me to again ask questions as to how to cope with the various problems he was facing in these new worlds.

Again I emphasize that even though he was turning to me for help, I still felt he was keeping his distance. He confirmed my feeling when he described a computer that had become a central element in one of his narratives. He would put money in this machine and it would answer his questions, clearly a replica of the way he viewed our relationship within the context of his transference projections. I did not feel depreciated when he assigned me the status of a machine, but I became aware of some stirrings of dissatisfaction.

I recognized what I labeled as a ridiculous urge to join him in his productions, not just as a computer prop but as a person. I did my best to keep this urge to myself, as I became increasingly aware of a need to have my presence felt. The patient must have sensed how I was reacting as evidenced by changes in the way he related to me. He began to make small talk and showed interest in activities unrelated to the treatment, such as to how I spent and enjoyed various holidays. He seemed to have developed some concern for me as a person, and we began to have short conversations after the session as he got up and prepared to leave. Frequently, he would tell me about interesting events taking place on the campus, implicitly suggesting that maybe I would find something that I might want to attend.

I conjectured that his stories at first referred to his past, which he constructed in prehistoric settings. He had actually set the scenes back in time as he traveled to them in a time machine. The first creatures he encountered were dinosaurs, before he proceeded to more civilized planets and advanced to the future. The patient was creating a space for himself in which he could emerge (from the cave) and feel relatively safe as he was able to expansively gain control by defying the laws of gravity. He was trying to convert the infantile environment into a secure, safe world in which he was master. He was not subjected to the unpredictable assaults of powerful forces rendering him helpless and vulnerable. Through the computer-machine, that is, through therapy, he was attempting to develop adaptive techniques that would enable him to cope with the ever-increasingly complex world he would encounter as he left childhood on his pathway to adulthood, that is, as he acquired further psychic structure.

At first, as Winnicott (1953) has described in his concepts of transitional space and transitional objects, the patient had to create both the space and the objects he put into it. Winnicott formulated that the child considered himself to be the source of his own nurture, a situation that was the outcome of primary psychic creativity. My patient was displaying a similar phenomenon as he blocked out any awareness of how I might have contributed to the world he was creating, a transitional world that would eventually lead him to a commonly shared reality. My interventions were nonintrusive to the degree that he could remain unaware of my influence on him. This is again similar to Winnicott's description of the nonobtrusive mother who blends with her child's needs in such a harmonious fashion that he does not recognize that the source of nurture resides outside the self.

I believe in both instances, that of the mother and the analyst, this nonintrusive contribution is possible because of fusion, that is, the mother's fusion with her child and, as discussed, the therapist's fusion with the patient.

When does interpretation, in the more traditional sense, enter the therapeutic setting? To some extent, the patient must deal with the analyst as separate and distinct in order to receive his communications. Though minimally, there must be some recognition of a nurturing source outside the self. When this occurs with patients suffering from primitive mental states, there have been significant treatment gains, as the patient has moved up the developmental scale in the direction of establishing object relations.

Gradually, the patient began to recognize my participation in his stories. He was, at first, frightened, because he believed that I would try to "take them away" from him. As strange as this may sound, he was genuinely afraid that, somehow, I would wrest the settings he was describing from him, make them my own, and cast him out.

Initially, I surmised that he was beginning to experience my fusing with him as destructive. This would have meant that he had achieved some capacity to fuse with me, but this was again an instance of attributing to his reactions more psychic structure than they actually possessed. As he continued to display anxiety, he did not present any data that would support the sophisticated hypothesis that he was experiencing a destructive fusion. Rather, he indicated in a concrete fashion that I would supplant him in his stories and take the leading role. I, too, began thinking about him concretely.

Literally, he was afraid that I would take over his space. He would become only a vassal of mine, whom I could use in whatever way suited me. I would be in total control, and he would be reduced to the status of a "nonperson." Instead of him treating me as a transitional object, he had become mine, and this represented a repetition of what had occurred during infancy. I will not go into details of his background, except to mention that his mother had compared him to a favorite doll she had during her childhood, and as he grew up she enjoyed showing him off to her friends because he was exceptionally bright.

I pointed out—that is, I made an interpretation—that his reactions were based on his fear that I would use him for my enhancement at the expense of his needs in the same manner that he had been using me in the past. Later I made some genetic connections, which he understood, because he responded by having vivid memories of how his mother had treated him. He was not able, however, to connect his infantile relationship with his mother with his current interaction with me.

I know that in some way my interpretation was over his head. He was too concretely oriented to fully understand its implications, especially those that referred to the repetition compulsion. Nevertheless, the fact that I responded to him in a fashion that indicated that I wanted to understand what was going on between the two of us rather than just continuing to threaten him caused him to gain some relief from his anxiety. He felt soothed and indicated that he was deriving some benefit from the therapeutic interaction. Perhaps within the context of attempting to establish an interpretative exchange, I had succeeded in establishing an effective holding environment. Though I was interpreting upwards, the patient did not need to comprehend totally the content of the interpretation; it was important that he was able to recognize me and that his relationship with me went beyond being simply a manipulator and a transitional object interaction. To some measure, he had achieved the capacity to see us as separate persons, and it was obvious to me that he had formed a dependent bond. He had entered the realm of beginning object relationships.

He continued with his stories, but his questions also intensified. Now, however, I felt he was not putting money into a computer. He often asked me how I would react to a particular situation or event, something he had never done in the past. I concluded that he was demonstrating two mutually supportive orientations, a state of absolute dependency, again a concept that Winnicott (1960) introduced, and a tendency to identify with me. In view of his primitive orientation, identification may be a too sophisticated psychic mechanism for his concretely oriented ego, but he was demonstrating some need to, at least, incorporate some elements of my ego executive system. This, most likely, was an attempt to fuse with the functional elements, vis-à-vis the external world, of my psyche.

There were many dramatic moments and regressions during this treatment, which lasted many years and which I have described in detail elsewhere (Giovacchini 1979). Here I emphasize that even though I responded toward him with mental mechanisms that were not yet part of his psychic equipment, he was eventually able to respond in kind, a mutual fusion, that was not experienced as destructive. Rather, it led to sufficient structuralization that permitted the treatment to proceed as an interpretative interaction, but first a holding environment had to be constructed. The beginning construction of the holding environment occurred during the prementational phase. Because he was fixated at this phase, he had a paucity of incorporative psychic mechanisms, but still his psyche had a certain permeable quality that enabled him to be soothed by the treatment process.

After having romped in the transitional space for many months, he was able to place me in the external world and eventually gained the capacity to reciprocate my fusing with him, which led to a treatment relationship that took us beyond states of physiological regulations and imbalances.

CONCLUSION

The authors of this volume were not specifically advised as to what areas they should focus on. They were simply told to include some facets of the psychoanalytic treatment interaction. It is extremely interesting how they all tended to concentrate on a homogeneous group of topics, all concerned with understanding the patient from a structural perspective and technical treatment problems as they concerned countertransference issues. Many authors stressed the psychic mechanism of projective identification as being the essence of the interaction between patient and analyst.

The patients, for the most part, were seriously disturbed patients suffering from severe character disorders and psychoses. Many of them were fixated at a prementational phase of development, a stage that precedes the construction of an ego state that is characterized by psychological processes and mentation. Although some of the authors used their own terms to describe the prementational phase, they discussed how such patients can become engaged in a treatment relationship based on psychoanalytic principles.

This book strives to accentuate processes that are involved in the integrative effects of psychoanalytic treatment. These patients need to acquire higher degrees of psychic structure rather than resolution of intrapsychic conflict. Patients fixated at the prementational stage, even though this is a phase that is not yet capable of psychological elaboration or recognition of potentially helpful caretakers, can still achieve a sense of security and inner soothing from the treatment setting. I describe an early neonatal interaction that is similar to the permeability of a cell membrane. The mother, rather than acting as a protective shield, is more like a filter, shutting out harmful stimuli and creating a soothing and nurturing ambience. Similarly in treatment, the analyst creates a holding environment.

There is a structural gradient between patient and analyst. The analyst, again similar to the mother, fuses with the patient, whereas both patient and infant are not capable of supporting complex psychological processes such as fusion. It is this differential, however, that makes treatment possible, which requires that the patient, at some point, acknowledge the existence of the therapist as a person who resides in the external world rather than remaining principally in the transitional space that the holding environment has helped create.

Generalizations about stereotyped courses of treatment are usually not valid when one is discussing most patients engaged in psychoanalytic therapy. Nevertheless, at the primitive, and perhaps the most advanced end of the developmental spectrum, clinicians might expect to discover certain features that regularly occur in varying proportions. The analyst may then anticipate certain movements and directions that can regulate countertransference evocations and cause them to be useful rather than disruptive.

REFERENCES

Alexander, F., and French, T. (1946). *Psychoanalytic Therapy.* New York: Ronald.

Aoki, C., and Siekevitz, P. (1988). Plasticity in brain development. *Scientific American* 259:56–68.

Bick, E. (1986). Further considerations on the function of the skin in early object relations. *British Journal of Psychoanalysis* 2:292–299.

Boyer, L. B., and Giovacchini, P. L. (1980). *The Psychoanalytic Treatment of*

Schizophrenia, Borderline and Characterological Disorders. Northvale, NJ: Jason Aronson.

Erikson, E. H. (1959). *Identity and the Life Cycle.* New York: International Universities Press.

Ferenczi, S., and Rank, O. (1923). *The Development of Psychoanalysis.* New York: Nervous and Mental Disease Publisher.

Fraiberg, S. (1969). Libidinal object constancy and mental representation. *The Psychoanalytic Study of the Child* 24:9-47. New York: International Universities Press.

Freud, S. (1905). Three essays on the theory of sex. *Standard Edition* 7:122-243.

——— (1911-1915). Papers on technique. *Standard Edition* 12:85-175.

——— (1914). On narcissism. *Standard Edition* 14:67-102.

——— (1915). Instincts and their vicissitudes. *Standard Edition* 14:109-141.

Giovacchini, P. L. (1979). *Treatment of Primitive Mental States.* Northvale, NJ: Jason Aronson.

——— (1986). *Developmental Disorders: The Transitional Space in Mental Breakdown and Creative Integration.* Northvale, NJ: Jason Aronson.

——— (1987). *A Narrative Textbook of Psychoanalysis.* Northvale, NJ: Jason Aronson.

Klaus, M., and Kennel, J. (1982). *Parent-Infant Bonding.* St. Louis, MO: Mosby.

Klein, M. (1946). Notes on some schizoid mechanisms. *International Journal of Psycho-Analysis* 27:99-110.

Langer, S. (1942). *Philosophy in a New Key.* New York: New American Library.

Loewald, H. (1960). On the therapeutic action of psycho-analysis. *International Journal of Psycho-Analysis* 41:16-33.

Mahler, M. (1968). *On Human Symbiosis and the Vicissitudes of Individuation.* New York: International Universities Press.

Money-Kyrle, R. E. (1956). Normal countertransference and some of its deviations. *International Journal of Psycho-Analysis* 37:360-366.

Schafer, R. (1968). *Aspects of Internalization.* New York: International Universities Press.

Spitz, R. (1941). Hospitalism. *The Psychoanalytic Study of the Child* 1:53-74. New York: International Universities Press.

Winnicott, D. W. (1953). Transitional objects and transitional phenomena. In *Playing and Reality*, pp. 1-26. London: Tavistock, 1971.

——— (1956). Primary maternal preoccupation. In *Collected Papers*, pp. 300-306. New York: Basic Books.

——— (1960). The theory of the parent-infant relationship. In *The Maturational Processes and the Infantile Environment*, pp. 37-56. New York: International Universities Press, 1974.

INDEX